Leisure cultures in urban Europe, c.1700–1870

Manchester University Press

STUDIES IN POPULAR CULTURE

General editor: Professor Jeffrey Richards

Already published

Christmas in nineteenth-century England   Neil Armstrong

Healthy living in the Alps: the origins of winter tourism in Switzerland, 1860–1914   Susan Barton

Working-class organisations and popular tourism, 1840–1970   Susan Barton

Leisure, citizenship and working-class men in Britain, 1850–1945   Brad Beaven

Leisure and cultural conflict in twentieth-century Britain   Brett Bebber (ed.)

British railway enthusiasm   Ian Carter

Railways and culture in Britain   Ian Carter

Time, work and leisure: life changes in England since 1700   Hugh Cunningham

Darts in England, 1900–39: a social history   Patrick Chaplin

Holiday camps in twentieth-century Britain: packaging pleasure   Sandra Trudgen Dawson

History on British television: constructing nation, nationality and collective memory   Robert Dillon

The food companions: cinema and consumption in wartime Britain, 1939–45   Richard Farmer

Songs of protest, songs of love: popular ballads in eighteenth-century Britain   Robin Ganev

Heroes and happy endings: class, gender, and nation in popular film and fiction in interwar Britain   Christine Grandy

Women drinking out in Britain since the early twentieth century   David W. Gutzke

The BBC and national identity in Britain, 1922–53   Thomas Hajkowski

From silent screen to multi-screen: a history of cinema exhibition in Britain since 1896   Stuart Hanson

Juke box Britain: Americanisation and youth culture, 1945–60   Adrian Horn

Popular culture in London, c. 1890–1918: the transformation of entertainment   Andrew Horrall

Popular culture and working-class taste in Britain, 1930–39: a round of cheap diversions?   Robert James

The experience of suburban modernity: how private transport changed interwar London   John M. Law

Amateur film: meaning and practice, 1927–1977   Heather Norris Nicholson

Films and British national identity: from Dickens to *Dad's Army*   Jeffrey Richards

Cinema and radio in Britain and America, 1920–60   Jeffrey Richards

Looking North: Northern England and the national imagination   Dave Russell

The British seaside holiday: holidays and resorts in the twentieth century   John K. Walton

Leisure cultures in urban Europe, c. 1700–1870

A transnational perspective

Edited by
PETER BORSAY AND
JAN HEIN FURNÉE

Manchester University Press

Copyright © Manchester University Press 2016

While copyright in the volume as a whole is vested in Manchester University Press, copyright in individual chapters belongs to their respective authors, and no chapter may be reproduced wholly or in part without the express permission in writing of both author and publisher.

Published by Manchester University Press
Altrincham Street, Manchester M1 7JA
www.manchesteruniversitypress.co.uk

British Library Cataloguing-in-Publication Data
A catalogue record for this book is available from the British Library

Library of Congress Cataloging-in-Publication Data applied for

ISBN   978 0 7190 8969 5 hardback

First published 2016

The publisher has no responsibility for the persistence or accuracy of URLs for any external or third-party internet websites referred to in this book, and does not guarantee that any content on such websites is, or will remain, accurate or appropriate.

Typeset by Out of House Publishing
Printed in Great Britain
by TJ International Ltd, Padstow

STUDIES IN POPULAR CULTURE

There has, in recent years, been an explosion of interest in culture and cultural studies. The impetus has come from two directions and out of two different traditions. On the one hand, cultural history has grown out of social history to become a distinct and identifiable school of historical investigation. On the other hand, cultural studies has grown out of English literature and has concerned itself to a large extent with contemporary issues. Nevertheless, there is a shared project, its aim, to elucidate the meanings and values implicit and explicit in the art, literature, learning, institutions and everyday behaviour within a given society. Both the cultural historian and the cultural studies scholar seek to explore the ways in which a culture is imagined, represented and received, how it interacts with social processes, how it contributes to individual and collective identities and worldviews, to stability and change, to social, political and economic activities and programmes. This series aims to provide an arena for the cross-fertilisation of the discipline, so that the work of the cultural historian can take advantage of the most useful and illuminating of the theoretical developments and the cultural studies scholars can extend the purely historical underpinnings of their investigations. The ultimate objective of the series is to provide a range of books that will explain in a readable and accessible way where we are now socially and culturally and how we got to where we are. This should enable people to be better informed, promote an interdisciplinary approach to cultural issues and encourage deeper thought about the issues, attitudes and institutions of popular culture.

Jeffrey Richards

Contents

List of figures	*page* ix	
List of contributors	xi	
General editor's introduction	xvi	
Acknowledgements	xvii	
1	Introduction – PETER BORSAY AND JAN HEIN FURNÉE	1
I	**Charting the flows: institutions and genres**	**19**
2	Art in the urban public sphere: art venues by entrepreneurs, associations and institutions, 1800–1850 – J. PEDRO LORENTE	21
3	Melodrama in post-revolutionary Europe: the genealogy and diffusion of a 'popular' theatrical genre and experience, 1780–1830 – CARLOTTA SORBA	49
4	Games and sports in the long eighteenth century: failures of transmission – PETER CLARK	72
II	**Processes of selection and adaptation: actors and structures**	**91**
5	Georgian Bath: a transnational culture – PETER BORSAY	93
6	Music and opera in Brussels, 1700–1850: a tale of two cities – KOEN BUYENS	117
7	Leisure culture, entrepreneurs and urban space: Swedish towns in a European perspective, eighteenth–nineteenth centuries – DAG LINDSTRÖM	140
8	Coffeehouses: leisure and sociability in Ottoman Istanbul – CENGIZ KIRLI	161

III Towards an 'entangled history' of urban leisure culture — 183

9 The rules of leisure in eighteenth-century
Paris and London – LAURENT TURCOT — 185

10 City of pleasure or *ville des plaisirs*? Urban leisure culture
exchanges between England and France through travel writing
(1700–1820) – CLARISSE COULOMB — 210

11 The role of inland spas as sites of transnational cultural
exchange in the production of European leisure culture
(1750–1870) – JILL STEWARD — 234

12 Coastal resorts and cultural exchange in Europe,
1780–1870 – JOHN K. WALTON — 260

Select bibliography — 278

Index — 287

List of figures

2.1   *La Grande Galerie du Louvre*, print by J.B. Allen from a
drawing by Thomas Allom, c. 1840.   *page* 36

3.1   Louis Léopold Boilly, *L'entrée du Théâtre de
l'Ambigu-Comique à une représentation gratis*, 1819. Musée
du Louvre, Paris.   57

3.2   Louis Léopold Boilly, *L'effet du mélodrame*, 1830. Musée
Lambinet, Versailles.   62

4.1   After Francis Hayman, *A Game of Cricket*, 1790s. Yale Centre
for British Art, Paul Mellon Collection.   73

4.2   Jean Louis Théodore Gericault, *Riderless Racers at Rome*,
1817. Collection Walter Art Museum (Wikimedia Commons).   76

4.3   Adriaen van Ostade, *The Pall Mall Court* [*Vertier bij een
herberg*], 1677. Collection Rijksmuseum Amsterdam.   79

5.1   Thomas Rowlandson, *Comforts of Bath: The Concert*, 1798.
Yale Center for British Art, Paul Mellon Collection.   95

5.2   Thomas Rowlandson, *Comforts of Bath: The Ball*, 1798. Yale
Center for British Art, Paul Mellon Collection.   106

6.1   *View of the Place de la Monnaie in Brussels*. Collection
Archive de la Ville de Bruxelles, D 881.   120

6.2   François Harrewijn, *Charles de Lorraine*. Bibliothèque royale
de Belgique.   123

6.3   Caricature of François-Joseph Fétis.   131

7.1   Assemblé och spektakelhuset, Linköping, 1900. Photograph
by Didrik von Essen. Didrik von Essens fotosamling,
DvE13, Östergötlands museum, Linköping.   142

List of figures

7.2 Strömparterren, Stockholm, 1841. Lithography by Fritz von Dardel, Stockholms Stadsmuseum, Stockholm. 154

8.1 Interior of a large coffeehouse at the square of Tophane at the end of the eighteenth century. Antoine Ignace Melling, *Voyage pittoresque de Constantinople et des rives du Bosphore*, Paris 1819. 166

8.2 Karagöz (right) and Hacivat (left). 173

9.1 Reinier Vinkeles, *The Tuileries in Paris*, 1770. Collection Rijksmuseum Amsterdam. 189

9.2 *Première vue des boulevards prise de la porte Saint-Antoine*, c. 1750. © Musée Carnavalet, Roger-Viollet, no. 46120–1. 197

9.3 Thomas Rowlandson, *An Audience Watching a Play at Drury Lane Theatre*, c. 1785. Yale Center for British Art, Paul Mellon Collection. 202

10.1 Joseph Highmore (attr.), *The Coffee House Politicians*, c. 1725 or after 1750. Yale Center for British Art, Paul Mellon Collection. 213

10.2 James Caldwall, *The Cotillion Dance*, 1771. Yale Center for British Art, Paul Mellon Collection. 221

11.1 E. Whymper, *The Baths at Leukerbad*, c. 1860, in S. Green (ed.), *Swiss Pictures drawn with Pen and Pencil* (London: Religious Tract Society, 1891, revised edn, p. 96). Collection of author. 242

11.2 J. Watter, *City People on the Alm: Sunny Days*, 1874, in H. Schmid and K. Steiler, *The Bavarian Highlands and the Salzkammergut with an Account of the Habits and Manners of Hunters, Poachers and Peasantry of these Districts* (London: Mills and Boon, 1874). Courtesy of the Literary and Philosophical Society: Newcastle upon Tyne. 251

12.1 San Sebastian, Gran Casino, 1860–1880. Collection Rijksmuseum Amsterdam. 268

12.2 Frederick William Woledge, *Brighton: The Front and the Chain Pier Seen in the Distance*. Yale Center for British Art, Paul Mellon Collection. 270

Every reasonable attempt has been made to obtain permission to reproduce copyright images. If any proper acknowledgement has not been made, copyright holders are invited to contact the author via Manchester University Press.

List of contributors

Peter Borsay is professor of history at Aberystwyth University (Wales), a member of the international advisory board of *Urban History* and a committee member of the British Pre-Modern Towns Group. His books include *The English Urban Renaissance: Culture and Society in the Provincial Town, 1660–1770* (Oxford University Press, 1989), *The Image of Georgian Bath, 1700–2000: Towns, Heritage and History* (Oxford University Press, 2000) and *A History of Leisure: the British Experience since 1500* (Palgrave Macmillan, 2006). He has also edited, along with G. Hirschfelder and R.-E. Mohrmann, *New Directions in Urban History: Aspects of European Art, Health, Tourism and Leisure since the Enlightenment* (Waxmann, 2000) and, with John Walton, *Resorts and Ports: European Seaside Towns since 1700* (Channel View, 2012). He is currently engaged in research on British spas and seaside resorts, and is preparing a monograph on *The Discovery of England*.

Koen Buyens took in 1988 a premier prix in violin at the Brussels Royal Conservatory. Afterwards he obtained degrees in law (1993/1997), philosophy (1993) and history (2000) at the universities of Antwerp, Leuven, Brussels, Heidelberg and Harvard. In 2004 he obtained a PhD in history at the Vrije Universiteit Brussel with a dissertation on the music life in Brussels from 1750 to 1850. Currently he is a lecturer at the Erasmus University College Brussels (Campus Brussels Royal Conservatory). He is the author of a monograph on the court chapel of Prince Charles Alexander of Lorraine: *Musici aan het hof, De Brusselse hofkapel onder Henri-Jacques de Croes (1749–1786)* (Vrije Universiteit Brussel Press, 2001).

Peter Clark is emeritus professor of European Urban History at Helsinki University and visiting professor at the University of Leicester, where he was director of the Centre for Urban History 1985–1999. In 2010 he received

xii List of contributors

an honorary doctorate from the University of Stockholm. He has published or edited more than 20 books on urban, social and cultural history, including the *Cambridge Urban History of Britain: II* (Cambridge University Press, 2000), *British Clubs and Societies 1580–1800* (Oxford University Press, 2000), *European Cities and Towns 400–2000* (Oxford University Press, 2009) and most recently, *The Oxford Handbook on Cities in History* (Oxford University Press, 2013), with more than 50 contributors.

Clarisse Coulomb is lecturer in the Department of History, University of Grenoble (France). Her PhD dissertation was on political culture and social relations in eighteenth-century Grenoble (*Les Pères de la Patrie*, Grenoble University Press, 2006). Her actual field of research is early modern urban history. She is interested in the question how local histories of particular towns, produced by antiquarians or historians, became a popular new expression of urban identity. She recently coordinated the writing of a special issue of *Histoire Urbaine*: 'Ecrire l'histoire de la ville à l'époque moderne' (2010).

Jan Hein Furnée is professor of European Cultural History at Radboud University, Nijmegen (The Netherlands). His research focuses on urban leisure culture, class and gender relations, and cultural policy in the nineteenth century. He has published widely on topics such as gentlemen's clubs, concert life, theatre culture, shopping streets, grands cafés, seaside resorts, ice-skating and cultural policy, as well as on the state of the art of Dutch and international urban history. Recent publications include *Plaatsen van beschaafd vertier: Standsbesef en stedelijke cultuur in Den Haag, 1850–1890* (Bert Bakker, 2012), *The Landscape of Consumption: Shopping Streets and Cultures in Western Europe, 1600–1900* (Palgrave Macmillan, 2014; edited with Clé Lesger) and ' "Le bon public de La Haye": local governance and the audience in the French opera in The Hague, 1820–1890', *Urban History* (2013). He is chief editor of the Flemish-Dutch journal *Stadsgeschiedenis*, editor of *De Negentiende Eeuw* and *Geschiedenis Magazine*, initiator and former coordinator of the Amsterdam Centre for Urban History and secretary of the European Association for Urban History.

Cengiz Kırlı is lecturer at the Ataturk Institute for Modern Turkish History, Bogazici University, Istanbul (Turkey). He wrote his dissertation on coffeehouses as places of sociability and entertainment in the eighteenth- and nineteenth-century Ottoman Istanbul. His publications include 'Surveillance and constituting the public in the Ottoman Empire', in Seteney Shami (ed.), *Publics, Politics and Participation: Locating the Public Sphere in the Middle East and North Africa* (SSRC, 2009); 'Coffeehouses: public opinion in the nineteenth-century Ottoman Empire', in Armando Salvatore and Dale F. Eickelman (eds), *Public Islam and the Common Good* (Brill, 2004); and a book in Turkish, *The Sultan and the Public Opinion*, in which he transliterated and examined everyday people's political conversations in public places recorded by informants in mid-nineteenth-century Istanbul.

Dag Lindström is professor of history at Uppsala University (Sweden). He has published widely on early modern Swedish urban history. His main publications in English include *Crime and Social Control in Medieval and Early Modern Swedish Towns* (Uppsala, 1988; with Eva Österberg); 'Urban order and street regulation in seventeenth-century Sweden', *Journal of Early Modern History* (2008; with Riitta Laitinen); 'Homicide in Scandinavia: long-term trends and their interpretations', in Pieter Spierenburg and Sophie Body-Gendrot (eds.), *Violence in Europe: Historical and Contemporary Perspectives* (Springer 2008); and 'Maids, noblewomen, journeymen, state officials, and others: unmarried adults in four Swedish towns 1750–1855', in Isabelle Devos, Ariadne Schmidt and Julie De Groot (eds.), *Single Life in the City* (Palgrave Macmillan, 2014). He is a member of the Gender and Work research project at Uppsala University, and he is currently also engaged in research on unmarried men in eighteenth- and nineteenth-century Sweden, and on the development of urban leisure culture in eighteenth- and early nineteenth-century Sweden.

J. Pedro Lorente is professor of art history at the University of Zaragoza (Spain), where he is the academic coordinator of the MA in museums: education and communication. He is a member of the scientific board of the journals *Museums and Society, Museum History Journal, Museos.es* and *Revista de Museología*. Among other publications, he is the author of the book *Cathedrals of Urban Modernity: The First Museums of Contemporary Art, 1800–1930* (Ashgate, 1998), which was published again in 2011 in an expanded edition under the title *The Museums of Contemporary Art: Notion and Development*.

Carlotta Sorba is professor of modern history at the University of Padua (Italy). She is director of the Centro interuniversitario di storia culturale (CSC – Universities of Padua, Venice, Bologna, Verona, Pisa) and co-director of the Italian journal *Contemporanea. Rivista di storia dell'800 e del 900*. In recent years she has published intensively on the social and cultural history of theatre, with special interest on the nineteenth century. She is the author of *Teatri: L'Italia del melodramma nell'età del Risorgimento* (Il Mulino, 2001) and *Il melodramma della nazione: Sentimento, politica e spettacolo tra Europa romantica e Italia risorgimentale* (Laterza, 2014). Her main publications in English include 'Ernani hats: Italian opera as repertoire of political symbols during the Risorgimento', in Jane Fulcher (ed.), *The Oxford Handbook to the New Cultural History of Music* (Oxford University Press, 2011) and 'Between cosmopolitanism and nationhood: Italian opera in the early nineteenth century', *Modern Italy* 19 (2014) 53–67.

Jill Steward is a visiting fellow at Newcastle University. Her interests are in the history of travel and tourism in the nineteenth century and its influence on urban culture. Publications include an edited collection (with Alexander Cowan), *The City and the Senses: Urban Culture since 1500* (Ashgate, 2006), and essays on exhibitions, spa culture and urban tourism. Recent publications include: 'Travel to the spas: the growth of health tourism in Central Europe 1850–1914', in Gemma Blackshaw and Sabine Wieber (eds.), *Journeys into Madness: Mapping Mental Illness in the Austro-Hungarian Empire* (Berghahn, 2012); 'Nineteenth-century Britons abroad and the business of travel', in Martin Farr and Xavier Guégan (eds.), *The British Abroad since the Eighteenth Century: Travellers and Tourists* (Palgrave Macmillan, 2013); 'The affective life of the spa', in: David Picard and Mike Robinson (eds.), *Emotion in Motion: Tourism, Affect and Transformation* (Ashgate, 2012). She is currently working on urban tourism and the media.

Laurent Turcot, professor at the Université du Québec à Trois-Rivières, is the recipient of the Canada Research Chair in the History of Recreation and Entertainment. He specialises in urban leisure culture from the sixteenth to nineteenth centuries, especially in the cultural transfer of and sociability in theatres, coffeehouses, cabarets, Wauxhalls and promenades. His recent publications include *Le promeneur à Paris au XVIIIe siècle* (Gallimard, 2007), *Flagrants délits sur les Champs-Élysées: Les dossiers de police du gardien Federici (1777–1791)* (Éditions du Mercure de France, 2008; with Arlette Farge), *La promenade au tournant des XVIIIe et XIXe siècles (Belgique – France – Angleterre)* (Éditions de l'Université de Bruxelles, 2011; edited with Christoph Loir) and *Les Histoires de Paris (XVIe–XVIIIe siècle): Tome 1 et tome 2* (Hermann, 2012; with Thierry Belleguic) and, with Jean-Clément Martin, *Au coeur de la Révolution: les leçons d'un jeu vidéo* (Vendémiaire, 2015).

John K. Walton had to retire suddenly in September 2013 from his post as an Ikerbasque research professor at the University of the Basque Country, Vitoria (Spain), to care for his wife in her life-threatening illness. They now farm a smallholding in the West of Ireland. Professor Walton was founding editor of the *Journal of Tourism History* and published extensively on the social history of tourism, regions and identities, sport and popular culture. His most recent books include *Constructing Cultural Tourism: John Ruskin and the Tourist Gaze* (Channel View, 2011; edited with Keith Hanley), *Riding on Rainbows: Blackpool Pleasure Beach and its Place in British Popular Culture* (Skelter, 2007), *The Playful Crowd: Pleasure Places in the Twentieth Century* (Columbia University Press, 2005; with Gary Cross), *Histories of Tourism* (Channel View, 2005; as editor) and *The British Seaside: Holidays and Resorts in the Twentieth Century* (Manchester University Press, 2000).

General editor's introduction

In this groundbreaking work, the very distinguished international and inter-disciplinary team of contributors assembled by Peter Borsay and Jan Hein Furnée undertake a comparative study of leisure cultures in urban Europe in the eighteenth and nineteenth centuries. The collection covers a broad span of countries and a wide variety of leisure activities. It sets out to trace the interconnections between countries and cultures, to identify the processes of continuity and change, and to place the leisure activities in their wider social, economic, political and spatial contexts. While recognising the importance of gender, the volume also seeks to reintegrate the ideas of class and social status that have tended to be downplayed since cultural history displaced social history as a dominant trend in historical writing. We are taken on an exhilarating cultural tour from Stockholm to Istanbul via Bath, Brussels, Brighton and Biarritz as well as the more familiar destinations of Paris and London. En route we stop off at art galleries, theatres, opera houses, salons, race tracks, sports grounds, public parks, promenades, coffeehouses, restaurants, pleasure grounds and spas. The whole collection is a rich mix that addresses all the key questions laid out by the editors, provides much food for thought and points the way forward to future research.

Jeffrey Richards

Acknowledgements

This book has its origins in the workshop 'The origins of modern mass culture: European leisure in a comparative perspective 1660–1870', convened on 16–19 September 2010 at Gregynog Hall near Newtown in Wales, United Kingdom. We are very much indebted to the European Science Foundation (ESF) who generously sponsored the meeting as an exploratory workshop. We have greatly profited from the illuminating remarks of Dr Jacques Carré (University Paris-Sorbonne, Paris IV), Dr Hugh Cunningham (University of Kent) and Dr Csaba Pleh (ESF representative), who acted as discussants at the workshop. We would like to thank all authors for contributing their chapters: it was intellectually and socially a pleasure working together on this project. We are especially grateful for the comments of the anonymous readers, whose constructive suggestions substantially enhanced the quality and coherence of the book. In the final stage, Dr Rosie McArthur did a marvellous job of polishing the English of various chapters, and we are grateful for the support and encouragement that we have received from the staff at Manchester University Press.

1

Introduction

PETER BORSAY

AND JAN HEIN FURNÉE

As early as 1801 the English antiquarian, engraver and historian Joseph Strutt (1749–1802) declared:

> in order to form a just estimation of any particular people, it is absolutely necessary to investigate the sports and pastimes most generally prevalent among them. War, policy, and other contingent circumstances, may effectively place men, at different times, in different points of view; but, when we follow them into their retirement, where no disguise is necessary, we are most likely to see them in their true state, and may best judge of their natural dispositions.[1]

Strutt's exhortation to study leisure is one that historians have generally speaking been reluctant to follow; 'war, policy and other contingent circumstances' have always and continue to attract the lion's share of the historical community's attention. Yet Strutt had a point. If we want to get under the skin of a people and their past, it may be best to catch them off-guard, at leisure and in 'their retirement'. Far from being a superficial facet of a person's life, studying leisure may allow us to reach parts of the human experience – in particular culture – inaccessible through more obvious channels such as politics or even work.

Although most European historiographical traditions seem to lack an established term to identify leisure history as a subdiscipline (equivalents such as 'Freizeitgeschichte' or 'histoire des loisirs' are relatively little-used), it is not too difficult to delineate its field of inquiry. Indeed, whether primarily originating from social history (such as in Britain),[2] from the history of mentalities (as in France),[3] from *Alltagsgeschichte* (as in Germany)[4] or from cultural history and the history of cultural institutions (as in Italy), it is exactly at the intersection of these different historical approaches that a history of leisure finds its most challenging and fruitful questions. How did various social classes, generations, ethnicities and men and women identify themselves and relate to each other in their spare time activities? What ideas, mentalities and daily routines structured their changing social behaviour and their cultural tastes and experiences? What role did entrepreneurs, artists and various authorities, but also the spatial settings of leisure institutions and recreational artefacts themselves play in shaping and changing the ways in which people enjoyed their leisure time and how they felt part of larger social, cultural or national communities?

This volume aims to advance the historical research on European urban leisure cultures in three different yet interrelated ways. First, it aims to juxtapose and integrate the historical research on a wide variety of leisure activities and institutions that are usually studied in isolation: ranging from visiting theatre, concert and opera performances, attending art exhibitions and residing in spas and seaside resorts, to enjoying sports and games, walking, promenading, attending balls and frequenting coffeehouses and restaurants. A more integrated approach will not only show interesting contrasts and similarities between various leisure experiences, but also help to get a better understanding of the underlying social, economic, political and spatial processes that linked them together. Second, the volume seeks to counter the still persistent practice in the majority of historical research on leisure of focusing exclusively either on the early modern or modern periods. This has led to an overemphasis on innovations at the expense of continuities, and has severely hampered any well-informed understanding of long-term developments. Third and finally, the volume aims to bridge the gap between national research traditions, which in many ways are still locked in their national or even nationalistic frames of reference. In this endeavour, our objective is not only to juxtapose and compare historical developments in various European countries, but also to focus on processes of cultural transfer and appropriation. The history of leisure cultures in urban Europe in the period 1700–1870, we would like to argue in this volume, *is* fundamentally a transnational history.

Leisure history: some problems and challenges

From the onset, one of the principal problems facing those who study the history of leisure has been its multifaceted nature. Leisure necessarily embraces a wide range of human activities, such as music, theatre, visual art, sport, tourism and popular culture and customs, all of which have become associated with distinct disciplines such as art history, musicology and theatre and folklore studies, or at least with specialist academic fields. To develop a genuinely holistic view, the historian of leisure needs to be able to accommodate all these different perspectives. Understandably this has proved difficult. Disciplinary borders are notoriously difficult to cross, each discipline having its own modes of discourse and language, so that although there are some excellent studies of the history of particular forms of recreation – such as horseracing, the seaside holiday and the music hall in Britain – the truly panoptic perspective is rarely to be found. One effect of this is often to fail to notice the interconnections between various forms of leisure but also the differences.[5] Why, for example did some recreations become commercialised and modernised more rapidly than others, or why did some cross national boundaries more easily than others? In drawing on the expertise not only of the social, cultural and urban historian, but also the art historian, musicologist and theatre historian, the essays in this volume will attempt to provide something of the interdisciplinary mix that allows a broader vision to be developed.

While the first interdisciplinary challenge of this book will appear quite self-evident (which is not the same as easy to tackle), the second one deserves a little more explanation. Next to the work done within the disciplinary boundaries of art history or music and theatre studies, the majority of historical research on leisure culture has tended to focus *either* on the early modern period – especially in the French and German traditions of the history of mentalities or *Alltagsgeschichte* – *or* on the nineteenth and twentieth centuries – notably in British historiography but also elsewhere. The fundamental assumption underlying much of this divide, and indeed influencing the majority of work on the modern period, has been that large-scale industrialisation, and the associated urbanisation, would have created the need and means for the very phenomenon that we now call leisure, particularly through the generation of wealth surplus to the basic necessities of life, and the introduction of new technologies. In pre-industrial society, the argument follows, the line that divided work from recreation was blurred, particularly in relation to time,[6] and the vast majority of the population did not have the means to engage in any sustained way in unproductive pastimes; in other words, there was no demand or market for leisure as we understand it, especially in its commercialised forms. Although, in the short-term, industrialisation may have reduced the time, resources and opportunities for leisure for many, over the longer-term it initiated a process of modernisation that changed the nature of work (accentuating the dividing line with play), and began to realise its full potential with the accession of the employed male working class into the rewards of economic growth (with the rise of real incomes) in the late nineteenth century, reflected in the emergence of mass spectator sports and holidays at this time.

4   Introduction

Although there can be little doubt about the long-term transformative effects of large-scale industrialisation and urbanisation on people's patterns of recreation, it would seem implausible to argue that leisure in the broadest sense did not exist in pre-industrial society – although there has been a debate as to whether it was 'invented' in the early modern period, or can be traced back to the medieval era.[7] But was it of such a different character as to be a qualitatively different phenomenon? As early as a lecture of 1972, J.H. Plumb drew attention to the increasing commercialisation of leisure in the 1690s, and argued that by the 1750s leisure was becoming 'an industry with great potentiality for growth'.[8] Much of Plumb's paper was taken up with the growth of print culture, but he also included gardening, shopping, theatre, concerts, dancing, sport and spa visiting, concluding 'the middle class culture which this commercialisation of leisure brought about expanded greatly in the nineteenth century, modified maybe, but not essentially changed, and lasted until our own time.'[9] Plumb's lecture was subsequently reprinted in an influential volume of essays, written with Neil McKendrick and John Brewer, *The Birth of a Consumer Society: the Commercialization of Eighteenth-Century England* (1982), which declared that the period saw a 'consumer revolution',[10] and which stimulated a series of studies demonstrating the vibrancy of consumer culture (of which recreations were a part) in the long eighteenth century.[11] Simultaneously, research on what was coined the 'English urban renaissance' in the late seventeenth and eighteenth centuries revealed the emergence, well before the classic period of the Industrial Revolution, of a leisure economy in the modern sense, based on towns.[12] It was a pattern also to be seen in parts of Europe, notably seventeenth-century Netherlands and Italy, and eighteenth-century France and Germany. All this suggests that in the search for the emergence of modern leisure, the spotlight has at the very least to be trained back to the start of the eighteenth century, and focused on the urban world. It was in the eighteenth and early to mid-nineteenth century that the origins of what we consider 'modern' leisure are to be found, as the essays in this volume argue.

This also brings us to the hotly debated issues of class and gender. Leisure history in the 1970s, in Britain but also elsewhere, mainly focused on working-class leisure, reflecting the prevailing ideological perspective of social historians, one that emphasised the overarching role of class in determining social interactions and processes of change. With the rise of the 'cultural turn' and post-modernism, and the declining influence of Marxist thinking, the dominance of the class model was undermined. Culture became a force in its own right, not necessarily tied to specific economic and social structures. The inclusion of the eighteenth century as the period that saw the emergence of modern leisure had tended to reinforce this trend, because compared to the nineteenth century many historians have seen it as a relatively classless society. Nevertheless, there is no doubt that the increasing numbers of visitors to theatres, concerts, parks or coffeehouses can at least partly be explained by their pleasure at expressing – or even sense of need to assert and confirm – their social status and group identities. The skilful tactics of cultural entrepreneurs and indeed of town authorities to capitalise on these social aspirations can even be regarded as one of the key explanations of the expanding world of urban leisure. Although most of the chapters in this volume primarily focus on the social and cultural worlds of urban elites, we can regard this new leisure culture at the same time as 'popular' and 'mass' culture in the sense that it catered for increasing numbers of visitors, was often highly commercial in its character and in many ways lacked the educated and individualistic refinement often – although sometimes unfairly – associated with elite leisure culture. To reintegrate the notion of class and social status in the long-term history of leisure is one of the challenges that several chapters address.

Although the 'cultural turn' has tended to downplay the role of class, it has undoubtedly had the benefit of recognising the role of leisure in mediating a range of identities other than class, especially gender. In the field of leisure, the construction of class and gender identities and relations were obviously closely interconnected. Aristocratic, bourgeois and working-class identities were to a great extent constructed on the basis of shared ideals of manliness and accepted female behaviour in public and semi-public sites of leisure. The contested but influential ideology of separate spheres problematised the presence of women in public spaces, even in venues such as opera and concert halls or ballrooms, where female presence was an absolute requisite for any successful cultural and social event. In the course of the eighteenth and nineteenth centuries, various sites of leisure (such as theatres, cafés and spas) facilitated different models of bourgeois experiences and expectation of masculinity and femininity. Especially interesting in this respect is the often leading role of cultural entrepreneurs, who at one moment facilitated a demand for male-only leisure spaces (albeit often including prostitutes), while at another carefully enhanced the inclusion of women in public leisure as a way of expanding their public and profit – often by carefully regulating the class composition of their amenities. A long-term analysis of the relation between class and gender formation in various types of urban leisure sites still needs to be written, but several chapters in this collection offer some new building blocks for this endeavour.

6 Introduction

A transnational perspective

One of the most problematic aspects of much of the scholarship on leisure history is that generally it has been locked tightly within national boundaries. Until now many of the scholarly efforts to move beyond the national framework by at least starting to compare developments in leisure cultures in various countries seem to have been confined to conference sessions and the 'book binder synthesis', juxtaposing historical developments next to each other and at most making an inventory of differences and similarities, without a joint effort to seek for explanations. Much of the arguments that have been developed for comparative history as a systematic method to enhance the quality of our historical explanations since the 1990s, especially by German scholars, have received little response in the field.[13] To a great extent, the same pertains for the transnational approach, focused on 'cultural transfer' and 'entangled histories', and developed by scholars such as Michael Werner and Bénédicte Zimmermann, and Akira Iriye and Pierre-Yves Saunier.[14] Indeed, over recent years a substantial number of publications have appeared on Anglo–French cultural and intellectual relationships in the eighteenth century.[15] Especially in the fields of music, theatre and museum history, there is a clear increase of interest in processes of cultural transfer in the eighteenth and nineteenth centuries.[16] The recent upsurge in the historiography of tourism has also substantially promoted a more transnational approach.[17] However, most of the work that is currently being done under the umbrella of transnational history tends to focus on the international dynamic of cultural change and innovation for the late nineteenth and twentieth centuries, while much less work has been undertaken on the transnational process across Europe in the crucial period of the eighteenth to late nineteenth centuries.

As a concept that challenges yet also presupposes the boundaries of the nation-state, it is not surprising that the transnational approach or the 'transnational turn' – recently described as 'the most important development in the historical discipline'[18] – has largely been forged in the context of modern history, especially the twentieth century, and in particular in the fields of political history, migration history and subfields such as the history of nationalism and urban governance.[19] Indeed, it is an approach that we should be cautious about applying crudely to earlier eras, since, as Chris Bayly has argued, 'before 1850, large parts of the globe were not dominated by nations so much as by empires, city-states, diasporas, etc.'[20] But although the majority of the period covered in this volume falls in the pre-1850 era, when the nation-state was still a phenomenon in formation, we believe that transnational perspective, loosely defined as studying cultural flows across political boundaries, is both a legitimate and helpful approach for this period. Not only does it offer us the possibility to stress and explore the continuities in the dynamic processes of cultural transfer throughout Europe between the eighteenth and nineteenth centuries, but it also enables us to radically break free from the national boundaries that still dominate the mental maps of most social and cultural historians.

That said, it is important to recognise the inherent complexity and messiness of the transmission process. In his recent study of London and Paris, Jonathan Conlin has warned:

> it might be possible to distil the story of the development of the two capitals as modern cities between about 1700 and 1900 into a game of cross-Channel tennis, of influence on one side, followed by reception on the other. As with a tennis serve, influences might be resisted, assimilated or diluted. Yet the interaction described here is too complicated and too reflexive for this concept to be helpful. The crossings were more than exchanges.[21]

Two factors are clearly critical. First, the movement of leisure forms and practices was rarely of a simple linear type from primary transmitter to receiver. More often than not the flow would be received via some intermediary, or intermediaries, and would itself then be transferred to other parties, and quite possibly return in a circular motion to the original source. Second, receivers were by no mean passive recipients, slavishly mimicking what they were sent. Rather they were quite able to refuse to participate in the cultural exchange; or, more likely, appropriate what they saw fit, and reject what they did not, modifying and adapting the imported forms to reflect their own cultural practices. Transnational history is therefore a deeply entangled process.

The chapters in this volume – spanning a geographical area as wide as Austria, Belgium, France, Germany, Great Britain, Hungary, Italy, Spain, Sweden and Turkey – aim to present a coherent set of examples of how to operationalise a transnational perspective in historical research on leisure culture in urban Europe in the period from 1700 to 1870. While the chapters in Part I of the volume predominantly deal with *charting the flows* of transmission throughout Europe – from a genre such as the Parisian melodrama and an institution such as public art venues to the 'failed' transfer of practices such as organised sport – the chapters in Part II primarily explore and explain the *processes of selection and adaptation* of foreign cultural influences in individual cities, specifically Bath, Brussels, Swedish provincial towns and Istanbul. Part

8   Introduction

III offers a range of examples of how to explore the history of European leisure culture from the perspective of *entangled history*: focusing on the cultural exchange between France and England by the use of travel diaries, travel guides and etiquette books, and finally studying the sites of transnational leisure culture par excellence: spas and seaside resorts.

What becomes clear from all the chapters in this volume is that during the period there was a rich and widespread flow of leisure ideas and practices across Europe. Some countries and locations may have been more to the fore in this than others. One thinks of the impact of French taste and fashion, German and Italian music and Britain's role in the commercialisation process; of the role of cities as engines of cultural innovation and dissemination; but also of the widening and dynamic range of encounters – particularly from the Americas, Asia and Africa – that forced the traditional centres of Western European culture to adapt to new influences The essays reveal the complex network of contacts, especially between urban centres, that paid little heed to national borders and helped shape an international leisure culture across Europe. Taken together, they offer a range of valuable insights on a range of recurrent questions and issues: on the vectors of transmission, on the role of cities and on the relation between the Enlightenment and nationalism.

Vectors of transmission

There can be no flows of ideas and practices, transnational or otherwise, without some form of carrier. What were the vectors of transmission available for leisure between 1700 and 1870? First and foremost we must think in terms of people. Particularly important are those whose work or lifestyles involve long-distance movement, and for whom political borders were no significant barrier. Several of the authors in this volume identify the likely groups. Wealthy foreign tourists have the means and motives to travel extensively. Peter Borsay, Jill Steward and John K. Walton note their presence at spas and seaside resorts, and Clarisse Coulomb affirms explicitly that 'tourists were the agents of cultural transmission. They could be called the "importers" of foreign entertainments.' They were also, of course, the group most likely to participate in the European Grand Tour, a form of travel that emerged in Britain in the sixteenth and seventeenth centuries, enjoyed its golden age in the eighteenth century, surviving in a modified form into the nineteenth century. The core route took in France, Italy and a number of iconic cities, notably Paris and Rome, but towards the late eighteenth century was modified to include more mountainous regions to satisfy the new romantic spirit.[22] Tourists of this sort might be expected to pick up tastes and fashions like bees attract pollen, and it might also be expected that what was acquired would be taken home and allowed to fertilise with their native culture. Certainly, those taking part in Grand Tours were assiduous, almost obsessive collectors of foreign art and antiquities, which they went to a great deal of trouble to display in their impressive homes, which were themselves modelled on designs observed abroad. The Grand Tour was seen to have an explicit educative function and was directed particularly at the younger generation, who were expected to stay away for a substantial period of time before returning versed in the most advanced European practices in dancing, swordsmanship, music-making and such like, along with an understanding of classical art. However, if this was the ideal, it was not necessarily the reality. For the adolescent and young male, the Grand Tour was as much an initiation ritual into sex, drink and gambling as more elevated pastimes, and tourists took their national prejudices with them, so that contact with foreign culture was as likely to reinforce these attitudes as to moderate or modify them.[23] In his study of the relationship between London and Paris in the eighteenth century in this volume, Laurent Turcot makes us aware of the fact that forms of interaction by travellers could involve resistance to cultural exchange as well as provide an impetus for it. Moreover, Walton notes that although eighteenth- and nineteenth-century English seaside resorts in many ways stimulated the European seaside holiday 'industry', the nation's own seaside resorts remained 'overwhelmingly domestic in demand and character, thereby limiting the scope for international cultural exchange'.

Beyond the well-heeled tourist, those whose jobs were inherently mobile could also act as a carriers of new ideas; Dag Lindström shows how the initiative to build the new theatre at Norrköping in Sweden in 1798 was taken by a man who had served as a diplomat in London, Paris and Constantinople, and was therefore not short of models to draw upon. Carlotta Sorba suggests that the intensification of theatrical activity (and perhaps wider circulation of melodrama texts) in Napoleonic Europe may have been due to the higher levels of troop mobility in the period. But perhaps the single most important group of culture carriers were those professionally engaged in delivering leisure. Art music was an international culture, and musicians and composers moved freely around Europe, drawn, like modern-day footballers, to where the most lucrative deals were to be found. Britain was able to use its burgeoning wealth to attract Europe's most prodigious talents – Handel, J.C. Bach, Haydn, Mozart, Farninelli, Rauzzini, Tenducci; the list is long.[24] Lindström shows

Introduction

how theatrical companies visited Stockholm from Germany, the Netherlands, France and Italy; Turcot, Borsay and Lindström how French dancing-masters visited England and Sweden; and Koen Buyens how the musician and impresario Charles-Louis Hanssens was trained in his native Ghent, completed his studies in Paris before returning at the head of a French company to tour the Netherlands and Belgium, and then in 1825 became conductor of the Théâtre de la Monnaie in Brussels. Sometimes it was purveyors of material recreational goods who crisscrossed Europe with their wares; Lindström notes how coffeehouses were introduced into Sweden by immigrants in the eighteenth century, especially French and Walloons; and how Swiss confectioners operated in Venice, and then – after problems with the authorities – emigrated to Berlin and Stockholm. J. Pedro Lorente records how the art dealer Goupil & Cie in the nineteenth century had its headquarters in Paris but branches in London, Vienna, Berlin, Brussels, The Hague and New York.

What made all this movement possible was wealth. Elite individuals had always been able to afford the means to travel, and more pertinently to attract the services of talented foreign artists and performers. What changed decisively in the eighteenth century was the generation of greater volumes of wealth, particularly in Northern and Western Europe, on the back of commercial expansion, and the spread of this to the upper elements within the middling orders, a process that continued in the nineteenth century supported by accelerating industrialisation. It has been argued that from the late eighteenth century the majority of those engaged in the Grand Tour were middle class, and this was reflected in the declining period of time spent away (from three years or more in the seventeenth century, to sometimes just four to six months by the 1820s).[25] Working people would have been involved in the transmission of commercialised entertainment as itinerant performers and the like, and the mass subsistence migrations of certain populations (such as the Irish to England and the USA after the Famine) would modify the 'popular' culture of the host community; but it is difficult, on the face of it, to see the working class possessing the wealth before the twentieth century to exert much impact as consumers on the international market in leisure. However, Peter Burke has emphasised the role of itinerant entertainers, who were 'no respecters of political boundaries', in giving early modern European popular culture its 'unity';[26] and both Coulomb and Sorba suggest that, in the special markets in leisure that existed in the huge cities of London and Paris in the later eighteenth century, melodramas (imported from France to London) and circus (imported from England to Paris) flourished because of demand from a popular audience – almost certainly the large pool of skilled artisans that both cities supported.

Institutions as well as individuals facilitated transnational transmission. Museums and art societies played an important part in spreading visual culture, as Lorente shows (although how far this was transnational in character would depend upon the content of displays), and Cengiz Kırlı makes the case for the coffeehouse in Turkey as an information hub for pan-European news, not least because of the presence of merchants and immigrants. Coffeehouses proliferated in late seventeenth-century England, especially London, and would have fulfilled a similar function, but the most ubiquitous secular social institution in village and town, and the one that lasted longest and was frequently the base for various recreations, was the hostelry – the inn, tavern and alehouse. The larger urban inns often acted as venues for fashionable assemblies, concerts and plays that were influenced by European taste, but it seems likely that the mass of smaller alehouses – catering for the generality of the population – promoted a more locally based culture.[27] Clark in his chapter argues that commercialised 'new style' sports developed more rapidly in England than on the Continent because hostelries were much more committed to – and effective at – promoting it. One reason for this, he argues, is that they held a far more central role in society.

In Europe as a whole, religious guilds and fraternities were still critical community organisations during the early modern period, and were important purveyors of recreational culture, whereas in England after the Reformation, religious organisations of this type were abolished or fell into decline, opening up space for inns and alehouses. This raises the question to what extent certain institutions were more receptive to cultural change and transfer, and others positively resistant. Elements in the Church of England, and indeed the growing nonconformist sector, protested frequently about the ungodly nature of popular pastimes, but it seem unlikely that they could effectively counter – without their own alternative organisations like guilds and fraternities – the appeal of the inn and alehouse. The growth of the ethic of muscular Christianity in the later nineteenth century, and of the parson who used sport to win back his congregation, suggests that by that time a policy of accommodation – if you can't beat them, join them – had been adopted. In truth, the Church of England in the eighteenth century became an important vehicle for promoting new fashions in religious and secular music, both native and overseas, establishing musical festivals, opening up its premises as performance venues, and its personnel – such as organists – actively developed the local

12 Introduction

musical scene.[28] Attitudes could also change very quickly. In 1798, the Bishop of Linköping vehemently tried to abolish theatre, while in 1805 he was one of the first shareholders of the Assembly and Theatre House Company.

The urban factor

In the rise of new leisure cultures and in particular in the processes of cultural transfer central to this volume, towns and cities played an enormously important role. In part this stemmed from their fundamental historic role as centres of marketing and trade. They were the engines of the economy, pumping goods around the regional, national and international commercial systems, and connecting producers and consumers. Leisure and cultural goods both took advantage of these existing networks and were part of their fabric. Towns invariably sat on the nodal points of the communications infrastructure – road, river/canal, sea and, from the 1840s, rail. Generally the chapters in this volume do not place a great deal of emphasis upon the impact on cultural exchange of the dramatic improvements and innovations in transport that occurred across Europe after 1700, perhaps wishing to avoid crude reductive arguments based on technological change. However, as both Walton and Steward indicate, the arrival of the steamship and railway had, of course, a tremendous impact on spa and seaside resort development, allowing access to previously remote locations. Not that we should underrate earlier improvements to traditional modes of transport. The introduction of turnpike roads and refinements in carriage technology reduced the journey from London to Bath from one of more than 60 hours before the 1680s to little more than ten hours by the end of the eighteenth century.[29]

All the chapters in this volume, directly or indirectly, argue that cities and towns were predominantly the sites in which innovations in leisure were first introduced and developed, and were the sites to which these innovations moved as their influence spread. The commercial pleasure garden, despite its green and rural overtones, was first introduced in London, and then enjoyed a remarkable dissemination, not only across British, but also European cities, with a rash of Vauxhalls, Vauxhallen and Wauxhalls emerging, as several of the authors in this volume demonstrate.[30]

Urban competition played a key role in stimulating the flow of ideas, as cities sought to imitate and excel each other in a process, as Turcot writes of the Paris–London relationship, of 'civilising emulation'. The city's capacity to create or adopt new forms of leisure owed a lot to the issue of numbers. It was

Introduction   **13**

the presence of a comparatively large and concentrated population that created the market that encouraged entrepreneurs to invest in leisure facilities. The sheer size of a London or Paris – the former increased its size from around half a million people in 1700, to a million by 1800 and almost four million by 1870 – and their capacity to attract those in search of pleasure placed them at the forefront of innovation in the recreational industries.

Cities were also home to the printing press. Not only were its products leisure items in their own right – indeed, reading became one of the great pastimes of the period – but they also played a key role in disseminating new fashions and ideas nationally and internationally. Turcot shows how courtesy literature in translation carried French fashions in behaviour to England and Sorba explains how an unprecedentedly large quantity of translations of texts from the French minor theatre helped to spread new forms of drama in Italy.

Some urban places were, of course, more powerful instruments of cultural transfer than others. The great national capitals radiated influence, setting models of pleasure-seeking that lesser towns, at home and abroad, were keen to imitate. They also attracted tourists who would absorb the norms and practices of the city and take them back home. One particular category of town, although individually often relatively small in size, and sometimes displaying semi-rural characteristics, also acted as a tourist magnet; the so-called 'watering place'. Spas and seaside resorts are well-represented in this volume – with the chapters by Borsay, Steward and Walton – because they were centres of leisure and at the cutting edge of cultural change, because they develop to maturity across the entire period 1700 to 1870 and because the more fashionable ones encouraged a transnational trade in people and their pastimes. It is also clear that because the more prestigious watering places were competitors in an international marketplace, they followed keenly what each other was doing, and were ready to import successful models of development; Steward shows how continental spas copied Bath, and Coulomb and Walton how the model of the English seaside resort spread to France.

The Enlightenment and nationalism

Leisure is part of the economic and cultural matrices of a society, and as the form of these matrices changes, so does the nature of leisure. The commercialising process evident in eighteenth-century society as a whole drew leisure into the marketplace, just as industrialisation remodelled the nature of leisure by changing the relationship between work and play. In the eighteenth century the

Introduction

dominant cultural matrix (although not necessarily that shared by the majority of people) was the Enlightenment. Leisure was not always the medium for articulating this; some forms of violent traditional recreations – such as cockfighting, bull baiting and hunting – embodied values seemingly at odds with the Enlightenment. Nonetheless, so often do we see fashionable institutions and pastimes – such as libraries and reading, assemblies and dancing, concerts and music-making, coffeehouses and clubs, debating societies and scientific lectures, and travel and tourism – acting as key vehicles for the cultivation and transmission of enlightened values, that it is hard not to see a close association, at least for the better off, between leisure and the Enlightenment. For some contemporaries there was a specific link between the economic and cultural matrices; as Roy Porter has argued, 'new lobbies of enlightened economists and progressive social commentators began to argue that market culture, sport, print and leisure were economically productive entities, forces for civilisation and social cohesion, and indices of improvement'.[31] Jürgen Habermas' canonical analysis of the rise of the 'public sphere' in eighteenth-century coffeehouses and reading rooms has been widely criticised for his optimistic vision on the democratic and accessible character of these leisure sites.[32] Nevertheless, the mixture of commercialisation and leisure, of the marketplace and pleasure, seemed the ideal breeding ground for the Enlightenment values of reason and reasonability, openness and toleration, sociability and civility, and improvement.[33]

Many of the chapters in this volume reflect this process. Both Borsay and Steward show how British and European spas cultivated Enlightenment values in the eighteenth century, Steward, for example, demonstrates how during the 1750–1790 phase of spa development central European potentates created 'ideal worlds' centred on a water facility and including leisure services such as a pleasure garden, promenade, theatre and library. The Enlightenment did not represent a static cultural model; its values were constantly mutating. Turcot's reference to 'a return to intimacy' in France as a reaction against the formalities of politeness, and Sorba's identification of a relationship between the rise of the cult of sensibility and the growth of melodrama, show how attitudes were changing in the later eighteenth century. This was also reflected in the rise of the '*jardin anglais*' or '*Englischer garten*', with its reaction against formalism in favour of more 'natural' forms, and its widespread adoption across Europe – one of the most striking examples of cultural transfer.[34] Just as the Enlightenment model was not a static one, so it also varied between regions and nations;[35] Turcot's comparison of Paris and London demonstrates the

Introduction   **15**

different national takes on the phenomenon. Nonetheless, underpinning the idea of the Enlightenment was a fundamental universalism. Even if in practice there were a variety of Enlightenments, in principle the values should be common ones, and the vernacular and the local were seen as representing barriers that interfered with the exchange of shared ideals and free social intercourse.

In this sense the Enlightenment was an inherently international culture, and this made it ideally suited to transference across national boundaries. Such fluidity did not, of course, sit easily with the rise of the nation-state. For much of the early modern period this was not a particular problem, given the fragmented nature of the European political map and the dynastic rather than nationalistic character of states. Rulers of minor states and polities could embrace the Enlightenment agenda as a means to bolster their credentials without engaging the forces of nationalism. But after the French Revolution such a stance became increasingly problematic, as Romanticism allied to wider political changes began to turn the nation-state and nationalism into an ideal, capable of countering the universalism of the Enlightenment. The rise of nationalism therefore emerged as one of the factors that inhibited transnational cultural flows. Whereas Turcot can write of eighteenth-century Paris and London being involved in 'larger cultural exchanges and affinities tending to transcend national character', signs of the new ideological climate can be seen, as Buyens demonstrates, in the anti-French Flemish Movement (although ironically drawing on German sources) in Belgium in the first half of the nineteenth century, and later in the rise of the 'thermal nationalism' referred to by Steward.

However, just as we should avoid being seduced by the universalist aspirations of the Enlightenment – not least because of its elitist and socially divisive character – so we should also resist being swept along into believing that the rhetoric of nationalism slammed the doors closed on cultural transfers. When it came to their pleasures and pastimes (such as their choice of music, literature and holiday destinations), European elites, and growing numbers of the well-off middle class, continued to treat national boundaries with disdain. Indeed, for some of the super-wealthy an international lifestyle of conspicuous leisure became the emblem of their superiority. Not only did tourism within Europe flourish, but with the growth of empire recreational travel took on an increasingly global character. It is true that as the more prosperous working class began to take holidays, they generally stayed close to home, but that was a function of economic necessity, and if it did express anything it was a regional rather than national identity. Leisure certainly became a vehicle of

16 Introduction

nationalist sentiment and a tool of the nation-state in the twentieth century; but the traditions of the Enlightenment, and the processes of commercialisation and cultural transfer in which leisure's modern forms emerged in the eighteenth century, ensured that it continued to exert a powerful transnational influence well into the modern era.

Notes

1 Joseph Strutt, *Glig-Gamena Angel Deod: Or the Sports and Pastimes of the People of England*, 2nd edn (London, 1810), p. i.

2 For an excellent introduction see Peter Bailey, 'Leisure, culture and the historian: reviewing the first generation of leisure historiography in Britain', *Leisure Studies*, 8 (1989), 109–122; Peter Bailey, 'The politics and poetics of modern British leisure: a late twentieth-century review', *Rethinking History*, 3 (1999), 131–175.

3 See, for example, Alain Corbin, *L'Avènement des loisirs, 1850–1960* (Paris: Aubier, 1995).

4 See, for example, Gerhard Huck (ed.), *Sozialgeschichte der Freizeit. Untersuchungen zum Wandel der Alltagskultur in Deutschland* (Wuppertal: Hammer, 1980).

5 For an outstanding study that does explore these kind of interconnections see J. Brewer, *The Pleasures of the Imagination: English Culture in the Eighteenth Century* (London: HarperCollins, 1997).

6 For Britain, see the following classic essays: K. Thomas, 'Work and leisure in pre-industrial society', *Past and Present*, 29 (1964), 50–62; E.P. Thompson, 'Time, work discipline and industrial capitalism', in E.P. Thompson, *Customs in Common* (Harmondsworth: Penguin, 1993), pp. 352–403.

7 P. Burke, 'The invention of leisure in early modern Europe', *Past and Present*, 146 (1995), 136–150; J.-L. Marfany and P. Burke, 'Debate: the invention of leisure in early modern Europe', *Past and Present*, 156 (1997), 174–191.

8 J.H. Plumb, *The Commercialisation of Leisure in Eighteenth-Century England* (Reading: University of Reading, 1973), p. 3.

9 Plumb, *Commercialisation of Leisure*, p. 19.

10 N. McKendrick, J. Brewer and J.H. Plumb, *The Birth of a Consumer Society: The Commercialization of Eighteenth-Century England* (London: Hutchinson, 1983), p. 9.

11 See, for example, J. Brewer and R. Porter (eds.), *Consumption and the World of Goods* (London: Routledge, 1993); A. Bermingham and J. Brewer (eds.), *The Consumption of Culture, 1660–1800: Image, Object, Text* (London: Routledge, 1997); M. Berg, *Luxury and Pleasure in Eighteenth-Century England* (Oxford: Oxford University Press, 2005).

12 P. Borsay, *The English Urban Renaissance: Culture and Society in the Provincial Town, 1660–1770* (Oxford: Clarendon Press, 1989). See also J. Stobart, A. Hann and V. Morgan, *Spaces of Consumption: Leisure and Shopping in the English Town, c. 1680–1830* (Abingdon: Routledge, 2007).

13 See especially: Heinz-Gerhard Haupt and Jürgen Kocka (eds.), *Geschichte und Vergleich: Ansätze und Ergebnisse international vergleichender Geschichtsschreibung* (Frankfurt: Campus, 1996); Heinz-Gerhard Haupt and Jürgen Kocka, 'Comparative history: methods, aims, problems', in D. Cohen and M. O'Connor (eds.), *Comparison and History* (New York: Routledge, 2004), pp. 23–40; Heinz-Gerhard Haupt and Jürgen Kocka (eds.), *Comparative and Transnational History: Central European Approaches and New Perspectives* (New York: Berghahn, 2009).

14 Michael Werner and Bénédicte Zimmermann, 'Histoire croisée – Penser l'histoire croisée: entre empirie et réflexivité', *Annales* 58 (2003), 7–36; Michael Werner and Bénédicte Zimmermann (eds.), *De la comparaison à l'histoire croisée* (Paris: Seuil, 2004); Michael Werner and Bénédicte Zimmermann, 'Beyond comparison: Histoire croisée and the challenge of reflexivity', *History and Theory*, 45 (2006), 30–50; Akira Iriye and Pierre-Yves Saunier (eds), *The Palgrave Dictionary of Transnational History: from the Mid-Nineteenth Century to the Present Day* (London: Palgrave Macmillan, 2009); Pierre-Yves Saunier, *Transnational History* (London: Palgrave Macmillan, 2013); Akira Iriye, *Global and Transnational History: the Past, Present and Future* (London: Palgrave Macmillan, 2013).

15 See, for instance, J. Grieder, *Anglomania in France 1740–1789: Fact, Fiction and Political Discourse* (Geneva: Droz, 1985); F. Ogee (ed.), *Better in France? The Circulation of Ideas between Britain and the Continent in the Eighteenth Century* (Lewisburg: Bucknell University Press, 2005); C. Charle, J. Vincent and J. Winter (eds.), *Anglo-French Attitudes: Comparisons and Transfers between English and French Intellectuals since the Eighteenth Century* (Manchester: Manchester University Press, 2007); S. Audidière, S. Burrows, E. Dziembowski and A. Thomson (eds.), *Cultural Transfers: Studies on Franco–British Intellectual and Cultural Exchange in the Long Eighteenth Century* (Oxford: Voltaire Foundation, 2010).

16 H.E. Bödeker, P. Veit and M. Werner (eds.), *Espaces et lieux de concert en Europe 1700–1920: Architecture, musique, société* (Berlin: BWV, 2008); A. Fauser and M. Everist (eds.), *Music Theater and Cultural Transfer: Paris, 1830–1914* (Chicago and London: Chicago University Press, 2009); C. Charle, *Théâtres en capitales. Naissance de la société du spectacle à Paris, Berlin, Londres et Vienne* (Paris: Albin Michel, 2008) ; J.-P. Lorente, *Cathedrals of Urban Modernity: The First Museums of Contemporary Art, 1800–1930* (London: Ashgate, 1998).

17 See, for a recent introduction, Eric G.E. Zuelow (ed.), *Touring Beyond the Nation: A Transnational Approach to European Tourism History* (Farnham: Ashgate, 2011).

18 Mae M. Ngai, 'Processes and perils of transnational history', Perspectives on History, American Historical Association, www.historians.org/publications-and-directories/perspectives-on-history/december-2012/the-future-of-the-discipline/promises-and-perils-of-transnational-history (accessed 22 May 2014).

19 The volumes in the Palgrave Macmillan Transnational History series are almost wholly on the post-1800 era, and predominantly on the twentieth century.

20 Chris Bayly, 'AHR conversation: on transnational history', *American Historical Review*, 111:5 (2006), 1442.

21 Jonathan Conlin, *Tales of Two Cities: Paris, London and the Birth of the Modern City* (London: Atlantic Books, 2013), p. 23.

22 J. Towner, *A Historical Geography of Recreation and Tourism in the Western World, 1540–1940* (Chichester: John Wiley, 1996), pp. 96–138.

23 J. Black, *The British and the Grand Tour* (London: Croom Helm, 1985), pp. 109–124, 162–248; R. Sweet, *Cities and the Grand Tour: The British in Italy, c. 1690–1820* (Cambridge: Cambridge University Press, 2012).

24 C. Ehrlich, *The Music Profession in Britain since the Eighteenth Century* (Oxford: Oxford University Press, 1985), pp. 16–19; H. Berry, *The Castrato and His Wife* (Oxford: Oxford University Press, 2011).

25 Towner, *Historical Geography*, pp. 97–98, 132.

26 P. Burke, *Popular Culture in Early Modern Europe* (London: Temple Smith, 1979), p. 97.

27 Borsay, *English Urban Renaissance*, pp. 144–145; P. Clark, *The English Alehouse: a Social History, 1200–1830* (Harlow: Longman, 1983).

28 Borsay, *English Urban Renaissance*, pp. 123–127; P. Borsay, 'Concert topography and provincial towns in eighteenth-century England', in S. Wollenberg and S. McVeigh (eds.), *Concert Life in Eighteenth-Century Britain* (Aldershot: Ashgate, 2004), pp. 31–32.

29 S. McIntrye, 'Bath: the rise of a resort town, 1660–1800', in P. Clark (ed.), *Country Towns in Pre-Industrial England* (Leicester: Leicester University Press, 1981), pp. 208–210.

30 D. Coke and A. Borg, *Vauxhall Gardens: A History* (New Haven and London: Yale University Press, 2011); J. Conlin (ed.), *The Pleasure Garden from Vauxhall to Coney Island* (Philadelphia: University of Pennsylvania Press, 2013); J. Conlin, 'Vauxhall on the boulevard: pleasure gardens in London and Paris, 1764–1784', *Urban History*, 35:1 (2008), 24–47.

31 R. Porter, *Enlightenment: Britain and the Creation of the Modern World* (London: Allen Lane, 2000), p. 268.

32 J. Habermas, *The Structural Transformation of the Public Sphere*, trans. T. Burger (Cambridge: Polity 1989); C. Calhoun (ed.), *Habermas and the Public Sphere* (Cambridge, MA: MIT Press, 1992).

33 P. Borsay, 'The culture of improvement', in P. Langford (ed.), *The Short Oxford History of the British Isles: The Eighteenth Century* (Oxford: Oxford University Press, 2002), pp. 183–210.

34 E. Kluckert, 'The landscape garden', in R. Toman (ed.), *Neoclassicism and Romanticism* (Potsdam: Ullmann & Könemann, 2007), pp. 230–249.

35 R. Porter and M. Teich (eds.), *The Enlightenment in a National Context* (Cambridge: Cambridge University Press, 1981).

1

Charting the flows: institutions and genres

2

Art in the urban public sphere: art venues by entrepreneurs, associations and institutions, 1800–1850

J. PEDRO LORENTE

A rt historians usually refer to the Enlightenment as a turning point in the public consumption of art, because many royal or aristocratic galleries were made accessible to the public. But the opening of collections in stately palaces was a concession emanating from the top and often revoked unpredictably. Even after the French Revolution, many museums seemed shaped by the patronising values of enlightened despotism: everything for the people, but without the people. However, throughout Europe in the first half of the nineteenth century an interesting series of more participatory initiatives arose from the bottom up that substantially increased the number of more modest venues exhibiting art to a general public. Many of these 'alternative' art venues were situated very close to the most distinguished museums and galleries. Together they enriched numerous capital and provincial cities with a diverse and relatively accessible landscape of art venues, where people from various classes found new ways of enjoying their leisure time by contemplating works of art, meeting friends and exchanging views and news. As this chapter will argue, these new venues substantially extended the existing infrastructure of cafés, clubs and salons analysed by Jürgen Habermas when he expounded the concept of the 'public sphere'. Interestingly, many of these new art venues resulted from a constant international flow and exchange of new models and ideas, adapted to the domestic situation, whereas at the same time some new institutions were very specific to certain nations and regions. This chapter aims to sketch the increasingly diverse and changing landscape of public art venues in a range of influential European capitals and provincial cities, with a special attention to its comparative and transnational dimensions.

Entangled commercial art venues: London and Paris, new capitals of the art market

In *ancien régime* society, artists used to work within the structure of the guild system, whereby apprentices and officers would depend on a master, who agreed the terms and conditions of commissions with art patrons. However, in the first half of the nineteenth century, artworks were no longer produced collectively and to order on a regular basis; instead, they became individual products released to the market, with variable worth according to public appreciation. This was formed through social assessments, reflecting not only aesthetic hierarchies, but also the range of the places where the art pieces came into contact with the public.

Leaving aside monuments placed in public spaces on a permanent basis, there have always been works of art shown to the public on certain occasions. A significant historical example would be the street exhibitions organised for religious celebrations by guilds whose members included painters or collectors. This was a widespread tradition in Catholic countries, particularly in Italy, where temporary displays of pictures or decorative arts during the feast of Saint Luke have been documented since the dawn of the Renaissance, in squares and streets or under porticoes – for example, in the cloister of the Annunziata in Florence, where an exhibition of 250 pictures was open for the public for three days in 1709; or in the square in front of the Scuola di San Rocco during the feast of Saint Roch, as pictured in a 1735 painting by Canaletto exhibited in the National Gallery in London. In principle, these festive-religious shows did not have a commercial purpose, nevertheless, sometimes transactions arose, and in particular cases artworks were part of a fair or street market, as at the 'Mercato della Sensa' represented in 1775 by Guardi in a beautiful painting in the Gulbenkian Museum in Lisbon, that portrays the market of handcrafts under the porches of the piazza San Marco in Venice during the feast of the Ascension.[1] In France, a traditional example was the open-air exhibition of pictures organised by the parish of St Bartholomew in the Ile de la Cité on the occasion of the feast of Corpus Christi, which gained momentum in the eighteenth century. Crowds strolled from the Place Dauphine to the Pont Neuf to visit this show, popularly called 'Exposition de la Jeuneusse', because it was where novice artists would present their works, although it also sometimes featured masterpieces by Coypel, Rigaud or Chardin.[2]

Similarly, some religious festivities in historical cities were celebrated with street festivals, fairs and markets that, because of their riotous and commercial

Art in the urban public sphere   **23**

nature, would progressively leave the main streets and squares: the neighbour-hood of churches or noble palaces seemed inadequate for the roar of itinerant vendors, cattle markets, acrobats and street musicians. But the assortment of trinkets, bric-a-brac and curiosities offered to the public would often include works of art, and not necessarily of little merit: it seems that by the end of the eighteenth century it was still possible to find exquisite art pieces in the street stalls of London's Bartholomew Fair held every August 24 at West Smithfield, or in the Paris fair of San Germain, on 28 May.[3] A similar occurrence in Madrid was pictured by Goya in his famous cartoon *The Fair*, painted in 1779 for the Royal Tapestry, featuring a merchant of Madrid flea market who shows paint-ings and crockery to a nobleman and his retinue.

Goya himself was not very discriminative about the spaces where his own works would be offered to the general public, for he put on sale in 1799 his series of prints *Los Caprichos* in a liqueur and fragrance shop, instead of trusting them to one of the retailers of art and antiquities emerging then in Madrid,[4] probably because he wanted to retain control of the sales and avoid profes-sional art dealers. Similarly, William Blake was so opposed to London art mer-chants that in 1809 he preferred to hold a one-man show of his paintings in the upstairs room of his brother's hosiery shop in Golden Square, Soho. But both instances are also famous examples of commercial failures, since both Goya and Blake sold very little in such arbitrarily chosen shops. Other artists personally took care of showing their artworks by simply opening their studios to the public;[5] but most soon learned to deal with retailers specialising in sell-ing art materials. A very revealing case is Watteau's professional and personal bond with the art dealer Edmé-François Gersaint, for whom he painted his last picture *L'Enseigne de Gersaint* in 1720: an attractive shop-sign purposely made to be hung in a Parisian street, over the entrance of the refurbished premises of his *marchand* and friend.

It is no coincidence that Antoine Watteau painted this shop-sign for his friend in Paris upon returning from London, a city where this art of street advertising was highly developed.[6] Indeed, it was a typical eye-catching fea-ture used by pubs and shops all over Britain, thus the growing number of art-related businesses thriving in the capital in the eighteenth century could not be an exception. In Georgian times professional art dealers of all sorts, especially print sellers, flourished there more than in any other European city: not all were as famous as Colnaghi's, founded in 1760, or Agnew's, in 1817, but shrewdly most were located, like the first public museums, in the West End.[7] Art lovers could pay a visit to browse their merchandise in the shop

24 Charting the flows: institutions and genres

stalls or even in the back rooms, and gaze appreciatively at potential purchases; but even penniless passers-by could enjoy the contemplation of artworks from outside, as caricaturist James Gillray portrayed in his 1808 print *Very Slippery Weather*: a wet London street with a mixed group of bystanders, including a young tramp, looking into the eye-catching shop window of a print seller, a spectacle that has distracted the attention of a gentleman passer-by who stumbles in the foreground. Compositions of this kind, showing a mixed social meeting on the street in front of the shop-windows of art dealers, would later become commonplace in prints, paintings and photographs representing the effervescence of urban life in Paris and other cultural capitals. One of the most famous illustrated books was *Le Diable à Paris: Paris et les Parisiens: Mœurs et coutumes, caractères et portraits des habitants de Paris, tableau complet de leur vie privée, publique, politique, artistique, littéraire, industrielle* (*The Devil in Paris: Paris and the Parisians: Manners and Customs, Characters and Portraits of the Inhabitants of Paris, Complete Picture of their Private, Public, Political, Artistic, Literary, Industrial Life*), published in two volumes in 1845 and 1846. The second one featured a print by Félix Leblanc based on a drawing by Bertall (the artistic pseudonym of Charles-Albert d'Arnould), picturing Balzac in the boulevards surrounded by a crowd of people of different class, gender and age, some passing by while others turn to look at the prints exhibited in the shop-window of an art dealer.

In many ways, this public experience of art on the street was very close to the highbrow experience of visiting museums and galleries. The different types of venue tended to be clustered in the same neighbourhood and somehow conceptually associated. In different languages, the term 'gallery' was used for shops and commercial arcades, as well as for all sort of venues offering exhibitions either for profit or with educative aims. But somehow the degree of prominence of these spaces reflected an urban hierarchy, those of great art capitals being more influential than their equivalent in provincial towns, and those in central districts often ranking higher than initiatives in the outskirts. That is why it is particularly interesting to consider a *histoire croisée* of art venues in the heart of London and Paris, the emerging meccas for art commerce in the early nineteenth century.

Commercial 'arcades', typical novelties of the public sphere in that period, were favourite places to experience a variety of leisure activities.[8] Art dealers' galleries and art museums frequently featured among amenities enhancing these arcades or their vicinities. Therefore, the wealthy West End neighbourhood in London, a popular location for venues such as the Royal Opera Arcade established in 1816 or the Burlington Arcade in 1818, was also chosen by the main British auction houses, such as Sotheby's or Christie's, whose origins go back to 1744 and 1766 respectively. But London was not alone in setting this international trend and indeed it seems in some respects to have followed the Parisian example of the Galeries du Palais Royal, opened to the public in the mid-1780s, where shoppers could also visit the neighbouring gallery of the Orleans family[9] – until the collection was sold in London in 1792, providing another fascinating example of the circular history of urban culture in both cities. The Galeries du Palais Royal was rivalled in the mid-nineteenth century by the creation of a great auction house near the arcades Vivienne and Colbert, which was surrounded by other art venues.[10] In any case, a similar urban concentration developed in other capitals, where these businesses, like museums, allowed everyone to enter their premises, especially before and during the auctions, spectacles attended by prospective customers, but also by socialites, rubbernecks, pickpockets, etc., as represented in the engraving *Christie's Auction Room*, created by Thomas Rowlandson and Augustus Charles Pugin for the illustrated book *The Microcosm of London*, published in 1810 by Rudolph Ackerman.

This German entrepreneur had moved to London in 1795, where he opened a print shop and drawing school in the Strand with such a success that two years later he established his famous Repository of Arts in the same street, a print and picture business where he not only sold prints and illustrated books, but also drawing paper, art supplies, old master paintings, miniatures and ornaments. Its luxurious premises could be considered a stage for random encounters and discussions, comparable to the cafés, clubs and salons where a relatively mixed public could spend their leisure time and shape public opinion. In fact, this very elegant shop, one of the first to be illuminated by gas, became one of the most fashionable places in London to visit and to be seen until its closure in 1856: tea and lectures were offered, and conversations originated from chance meetings of sophisticated Londoners who kept themselves up-to-date about the latest designs for clothing or interiors. Such imitation of private domesticity would certainly become a typical strategy for art dealers to welcome their customers and make them feel at home, to the point that, unlike in museums and public galleries, patrons could touch and browse undisturbed through the books and prints or other artworks, as pictured in the illustration corresponding to Ackerman's Repository of Art in the above-mentioned book *The Microcosm of London*. But apart from some sophisticatedly dressed ladies and gentlemen depicted there, other customers in the shop seem to wear more modest

26   Charting the flows: institutions and genres

clothes: they are probably artists since, as mentioned above, the Repository of Arts also sold art materials. In fact, offering a meeting point for artists and their patrons was part of the charm of this celebrated enclave in London's public sphere, and its equivalent in Manchester, the shop of the immigrant Italian entrepreneur Vittore Zanetti and Thomas Agnew, also called the Repository of Arts. As the nineteenth century advanced, this doubling of commercial venues as cultural meeting-points would also become common practice for famous internationally operating art dealers such as Goupil & Cie, an emporium with branches in London, Vienna, Berlin, Brussels, The Hague and New York and its main headquarters in Paris, in a luxurious building including artists' studios upstairs where very important customers could be quickly introduced to their favourite painters and see their freshly painted works.[11]

To offer artists and art lovers a shelter would be, in many ways, an ambition of most art dealers: even nowadays many of them often say that they are not in the business in order to earn money. That was also common in the early nineteenth century, when some commercial art galleries gave remarkable examples of altruism. One of the best known was the Lebrun Gallery, a commercial space open to philanthropic collaborations with artists in Paris during the Romantic era.[12] But it is interesting here to highlight a similar case that was inaugurated by Henri Gaugain in November 1829 in the Arcade Colbert: although it offered paintings for sale, this gallery had high aspirations to resemble a museum, and was commonly called Musée Colbert, while its pompous official name was Exposition permanente de tableaux, statues, bronze, etc, des artistes modernes, français et étrangers.[13] A special case – showing again how the term 'museum' was sometimes used even for partly lucrative businesses – was the so-called Museum des Arts Modernes, installed in 1802 in Rue Grenelle-Saint-Honoré: it held changing exhibitions open to the public every day with an admission fee of one franc and 20 cents – a third of the takings went to the artists of the paintings, who could also sell them there.[14]

These three Parisian examples had their counterparts in London, not only regarding their highbrow aspirations but especially in respect of the practice of charging visitors an entrance fee: an old custom emulated in many other cities.[15] But the British capital offered a more influential model of commercial display resembling a museum. It constituted a special category of public recreation spaces that charged visitors to see works not for sale: these pay-per-view shows with high aspirations were often called 'museums' and it is difficult to distinguish them from proper museums or galleries, according to the present distinction in English.[16] Nowadays the code of ethics of the International

Council of Museums (ICOM) makes clear that museums are non-profit venues; but at their origin such discrimination was rather difficult to establish. The genealogy of mixed educational/commercial 'museums' can be traced back to the exhibition of paintings, stuffed animals, fossils and other attractions opened by Charles Wilson Peale in 1786 in Philadelphia. Peale charged the public for entrance and his financial success prompted his sons and other 'businessmen' to follow suit in Baltimore, New York and Utica.[17] But London became the main metropolis to feature these so-called museums, akin to low-brow fairground stalls with a variegated range of exhibits that changed periodically in order to assure the continuous flux of customers and cash.[18]

Likewise, the London Museum established in 1812, also known as the Egyptian Hall because of the neo-Egyptian decoration of its façade in Piccadilly – whose caryatides are at present displayed at the entrance of the Museum of London, as an homage to its predecessor – should in fact be considered a lucrative establishment. Its founder, William Bullock, was an entrepreneur who made plenty of money from entrance tickets: initially crowds would pay to see his large collection of artworks, armoury, stuffed animals and other curiosities, which he had previously displayed in his native Sheffield and in Liverpool, but in 1819 he sold most of his collection at auction, converting the 'museum' into an exhibition hall specialising in large paintings. He would often strike agreements with artists of renown, such as Benjamin Robert Haydon, James Ward, John Martin and Théodore Géricault, whose picture *The Raft of the Medusa* attracted 30,000 people in 1820. Ordinarily the admission fee was one shilling, of which Bullock kept two-thirds and the other third went to the painter.

Another example in London also featuring contemporary art as a crowd-puller was the Adelaide Gallery, open to the public in the Lowther Arcade of Adelaide Street, between Charing Cross and the Strand. It was founded in 1832 as the Gallery of Practical Science with the aim of publicising various scientific inventions, especially those related to electricity. These were shown and explained on the main floor, while the upstairs gallery featured innovative pieces of recent art. Thanks to this double attraction, in 1835 it welcomed more than 80,000 visitors, who each paid a shilling entrance fee, but this popularity declined in the 1840s and by 1852 the gallery had become a marionette theatre.[19]

The diffusion of this London model of pay-per-view museums to other European cities is an interesting research topic awaiting a new wave of comparative cultural studies. The social success of these shows encouraged other entrepreneurs to open all sorts of exhibition spaces, not necessarily to earn money but for the returns in public appreciation to be gained by the firm. Taking into account the great quantity of nineteenth-century illustrated journals and magazines that used the word 'museum' in their titles, it is not surprising that, beyond such metaphorical association, a number of periodicals had exhibition spaces in their headquarters where works by artists featuring in their pages or close to the journal would be publicly displayed for sale. But such exhibitions rarely made a profit for the venue, thus they could be considered as just a step below collective art patronage initiatives, which will be discussed next.

Art halls and exhibitions run by cultural associations

In addition to all these commercial venues run by private entrepreneurs seeking economic profit, in the first half of the nineteenth century, European cities also witnessed the rise of new types of art shows that were collectively managed. These exhibition spaces can be classified in three categories according to the degree of specialisation of their relative associations: first of all cultural societies of 'encyclopaedic' occupations; then art unions promoting local artists through lotteries and exhibitions; and finally the professional associations of artists and artists' clubs.

The more basic level corresponds to societies whose interest in the arts was only a part of their range of multiple cultural concerns. They would often hold art exhibitions scarcely open to the general public and this was especially true of societies for the encouragement of the economy, sciences and the arts, whose membership came from the very high social classes. That was the case for the Society of Dilettanti, founded in 1732 by noblemen and scholars, which was one of the most elitist clubs in London. Following this precedent, the Royal Society for the Encouragement of the Arts, Manufactures and Commerce was founded in 1754 and is still active today in its historic building on John Adam Street commissioned from Robert Adam. A similar case was the very exclusive – no artists were admitted as members – British Institution founded in 1795 and dissolved in 1867, also located in a purpose-built edifice on the aristocratic Pall Mall. The Royal Irish Institution, established in 1813, also erected a gallery in the centre of Dublin, close to Trinity College. Yet, notwithstanding their exclusivity in recruiting members or their highbrow art preferences, favouring old masters, they would sometimes welcome to their shows all sorts of visitors, regardless of gender, age and social situation; occasionally they even rented or borrowed theatres or other vast buildings for their art exhibitions. In the United Kingdom that was the usual option for public shows arranged by this kind of society, since they rarely had appropriately spacious premises, with the exception of the Royal Manchester Institution, active between 1823 and 1883, which erected a great neoclassical mansion that housed art galleries in the centre of that industrial city, with no equal in other provincial cities.[20] During the Enlightenment these upper-class associations became very common in the rest of Europe. Rarely including artists as full members, they encouraged local economic progress in general and the arts in particular through scholarships, awards and exhibitions. In France, this British prototype took some time to develop, but it was emulated earlier in Central European cities: some of the oldest examples were the Wirtschaftliche Gesellschaft von Bern, founded in 1762 in the Swiss capital, and the Leipziger Ökonomische Sozietät, created in 1763. In Spain, they were called *Reales sociedades económicas de amigos del país*, the oldest being the Real Sociedad Bascongada, dating from 1765, followed shortly afterwards by almost 100 similar societies in cities of the peninsula and the overseas territories.

More socially mixed were masonic lodges and cultural circles that proliferated throughout Europe in the same period. They would also organise public activities for the promotion of art, or at least some of them did. In the French capital, La Loge Les Neuf Soeurs, founded in 1776, arranged public exhibitions and lectures devoted to some pictures, and even opened a pompously named Musée de Paris in 1782 in the Rue Dauphine, a 'museum' in the etymological sense, since it was a place for educational meetings and discussions, but also exhibited the art collection of the society and artworks on loan.[21] On the other hand, the Colisée, a great night club situated in the western end of the Champs-Élysées, arranged an exhibition of contemporary art in 1779; an initiative already put in place the previous year by its main competitor, the society founded in 1778 by entrepreneur Pahin de la Blancherie called Salon de la Correspondance, which combined popular exhibitions of art and curiosities with a permanent collection of scientific objects and contemporary artworks. Three temporary art exhibitions were organised on its premises between 1782 and 1783.[22] Its fame reached the ears of Count d'Angiviller, director of the Bâtiments Royaux and organiser of the Louvre's official Salon, who felt threatened by this competition and in 1784 ordered the closure of all of these shows, arguing that these modest independent ventures were acceptable in England, given the lack of a governmental policy in support of the arts there, but they were not to be tolerated in France.[23]

Charting the flows: institutions and genres

Perhaps in order to avoid these problems, the name *musée* was avoided by many similar venues managed by cultural associations, preferring others such as *lycée* or *athénée*. Some early examples were the Lycée de Paris, founded in 1784 or the Lycée des Arts, dating back to 1788, and especially the Athénée in Paris, which had already been established in 1775.[24] Henceforth the nouns *athenaeum* and *lyceum* were favourite designations across Europe in the nineteenth century for middle-class associations devoted to art and literature.[25] In the British capital, the famous Lyceum Theatre had existed since 1765, and hosted many activities – including the first London exhibition of waxworks by Madame Tussaud – although it would be better known for hosting the English Opera House in the Romantic period. Thus it was not pure coincidence that the name Círculo del Liceo was used in Barcelona for the society that opened a large opera house in 1847; while other Spanish examples of this terminology followed Parisian precedents, such as the Liceo Artístico y Literario de Madrid, founded in 1837.[26] The athenaeums had a glorious English model, the Athenaeum Club, founded in London in 1824, whose members were mostly high-ranking civil servants, but that also admitted eminent artists, writers and scientists: its central headquarters in 107 Pall Mall, with a beautiful neoclassical façade, continues to attract many lovers of art to its great library, well equipped with nineteenth-century publications.[27] This interest in the arts was not equalled by any other English club but was a typical recreational association of gentlemen, with origins in the Tudor era, although it was in the nineteenth century that it reached its heyday.[28] Some clubs had headquarters richly decorated with works of art or featured other kinds of patronage, but in the most exclusive clubs, public access without invitation was quite complicated, and the attention to preserve the intimacy of members was always a handicap in organising activities open to the public. More accessible to the general public were the events and the building of the Ateneo Científico, Literario y Artístico de Madrid, founded in 1835, or its equivalents in other Spanish cities. Its spacious premises had rooms reserved for members, who could converse, read newspapers and illustrated magazines, etc., but on special days certain rooms were also open to the public for social gatherings: concerts, dances, lectures and various exhibitions. These sophisticated institutions were then emulated among the working class by *ateneos* and *liceos populares*. Yet, the most notable successors of such recreational societies providing a mixture of culture and leisure would be the casinos and *círculos de amistad*, proliferating later on in all Spanish cities, especially under the Bourbon Restoration. The marginal role of the arts in such associations was a common feature in nineteenth-century European cities in general.[29]

A second category deserving special attention were spaces managed by a type of association specifically dedicated to the promotion of the arts through exhibitions and other initiatives of collective patronage. We should look particularly at a type of group still ubiquitous in almost every important city of the German cultural area, where it is usually called *Kunstverein*, a denomination that could be translated as 'art circle' or 'art union', which was the name this kind of society used to have in English. It was a typically patriotic venture, uniting citizens of all social classes who would pay an annual fee to sustain local artists by means of different strategies, such as the collective subscription of prints, raffles of paintings or sculptures of local artists, the organisation of exhibitions and even the creation of an art collection owned by the institution. A comparative international study of their development has never been undertaken, and it would be rather difficult to tackle due to the many cultural nuances and peculiarities to be taken in consideration. Nevertheless, it is interesting to sketch a few major trends.

One of the better known is the French case, because Paris was the cradle of the most influential example, the Société des Amis des Arts, established in 1791, which organised shows of contemporary art distributed by lottery between subscribers, arranged first in the Louvre and since 1791 in an exhibition hall opened near the Palais-Royal – a venue eliminated during the Revolution and re-established in 1814, under the protection of the Duke of Berry.[30] It was an initiative in solidarity with the artists, impoverished by the disappearance of aristocratic patronage and the abolition of the guilds. The idea came from architect Charles de Wailly, inspired by the complaints of artists who now had to produce works without assured buyers. This Société also had the sympathy of the Ministry of the Interior, who endorsed its expansion elsewhere – not only in Paris, where the Société de la reunion des beaux-arts, created in 1792, arranged exhibitions in its premises at Rue d'Orléans St Honoré,[31] but all over France and the territories annexed by the Republic. For example in the city of Antwerp, a Société d'Emulation, was founded in 1802, while another one emerged the following year in Brussels, and under the Napoleonic Empire equivalent cases sprung up in Ghent, Liège, Malines, etc.[32] After the Restoration, these societies reached their zenith in France, with prominent examples such as the Cercle des Arts, which from 1819 onwards published a newspaper, commissioned etchings and sold paintings,[33] while in the provinces they flourished during the Romantic period, often with the support of each municipality: Avignon in 1826, Strasbourg in 1831, Marseilles in the following year, Rouen and Metz in 1834, Lyon and Nantes in 1836, Bordeaux in 1851, Toulon in 1854, and so on.

Modelled on these Parisian forerunners, the Società Promotrice di Belle Arti of Milan was founded in 1822, followed in Rome by a Società degli Amatori e Cultori di Belle Arti, publishing its statutes in 1830, and in Trieste its equivalent emerged in 1839/1840, while the Società Promotrice delle Belle Arti of Turin was established and mounted its first exhibition in 1842.[34] The Florence association was founded in 1843, and it is perhaps the most cited by historians of nineteenth-century art, because one of its exhibitions in the fall of 1862 was dedicated to the Macchiaioli group, who were unable to get their paintings admitted to the Academy, but henceforth became highly successful among the Tuscan bourgeoisie. Since 1850 the society in Genoa also organised annual exhibitions with abundant sales, and the Naples association started as late as 1862, but it is still active. Following these Italian examples and their French prototype, some similar associations would flourish later on in the capitals of Argentina, Mexico and other Latin American cities. It might be assumed that an earlier development of such associations for the promotion of art through lotteries and art shows would have taken place in Spain; but it seems that they hardly materialised in the first half of the nineteenth century, some of the earliest examples appearing as late as 1852 in Barcelona, or 1856 in Madrid and even later in other cities.[35]

In Central European cities too, other examples of these kind of societies can be traced; but their nomenclature is not so directly connected to the Parisian model and they eventually constituted a new urban paradigm. One of the oldest was the Kunst-Societät founded in 1792 in Nuremberg, while in Karlsruhe the Badische Kunstverein was instituted in 1818, the Hamburg Kunstverein in 1822 and the Kunstverein Bremen in 1829.[36] By the 1840s they had become commonplace in cities of the German cultural area. But what makes them a fascinating urban phenomenon was the fact that they often generated a specific art space, the Kunsthalle. Under this or any other name, as there are several variants in different Germanic languages, these pavilions purposely designed as exhibition halls became a widespread feature: the Kunsthalle of Basel was founded in 1839, the Kunstgebäude of Stuttgart were built in 1843, the Kunsthalle of Karlsruhe goes back to 1846 and that of Bremen dates from 1849, Kiel had one from 1857, Hamburg from 1869, etc. Some of them, in time, would achieve remarkable permanent collections of their own and could therefore be considered museums of contemporary art, although this was not at all a declared speciality. In fact, each Kunsthalle exhibited all sorts of objects, sometimes including archaeological, scientific and technological material.[37]

By contrast, the equivalent associations in the United Kingdom never built their own exhibition galleries. The rather middle-class London Art Union, founded in 1837, only had a modest office in the Strand and it used other buildings for its major annual exhibition each April, prior to the lottery of hundreds of contemporary artworks. On the other hand, the American Art Union established in 1839 had a 'Perpetual Free Gallery' since its inception – as the name indicated, access was free, at least for members, while other visitors paid a reasonable entry price – which soon became a popular place for meeting and socialising in the middle of Broadway Avenue.[38] In order to make it clear that members did not want to profit at the expense of the public, these societies sometimes gave the money raised through entrance fees to charitable causes, as the Royal Irish Art Union did in 1847, donating the total of £500 earned from an exhibition of old masters in Dublin to people affected by the famine of that year.[39] The great success of art unions was also emulated at mid-century in Australia and New Zealand. Yet in the English-speaking world their decline was very quick, due to a combination of obstacles, including legal impediments (laws prohibiting lotteries banned raffles of artworks), the lobbying hostility of the printing industries (opposing the distribution of prints among art union members) and conflicts between rival organisations, which meant that by the end of the nineteenth century the art unions had all but vanished and even members who had served for years in their steering committees seemed embarrassed to mention their prior involvement in such antiquated institutions, according to a recent cross-Atlantic study.[40]

Finally, a third category of exhibition spaces run by cultural associations relates to grassroots groups of artists who made themselves known to the public on their own initiative. It seems that British pioneers were setting the world standard from the Enlightenment onwards, although such initiatives found early precedents in all of the great capitals of the Western world. In London, the first exhibitions of contemporary art of this kind were organised during the 1740s by groups of artists such as Hogarth and Hayman at the children's orphanage called the Foundling Hospital. This type of initiative managed by artists in formal associations became ever more numerous, especially in the British capital, where they attained great prominence in the public sphere. Some of the earliest examples of artists' groups running their own exhibition galleries were the Society of Arts founded in 1754, the Society of Artists established in 1760 (and known from 1761 to 1783 as the Free Society of Artists, in order to avoid confusion with the Society of British Artists) and the British School, founded in 1823.[41] Meanwhile, others appeared that were

34   Charting the flows: institutions and genres

highly specialised with regard to art genre or technique used. For example the London-based Society of Painters in Water Colours (now known as the Royal Watercolour Society or RWS) was founded in 1804 by some secessionists of the Royal Academy dissatisfied by the lack of interest given the watercolours in their Summer Exhibitions; but in 1831 another group created the New Society of Painters in Water Colours, whose art shows would also accept works by artists not associated. Others followed suit, affiliating pastelists, etchers, sculptors, medallists etc., including the special case of the Society of Female Artists, which was founded in 1855 and opened its first annual show with 358 exhibits two years later.[42] Most of these associations of artists had their premises in buildings that were elegantly decorated with portraits of great artists or allegories of the arts that would catch the attention of passers-by in central London. This artistic lure attracted people indoors, where some rooms where open for visitors including some kind of exhibition gallery featuring shows related to the respective art speciality of each association. The fact that their programmes of events were so specialised often meant that their discerning public was a sophisticated minority, to the delight of snobbish artists like Whistler.

In contrast, during this period in Paris spaces run by artists' associations kept a low profile, and were usually housed in 'alternative' spaces of a mixed and somewhat downmarket nature. For example, the Galeries de l'Agence Générale Artistique opened in 1838 in a passage of the Boulevard Bonne-Nouvelle, commonly known for this reason as the 'Bazar Bonne Nouvelle'.[43] The nominal connection to bazaars tells us a lot about its low standing, although in order to attract socialites, such artists' associations would put on charity exhibitions – in this case, for example, the one held in 1843 in aid of the victims of Guadalupe Island. But poor artists themselves were often in need of social aid, thus one of the many associations of mutual assistance created under the reign of Louis Philippe at the behest of Baron Taylor was the Association des artistes peintres, sculpteurs, architectes, graveurs et dessinateurs, established in 1844, so that their sick or prematurely deceased members and their families would receive help using the money obtained from annual fees (of only six francs, to ensure a substantial membership, which soon amounted to 3,000 members) plus the income from art shows organised by them. The most celebrated was the ambitious retrospective, starting with paintings by David – whose *Marat Dead*, on loan from Brussels, was a rediscovery for the Parisian public – and culminating with works by Ingres – who had not exhibited at the official Salon for 12 years – held from 11 January to 15 March 1846 at the Bazar Bonne

Nouvelle.[44] From this lineage a long-lasting mutuality emerged in Madrid called Fomento de las Artes, founded in 1859, which offered drawing classes and other educational activities to its members, while non-members only had free access on special occasions such as the public exhibition of designs and crafts organised every year.

Such philanthropic societies succeeded in making the payment of entrance charges at art exhibitions in continental Europe more socially acceptable. A charitable exhibition, held in February–March 1860 at the Bazar Bonne Nouvelle was the origin of the Société National des Beaux-Arts, founded two years later by the painter, engraver and art dealer Louis Martinet, whose gallery at number 26 Boulevard des Italiens, became a regular venue for their exhibitions of contemporary art. But they never rivalled the public prominence of official exhibitions.[45] Undoubtedly, the explanation for this meagre development in Paris of public shows arranged by groups of artists was, as it will be discussed hereafter, the great importance of the salons organised by public powers. However, under the Third Republic, the situation shifted radically and the exhibitions arranged by artists' associations became a common feature in France, sometimes emulated in other countries.[46]

Major national and international institutions and exhibitions

Positioned high above all these different types of associations stood the Royal Academy of London, the Académie des Beaux-Arts in Paris and their international equivalents, whose elected members were prominent artists and representatives of the socio-political elite. But the most distinctive honour of these high-ranking institutions, making them a case apart was that they enjoyed some degree of support from the state.[47] This was particularly the case in France, where the monarchy financed the Académie des Beaux-Arts and its exhibitions of contemporary art held yearly or with biannual regularity at the Louvre since 1737. It was known as the Salon as a result of the metonymic link with its location, the so-called Salon Carré and adjacent corridors.[48] This model would be emulated in many other European nations, competing to organise their own official fine arts exhibitions.

The Royal Academy in London was a very particular case, because it only received minimal financial support from the crown or public purse, with the exception of its magnificent premises at Somerset House. This had two consequences for its public approach. Instead of the official taste, conservative restrictions and tough juries typical of the French Salon, or the other official

Figure 2.1 *La Grande Galerie du Louvre*, print by J.B. Allen from a drawing by Thomas Allom, c. 1840.

exhibitions organised by academies with the financial support of the state, the annual Summer Exhibition of the Royal Academy was more populist and inclusive in taste, because the institution earned a percentage from art sales that it desperately needed. Entrance tickets and exhibition catalogues were sold to the public by the porter, as pictured by John Russell in a pastel painting of around 1792 in the collection of the Courtauld Gallery, where the artist represented a tumultuous crowd in the background hurrying upstairs. Such rowdy behaviour was not uncommon for Paris Salon visitors. In a witty 1808 picture by Louis-Léopold Boilly, *The Public at the Salon of the Louvre Looking at the Sacré Napoleon*, owned by the National Gallery in Washington, a thronging crowd is represented in front of David's big masterpiece, but not all characters are looking at it in silence; there are family groups chatting, flirting lovebirds, crying children and so on.[49] At the gates, street vendors called out offering pamphlets and prints or explanatory booklets, published by art critics – in fact a 24-year-old Baudelaire published a booklet on the Salon of 1845, convinced that the sales were going to reap huge profits. Similarly, there were stalls selling drawings and prints under the arches of the Institute.[50] These neighbouring forms of art consumption were still very related in terms of urbanity.

As the nineteenth century advanced, a disciplinary emphasis would succeed in civilising the crowds attending massive exhibitions and other amenities.[51]

Britain played a leading role with its boom of national and international exhibitions during this period, such as the Universal Exhibition of London in 1851 and the celebrated show 'Art Treasures of the United Kingdom', held in Manchester in 1861. Both have been studied by a large number of scholars, some of whom have shed new light on social consumption of art in the public realm, contrasting for example the solitary gaze of the elegant *flâneur*, to the group behaviour of family visitors and the quick march of masses of workers reviewing the displays accompanied by brass-bands, drums and fifes[52] – a case that could well be added to those analysed in other surveys on promenading as a cultural urban phenomenon at the end of the eighteenth century and much of the nineteenth.[53] This period witnessed the rise of a new profession, the art critic, a key figure in the creation of public opinion through comments made sometimes orally but more often published in newspapers, art journals or books; but not without social contestation. This kind of commentator was especially conscious of artworks extolled in great official exhibitions and museums, frequently establishing comparisons with referential art shows in foreign capitals. But all sorts of polite travellers, usually enthusiastic consumers of city almanacs and tourist guides, should also be taken into account, as they questioned established hierarchies and fashioned cultural exchanges across Europe, facilitating shifting approaches: in this respect, official art shows were akin to other leisure attractions, supposedly catering for a broader spectrum of publics and changing perspectives.

Public museums and art galleries, considered the apex of cultural offerings, were not unfamiliar with these shifting policies and urbanities in action all over Europe from the Enlightenment through Romanticism: on this subject, a new strand of international comparative critique could be developed.[54] Undeniably, one of the main achievements of the Enlightenment was to offer a greater availability of cultural heritage to lay citizens through the creation of national museums, such as the British Museum in London and the Louvre, or through the opening to the general public of palatial collections like the Capitoline Museum in Rome, the Uffizi in Florence, the Luxembourg Museum in Paris, the Belvedere in Vienna, the Stalhof in Dresden and the Royal Museum in Stockholm.[55] Yet, regardless of their royal or national status, they originally offered a very limited degree of accessibility. The latter term is nowadays commonly associated with special arrangements for disabled visitors, whose ability to navigate palatial stairs was not considered in this earlier period. But there were other social barriers then as well, taking into account that etiquette rules were *de rigueur* in the case of some galleries of the English nobility and

Charting the flows: institutions and genres

in some court galleries such as the Hermitage in Saint Petersburg, while in the Prado, barefoot or shabby-clothed visitors were not admitted and in French museums not having a 'decent' dress could lead to refusal of entry by the guards, who used to wear smart uniforms.

Furthermore, opening times and conditions were very restrictive. In Rome, the Capitoline Museum founded in 1734 aimed at a target public of *eruditi* admitted on appointment only, under the guidance of the keeper or his son, who expected to receive tips from visiting scholars, artists and travellers; time-tables of public opening hours were only established in the early nineteenth century.[56] Similarly, visiting the British Museum in the early years was not a simple process: one had to first go there to formally apply for entrance when a place would be available, then return another day to collect the admission pass valid for a specific date and time, and finally be there at the appointed moment, to follow a group led by a guide who would not allow individual visitors to stop at their own will if something caught their eye.[57] In Paris, when the French royal gallery opened in 1750 at the Luxembourg palace on the city's *rive gauche*, general visitors were admitted twice a week, on Wednesdays and Saturdays, from 10am to 1pm in winter and from 4pm to 7pm in summer; art-ists enjoyed a particular treatment and were allowed more days and hours, but for security reasons they were strictly forbidden to paint, for fear they might stain the paintings or swap an original for its copy.[58] Public visiting days were also quite limited when the new French Republic opened the Museum Français at the Louvre in 1793,[59] where general visitors were given free access three days per week. In fact, the museum was closed to the public three years later and only reopened to all citizens on 14 July 1796. But things seemed even worse in other countries, for example in Spain, where the Prado was originally open to the general public only on Sundays, and for most of the nineteenth century just twice a week, save on days of wet weather when it would be completely closed to avoid mud being trodden around the galleries.

However, some revolutionary novelties should not be overlooked; for example, a greater freedom of entry and behaviour at the Louvre: barriers and armed guards were placed to prevent vandalism, but they would not deter peo-ple from making loud comments that could be overheard by other visitors.[60] Museums came to be crowded public spaces where the spectacle of the build-ing and its collections was supplemented by the merriment of interacting with fellow visitors. Sometimes museum audiences were so politically conscious of their own right to enjoy these amenities as a common public space that they even wanted to take in their dogs, food or beverages![61] The Enlightenment is

Art in the urban public sphere **39**

associated with greater freedom to speak out and to exchange personal opinions, but that was not only the case for social gatherings in salons, bookshops and cafés. Romanticism is identified with individual emotions, but these were also expressed in public. We should remember that reading became a silent and intimate activity little by little, but for many people reading aloud remained a common habit, especially when they had to share a catalogue with other visitors or read out labels to illiterate companions.

Museums, like theatres and concert houses, favoured dim light, silence and intimacy in the late nineteenth century;[62] but in the period considered here they were more like a social playground, a public space for intermingling, with even more equalitarian conditions than street promenades: down from their horses and carriages, the elites had to walk there on foot, and they even had to hand in their canes and umbrellas at the door – except at the Prado Museum, where high-ranking military or civil dignitaries were accorded the privilege of keeping their walking canes.[63] Museum regulations in French provinces insisted on asking for silence, decorum and appropriate behaviour, and prohibited knitting or other such activities, but it seems that this emphasis was precisely due to the very different reality they experienced, especially on Sundays, when the masses would arrive, commenting aloud and even touching artworks, particularly political pictures, for these often sparked partisan discussions, documented in the local museums of Bordeaux and Marseilles.[64]

Moreover, besides cafés, ateliers and other bohemian haunts, art museums were also favourite places where artists would meet colleagues and encounter other people. In fact, the aforementioned restrictions of entrance to early museums did not apply to artists, who could go every day to the Louvre or any equivalent institution. In Berlin, the Altes Museum was built near the Academy of Fine Arts, so that art students could see and discuss artworks daily and, in the mid-nineteenth century, some university lectures on art history were routinely given at the museum in front of relevant masterworks.[65] At that time, artists and connoisseurs often shared their enthusiasm and criticisms in museum rooms: there is an abundant romantic iconography of painters portrayed in public art galleries copying their favourite masterpieces, but some drawings, prints and pictures show artists in museums engaged in visual or verbal interaction with other colleagues or, more interestingly, with other visitors. Where else could unacquainted art enthusiasts and artists meet and casually interact? Art scholars and foreigners were granted the same timetable of museum opening enjoyed by artists. All of them were instrumental in creating collective opinion on art matters, and no doubt in looking at artworks

40   Charting the flows: institutions and genres

together, in sharing appreciative comments and in nurturing the continuing social re-evaluation of academic canons in museum spaces.

This is even more significant regarding museums of contemporary art, where public appraisal or dismissal of works on show could offend living artists or their supporters. When Louis XVIII opened the Musée des Artistes Vivants in 1818, lay citizens could only enjoy it on Sundays and public holidays, as a leisurely complement to the popular promenades in the Luxembourg Gardens. On weekdays, most people were supposed to work, thus only tourists and artists were admitted then at the Luxembourg Museum, a site removed from the hub of busy life in the centre of Paris. In many ways, this kind of museum specialising in contemporary art responded to new urban hierarchies: every medium-sized town already had its 'temple' of art and antiquities, generally in a central location, but only the big cities would erect 'cathedrals of urban modernity', often in sprawling districts.[66] In London this dichotomy was compounded by the opposition between two cultural counterparts: on the one hand the National Gallery, founded in 1824 and definitively housed 14 years later in Trafalgar Square, where old masters were accessible without payment in the heart of a polluted and populous metropolis; on the other hand, the museum complex of South Kensington, a district of green fields and new mansions, where since 1857 an amalgam of didactic institutions offered complementary charms.

However the bus ride from the city centre would cost sixpence, to which another sixpence had to be added as an entrance fee, except for artists and on Mondays, Tuesdays and Saturdays, when admission was in general free for all. Fee-paying days ensured quieter visits for the well-off and better working conditions for artists copying works as part of their professional training. This implicitly involved a social division of time-sessions for different publics, which became very common in Victorian society at concert or theatre performances.[67] The South Kensington Museum pioneered night-openings by gaslight supposedly for the benefit of workers, but there was a charge for these sessions: a social filter to be taken into account. Similarly, in the late 1860s it was the first museum to provide a cafeteria, a grill-restaurant and a dining room; but the kind of public they were catering for can be gauged from their luxurious decorations, designed by James Gamble, Edward Poynter and William Morris respectively. Later on, new political and social efforts would bring new art galleries to the slums and to industrial settlements. But by then the infancy of museums was over: an age of innocence when they had been the pinnacle in the emerging art world of the Enlightenment and

Romanticism, an intricate public sphere concentrating all sort of venues in the centre of great cities, where experiencing art provided social encounters and potential conflicts, intermingling the uneducated and the elite, art lovers and artists.

Conclusion

Arranged for enjoyment, all places where people would find art on show in the first half of the nineteenth century served as a backdrop to random conversations and disquisitions vindicated in this chapter as key elements in the emergence of a modern 'public sphere'. This concept, following Habermas, had been mostly associated with the creation of public opinion generated in cafés, clubs and salons or other venues for social debates and conversations triggered by the reading of newspapers or books. But it has been argued here that looking at public displays of art also generated dialectic appraisal shaping social judgement. This is not to deny that exhibitions and museums would also act as cultural transmitters of upper-class values in common citizens and outsiders, as it has been appropriately demonstrated by interpretations drawing on Foucault's analysis of the history of disciplinary control. Yet, another perspective could also be considered, alleging that art shows and museums in this early stage were not too different from other urban spaces for socialisation and leisure: in fact, they grew very close both topographically and conceptually. Three different categories have been discussed in this chapter, corresponding to public displays organised by individuals, associations and official institutions. They nurtured modern visual culture, sometimes emulating paradigms imported from influential capitals and occasionally exporting new models to other cities.

Notes

1 Lina Padoan Urban, 'La festa della Senta nelle arti e nell'iconografia', *Studi Veneziani*, 10 (1996), 291–353.
2 Prosper Dorbec, 'L'exposition de la Jeunesse au XVIIIe siècle', *Gazette des Beaux-Arts*, 33 (1905), 456–470 and 34 (1906), 77–86; Thomas E. Crow, *Painters and Public Life in Eighteenth-Century Paris* (New Haven and London: Yale University Press, 1985), pp. 83–86; Oskar Bätschmann, *The Artists in the Modern World: The Conflict between Market and Self-Expression* (Cologne: Dumont, 1997), pp. 13–14.
3 Crow, *Painters and Public Life*; Richard Altick, *The Shows of London* (Cambridge, MA and London: Belknap Press 1978).

Charting the flows: institutions and genres

4 Some of these Madrilenian retailers are mentioned in a recent study by Jesusa Vega, where the famous painting by Luis Paret y Alcázar owned by the Museo Lázaro Galdiano usually entitled *The Antiquarian's Shop*, has been identified as the shop of Antonio Geniani. Jesusa Vega, *Ciencia, arte e ilusión en la España ilustrada* (Madrid: Ministerio de Cultura, CSIC, Ediciones Polifemo, 2010), pp. 268–269.

5 This was very common in London, where Gainsborough advertised such an initiative in newspapers in 1785. The same year, David opened his studio in Rome to show *The Oath of the Horatii*. In 1808, Caspar David Friedrich did likewise in Dresden, where he threw open his studio to exhibit *The Cross in the Mountains*. See Elizabeth Gilmore Holt, *The Triumph of Art for the Public, 1785–1848, The Emerging Role of Exhibitions and Critics* (Garden City: Anchor Books, 1979), pp. xxiv–xxv, 12–28, 52–57, 121–133, 148–168, 206–210, 235–237. Furthermore, in the early nineteenth century the first monographic art galleries developed showing the works of a single artist, like the posthumous picture gallery of Benjamin West, and Turner's personal gallery open by appointment to visitors next to his house. Giles Waterfield (ed.), *Palaces of Art: Art Galleries in Britain 1790–1990* (London: Dulwich Picture Gallery, 1991), pp. 77–78.

6 Shop-sign paintings were so popular in Britain that an exhibition of this kind of art was arranged in London from April to June 1762, competing for visitors with those organised by the Royal Academy, according to Jonathan Conlin, 'At the expense of the public: the sign painters' exhibition of 1762 and the public sphere', *Eighteenth-Century Studies*, 36:1 (2002), 1–21. Other art historians had previously studied the proliferation of such paintings on the streets of Georgian London, well documented in some prints by Hogarth: Ambrose Heal, *The Signboards of Old London Shops: A Review of the Shop Signs Employed by the London Tradesmen during the XVIIth and XVIIIth Centuries, compiled from the Author's Collection of Contemporary Trade-Cards and Billheads* (London: Portman, 1988).

7 Waterfield (ed.), *Palaces of Art*, pp. 159–167; Gordon Fyfe, *Art, Power and Modernity: English Art Institutions, 1750–1950* (London and New York: Leicester University Press, 2000), pp. 64–65.

8 The ever-increasing influence of Walter Benjamin, who was not able to finish his great treaty *Das Passagen Werk*, has meant that commercial arcades are very popular as a topic of study from different points of view, especially their architecture, which has been studied across Europe in a voluminous book by another German scholar, Johann Friedrich Geist, *Passagen: ein Bautyp des 19. Jahrhunderts* (Munich: Prestel Verlag, 1982).

9 Some of the oldest and best examples were the arcades of the Palais Royal in Paris, opposite the Louvre, where shoppers could also visit the neighbouring gallery of paintings of the Orleans family. Its owner, the spendthrift Duke of Chartres, did well out of developing the site in the rear garden in 1784: one of the lures of the place for polite society was visiting his art collection but also important was for lots of people to enjoy the other charms of the three enclosed galleries accommodating shops, meeting halls and cafés on the ground floor, while on the top floor rooms were rented out to 'bachelors, prostitutes and artists'. Mark Girouard, *Cities and*

People: A Social and Architectural History (New Haven and London: Yale University Press, 1985), p. 203.

10 An art district emerged in the arcades near the Hôtel des ventes Drouot, a great building erected in 1852 in the vicinity of these commercial spaces and the Bourse, as epicentre of the new world capital of the pictures trade. Monica Preti-Hamard and Philippe Sénéchal (eds.), *Collections et marché de l'art en France, 1789–1848* (Rennes: Presses Universitaires de Rennes-Institut National d'Histoire de l'Art, 2005).

11 Hélène Lafont-Couturier (ed.), *État des Lieux*, I (Bordeaux: Musée Goupil 1994).

12 The Lebrun Gallery at Rue Gros-Chenet in Paris had been originally built by art dealer Jean-Baptiste-Pierre Lebrun, but it was bought after 1790 by Quillet and managed by the honorary curator of the Louvre, Charles Paillet, who organised a highly successful exhibition there in 1826 in aid of Greek pro-independence campaigners, where Delacroix showed his painting *Greece Expiring on the Ruins of Messolonghi*. In 1829, Paillet organised another charity exhibition of contemporary art in the same gallery, for which he dared ask the royal household to lend him two paintings by Gros, *Napoleon Visiting the Pest-house of Jaffa* and *The Battle of Eylau*, stored at the Louvre, arguing that the profit would be used to combat mendicity (on these and other instances see Marie-Claude Chaudonneret, *L'État et les artistes: De la Restauration à la monarchie de Juillet (1815–1833)* (Paris: Flammarion 1999), pp. 110–116.

13 Beth Wright, 'Henri Gaugain et le musée Colbert: L'entreprise d'un directeur de galerie de d'un d'éditeur d'art à l'époque romantique', *Nouvelles de l'estampe*, 114 (1990), pp. 24–31.

14 Chaudonneret, *L'État et les artistes*, p. 102.

15 Exhibitions with entry fees arranged by artists were very common in London, where lucrative precedents had been set by John Singleton Copley in 1784 and Benjamin West in 1785. But in Berlin Friedrich Bury caused general outcry when he painted a portrait of Goethe in 1800 and exhibited it charging an entrance fee. Meanwhile, in Paris, nobody had protested a few months earlier when David had opened his studio at the Louvre, asking visitors to pay a small fee to see *The Intervention of the Sabine Women*: so many customers came from 1799 to 1802, when Napoleon ordered its closure, and the show continued at the former church of Cluny until 1805, that the painter earned more than 60,000 francs, which allowed him to buy land and a cottage, while he sold this painting in 1819 to the restored monarchy for 10,000 francs. This example illustrates the growing importance, even in economic terms, of showing artworks in the public sphere instead of selling them. Some art historians consider this the prelude of other famous cases later set by Courbet who tried his first *exposition payante* in 1850, renting premises in Ornans, Besançon and Dijon to show his recent works, charging 50 centimes with irregular success: in Besançon there were up to 250 visitors, while in Dijon he had to close after three days for lack of customers. Better known is his Pavillion of Realism open by Courbet on the occasion of the 1855 and 1867 Universal Exhibitions in Paris, the latter emulated by Manet, who arranged a show with an entry charge at the same time.

16 This English differentiation between museum and art gallery, to describe those specifically dealing with art, generally refers just to content, because a gallery can also be a building – even if it is for private use – erected for the purpose of housing paintings. But a hedonist connotation is also attached to this term due to its etymology – a Gallicism from the old French word *galerie*: amusement, revelry. Thus, while one may go to a museum to learn, it is understood that one goes to a gallery for the sake of mere visual enjoyment. Javier Gómez Martínez, 'Museo y galería, pragmatismo y hedonismo en la museología anglosajona', *Trasdós. Revista del Museo de Bellas Artes de Santander*, 4 (2000), 77–97, pp. 78 and 82.

17 David R. Brigham, *Public Culture in the Early Republic: Peale's Museum and its Audience* (Washington, DC and London: Smithsonian Institution Press, 1995).

18 More specialised and permanent contents, closer to the notion of a museum proper, were riskier investments; but some examples emerged towards the end of the eighteenth and the beginning of the nineteenth centuries. That was the case of the Shakespeare Gallery in London, a permanent exhibition of paintings on Shakespearean topics commissioned from prestigious artists, inaugurated by businessman John Boydell in 1789 in Pall Mall, where it was active until 1804, when it went bankrupt.

19 Celina Fox, *The Arts of Industry in the Age of Enlightenment* (New Haven and London: Yale University Press, 2009), p. 455.

20 Equivalent institutions were founded in Derby (1783), Manchester (1781), Newcastle (1793), Birmingham (1800), Glasgow (1800), Bristol (1808), Plymouth (1812), Liverpool (1814), Leeds (1818), Cambridge (1819), York (1822), Sheffield (1822), etc. (most of them described at www.scholarly-societies.org). But all sorts of mechanics' institutions also had paintings, statues, natural history specimens, maquettes or technological equipment on show in their premises, where they organised public meetings, conferences, and exhibitions. Fox, *The Arts of Industry*, p. 228.

21 Hervé Guénot, 'Musées et lycées parisiens (1780–1830)', *Dix-Huitième Siècle*, 18 (1986), 249–67.

22 John Goodman, 'Altar against altar: the Colisée, Vauxhall utopianism and symbolic politics in Paris (1769–77)', *Art History*, 15 (1992), 434–469; Laura Auricchio, 'Pahin de la Blancheri's Commercial Cabinet of Curiosity (1779–87)', *Eighteenth-Century Studies*, 36 (2002), 47–61.

23 Dominique Poulot, *Musée, nation, patrimoine, 1789–1815* (Paris: Gallimard, 1997), p. 97.

24 Guénot, 'Musées et lycées parisiens', pp. 252–253.

25 Jean-Pierre Chaline, *Sociabilité et érudition: les sociétés savantes en France, XIXe-XXe siècles* (Paris: Editions du CTHS, 1995).

26 Aránzazu Pérez Sánchez, *El Liceo Artístico y Literario de Madrid (1837–1851)* (Madrid: Fundación Universitaria Española, 2005).

27 Frank Richard Cowell, *The Athenaeum: Club and Social Life in London, 1824–1974* (London: Heinemann, 1975).

28 Peter Clark, *British Clubs and Societies, 1580–1800* (Oxford: Clarendon Press, 2001).

29 Graeme Morton, Boudien de Vries and R.J. Morris (eds.), *Civil Society, Associations and Urban Places: Class, Nation and Culture in Nineteenth-Century Europe* (Aldershot: Ashgate, 2006).

30 Udolpho Van De Sandt, *La Société des Amis des Arts (1789–1798): Un mécénat patriotique sous la Révolution* (Paris: ENSBA, 2006).

31 Preti-Hamard and Sénéchal, *Collections et marché de l'art*, p. 80.

32 Christophe Loir, *L'emergence des Beaux-Arts en Belgique: Institutions, artistes, public et patrimoine (1773–1835)* (Brussels, Éditions de l'Université de Bruxelles, 2004), pp. 131–133.

33 Louis Lagrange, 'Des Sociétés des Amis des Arts en France: Leur origine, leur état actuel, leur avenir', *Gazette des Beaux-Arts*, 9 (1861), 291–301; 10 (1861), 29–47, 102–117, 158–168 and 227–242; Gérard Nonnier, *L'art et ses institutions en France. De la Révolution à nos tours* (Paris: Gallimard, 1995), pp. 167–176.

34 Maria Cristina Gozzoli (ed.), *Istituzioni e Strutture Espositive in Italia. Secolo XIX: Milano, Torino* (Pisa: Scuola Normale Superiore, 1981).

35 In Spain the history of these kinds of associations is little-known, perhaps because they never made great progress, but maybe also because Spanish historiography is not much interested in studying them. Jesús-Pedro Lorente, 'Las asociaciones de amigos de las artes y sus exposiciones en el siglo XIX: Modelos internacionales, e interrogantes sobre su desarrollo en España', in Isabel Álvaro, Concha Lomba and José L. Pano (eds.), *Estudios en homenaje a Gonzalo Borrás* (Zaragoza: IFC, 2012), pp. 454–464. It is no coincidence that the first general study thereon was offered in a North American doctoral thesis: Óscar E. Vázquez, *Inventing the Art Collection: Patrons, Markets, and the State in Nineteenth-Century Spain* (Philadelphia: Pennsylvania State University Press, 2001), pp. 94, 95 and 248, footnotes 97, 98, 104, where the earliest example quoted is the Societat d'Amics de les Belles Arts, founded in Barcelona in 1852, followed by short-lived equivalents in Madrid in 1856 and in 1867. Both Madrilean societies apparently failed due to their elitist character, because middle-class people could not afford their high fees. Much cheaper was the annual subscription paid by members of the aforementioned Barcelona association, which had more than 1,000 shareholders when it was re-founded in 1868, residing then in calle de las Cortes, to the right of the Paseo de Gracia, a nice room for exhibitions. Ana María Revilla Hernando, 'Promoción de las artes y vitalización cultural Informaciones en La Ilustración Española y Americana, 1870–1895', *AACADigital*, 14 (2011). Others emerged in Cadiz, Seville, Málaga and Valencia, but much later and not always having premises of their own to show exhibitions.

36 Joachim Großmann, 'Verloste Kunst. Deutsche Kunstvereine im 19. Jahrhundert', *Archiv für Kulturgeschichte*, 76 (1994), 351–364; Christoph Behnke, 'Zur Gründungsgeschichte deutscher Kunstvereine', in Bernd Mila and Heike Munder (eds.), *Tatort Kunstverein* (Nuremberg: Verlag für moderne Kunst, 2001), pp. 11–25.

37 James J. Sheehan, *Museums in the German Art World from the End of the Old Regime to the Rise of Modernism* (Oxford and New York: Oxford University Press, 2000), pp. 111–112.

38 Rachel N. Klein, 'Art and authority in antebellum New York City: the rise and fall of the American Art Union', *Journal of American History*, 81:4 (1995), 1534–1561.

39 Eileen Black, 'Practical patriots and true Irishmen: the Royal Irish Art Union, 1839–1859', *Irish Arts Review Yearbook*, 14 (1998), 140–146, p. 143.

40 Joy Sperling, 'Art cheap and good: the art union in England and the United States, 1840–60', *Nineteenth-Century Art Worldwide*, 1 (2002).

41 Algernon Graves, *The Society of Artists of Great Britain, 1760–1791; the Free Society of Artists, 1761–1783; A Complete Dictionary of Contributors and Their Work from the Foundation of the Societies to 1791* (London: G. Bell and Sons, 1907); John Whiteley, 'Exhibitions of contemporary painting in London and Paris, 1760–1860', in Francis Haskell (ed.), *Saloni, galerie, musei, e loro influenza sullo sviluppo dell'arte nei secoli XIX e XX* (Bologna: Clueby, 1982), pp. 69–79, footnote 8; Bätschmann, *The Artists in the Modern World*, pp. 24–26.

42 The Royal Institute of Oil Painters, the Society of Pastelists, the Royal Society of Painter-Etchers, the International Society of Sculptors, Painters and Etchers, two Societies of Watercolorists, the Royal Society of Marine Painters, the Royal Society of Portrait Painters, the Society of Medallists, the Society of Wildlife Artists, etc. The list is long and this is just a selection of those mentioned by Julie F. Codell in Brian Allen (ed.), *Towards a Modern Art World* (New Haven and London: Yale University Press, 1995), pp. 169–188.

43 This shopping arcade, where the diorama was installed after 1840, had a market in the basement and 300 shops in the ground floor, while the upper floor, with zenithal lighting, was meant to 'permanent exposition des produits de l'industrie et des arts de deux, tels que tableaux, engravings, etc.'. See Luc Marco, *Histoire mangeriale du Bazar Bonne-Nouvelle: Galeries marchandes à Paris, 1835–1863* (Paris: L'Harmattan, 2009).

44 Bruno Foucart et al., *Le Baron Taylor, l'Association des artistes et l'exposition du Bazar Bonne-Nouvelle en 1846* (Paris: Fondation Taylor, 1995).

45 In 1863 Martinet turned down a proposal presented by Doré and Manet, who tried to display in his gallery some of their paintings rejected at the Salon. This was finally granted by Napoleon III who scored a point by opening a Salon des Refusés in 1863, despite the negative reports from officials of his cultural administration.

46 In this context the exhibitions of the Impressionists and other artistic groups would arise, and even the French government left the official organisation of the Salon from 1880, leaving the management of future events in the hands of associations of artists. Other nations would not emulate this U-turn in cultural policies, but groups of artists also proposed alternatives to the official exhibitions, and thus in Madrid an artists' association created one of the busiest exhibition centres – still today – which is the *Círculo de Bellas Artes*, founded in 1880. Other internationally renowned venues would be created by the Group of the XX in Brussels or the Secessionists in Germany and Austria – the Haus der Secession built in Vienna 1898 is perhaps the best-known example worldwide, but comparable to the Konsthuset in Stockholm and many others all around Europe. On the development of artists associations in Europe during the second half of the nineteenth century, see J. Pedro Lorente, 'Asociaciones de artistas y sus espacios expositivos en el siglo XIX', in M. Carmen Lacarra (ed.), *Arte del siglo XIX* (Zaragoza: IFC, 2013), pp. 279–312 (esp. pp. 285–312).

47 Nikolaus Pevsner, *Academies of Art, Past and Present* (New York: Da Capo Press, 1973).

48 Although this great exhibition was forced to temporarily withdraw the museum's permanent collection from public view, the Salon continued to be held during this period at the Louvre, moving later on to the Palace of Exhibitions and Industry, built in 1855.

49 The audience at the Paris Salon was a variegated spectacle in itself, starting outdoors, with jugglers and puppet shows on the streets, while in the showrooms it was often difficult to see the pictures due to the crush of people, but some onlookers were much amused by watching groups of visitors and listening to their comments. See Eva Boutillo, 'Le fréquentation du Salon de 1817 à 1827', in James Learns and Pierre Vaisse (eds.), *Ce Salon à quoi tout se ramène: Le Salon de peinture et de sculpture, 1791–1890* (Bern: Peter Lang, 2010), pp. 23–43.

50 These stalls were only abolished in 1863, according to Anne Martin-Fugier, *La vie d'artiste au XIXe siècle* (Paris: Audibert, 2007), p. 171.

51 Eilean Hooper-Greenhill, *Museums and the Shapping of Knowledge* (London and New York: Routledge, 1992); Tony Bennett, *The Birth of the Museum: History, Theory, Politics* (London and New York: Routledge, 1995).

52 Titus Salt, a textile tycoon, sent 2,500 workers from his Bradford factory to Manchester on a Saturday to visit the Art Treasures Exhibition, where they marched behind their banners and two music bands, who continued to play in the upstairs gallery during lunchtime and for the rest of the workers' visit, entertaining them and all visitors, including some who found popular music unfit for the enjoyment of high art, but acquiesced cheerfully to this exceptional behaviour. Helen Rees Leahy, 'Walking for pleasure? Bodies of display at the Manchester Art Treasures Exhibition in 1857', in Deborah Cherry and Fintan Cullen (eds.), *Spectacle and Display* (Oxford: Blackwell Publishing, 2008), pp. 71–91, 86.

53 Christophe Loir and Laurent Turcot (eds.), *La promenade au tournant des 18e et 19e siècles (Belgique/Europe)* (Brussels: Editions de l'Université, 2011).

54 Testimonies by artists, scholars and curators are a promising source for comparative international essays, such as those compiled in Andrea Meyer and Bénédicte Savoy, *The Museum is Open: Towards a Transnational History of Museums, 1750–1940* (Berlin and Boston: De Gruyter, 2014).

55 Per Bjurström (ed.), *The Genesis of the Art Museum in the 18th Century* (Stockholm: Nationalmuseum, 1993); Andrew Mcclellan, *Inventing the Louvre: Art, Politics, and the Origins of the Modern Museum in Eighteenth-Century Paris* (Cambridge and New York: Cambridge University Press, 1994); Édouard Pommier (ed.), *Les musées en Europe à la veille de l'ouverture du Louvre* (Paris: Klincksieck-Musée du Louvre, 1995).

56 Carole Paul, 'Capitoline Museum, Rome: civic identity and personal cultivation', in Carole Paul (ed.), *The First Modern Museums of Art* (Los Angeles: J. Paul Getty Museum, 2012), pp. 27 and 41.

57 Karsten Schubert, *The Curator's Egg: The Evolution of the Museum Concept from the French Revolution to the Present Day* (London: One-Off Press, 2000), p. 17.

58 Mcclellan, *Inventing the Louvre*.

59 In 1796 the Louvre was called Musée Central des Arts in order to define its speciality – because two other national museums had also been opened, the Museum

48   Charting the flows: institutions and genres

d'Histoire Naturelle and the Conservatoire des Arts et Métiers – and in 1803 it became Musée Napoléon. In 1801, a decree by Minister Jean-Antoine Chaptal created museums in 15 other 'French' cities – including Brussels and Geneva.

60 It was not only the connoisseurs who would give explanations to accompanying friends, but the uneducated would also make loud comments and burlesque exclamations to be heard by everyone, as the German knight Carl Christian Berkheim noted after visiting the Louvre. Andrew Mcclellan, *The Art Museum from Boullée to Bilbao* (Berkeley: University of California Press, 2008), p. 161.

61 I cannot confirm, as a museologist has recently argued, that visitors of the Louvre and the British Museum would even picnic in the galleries (Jennifer Barrett, *The Museum and the Public Sphere* (Hoboken, NJ: John Wiley and Sons, 2011), p. 58); but I agree with her when she defines exhibition spaces as places of leisure, casual talk and social interaction. Following Foucault's theories on social control, many museologists have hitherto emphasised the role of museums and public art galleries in civilising a rough populace; but in the period studied here the public sphere of art was an arena of collective passions. Michael Fried, *Absorption and Theatricality: Painting and Beholder in the Age of Diderot* (Chicago-London: Chicago University Press, 1980); Paul Barlow and Colin Trodd (eds.), *Governing Cultures: Art Institutions in Victorian London* (Aldershot: Ashgate 2000), pp. 2–12.

62 In order to eliminate distraction and heighten attention, Wagner chose the rural location of Bayreuth to erect his opera house in 1871 rather than building it in Munich, hoping that the trip to the distant town of Franconia would provide detachment for his audience from life's petty concerns The building was not eye-catching, and had a Spartan interior, where the orchestra was hidden from sight in a *mysticher Abgrund*. The room lights were no longer left on during the function, but turned completely off to concentrate the attention of viewers on the scene. The audience were forbidden to yell bravos or to applaud until the end – these innovations and their parallelism in art displays at Whistler times are discussed in John Walsh, 'Pictures, tears, lights, and seats', in James Cuno (ed.), *Whose Muse? Art Museums and the Public Trust* (Princeton: Princeton University Press, 2004), pp. 77–101, 93–94.

63 Pierre Géal, *La naissance des musées d'art en Espagne (XVIIIe-XIXe siècles)* (Madrid: Casa de Velázquez, 2005), p. 325.

64 Daniel J. Sherman, *Worthy Monuments: Art Museums and Politics of Culture in Nineteenth-Century France* (Cambridge, MA and London: Harvard University Press, 1989), pp. 118 and 239.

65 Thomas Adam, *Buying Respectability: Philanthropy and Urban Society in Transnational Perspective, 1840s to 1930s* (Bloomington and Indianapolis: Indiana University Press, 2009), p. 22.

66 Jesús-Pedro Lorente, *Cathedrals of Urban Modernity: The First Museums of Contemporary Art, 1800–1930* (London: Ashgate, 1998).

67 Brandon Taylor, *Art for the Nation: Exhibitions and the London Public, 1747–2001* (Manchester, Manchester University Press, 1999), p. 75.

3

Melodrama in post-revolutionary Europe: the genealogy and diffusion of a 'popular' theatrical genre and experience, 1780–1830

CARLOTTA SORBA

In September 1820 a newspaper from the city of Pau, Department of the Pyrenees in the south-west of France, recounted a journalist's tale of how, finding himself in a deep and remote valley in the Béarn, he approached a child carrying a bundle of wood on her head. Upon being asked what she was called, she did not reply, as one might have anticipated, Jeanne or Marguerite, but rather Coelina, the far-from-common name of the heroine in a novel by Ducray-Duminil, a French follower of Ann Radcliffe and, crucially, in a very celebrated melodrama that Guilbert de Pixérécourt had staged in Paris in 1800 in one of the numerous, very rowdy boulevard theatres. Intrigued, the journalist then learnt that the child's family had seen this same work performed by the local dramatic society on a holiday and had thereupon resolved to give her at birth the name of the ill-starred but ultimately triumphant protagonist.[1] As with present-day soap operas, early nineteenth-century melodramas tended to serve as a source of proper names and of particular fashions, in a very widespread process of reception and appropriation of fictional plots and characters which in the above case even ended up having an impact upon a peasant milieu.[2]

The above example gives some idea of how melodrama – a hybrid theatrical genre generally reckoned to have arisen in France at the beginning of the nineteenth century, employing the spoken word and music and the parading

50 Charting the flows: institutions and genres

of intense emotions – should be regarded as not only a literary but also a social phenomenon. Indeed, this genre is an early and highly significant indication of the emergence of an entertainment industry that was taking its first tentative steps in those years, in the context of intense exchanges on a European level. What were the intellectual and social origins of the genre? And how did the genre travel throughout Europe in the first half of the nineteenth century? This chapter will demonstrate that melodrama, more than often acknowledged, built on a mix of French, German and English intellectual writings and practices. Although developing its canonical form in Paris and spreading from there all over Europe, the genre was appropriated in other European contexts, for example in Britain and Italy, in strikingly different ways.

Emotions for everyone

All accounts, both by contemporaries and later historians, agree when tracing back the 'birth' of the melodrama to a specific place and time; namely, Paris, the Théâtre de l'Ambigu comique in the year 1800. It is obviously hard to credit the notion that on one particular evening of the year inaugurating the new century, in a theatre on the Boulevard du Temple, there was born a form of drama, and by the same token a narrative apparatus, which was destined to recast both the traditionally accepted and entrenched system of theatrical genres and the theatrical experience itself, and even to have an impact upon the political narratives of the early nineteenth century.[3] The codification of a genre that was to go by the name of 'melodrama', a term until then traditionally used to describe the lyric opera, was of course in reality a drawn-out affair, unfolding during the decades at the turn of the eighteenth century, and one that reflected a whole series of different pressures, including extra-theatrical ones, which were grafted on to the social structure and on to the system of cultural production of the period. It is precisely this process in its various aspects that interests the historian: both the genealogical aspects and those relating to later developments involving transpositions and appropriations of the genre in different national contexts and cultural traditions.[4] In this regard, investigating the trajectories, motivations and variant forms of the genre of melodrama sheds light upon important aspects of the early development of what has been defined as a proto-mass culture, that is to say, a mode of cultural production in effect conceived with a view to extending consumption.[5] It is no accident that at the beginning of the century the melodrama precipitated a fierce debate involving many different parties, wholly analogous to, but anticipating by at least two decades, the better known *querelle* that was to develop around the *feuilleton*, the new form of serial novel that began to appear in the daily newspapers in 1836, immediately earning, along with a noteworthy success, the scornful label of 'industrial literature'.[6] Contemporaries clearly seem to have recognised the elements of the melodrama that served radically to undermine established social and cultural hierarchies, to the extent of identifying it as the most telling expression of a 'degeneration' of artistic and cultural production occasioned by the violent assault of commercial imperatives.[7]

Yet where exactly had melodrama sprung from? At least two trajectories – markedly different as regards agency, objectives and instruments – converged to give rise to this new kind of production, and both will be borne in mind in our account in broad outline of its genealogy. The first trajectory is associated with an intellectual and philosophical milieu of Enlightenment provenance; the second by contrast pertains to a social and urban experience linked to the development within the Parisian metropolis of a zone of entertainment located on the north-eastern edge of the city. Its cultural and imaginative context was represented by the extensive development in the course of the eighteenth century of a culture of sensibility that flourished in the fine arts, literature and the theatre, but that also, as a good number of studies in recent years have shown, reflected the consolidation of a psycho-perceptual paradigm centred upon sentiment and sensitivity and having an impact upon the imaginary and the social order alike. Melodrama may be said to represent in a sense the development, at once later and more pronounced, of this same paradigm.[8] We are therefore concerned here with a genre that, as we shall see, would permeate early nineteenth-century Europe, but that in reality had its roots in the Age of the Enlightenment, being linked surprisingly enough to a fierce debate about theatre and its 'effects' upon the audience that was conducted throughout Europe as part of a more wide-ranging reflection on the relationship between language, the public sphere and the power of the emotions. This same debate was associated with a projected reform of dramaturgy involving both French and German Enlightenment milieux and the English theatre world, where earlier than anywhere else a genre had crystallised that in many respects broke with the traditional rules governing writing for the stage, namely, the 'sentimental drama'.

The key protagonists in these proposals for a reform of the theatre, a campaign characterised by a high degree of internationalisation of interventions and exchanges, were theorists and playwrights such as Denis Diderot and Sebastien Mercier in France, Gotthold Ephraim Lessing and August von Kotzebue in the Germanic lands and, a little later, Thomas Holcroft in England.[9] It was in this

52 Charting the flows: institutions and genres

same context that the idea gained ground that the theatre could become the most effective vehicle for educating the public in moral and political virtue, provided that a profound recasting of its systems occurred, not to mention its themes. Austerely abstract classical declamation was to be replaced by a staging closer on the one hand to the communicative potentialities of painting and, on the other hand, to the affective capacities of music.[10] As well as spawning many theoretical writings and theatrical texts with varying degrees of suitability for actual performance, this at once philosophical and theatrical enquiry had given rise to a number of 'experimental stagings' in the course of the 1770s, conducted on both banks of the Rhine, with a view to identifying a form of representation capable of offering the public the language of emotion in its pure state, and as such comprehensible to everyone. It is here that we first encounter a revival of the term 'melodrama', used by Zeno and Metastasio to denote lyric opera's marriage of music and speech. At the heart of the proposed theatre reforms, which had all too obvious political repercussions, not to speak of a range of variations, there was in fact the audience (or what Mercier, perhaps the most radical of these writers, had defined as the 'citizen-spectator'[11]), an audience that was supposed to include every order and rank of citizen, or at any rate all those capable of being moved by the travails of the innocent and by the persecution of virtue.

The '*scènes lyriques*' – subsequently termed melodramas – originally introduced by Rousseau in the guise of his *Pygmalion* (first staged in Lyons in 1770 but appearing in countless editions and stagings throughout Europe in the years that followed[12]), but then by the Bohemian composer George Benda in the form of a series of scenes such as *Ariadne in Naxos* (1774) and *Medea* (1775), were designed to point the way to a new relationship between music, words and gestures; they were, in other words, short plays in prose involving no more than two characters whose amorous approaches, by turns welcomed or rebuffed, were presented, as it were, in a single take. This effect was made possible by the musical accompaniment, which, like a modern soundtrack, marked the entrances of the characters and underlined all the nuances of their emotional states, and by an emphatically gestural language, which reflected the idea – advanced with notable success by G.G. Engel's influential treatise – that the gesture was the most spontaneous and the most universal of communicative forms.[13]

Plays of the above type represented philosophical experiments rather than genuine performances, interpretable as attempts to give theatrical form to the cult of sensibility. From a Rousseauist perspective, they aspired to transcend the mystifications and duplicities characteristic of theatrical fiction, itself a

Melodrama in post-revolutionary Europe

perfect mirror of the aristocratic world, in order to represent – in a fashion that was wholly transparent, comprehensible to all and unmediated – the individual essence, in which sentiment and morality were conjoined. Only in this way, Rousseau reckoned, could the theatre rouse, without hypocrisy, the souls of the onlookers and have an impact upon the natural moral sentiment that every man, irrespective of his social and cultural circumstances, bore within himself. The writer responsible for calling such 'scènes lyriques' melodramas was in fact the German George Benda, while his French translator took it upon himself to theorise this usage, thereby recasting a term that in Italy continued (and still continues) to be used in its original sense.[14]

Boulevard plays

What I have cursorily described above is an intellectual, as well as a dramaturgical debate, certainly on a European scale, that unfolded in the middle decades of the eighteenth century, and gave rise to a veritable flood of editions, translations and adaptations. The second trajectory we must follow in order to understand the genealogy of the melodrama is more specifically French, indeed Parisian, and it is linked on the one hand to a series of urban and social transformations more directly associated with the sphere of leisure and, on the other hand, to institutional mechanisms peculiar to the theatre system in France.

In the French capital, a substantial change in the structure of the theatrical landscape was in fact taking place, thanks to the gradual growth of a new urban zone of recreation and amusement concentrated in the Boulevard du Temple in the north-east of the city, which had developed after the definitive decline suffered by performances at fairs and the public authorisation in 1759 permitting the *amuseurs* of the capital (acrobats, puppeteers, small-time entertainers) to go into business on the outer ring of the boulevards.[15] In the 1780s a bustling quarter had grown up on the northern fringe of the city, which came to life from late afternoon onwards, paved by 1772 for those promenading on foot and for carriages, and endowed with the attributes of a permanent site of festivity, in the heart of which there stood halls for theatrical performances.[16] At least six new theatres had been built in the course of the 1770s, all a few paces away from one another, and in the following years they would undergo various transformations, extensions and rebuildings (the Théâtre de la Gaîté had been inaugurated in 1764, as was the new Théâtre de l'Ambigu Comique in 1786; the Théâtre des Associés in 1774, later renamed Patriotique; the Théâtre des Variétés amusantes in 1779 and the Théâtre des Délassements comiques in the following year).[17] In and among these new theatres there then sprang up the first cafés offering musical entertainment, a number of Vauxhalls – dance halls surrounded by gardens inspired by the eponymous space beside the Thames in London – and other attractions such as the *Cabinet des figures de cire* (1787), a waxworks exhibition, and the Russian Mountains, artificial slopes down which wooden-wheeled carts careered.[18]

A quarter had thus taken shape of an entirely novel appearance, with an eminently, if not exclusively spectacular function, a 'land of marvels' as a newspaper put it in 1815. Its emergence had also been facilitated by the early articulation in the French capital of an urban transport system based upon horse-drawn trams, already fairly efficient and widespread at the end of the eighteenth century, and which linked both the population of the suburbs and the historic city centre to the boulevards.[19] By the turn of the century, what had initially been shacks for acrobats and puppeteers had become large halls for 1,500–2,000 spectators, enhanced with monumental façades and carefully fashioned, attractive decors, whose projection and subsequent extension had been entrusted to well-known professionals. Not long after this date, many writers and journalists, first and foremost Honoré de Balzac, who gave unrivalled descriptions of the boulevards in his novels and elsewhere, would stress how such zones constituted a sort of crucible of modernity.[20]

The normative regime regulating theatrical life rendered the boulevards in many respects a separate world from the rest of the theatre system, clearly counterposed to the theatres endowed with 'privilege', that is, a royal patent, located in the heart of the right bank and officially entitled to stage performances in the classical theatrical genres: tragedy, comedy, *opera seria* and *opera buffa*. In France, as in England, although not in Italy, there was a system of strict public supervision enforced over theatrical activity, such that only a handful of grand, officially sponsored theatres had the authorisation to perform the classical theatrical genres, in prose and in music – at this date the Théâtre Français, the Académie de Musique and the *comédie italienne*, later the *opéra comique*. This circumstance, much as in London in the course of the eighteenth century, had led to the emergence of a commercial theatre or theatre of entertainment, wholly separate and distinct, at once spatially and culturally, from the larger grand theatres.

As many historians of the theatre have noted, such a sphere of activity proved to be more flexible and receptive in the decades at the turn of the eighteenth century, both in relation to the innovations proposed by the Enlightenment critics and as regards a demand for theatrical entertainment that is hard to

Melodrama in post-revolutionary Europe **55**

quantify but that struck contemporaries as steadily increasing. Here then arose, and soon became subject to genuine codification, a series of new genres with a powerful theatrical impact and the capacity to attract large audiences.

The impact of the normative regime upon the division of such modes of performance into actual genres was decisive. As was the case for the so-called illegitimate theatres, those who ran the boulevard theatres were in fact only permitted to stage theatrical forms that did not pose a threat to theatres vested with a patent: performances featuring mime, music or acrobatic feats, or at any rate performances that were not based upon a text, whether declaimed or sung.[21] In step with the gradual development of the new quarter, disputes between the two poles of the Parisian theatrical world, royal and commercial, had thus also grown more acrimonious during the latter half of the eighteenth century. I am referring here on the one hand to the constant pressure exerted by the primary theatres upon the authorities with a view to limiting and circumscribing the proliferating activities of the secondary theatres, accused of attracting a growing audience to performances of low quality; and on the other hand to the tenacious efforts of the latter to breach the normative system and its rules so as to win broader spaces of representation, planning performances that were longer, more structured and more reliant upon dialogue. On the very eve of the Revolution, as Hemmings has done well to emphasise, public supervision in the choice of the repertoire was very marked and had led to actual litigation, culminating in the banning on boulevard stages both of parodies of plays that had already appeared on the royal stages and even of the deployment in pantomime of very well-known characters such as Beaumarchais' Figaro.

The Revolution would, however, prove to be a watershed. In 1791 the Le Chapelier law had in a few brief lines brought about the liberalisation of the theatre system; that is to say, the abolition of the so-called 'privileges' and the introduction of unrestricted competition between the official theatres and those on the boulevards. This historical phase was dominated by the image of the citizen-spectator delineated by Mercier, and by the notion that theatres ought to constitute the best possible school for the masses and the most direct and effective means of educating the people in republican virtue. The 1790s thus witnessed a veritable proliferation of new theatre halls, which often nonetheless proved to be ephemeral, and a substantial increase in the supply of performances accessible to an audience tending now to be larger than that habitually frequenting the established theatres, attracted by fixed prices and sometimes by free performances. These circumstances also reflected a sort of collapse of the entrenched cultural hierarchies and did much to further the

56 Charting the flows: institutions and genres

consolidation on the boulevards of a mixed kind of performance, in which tragedy, comedy, patriotic tableaux and so-called dramas *à grande spectacle* were blended together in a temporary suspension of the system of genres that in France had been a firmly entrenched and hitherto uncontested tradition. Along with an extensive politicisation of the stage and the proliferation of occasional pieces – patriotic pantomimes or enactments of 'immediate history' through which the spectators were swept into the midst of recent events such as the Storming of the Bastille – the revolutionary political conjuncture also served to accelerate the commercialisation of entertainment and performance, which certainly had not been one of its objectives, and that gave rise to no end of polemics and even protests on the part of a workforce initially favourably disposed towards liberalisation.

A closer look at theatre performances in those years reveals an intertwining of political and more straightforwardly commercial productions, sometimes in works by the very same authors.[22] Consider, for example, the important case of one of the first melodramatists, Jean Cuvelier de la Trye, a writer employed in the revolutionary vanguard and the author in June 1794 of a patriotic tableau for the Festival of the Supreme Being. In 1798, when the political climate had greatly altered, he would stage by turns at the Ambigu Comique two productions defined by the flyers as 'lyrical and melodramatic scenes with pantomimes, fights and dances', although each was in fact completely different in nature. The first, performed over only two nights, was a political drama depicting topical events, alluding to the wars underway against the English and pitting some French peasants against a group of Englishmen who were attempting to sabotage a liberty tree but who were put to flight by their intrepid adversaries.[23] The second performance, by contrast, deployed a classic Gothic plot, packed with action scenes, flamboyant disguises and mistaken identities, which went by the title *C'est le Diable, ou la Bohemienne*, and met with an altogether more sensational success, to judge by the fact of its running for 97 whole nights.[24] In that same year at the Ambigu-Comique, Guilbert de Pixérécourt, a young writer fresh from the provinces and in search of fame and fortune as if in a novel by Balzac, set before the audience the first of a long series of plays that would mark the advent of the melodrama as such.[25] *Victor, ou l'enfant de la forêt* was drawn, like the above-mentioned *Coelina*, from a novel by Ducray-Duminil and it dramatised a story rich in *coups de théâtre* of an orphan, adopted and raised as a son of an aristocratic family, who discovers that his natural father is a celebrated and much-feared brigand. After many trials and tribulations, Victor succeeds in establishing his virtue and vindicating his honour, and thereupon marries the daughter of the baron, his adoptive father, a girl he has always loved and by whom he is loved in return. A virtually identical narrative structure recurred the following year in *Rosa, ou l'ermitage du torrent*, likewise a runaway success with the public, so much so that, according to the accounts in the newspapers, a huge crowd thronged the theatre doors. These plays were all intensely emotional affairs, hinging upon the persecution of a weak, defenceless victim by a villain, with musical accompaniment in the form of a score, the central premise of which was the indissoluble equation between sentiment and virtue, and as a consequence such dramas were inevitably destined to have a happy ending.

The narrative structures deployed were in reality far from original. Such plays in fact adopted the plots and settings characteristic of the Gothic dramas of Matthew 'Monk' Lewis or of August von Kotzebue, which were already familiar in theatres across Europe. Yet they translated these settings and situations into modes of performance that were quite new, a novelty due to their brevity (three acts), their extreme simplicity and predictability, the turning of the characters into readily recognisable types, and also the masterly use of music, mime and of highly diverse settings. All the above elements rendered these melodramas ideally suited to large and even illiterate audiences.

Figure 3.1 Louis Léopold Boilly, *L'entrée du Théâtre de l'Ambigu-Comique à une représentation gratis*, 1819. Musée du Louvre, Paris.

As if to confirm the important role of institutional factors in the trajectory sketched out above, a later legislative development served to sanction the definitive codification of the melodrama as a genre that was autonomous and acknowledged as such. A Napoleonic decree of 1807 in fact re-established state supervision over theatrical activities and reinstated the system of privileges that had been temporarily suspended in 1791. It did, however, take into account the upheavals of the previous 15 years, and in a bid to impose order upon what was defined as 'the anarchy' of the boulevards, it recognised only four of the minor theatres that were in business there as legitimate, attributing to them specific competences in the so-called secondary genres, never before featuring in legislation. The Gaîté and the Ambigu thereby became the theatres officially dedicated to melodrama. The decree recognised for the first time the legitimate existence of two distinct dimensions of theatrical performance, one loftily artistic and the other devoted to lowly entertainment, subjecting the latter, or at any rate attempting to subject it, to the supervision of the authorities, by extending the system of genres so as to encompass the so-called minor ones.[26] August von Schlegel, when publishing two years later his influential *A Cours of Lectures on Dramatic Art and Literature*, which would have a major impact upon the early nineteenth-century debate on the theatre, showed a very clear understanding of the particularity of the French situation, which in his judgement lay precisely in the close connection prevailing there between public supervision of the theatre and the system of genres, the outcome being an extreme formalisation of the latter. Half critical and half surprised, he wrote that 'the Parisian theatres are at present tied down to certain kinds, and [...] poetry has here a point of contact with the police'.[27]

The melodrama industry

In the early years of the nineteenth century, a veritable factory of sentiment therefore started up in the boulevard theatres, churning out hundreds of texts and thousands of productions, and it involved a huge workforce (authors and actors, but also scene painters, costumiers, musicians, etc.), in a process of unceasing creation in which novelty was at a premium.[28] Melodrama may in this regard be viewed as the first thoroughgoing example of a commercial theatre product that addressed an uneducated audience and whose nature was all but serial. If Guilbert de Pixérécourt and Louis Caignez are the most prominent authors of the period, dozens of other writers for the theatre, whose names are even less well remembered, oversaw a vast production in the first two decades of the nineteenth century, in part lost but in part collected in 20 volumes of theatre texts published in 1824 in a series called 'Masterpieces of Melodrama'. This initiative was due to a Parisian publisher intent upon exploiting the enduring success obtained by similar plays in the boulevard theatres.[29] This was a substantial work, featuring a long list of texts and writers – four volumes are devoted to works by Pixérécourt, three to Caignez and the rest to a motley selection of other authors – and often also including those responsible for the music, the stage sets or the choreography, thereby giving us a sense of the expressly composite character of this productive set-up. The second publishing venture – focused upon melodrama and immensely valuable, despite its evidently self-congratulatory nature, to those researchers who today are concerned to recover its profile – is Pixérécourt's *Théâtre choisi*. This work consists of four volumes published between 1841 and 1843, a meticulously systematic attempt by its author to legitimise once and for all his literary oeuvre.[30] A chronological table of his texts presents 120 works composed between 1793 and 1835, 26 of which had never been performed; it was flanked by a list of the productions realised within that time span, subdivided between Paris and the provinces. The numbers involved are genuinely impressive; indeed, many of his plays went through more than 1,000 productions. The figures cited by Pixérécourt admittedly do not bear comparison with the 425 *pièces* produced from the 1820s onwards by Eugène Scribe, one of the most widely produced authors of comedies and vaudeville in nineteenth-century Europe and, in the judgement of some historians, the first figure to produce theatre entertainment on a genuinely 'industrial' scale. The latter case concerns a mode of literary production akin to a mountain range, given that a good proportion of Scribe's texts were written in collaboration with minor authors, who were nonetheless mentioned in the librettos.[31] Notwithstanding the differences between Pixérécourt and Scribe, one can plausibly maintain that the melodrama factory anticipates and serves as a prelude to this later circumstance, constituting an important precedent and a sort of generative matrix.[32] If we take into account the contrasting lengths of career of the two authors, the gap between them is in fact not so very great and their productivity proves to be analogous. Bear in mind that in the early years of the century Pixérécourt staged from four to eight new texts a year in the boulevard theatres, precisely the number Scribe's theatre contracts from the 1820s committed him to writing.

What allowed a truly frenetic rhythm in the production of melodramas *à grande spectacle* was also the practice, not only customary but also virtually structural, of 'adapting' pre-existing texts. 'The texts of well-known novels or plays (Radcliffe, Defoe, Schiller or Ducray-Duminil) were adapted and rejigged, drastically reducing the number of characters and simplifying the plots, without any sign of this being evident in the libretti.'[33] The transfer of plots and characters between different literary genres – from the novel to the stage, but also between different forms of play: from tragedy to melodrama, to opera or to pantomime ballet – serves to show just how porous literary genres were, a porosity that represents a hallmark of the period under consideration here, linked among other things to a very summary legal recognition of an author's rights, and finds its most perfect expression precisely in the melodrama. Only with the normative legitimisation of authorial status on the one hand, and the Romantic aesthetics of artistic originality on the other, would the principle of this relaxed decanting between different literary genres and forms, which we encounter with such extraordinary frequency in the cultural production of the period, enter into crisis in the course of the 1830s.[34]

If on the supply side we can therefore say that we are faced with a proto-industry of the spectacle, the demand side – and of actual attendances at these same performances – is much harder to decipher. We cannot in fact recover reliable data on the daily influx of persons into the theatres, still less on the social profile of the audience. What we do find in significant quantities, when we consider the very intense debate that melodrama provoked, are representations and discourses 'upon' the audience, in which it is hard to differentiate between social description and the fiercely moralistic polemic against the *mélo*. Contemporaries were evidently struck by the apparent democratisation of the theatre audience in post-revolutionary France.[35] Quite how far such a phenomenon also amounted to an actual 'popularisation' of the public is hard to say, it being a question moreover of individual accounts, which are prone to casting aspersions or to caustically parodying mass theatrical entertainment. The campaign against the *mélo*, widespread in the years between 1810 and 1820, gave rise to numerous interventions, both in verse and in prose, the tone adopted being sometimes caustically satirical and sometimes damning and gloomily anxious. In every case, however, the genre tended to be presented as a characteristic product of the times, and as one of the most terrible outcomes of the recent upheavals. In such performances, critics felt justified in tracing all the evil consequent from the dismantling of the social and cultural hierarchies occasioned by the demise of a caste society, and by the unfamiliar mobility that the revolution had instilled in contemporary society, a mobility at once social and geographic, owing to the geographical fluidity to which revolutionary events and the great shifts in the position of the masses connected to them had given rise, thereby accelerating the creation of a metropolitan Paris.[36]

In the pamphlets, parodies and literary squibs that appeared in great numbers between the 1810s and 1820s and that had the melodrama in their sights, the figures most often taken to typify its audience are drawn from the world of petty tradesmen or artisans; a baker, a cobbler or a maker of playing cards are all described as they hurry along the boulevards to attend the latest melodramatic production. This serves to make the corrupting effect that melodrama could have on such an audience, given its violent emotions, seem all the more risky. In his reflections on the current state of the theatrical art, published in 1811, Alexandre Ricord writes that 'the bourgeois, the tradesman, all those who do not have sufficient resources, take their families to the *boulevard* theatres where the *mélo* corrupts their taste'.[37] Here too features the sad tale of a honest cobbler with his wife, a housemaid, both of them illiterate, who see their two children led astray and ruined thanks to the boulevard performances at which they spend a large part of their days.[38]

Perhaps the best known of the protagonists featuring in these polemical interventions is a generic '*bonhomme*' from the Marais, who represents the population of a quarter given over to the minor urban trades, or else a baker from Gomesse, a suburb to the north of the capital, who declares himself to be a poet and the president of the local athenaeum. Both are obviously taking part for the very first time in the theatrical life of the city, and are described as rough and ready folk in thrall to the heightened emotion of the melodramas. Pixérécourt himself did not stay out of the controversy, and indeed on several occasions responded to his critics with pamphlets, often equally ironical in tone, in which he presents himself as a staunch advocate of the melodrama, identifying himself with the abovementioned 'bloke' and maintaining that the war against the new genre was 'a sinister cry starting out from Lord knows where and echoing down at last to the Marais'.[39] Such a cry was intended, Pixérécourt wrote, to render the *mélo* 'a universal synonym; it means everything that is ugly, dangerous or even downright criminal. As a certain Voltaire once said, an abomination and a desolation.'[40]

Detractors and supporters alike did, however, acknowledge that the public were flocking to the melodramas. It was a veritable 'throng', the newspapers frequently said when describing the crowds at the entrances to the theatres, and we do sometimes come across pictorial or lithographic images of it, the implication being that it was one of the most remarkable features of Paris at the beginning of the nineteenth century (Figure 3.1). In any case, the quest for a large and not necessarily educated audience had been one of the original motivations behind the melodrama, one could say both in its original guise as a philosophical experiment and in commercial practice. Pixérécourt had made this one of his rallying cries. Thus, in the preface to the abovementioned series of masterpieces of *mélo*, unsigned but presumably by him, we read that the new genre had aspired to reach the masses, who, although illiterate, were imbued with intelligence and good sense, craved adventure and wanted to be pleasantly entertained with deeds of derring-do and of virtue, and performances that were vigorous, animated and full of *coups de théâtre*.[41]

Finally, women were deemed to be particularly well-suited to melodrama. The producers themselves, Pixérécourt at their head,[42] were only too aware that women were sensitive to emotionally charged plots and to melodramatic tear-jerkers. This image of a female audience devoted to the melodrama soon became commonplace in descriptions of theatres from this period, as is evident from the fine painting by Boilly in which a lady faints in a box and is immediately helped to her feet by those around her. This canvas, entitled *The Effect of the Melodrama*, dates from 1830.[43]

Figure 3.2 Louis Léopold Boilly, *L'effet du mélodrame*, 1830. Musée Lambinet, Versailles.

European circulation and adaptation: Britain and Italy

As we have already noted, the melodramatic performance of eighteenth-century origin was the outcome of philosophico-theatrical experiments of European, or at any rate of Franco–German scope. The production of melodramas on the boulevards was likewise characterised by the involvement of several different national literatures, and by the adaptation and reassembling of existing texts. As if to confirm this markedly transnational character, the new genre was circulated in an extraordinarily rapid and intense fashion, which moreover helped to standardise its features in its country of origin also and made it one of the liveliest and most enduring expressions of popular theatre production. It is, however, worth noting how, by comparison with other theatre systems and cultural milieux, melodrama had a wide range of different outcomes and met with greatly varying degrees of success. Such trajectories deserve to be explored in more detail, especially in the context of the putative development of a proto-mass culture. I will limit myself here to a number of hypotheses relating to melodrama's original 'naturalisation' in non-French milieux.

The most common destination was indubitably Great Britain, or rather, initially at any rate, London, where shortly after their French productions all the major texts by Pixérécourt, Caignez and Victor Ducange in the 1820s were brought to shore. The original mediator between the minor Parisian stages and the great London theatres was Thomas Holcroft, a radical playwright who in the 1780s had been at the centre of a dense network of cultural exchanges between French and English theatrical milieux; for example, taking it upon himself to adapt Beaumarchais' comedies for an English audience.[44] After an enforced absence from the stage in the early 1790s on account of his avowedly pro-French stance, Holcroft entered a new phase of his career, becoming an importer of the melodramas he had attended on the Boulevard du Temple. In the grand performances put on by Pixérécourt – in which the *mise en scène*, the decor, the costumes, the music and the dances were as important as the text – Holcroft seemed to glimpse the possibility of implementing that reform of acting based upon the gestural-emotional language that he had himself advocated in a series of theoretical writings and that was destined to bring a wider and more diverse audience within closer reach of the theatre. The earliest English versions of melodrama therefore reconstituted the double trajectory that had characterised its genesis: the politico-pedagogic impulse, on the one hand, and the response to a pressing demand for entertainment on the other. In the preface to the second edition of his *A Tale of Mistery*, the English version of *Coelina* staged at Covent Garden in 1802, Holcroft was at particular pains to emphasise that the novelty of such performances consisted far less in the narrative set-up hinging upon victims and persecutors (figures of innocence and guilt to which London audiences were already fairly well attuned), than in the weight placed upon spectacle and music. For this reason, he wrote, the credit for their success was shared among the many different producers: the musician, the director, the composer and the costumier.[45]

The crossing of the Channel had, however, brought about a by no means insignificant variation: Holcroft's text and the many adaptations of French melodramas that arrived in London at regular intervals in the first two decades of the nineteenth century were in fact accommodated by the grand theatres, where they took on the role of 'afterpieces', that is to say, interludes between the main performances of works in the traditional genres. The fact of melodrama being a genre for export, coming directly from the Parisian theatres, essentially allowed it access to the legitimate theatres, in which, as studies in the history of theatre tell us, it favoured further contamination between theatrical genres and languages, and an enrichment of stage codes.

The circulation of such texts was in reality somewhat wider in Napoleonic Europe, where moreover one encounters a remarkable intensification of theatrical activity, apparently due also to the increased mobility of armies and of troops.[46] In the first two decades of the nineteenth century, translations – or rather adaptations – of Pixérécourt's productions flooded into Holland, Germany, Russia, Portugal and Spain, bringing with them all the main attributes that had characterised the original staging of melodramas, namely an absolute moral Manicheanism, the exaggerated use of gesture, a highly physical style of acting and the use of music to underscore emotion.[47]

In Italy such performances were not defined as 'melodrama' – to Italians the term still signified lyric opera – but rather as 'azione scenica' or as 'rappresentazione spettacolosa'.[48] Between 1802 and 1806 various translations were staged in Venice, and a number of productions in Milan and Turin, often with a change of title and with 'sundry alterations in the light of the usual practice in the Italian theatre'.[49] An unprecedentedly large quantity of translations of texts from the French minor theatre are recorded in Italy between 1790 and 1820, in the context of a noteworthy growth of theatrical publishing in the form of collections and repertoires of contemporary theatre, with melodramatists featuring very prominently up until the 1830s. Productions of such performances in the theatres did, however, become rarer after the Napoleonic period, since in Italy the combining of music and speech saw an uncontested hegemony of opera performance, and hence of singing and of its consolidated productive system. It is therefore not surprising to discover that in Italy it was opera in particular that was deeply influenced, in those early decades of the century, by the Parisian *boulevardier* theatre, from which the composers of the period derived important clues for their own narrative, scenographic and dramaturgical devices. In a good number of instances opera took its plots directly from the *mélo* repertoire.[50] This is the case with the composer Simone Mayr's *La rosa bianca e la rosa rossa* (Genoa, 1813), drawn from Pixérécourt, or likewise with Gioacchino Rossini's *La gazza ladra* (Milan, 1817), drawn from Caigniez's *La Pie voleuse*; or with *Margherita d'Anjou* (Milan, 1820), the plot for which Meyerbeer once again borrowed from Pixérécourt. More generally the *mélo*, as we have seen, dramatised and helped to popularise the plots of eighteenth- and nineteenth-century novels, setting up an intertextual chain whose strongest link in Italy was always opera. Thus, Walter Scott's *The Bride of Lammermoor* would be known to Donizetti, and to other opera composers who in the same period tried their hand at this same subject, through its melodramatic version, staged on the boulevards by Victor Ducange in 1828.

The circulation of the first French melodramas in Great Britain and in Italy therefore had outcomes that were in certain respects wholly at variance, and display the different possibilities of development of that form of spectacle once it had been inserted into the existing systems of theatrical production of the various countries. In Italy the new genre did not achieve its own autonomous position as a spectacle conceived for a broad and diversified public. Many of the dramatic devices of the *mélodrame* were, however, gradually absorbed by opera theatre, which moreover shared with the former the fact of being a spectacle conceived for the open market and for entertainment. In the 1830s and 1840s this gave rise to what has been defined as the 'melodramatic melodrama', a production marked by an identification between sentiment and virtue.[51]

In London, by contrast, the *mélo* was not only a resounding success but also underwent a rapid naturalisation, giving rise in the illegitimate theatres to an intensive English melodramatic production that identified in the formula for performance tried out on the boulevards (three acts, with musical accompaniment and dialogue), a perfect solution to the problem posed by the restrictions imposed by the existing regulatory system.[52] Here, however, the melodrama soon acquired a social inflection wholly lacking in the original French *mélo*. Rather than being an attribute of human nature as such, in many plots villainy tended now to lurk within the social order, and it was therefore against the latter's iniquities that the audience's emotions were roused. The consolidation of the melodramas thus ended up accentuating the distinction between two separate and distinct theatrical spheres: one deemed 'legitimate', and more strictly supervised by the censor, where the French *mélos* long continued to be performed as 'afterpieces', but where the great vogue for lyric opera also gradually took hold; and another more commercial and popular one, which also appealed to an audience composed also of artisans. There arose a new generation of dramatists called upon to write plays in quick succession, and at the same time a form of literary production that was in a political sense markedly radical in tone.[53] One of the most significant examples of a convergence between these two trajectories is furnished by the case of William Thomas Moncrieff, a sort of 'stock author' who dished up for the secondary theatres farces and melodramas at a furious pace, in which plebeian heroes bestrode the stage and traditional class relations tended in various ways to be undermined.[54]

Conclusion

What was happening in the meantime in the French boulevard theatres? Strangely enough, our starting-point, the French *mélo* was in reality very short-lived – in stark contrast to English melodrama, which was to pass through a whole series of different incarnations in the course of the nineteenth century, being finally supplanted as popular entertainment only by the cinema. The term began to disappear from theatre programmes after the revolution of 1830, when the minor theatres there witnessed the heyday of the Romantic drama, on the one hand, and of vaudeville on the other. All that remained was perhaps the epithet 'melodramatic', employed for the most part as a pejorative term indicating a lamentable excess of emotionality and an undue simplification of reality.

The experience of the *mélodrame* may thus be reduced to an extremely limited timespan, but one that was no less crucial in marking out the prelude of a form of theatre production in post-revolutionary Europe that, through the ostentatious striving after effect, a heightened sentimentalism and a marked taste for spectacle, sought for the first time to stage emotions for everyone.[55]

It is around this seemingly marginal goal, that the two trajectories came together and produced, as we have tried to show, the singular experience of the genre: the political and philosophical impulse linked to the idea of democratising theatrical access, and the commercial one corresponding to the growing development of a leisure market. What is more significant is the fact that, in the decades around 1800, both trajectories had a strong transnational

Melodrama in post-revolutionary Europe **67**

character. The *mélodrame*, formally established as a new codified genre on the Paris boulevards, combined a dramatic and narrative device of great effectiveness and readability (brevity, simplicity, predictability, emotional use of music), plots, settings and situations borrowed from novels or dramas coming from different national literatures. It arose from the widespread practice of the adaptation of often pre-existing and sometimes well-known texts for the stage, in highly spectacular forms. Equally important is its wide and rapid European (and global[56]) circulation and the variety of forms taken by the melodramas in their naturalisation within different systems of theatrical production and dissemination. What they show is a transnational network of reflections and experiences that in the early nineteenth century did not only concern high theatrical culture, the great authors and genres of tradition, but also the practices of a proto-mass culture that still deserve more research in our current age.

Notes

1 *Coelina* is the story of a young orphan, whose precise origins are veiled in mystery, and who is persecuted with cruel persistence by the resident villain, the perfidious Truguelin, destined to be unmasked and punished in a final crescendo under the aegis of the triumph of good over evil. The article from the *Journal de Pau* for 8 September 1820 is cited in *Théâtre choisi de G.R.C. de Pixérécourt*, preceded by an introduction by Charles Nodier (Paris: Nancy, 1841–1843), vol. I, p. 11.

2 It is reasonable to entertain some doubts as to the plausibility of the account given above, especially as regards the actual penetration of the melodrama into country theatres. Such doubts have in fact been raised by C. Gaspard, 'Coelina à l'aube de la littérature industriel', in *Mélodrames et romans noir (1750–1890)*, texts assembled and presented by S. Bernard-Griffith and J. Sgard (Toulouse: Presses universitaires de Mirail, 2000), who wonders whether such a diffusion of theatrical performances into rural zones is in fact plausible, and posits instead a borrowing from the novel by Ducray-Duminil, which went through at least 20 editions between 1818 and 1876, and was distributed in large quantities throughout the whole of France. The example given does nonetheless strike me as highly significant. Whether in novel form or in a theatrical guise, melodrama plots represent narratives which were widely consumed, and in this regard anticipate the *feuilletons* of the 1830s and 1840s.

3 For an account of the complex interaction between melodrama and political communication, I would refer the reader to my 'Le mélodrame du Risorgimento: Théatralité et émotions dans la communication politique des patriotes italiens', *Actes de la recherche in sciences sociales*, 4 (2010); for some comment on the excesses to which the 'melodramatic turn' in the interpretation of Victorian mentalities may perhaps have led, see R. McWilliam, 'Melodrama and historians', *Radical History Review*, 78 (2000), 57–84.

4 On the usefulness of an inquiry regarding the 'genre' of narrative, understood as process rather than discursive structure, see the classic essay R. Cohen, 'History and genre', *New Literary History*, 17:2 (1986), 203–218.

5 There is discussion of a proto-mass culture, or 'media culture', in J.-Y. Mollier, J.-F. Sirinelli and F. Vallotton (eds.), *Culture de masse e culture médiatique en Europe et dans les Amériques 1860–1940* (Paris: PUF, 2006), a volume that, although taking 1860 as its terminus *a quo*, identifies its origins in the early nineteenth century. See also D. Kalifa, 'L'Ère de la culture marchandise', *Revue d'Histoire du XIXème Siècle*, 19 (1999), 7–14.

6 On the early nineteenth-century polemics regarding the new popular literature and their impact upon cultural production, see L. Quellebec Dumasy, *La querelle du roman-feuilleton: Littérature, presse et politique. Un débat precurseur (1836–1848)* (Grenoble: Ellug, 1999).

7 The controversy was not conducted in newspapers, as would be later be the case in relation to the feuilletons, but rather through a flurry of pamphlets, parodic or critical. The opening salvo was, I believe, *Le mélodrame aux boulevards. Facetie littéraire, historique et dramatique par Placide le Vieux, habitant de Gomesse, de l'Athénée du même endroit et des sociétés littéraires de Saint Denis et d'Argenteuil* (Paris: De l'Imprimerie de la rue Beaurepaire, 1809); in reality its author was one Jean-Armand Charlemagne, a man of letters and of the theatre, responsible for anti-Jacobin squibs such as *Le souper des jacobins* (1795).

8 See G.J. Barker-Benfield, *The Culture of Sensibility. Sex and Society in Eighteenth-Century Britain* (Chicago: University of Chicago Press, 1992); D.J. Denby, *Sentimental Narrative and Social Order in France 1760–1820* (Cambridge: Cambridge University Press, 1994); P. Stewart, *L'invention du sentiment: roman et économie affective au XVIII siècle* (Oxford: Voltaire Foundation, 2010).

9 On the internationalisation of the debate regarding how a National Theatre was to be defined, see, for example, C. Sorba, 'National theatre and the age of revolution in Italy', *Journal of Modern Italian Studies*, 17:4 (2012), 400–413; more generally, P. Casanova, *La république mondiale des lettres* (Paris: Seuil, 1999).

10 See in this regard the reflections of D. Diderot, *Écrits sur le théâtre*, 2 vols (Paris: Pocket, 2003). For a recent treatment of this topic, see B. Didier, *Diderot dramaturge du vivant* (Paris: PUF, 2001).

11 S. Mercier, *Du théâtre, ou Nouvel essai sur l'art dramatique* (Paris 1773), p. 41.

12 *Pygmalion, 'scène lyrique' de Jean-Jacques Rousseau*, critical edition edited by Jacqueline Waeber (Geneva: Editions Université-Conservatoire de Musique, 1997).

13 *Ideen zu einer Mimik*, 2 vols (Berlin: Mylius, 1785–1786). An analysis of this work and its wider significance may be found in J. Veltrusky, 'Engel's ideas for a theory of acting', *The Drama Review*, 24 (1980), 71–80.

14 A long and detailed introduction to the French version of *Ariane abandonnée*, a melodrama in imitation of a German original, music by M. George Benda (Paris: Thomas Brunet Libraire, 1781), provided a first codification of the new genre of the '*mélodrame*', a term that nevertheless in the musical treatises of the period was still used to designate opera.

Melodrama in post-revolutionary Europe   **69**

15 The particular concern of the public authorities from the 1760s onwards to promote in Paris performances linked to entertainment may be viewed as a response to urbanisation, an increasingly rapid process and, as such, occasioning ever greater disquiet, as M. de Rougemont argues in *La vie théâtrale en France au XVIII siècle* (Paris: Librairie Honoré Champion, 1988), pp. 213–232.

16 On the gradual structuring of the *boulevards* as a space that was in reality multi-functional – recreational, commercial and residential – see L. Turcot, 'L'emergence d'un espace plurifonctionnel: les boulevards parisiens au XVIIIe siècle', *Histoire Urbaine*, 12 (2005), 89–115.

17 On the theatrical life of the quarter see M. Albert, *Les théâtres de boulevard (1789–1848)* (Geneva: Slatkine Reprints, [1902] 1978); M. Root-Bernstein, *Boulevard Theater and Revolution in Eighteenth-Century Paris* (Ann Arbor: UMI Research Press, 1984); more recently, B. Brunet, *Le théâtre de boulevard* (Paris: Colin, 2007).

18 See G.-A. Langlois, '"Les charmes de l'égalité": Eléments pour une urbanistique des loisirs publics à Paris de Louis XV à Louis-Philippe', *Histoire Urbaine*, 1 (2000), 7–17.

19 N. Papayanis, *Horse-Drawn Cabs and Omnibuses in Paris: The Idea of Circulation and the Business of Urban Transit* (Baton Rouge: Louisiana State University Press: 1996).

20 Aside from the many references in the novels, above all in *Les illusions perdues*, see also H. de Balzac, *Histoire et physiologie des boulevards de Paris, de la Madeleine à la Bastille* (1845), in *Oeuvres diverses* (Paris: Conard, III, 1940). On the *boulevards* as *foyer* of modern life see the special issue of *Romantisme*, 134 (2006), dedicated to 'Les Grands Boulevards', edited by J.D. Goffette.

21 On the French theatre system see F.W.J. Hemmings, *Theatre and State in France, 1760–1905* (Cambridge: Cambridge University Press, 1994); on the English one, J. Moody, *Illegitimate Theatre in London, 1770–1840* (Cambridge: Cambridge University Press, 2000).

22 For an accurate account of the theatrical repertoire during the Revolution, see the two volumes by A. Tissier, *Les spéctacles à Paris pendant la révolution: Répertoire analytique, chronologique et bibliographique* (Paris: Droz, 1992 and 2002).

23 *L'anniversaire ou la fête de la souverainété*, words by J.C.A. Cuvelier and J. Mittié, music by O. Vanderbroek (Paris: Barba, 1798). On the powerful impact the Napoleonic Wars had upon the English stage, in terms of both repertoire and the politicisation of the theatres, see G. Russell, *The Theatres of War: Performance, Politics and Society, 1793–1815* (Oxford and New York: Clarendon Press, 1995).

24 On Cuvelier see R. Martin, *La féerie romantique sur les scènes parisiennes 1791–1864* (Paris: Honoré Champion, 2007).

25 J.P. Marcoux, *Guilbert de Pixérécourt: French Melodrama in the Early Nineteenth Century* (New York: Peter Lang, 1992).

26 J.-C. Yon, 'Les théâtres parisiens à l'ère du privilège (1807–1864): l'impossible controle', in J.Y. Mollier, P. Régnier and A. Vaillant (eds.), *La production de l'immatériel: Théories, représentations et pratiques de la culture au XIXs* (St Etienne: Publications de l'Université de St Etienne, 2008).

27 A.W. Schlegel, *A Course of Lectures on Dramatic Art and Literature (1809)* (London: Henry G. Bohn, 1846), p. 334.

28 The most exhaustive account of French melodramatic production is still J.-M. Thomasseau, *Le mélodrame* (Paris: Presses Universitaires de France, 1984).

29 *Chefs-d'oeuvre du répertoire des mélodrames joués à différents théâtres*, 20 vols (Paris: Veuve Dabo, 1824–1825).

30 *Théâtre choisi de G.R.C. de Pixérecourt.*

31 See J.C. Yon, 'L'industrialisation de la production théâtrale: l'exemple de Scribe et de ses collaborateurs', *Revue d'histoire du XIX siècle*, 2 (1999), 77–88.

32 J. Przybos, *L'entreprise mélodramatique* (Paris: Librairie José Corti, 1987).

33 J.-M. Thomasseau, *Le mélodrame* (Paris: Presses Universitaires de France, 1984).

34 M.-P. Le Hir, 'Authors vs. playwrights: the two authorship systems of the Old Regime in France and the repercussions of their merger', *Theatre Journal*, 44:4 (1992), 501–514. See also O. Bara, 'Balzac en vaudeville', in P. Bourdin and G. Loubinoux (eds.), *La scène bâtarde: Entre Lumières et Romantisme* (Clermond Ferrand: Presses Universitaires Blaise Pascal, 2004).

35 In *Le romantisme aux enchères: Ducange, Pixérécourt, Hugo* (Amsterdam and Philadelphia: Benjamins, 1992), M.-P. Le Hir writes of the democratisation, rather than of the popularisation, of the theatre, and interprets the controversy surrounding the *mélo* as a classic struggle over the structuring and supervision of the theatrical 'field'.

36 See D. Garrioch, *The Formation of the Parisian Bourgeoisie (1690–1830)* (New Haven: Harvard University Press, 1996), and also D. Davidson, *France after Revolution: Urban Life, Gender and the New Social Order* (New Haven: Harvard University Press, 2007).

37 A. Ricord, *Quelques Rèflexions sur l'art théâtrale, sur les causes de sa decadence et sur les moyens à employer pour rappeler la scène française à son ancienne splendeur* (Paris: Pilez, 1811), p. 44.

38 J.B.L. Camel, *De l'influence des théâtres et particulièrement des théâtres sécondaires sur les moeurs du peuple* (Paris, 1822), p. 2.

39 G. de Pixérécourt, *Guerre au mélodrame* (Paris: De l'Imprimérie de Hocquet, 1818), p. 3.

40 de Pixérécourt, *Guerre au mélodrame*, p. 6.

41 *Essai sur le mélodrame*, the preface to the first tome of the series *Chefs d'oeuvres des mélodrames*, 1824.

42 In his umpteenth intervention on this theme (*Le mélodrame*, in *Le livre de cent et un*, 1831) Pixérécourt imagines a conversation in a salon. Melodrama's detractors in this case are a pomaded old man, two academicians, two presidents from the law courts and a member of the charity commission. Ranged against them is the salonnière herself, a young lady who loves art and who claims to speak on behalf of all women, who are, she says, fascinated, moved and thrilled by the plots of the *mélos*.

43 On the painter Boilly as an astute illustrator of Parisian modernity at the dawn of the nineteenth century, see S.L. Siegfried, *The Art of Louis-Leopold Broilly: Modern Life in Napoleonic France* (New Haven: Yale University Press, 1995).

44 See D. Karr, ' "Thoughts that flash like lightning": Thomas Holcroft, radical theater and the production of meaning in 1790s London', *Journal of British Studies*, 40:3 (2001), 324–356.

45 T. Holcroft, *A Tale of Mystery: A Mélo-drame*, 2nd edn (London: R. Phillips, 1802).

46 See G. Russell, 'Theatre', in *An Oxford Companion to the Romantic Age 1776–1832* (Oxford: Oxford University Press, 1999).

47 See W.G. Hartog, *Guilbert de Pixérécourt: Sa vie, son mélodrame, sa technique et son influence* (Paris: Honoré Champion, 1913); F. Rahill, *The World of Melodrama* (Philadelphia: Pennsylvania State University Press, 1967).

48 A staggering quantity of translations from French originals are recorded for the years between 1790 and 1820, see G.S. Santangelo and C. Vinti, *Le traduzioni italiane del teatro comico francese dei secoli 17 e 18*, bibliographical enquiry directed by M. Spaziani (Rome: Edizioni di storia e letteratura, 1981).

49 As we are told in, for example, the libretto of *Il conte dè castelli* (Venice: Rosa, 1806), the Italian version of Pixérécourt's *Le pelerin blanc*.

50 E. Sala, *L'opera senza canto: Il mélo romantico e l'invenzione della colonna sonora* (Venice: Marsilio, 1995).

51 M.G. Accorsi, 'Il melodramma melodrammatico', *Sigma*, 30 (1980), 109–127.

52 M. Booth, *English Melodrama* (London: Herbert Jenkins, 1965).

53 On the early manifestation of a plebeian dramatic sphere see D. Worrall, *The Politics of Romantic Theatricality, 1787–1832: A Road to the Stage* (London: Palgrave Macmillan, 2007).

54 On Moncrieff, see D. Worrall, 'Artisan melodrama and the plebeian public sphere: the political culture of Drury Lane and its environs, 1797–1830', *Studies in Romanticism*, 39:2 (2000), 213–227.

55 The disappearance of the area of Paris devoted to entertainment occurred at the time of the reorganisation of the city by Haussmann, a process that would lead to the demolition of the theatres on the Boulevard du Temple in 1862. The theatrical landscape of the city as it appeared in the latter half of the nineteenth century has been analysed with great care by C. Naugrette-Christophe, *Paris sous le II Empire: Le Théâtre et la ville. Essai de topographie théâtrale* (Paris: Librairie théâtrale, 1998).

56 D. Grimstead, *Melodrama Unveiled: American Theater and Culture 1800–1850* (Chicago and London: Chicago University Press, 1968); F. Kelleter, B. Krah and R. Mayer (eds.), *Melodrama! The Mode of Excess from Early America to Hollywood* (Heidelberg: Universitätsverlag Winter, 2007).

4

Games and sports in the long eighteenth century: failures of transmission

PETER CLARK

One the most important types of modern cultural and leisure activity, organised sport, did not have its European origins – unlike many of those other areas discussed in this book such as voluntary associations, concert music, leisure resorts, commercial theatre and promenades – during the Age of the Enlightenment. Or to be precise, while there was a major breakthrough, to use Norbert Elias' term, in the 'sportisation process' in Georgian England – as a number of traditional games developed written rules, standardisation, commercialisation, designated players, regulatory clubs, officials and spectators[1] – this was paralleled only to a minor extent in Continental Europe. The true explosion of sports across Europe (and beyond) occurred in the late nineteenth century when games such as football, athletics, rowing, cycling and rugby spread quickly from England across the Continent and British Empire, promoted by urbanisation, the media, state formation, new concepts of masculinity, associations, nationalism and national and international competitions.[2] So how can we explain the failure of sporting 'modernisation' in early modern Europe, and the failure of cultural transmission from England during the long eighteenth century? This chapter offers a first attempt to explore this complex and difficult question. Perhaps not, as we will see, to fully answer this key question, but rather as a strategy to shed some new light on a number of major themes relevant to this volume: issues of convergence and divergence, comparability, and processes of cultural transmission.

The transformation of English sports

In the historiography of sport, the rise of English sports in the eighteenth century has attracted a great deal of scholarly attention, much more than contemporary developments on the Continent. But for once this may reflect the reality on the ground. In England, as Peter Borsay, Bob Malcolmson and others have demonstrated, major developments occurred from the late seventeenth century.[3] The traditional ballgame of cricket, played largely in the villages of southern England was organised, urbanised and commercialised by 1750. By then, matches were regularly played in London and southern provincial towns, often under the aegis of cricket clubs, in front of large crowds of spectators. Around 1744 there was an early attempt to regulate the sport by the Star and Garter club in London, although it was not until the 1790s that the Marylebone Cricket Club finally took charge of the game. During this period, cricket slowly spread from southern England to the rest of the country.[4]

The ancient practice of archery had a tenuous existence in the seventeenth and early eighteenth centuries, but under George III numerous archery clubs shot up, encouraged by a revived cultural fascination for the Gothic. By the 1780s, clubs and grounds are found across the country, often in towns, and by the end of that decade a great annual archery tournament was held at Blackheath near London with important fashionable patronage but also a

Figure 4.1 After Francis Hayman, *A Game of Cricket*, 1790s. Yale Centre for British Art, Paul Mellon Collection.

considerable popular following. Archery benefited from royal patronage, which was not the case, it would seem, for cricket.[5]

Animal sports had turned into organised sports earlier. With active royal patronage under the Stuarts, horse races proliferated at the start of the eighteenth century with 138 venues listed by 1739 and many small towns hosting events. The 1740 Racing Act regulated and curtailed the number of venues but also confirmed the wide national following for the sport, races being held in almost every county from Cornwall to Cumberland.[6] Fashionable landed involvement in horse-ownership, racing and gambling was matched by large popular interest and great crowds of onlookers at major races such as those held at Newmarket, Epsom or York.[7] From the mid-eighteenth century, the Jockey Club – meeting both at the Star and Garter in London's Pall Mall and at Newmarket – began to control the sport in England.[8] Paintings and drawings of race meetings (and racehorses) are numerous and, although stylised, highlight the mixed attendance, with the elite classes accommodated in stands away from the *menu peuple*.[9] Fox and deer hunting also became organised during the eighteenth century through subscription hunts that operated increasingly on an associational basis with their own rules, costumes for participants and sociable gatherings, although there was no national regulatory body.[10]

Admittedly, not all games were so transformed. Semi-organised sports such as bowls and cockfighting went into decline. In the former case, this was rather surprising given civic sponsorship of the sport, the investment in greens and some games organised on a local club basis.[11] If anything cockfighting was even more organised, with published rules from the seventeenth century, prestigious matches between the birds of county landowners at provincial and London inns, although one weakness may have been the absence of any clear associational structure.[12] Competition from more fashionable sports together with increasing (if selective) criticism of animal cruelty seems to have led to the sport's inexorable decline.[13]

Other traditional popular games such as street football, cudgeling, bullbaiting and cock-throwing often with strong regional or local identities but, lacking elite sponsorship or much organisation, suffered criticism and repression, particularly from the close of the eighteenth century. In a recent study, Emma Griffin argued that growing action against such games by the authorities was motivated primarily by official concern to assert control over the public spaces (often streets and squares) where they were played.[14]

Unlike the late nineteenth-century sports revolution, the eighteenth-century phenomenon was not truly British: it hardly extended outside England. Horseracing and hunting clubs expanded in Scotland late – from the

Games and sports in the long eighteenth century **75**

1780s – and we find only one archery club in Scotland before 1800 and no organised cricket (although there were several golf, curling and skating clubs by 1800).[15] In Ireland, race meetings flourished from the late seventeenth century, as in England, with towns sponsoring events; by the 1750s a Jockey Club had been formed to regulate meetings and in the 1780s the Turf Club took over this role.[16] There was also a large number of hunt clubs, with the main surge from the 1770s. Thus in Münster we find well over a score during the years 1734 to 1800.[17] We also observe a few boating and racket clubs and traditional village hurling matches, but no cricket or archery clubs.[18]

In a similar fashion, cricket and archery failed to make a successful transatlantic crossing to the American colonies. While there are references to cricket matches in Virginia and Georgia, there is little to suggest the sport took off among the colonists, with no established clubs.[19] However, horseracing was much more widespread, although with no single format – in New York, English style distance racing was in vogue, while in the Chesapeake valley, quarter-mile sprints were the norm.[20] By the 1750s provincial jockey clubs had appeared to regulate the sport. Races at Williamsburg, Annapolis and Richmond attracted thousands of spectators and gambling was heavy.[21] Hunting was widespread but was mostly semi-organised, although some hunting clubs appeared.[22] Among other activities, small group sledging and skating flourished in New England as well as traditional bearbaiting, fist-fighting, cockfights and bowls.[23] But none turned into fully fledged sports at this time. As national identity emerged, the Americans developed their own distinctive ballgames, such as baseball and basketball, during the nineteenth century.[24]

Sports on the European continent

In Europe it would seem that the advent of English-type commercial sports was generally of minor significance during the early modern period. According to Wolfgang Behringer, increased formalisation of games occurred during the sixteenth and seventeenth centuries with the spread of written rules and textbooks, sports grounds and spectators, professional players and the like, mostly linked to traditional institutions such as royal courts or guilds. But Behringer produces little evidence for commercial, organised sport on the English model.[25] What data there is for new-style sport on the Continent seems very patchy and local. There are references to cricket at Prato, Florence and Naples (played by a team of Old Etonians against the world) and in Vienna.[26] We find English-style horseracing at Toulouse in 1760, but most accounts of horseracing in Italy or Malta stress the traditional character, disorder and contrast with English racing.[27] Thus a British visitor to Rome noted that the horseraces during the carnival involved bystanders throwing squibs or fireworks at the runners, while 'all the rivalry is in the start – the reverse of an English horse-race … [where] the start is nothing and the contest is reserved for the goal'.[28] In Florence about 1820 the English established races 'after the English manner and ride their own horses with the caps and jackets of English jockeys'.[29] Fox hunting appeared in and around Paris; and at Rome an Englishman apparently imported a 'a pack of hounds from England' and 'hunts regularly during the season to the great astonishment of the natives'.[30] Observers frequently commented on the adoption or introduction of English models, but there is not much evidence that these innovations really took hold and became an integrated part of local leisure cultures.

Some sources suggest that local games adapted the English models of association and racing. In western France the sport of *boule* seems to have been organised by societies from the 1740s, with increasing numbers of rules and regulations; there is a suggestion that they may have imitated English clubs given British merchants traded in the area.[31] Further afield, we find Nordic ski-races from 1776, while fencing clubs appear in a number of countries.[32]

Figure 4.2. Jean Louis Théodore Gericault, *Riderless Racers at Rome*, 1817. Collection Walter Art Museum (Wikimedia Commons).

However, with these possible exceptions, sports clubs do not appear as an important type of association on the continent, and the overall impression is of a minimal advent or dissemination of new-style commercial sports in Europe before the second half of the nineteenth century.

In the games and sport literature, several explanatory theories are suggested for the variable dissemination of new-style sports. One explicit or implicit in the narratives offered by sports historians such as Eric Dunning, Annette Hofmann and others is that that the contrast between traditional games and new sports was so great that the former did not provide a platform for such a transition.[33] Richard Holt by contrast would suggest from the British evidence that a transition from games to sports could and did occur, but does not explain the divergence with Europe before the late nineteenth century.[34] Wolfgang Behringer is more radical and denies any such divergence, arguing that the early modern period was indeed 'the formative period of modern sport' on a European scale, although – as we will see – there are some problems with his analysis.[35] What I would like to propose is that from the seventeenth century parts of Europe witnessed a partial or abortive transition from traditional games to sports; a transition that was only realised in England during the long eighteenth century. The reasons for this abortive transition will then be discussed.

From games to sports

To try and understand this issue it is necessary, first of all, to make a few summary points about traditional games. Conventionally, they were informal, and socially, gender and age mixed: they were also promiscuously urban and rural. Although eight main types have been identified – ballgames, bowling games, throwing, shooting, fighting, animal, locomotion games and acrobatics – in fact, as the many detailed studies show, there was enormous local and regional variation.[36] For example, many different versions existed of street football. Thus *soule* in north-western France involved teams of players from different communities using feet, hands or sticks to play the ball, with matches often held on feast days and holidays. Or *cnapan* or *knappan* played mostly in the western part of Wales, where it was said in 1603 to be 'extremely popular in Pembrokeshire since great antiquity'. Or *caid* in Ireland, which was a largely rural game (although some games also took place in Dublin) played by large teams and probably the forerunner of the later Gaelic football. Or *calcio* in Italy, played in town piazzas between teams of 27 men dressed in uniforms.[37] Across Europe, major regional variations are also notable in the number and

78 Charting the flows: institutions and genres

types of games played over time: fewest in less urbanised areas, denser in more advanced regions.[38] In relatively backward, under-urbanised countries such as Finland there were few organised ballgames at all, instead we find more individual activities like weightlifting and skiing.[39] In more urbanised regions, like the Low Countries, western Germany and Italy, traditional games were much more formalised, linked to institutions such as the royal court, guilds, the church and church festivities. In Flanders, traditional shooting games were associated with archery guilds from the late Middle Ages, often supported by towns, and these participated in intercity competitions.[40]

Two developments impacted on this complex, highly variegated universe of traditional games from the end of the Middle Ages. First and most evidently on the Continent, increased institutionalisation, as Behringer has stressed. This was particularly the case in the more advanced parts of Europe – Italy, the Low Countries and Germany – where, as we have noted, traditional games were already more organised and structured. In this context, new printed rulebooks and manuals appeared, often written for rulers; sports grounds and halls were constructed – commissioned by princes, cities and confraternities; local sporting competitions proliferated, patronised again by rulers (several French kings and German princes appear to have been avid sports enthusiasts). Fashionable sporting events attracted large crowds of spectators. Other developments included the spread of sport instructors fine-tuning the skills of young gentlemen. As Behringer notes, these developments were clearly elite-driven, often linked to established institutions or state structures, and largely uncommercial. Voluntary organisations, so important for later new-style sports, seem strikingly absent.[41]

The second development after the Renaissance was rather different and involved a measure of proto-commercialisation taking place, as games became linked to public drinking houses. Why was this the case? Across Europe there seems to have been a general growth in the number of legal and illicit drinking houses during the sixteenth and seventeenth centuries. At Antwerp by 1584 we find 376 public houses or one for every 32 houses; in London before the Civil War there was one licensed house for every 16 houses. Factors influencing this development included the general growth of population, urbanisation, migration and the expansion of trade. While better-off traders, masters and the like patronised more established inns, *alberghi*, *gasthouses* and *auberges*, labourers, artisans and poorer migrants flocked to popular alehouses, cabarets, *taverne*, *buschenwirte* and *fratschler*.[42] As Beat Kümin, John Chartres and others have shown, drinking premises became increasingly important as economic, social and cultural centres; thus it is hardly surprising that traditional games drifted into their orbit. Already in England by the early seventeenth century one finds games of bowls and football, as well as animal sports, taking place in and around popular drinking houses. Alehouse keepers actively promoted such games. A Yorkshire publican kept 'a common football for the young men of the town to play with', while victuallers began to build bowling greens or alleys by their premises. In the same way, English inns with purpose-built cockpits became important venues in the seventeenth century for cockfights.[43]

There are indications of similar trends in some other parts of Western Europe. Thus for the Low Countries in the seventeenth century we have pictorial evidence of: groups of peasants bowling outside taverns; inn courtyards with alleys and equipment for quoits and bowls (by the Dutch painter Adriaen van Ostade, 1610–1685, who developed the genre of inn paintings in this period); and ice-skating outside taverns.[44] Here (and across Europe) card games were also widely played inside inns and drinking houses.[45] There may have been commercialising developments in German towns too. Thus Bavarian inn facilities included outdoor skittle alleys, shooting ranges and billiard tables; another tavern at Straubing organised stone throwing competitions. In France, *boule* games in the Mayenne area had links with local taverns.[46] In Sweden there are images of a competitive game of skittles about 1770 outside an inn on Södermalm in Stockholm, although this may be a famous exception to prove the rule.[47]

Figure 4.3. Adriaen van Ostade, *The Pall Mall Court* [*Vertier bij een herberg*], 1677. Collection Rijksmuseum Amsterdam.

Six explanations

Despite all this evidence, only in England did the shift towards more organised, commercial activities lead to the seminal growth of modern-style commercial sports with large numbers of spectators and voluntary regulatory bodies. How could we explain the abortive transition elsewhere?

At least six main variables and (partial) explanations need to be considered, in a comparative perspective with the general take-off and dissemination of new-style sports in the late nineteenth century. First, there was urbanisation. Given that many of the new sports were based in towns, the role of urbanisation, generating enlarged demand for new entertainments, may well be important in the contrasting experience of England and the Continent. As is well-known, urbanisation levels stagnated in most of Europe during the eighteenth century. Western Europe saw some modest growth, but here there were significant variations. In the Dutch Republic, the strong urban surge of the seventeenth century went into reverse during the eighteenth century, as de-urbanisation took hold. In Germany, growth was at best selective, advantaging specific regions and types of town more than others. In France, growth was more widespread up to the French Revolution.[48] But England enjoyed the most dynamic and wide-scale urbanisation. London's population soared from 575,000 at the end of the seventeenth century to a million by 1800. Many traditional regional centres and county towns put in strong performances, but so too did many small towns. New industrial towns and port cities likewise grew in size. And it was not just demographic growth – urban living standards improved significantly.[49] Other parts of the British Isles, such as Scotland and Ireland, which trailed England in terms of the development of commercial sports, also experienced more limited or tardy urbanisation during the eighteenth century: Scottish urban growth only accelerated from the 1780s.[50] By comparison to the generally erratic pattern of European urban growth in the eighteenth century, the late nineteenth century saw urbanisation rates rise sharply, especially in Western Europe, where the rate doubled between 1850 and 1910, creating large new markets for sporting and other leisure activity.[51]

A second variable to consider is the media. It was probably not without significance that the media and communication advances on the Continent were less developed and more subject to censorship in the eighteenth century than was the case in England. Certainly in England the end of censorship in the 1690s triggered an upsurge of metropolitan and later provincial newspapers, carrying advertisements and reports of sports events, such as horseraces, cricket matches, archery contests and so on. By the 1780s, English readers could choose from a dozen London papers and 50 or so other regional ones (there was a more limited expansion elsewhere in the British Isles). In addition, in the eighteenth century an important sports press emerged in England with the publication of the *Racing Calendar* after 1727 (and *General Stud Book* in 1791) and the *Sporting Magazine* (which carried reports of all types of fixtures) after 1792.[52] Nothing on this scale occurred in Western Europe. Dutch newspapers in the eighteenth century were strictly regulated, needing permits to print and with numbers strictly limited. There was repressive control over content, although not always effectual, and regulation collapsed during periods of political upheaval, as in the 1780s. The French and German press expanded during the eighteenth century, but censorship remained a recurrent problem. In contrast to this period, popular newspapers and specialist magazines were vitally influential in the spread of new-style sports across Europe in the late nineteenth century, with radio crucial after the First World War.[53]

This brings us to a third variable: power. In England the more relaxed political regime after the Glorious Revolution of 1688 and especially after the Hanoverian succession in 1714 offered favourable conditions of political freedom, toleration and space in which all kinds of leisure activity could expand and develop. In many areas of national and local administration, the government withdrew from active engagement and state officials exercised limited control over public sociability including sports. Parliament intervened sporadically as we noted with the racing legislation of 1740, but in general the organisation of sporting activity was left to local initiative. In England, new-style leisure activities, including sports, ideally benefited from their configuration as neutral political space, where Whigs and Tories, landowners and merchants, might meet together socially (although conflict was not always exorcised). On the Continent, in contrast, rulers were generally more nervous of large urban crowds assembling outside traditional or institutionalised settings. By the late nineteenth century, the European political context was more tolerant: sport was increasingly regarded by militarising states in a positive light, boosting the physical fitness and training of male populations.[54]

The role of elites is a fourth variable in the explanation. As we have seen, landowners were important for English sports such as horseracing, hunting, cricket and archery. Elias argued that this was because English landowners were 'pacified' after the Glorious Revolution and incorporated into parliamentary government. 'The "parliamentarisation" of the landed classes of England had its counter part in the "sportisation" of their pastimes,' he suggested, while on the Continent royal courts took landowners away from the countryside.[55] In fact, English landowners became heavily urbanised in the eighteenth century as wealthy magnates spent part of the year in London and Bath, and even smaller gentry took up residence in or patronised country towns. With time on their hands they organised and pursued a range of urban leisure activities, not least sports – hence the proliferation of new-style sports in and around cities and towns. But the indications are that landed residence in towns was also quite common across Europe during the eighteenth century, as the countryside was increasingly seen as dirty and backward. What may distinguish English land-owners from their continental counterparts was their general affluence, visible not only among the magnate class but percolating down to the smaller gentry as well. With affluence came a high propensity for gambling, which was partic-ularly vital for English horseracing, cricket and indeed all the new sports.[56] In the late nineteenth century it was a new urban elite, the bourgeoisie, that led the promotion of new-style sports, both in Britain and elsewhere.[57]

A fifth variable involves public houses. As we have seen, in England many new-style sports were enthusiastically promoted by publicans, who provided equipment for them, gave prizes, advertised sporting events heavily in the media and paid special taxes in some towns to support them. Taverns and other drinking houses were the venue for many of the important sports clubs that sprang up and also hosted banquets and other social events associated with them. In turn, famous sportsmen became publicans. This trend resulted from several factors. In eighteenth-century England, the drink trade became heavily regulated through the licensing system, the growing spread of tied houses (controlled by leading town brewers) and the excise system (as the drink trade became one of the pillars of the fiscal-military state). Inns and other public houses (the term appears from the 1650s) became bigger, with new purpose-built premises constructed having specialist rooms, and many land-lords turned into prosperous, respectable figures in the local community – as we can see from various portraits and paintings. As such they developed as leading cultural entrepreneurs – promoting not just sports but many other leisure activities including music concerts, assemblies and clubs. Sports and other leisure activities were clearly designed to generate important additional income for drink traders.[58] Rather less is known about the retail drink trade on the Continent. In the Netherlands and Germany, as seen earlier, we do find publicans promoting sports to some extent. In Germany and Switzerland, Beat Kümin has suggested, drink traders became increasingly prosperous. But on the Continent in general the drink trade seems less organised, less developed, and less respectable than in England. This may explain why fashionable elite activities such as clubs and societies generally avoided meeting in drinking houses. Although one should be rightly sceptical about travellers' accounts (which tell us more about the visitor than the visited), English travellers were invariably critical of European inns from Scandinavia to Italy, complaining of their disorganisation and dirtiness, at least underlining the contrast with England.[59] New-style sports may have been an incidental casualty before 1800. In the modern era, the role of drink retailers has been taken over by drink producers, including soft drink manufacturers, who have become increasingly powerful sponsors of international sporting competitions such as football championships and the Olympic Games.[60]

A sixth and final point is the variable importance of competing cultural spaces. As we noted above, in considerable parts of Continental Europe traditional customary games were often linked to established community institutions such as fraternities, guilds, neighbourhood organisations or churches. As Behringer argues, this kind of institutionisation may well have increased during the sixteenth and seventeenth centuries. Communal institutions often continued to host customary events into the modern era and so may well have impeded or obstructed the advent of new activities.[61] In England, communal institutional support for traditional games seems less important before the Reformation – there were no shooting guilds, for instance, as in the Low Countries. Traditional games not only suffered from fierce Puritan attack after the Reformation but, more important, there was a decline in the institutional support they had previously enjoyed. Fraternities were suppressed from the 1540s, trade guilds had disappeared in many southern towns by the seventeenth century and churches became more pluralistic with the rise of dissenting congregations. Thus in England, unlike on the Continent, there were fewer established competitive centres to stop the development of new commercial sports from the late seventeenth century.[62] Strikingly, in the late nineteenth century, when sports really take off across Europe, many of the traditional communal institutions such as fraternities and guilds had disappeared and churches were increasingly attracting only a small urban minority.

This checklist of factors, however important, can obviously not afford the whole answer. When we pursue the comparison with the late nineteenth-century development of sport on a European scale, other points present themselves. How important was gender and associated notions of masculinity? Although many of the new sports activists in England were men, this was not invariably the case. Women were involved in archery contests and also participated as spectators

84   Charting the flows: institutions and genres

in cricket and horseracing. This was in marked contrast to the most important new form of leisure activity in the long eighteenth century, clubs and societies, which in England (unlike on the continent) were heavily male-dominated. It is has been suggested elsewhere that male associational exclusivity in England may well have displaced female leisure activity to other cultural fields such as music and assemblies: new-style sports may also have benefited.[63] It might be possible that on the continent a different pattern of male and female participation in urban leisure resulted in a different route to modern sport.

In the eighteenth century, foreigners sometimes drew attention to what they saw as the distinctive Englishness of sports in England. Did this in some way hamper the dissemination of sport in this period, as something too specifically 'foreign' or 'English'? It seems unlikely. Overseas commentators made the same point about English clubs and societies, yet some types of association such as freemasonry spread widely on the Continent.[64] Nevertheless, the meagre adaptation of English sports on the Continent may partly be explained by the lack of some sort of international competition, which is so typical for the late nineteenth century. In the modern period competitions such as the Tour de France, football championships and, from the 1890s, the Olympic Games played a key part in promoting public interest in sports, mobilising media attention, transforming sportsmen into national heroes and encouraging the international mobility and visibility of sportsmen. Nothing similar happened in the eighteenth century and sportsmen did not travel widely, unlike those musicians, scientists and other Enlightenment figures who helped to disseminate new ideas and innovation in their fields across Europe.[65]

Conclusion

In conclusion, one must confess to not having a real answer to the initial conundrum. Much more research needs to be done, particularly on Continental sports. Is there more competitive commercial activity to be discovered outside England? Probably. Still, the analysis above with all its limitations and sketchiness may shed some useful light on the variables involved in cultural dissemination – and its limitations – during the eighteenth and early nineteenth centuries. Urbanisation, the media, political conditions, the role of elites, the dynamic role of publicans and competing cultural spaces all seem to be crucial for major changes in the cultural and leisure world of early modern Europe. If the first three are sufficient causes, the last three may well be the necessary preconditions for change.

Notes

1 E. Dunning et al. (eds.), *Sports Histories: Figurational Studies of the Development of Modern Sports* (Abingdon: Routledge, 2004), p. 9.

2 R. Holt, *Sport and the British* (Oxford: Clarendon Press, 1989), especially chapters 2 and 4; R. Holt, *Sport and Society in Modern France* (London: Macmillan, 1981); J. Lowerson, *Sport and the English Middle Classes 1870–1914* (Manchester: Manchester University Press, 1993); H. Meinander, *Towards a Bourgeois Manhood* (Helsinki: Finninsh Society of Sciences and Letters, 1994).

3 P. Borsay, *The English Urban Renaissance: Culture and Society in the Provincial Town, 1660–1770* (Oxford: Clarendon Press, 1989); R.W. Malcolmson, *Popular Recreations in English Society, 1700–1850* (Cambridge: Cambridge University Press, 1973), especially chapter 3; D. Underdown, *Start of Play: Cricket and Culture in Eighteenth-Century England* (London: Allen Lane, 2000).

4 Underdown, *Start of Play*; P. Clark, *British Clubs and Societies: The Origins of an Associational World 1580–1800* (Oxford: Clarendon Press, 2000), pp. 81, 125.

5 Clark, *British Clubs*, pp. 124–125.

6 Borsay, *English Urban Renaissance*, pp. 180–196; also P. Borsay, 'Town and turf: the development of racing in England, c.1680–1760', in *Life in the Georgian Town* (Georgian Group Annual Symposium, London, 1986), p. 53.

7 Borsay, *English Urban Renaissance*, pp. 189–190; Malcolmson, *Popular Recreations*, pp. 50–51. The German Count Kielmansegge noted at Newmarket in 1761: 'Everybody bets here down to the smallest boys who wager their pennies, just as the lords their two to three hundred guineas or more' (F. Kielmansegge, *Diary of a Journey to England in the Years 1761–2* (London: Longmans, Green and Co., 1902), p. 48).

8 Clark, *British Clubs*, p. 125; R. Mortimer, *The Jockey Club* (London: Cassell, 1958).

9 See *Horse Race at Newmarket*, painted 1730–1752 by James Seymour (1702–1752), National Trust, Petworth House, www.nationaltrustcollections.org.uk/object/486283 (accessed 10 February 2014); J. Whessell, *The Famous Match between Harry Tempest Vane's Horse Hambletonian* (1800), British Museum, Prints Department: 1917, 1208.2433.

10 R. Carr, *English Fox Hunting* (London: Weidenfeld and Nicolson, 1976); Clark, *British Clubs*, pp. 123–124; also T. Collins et al., *Encyclopaedia of Traditional British Sports* (Abingdon: Routledge, 2005).

11 Borsay, *English Urban Renaissance*, pp. 173–175. Bowls may have suffered from late attempts at regulation: N. Wrigglesworth, *The Evolution of English Sport* (London: Psychology Press, 1996), p. 27.

12 Borsay, *English Urban Renaissance*, pp. 16–18.

13 K. Thomas, *Man and the Natural World: Changing Attitudes in England 1500–1800* (London: Allen Lane, 1983), especially pp. 159–160.

14 E. Griffin, *England's Revelry: A History of Popular Sports and Pastimes 1660–1830* (Oxford: Oxford University Press, 2005), p. 251.

15 B. Harris and C. McKean, *The Scottish Town in the Age of Enlightenment 1740–1820* (Edinburgh: Edinburgh University Press, 2014), chapter 6; Clark, *British Clubs*, pp. 81, 126; Collins et al., *Encyclopaedia of Traditional British Sports*.

16 J. Kelly and M.J. Powell (eds.), *Clubs and Societies in Eighteenth-Century Ireland* (Dublin: Four Courts Press, 2010), pp. 413–424.

17 Kelly and Powell, *Clubs and Societies in Eighteenth-Century Ireland*, pp. 394, 441.

18 Kelly and Powell, *Clubs and Societies in Eighteenth-Century Ireland*, pp. 392–393, 442.

19 N.L. Struna, *People of Prowess: Sport, Leisure and Labor in Early Anglo-America* (Urbana: University of Illinois Press, 1996), pp. 76, 132.

20 Struna, *People of Prowess*, pp. 76, 96.

21 Struna, *People of Prowess*, p. 125; Clark, *British Clubs*, pp. 391, 392, 399; also T.H. Breen, 'Horses and gentlemen: the cultural significance of gambling among the gentry of Virginia', *William and Mary Quarterly*, 3rd series, 34 (1977), 239–257.

22 Clark, *British Clubs*, pp. 397, 418–419; Struna, *People of Prowess*, p. 125.

23 Struna, *People of Prowess*, pp. 76, 84, 122; Clark, *British Clubs*, pp. 396–399.

24 H. Seymour and D. Seymour Mills, *Baseball: The Early Years* (Oxford: Oxford University Press, 1960); J. Naismith, *Basketball: Its Origin and Development* (New York: Association Press, 1941); A. Danzig, *The History of American Football: Its Great Teams, Players, and Coaches* (Englewood Cliffs, NJ: Prentice-Hall, 1956).

25 W. Behringer, 'Arena and Pall Mall: sport in the early modern period', *German History*, 27 (2009), 331–357. I am grateful to Professor Behringer for bringing this article to my attention.

26 Information kindly provided by Professor Roey Sweet; see also H. Matthews, *The Diary of an Invalid*, 2nd edn (London: John Murray, 1820), p. 171.

27 P. Clark, *European Cities and Towns 400–2000* (Oxford: Oxford University Press, 2009), p. 194; T. Martyn, *A Tour Through Italy* (London: C. and G. Kearsley, 1791), p. 385; J. Baretti, *An Account of the Manners and Customs of Italy* (London: T. Davies, 1768), vol. II, p. 239; P. Brydone, *A Tour Through Sicily and Malta* (Paris: J.G.A. Stoupe, 1780), vol. I, p. 256; vol. II, p. 153.

28 Matthews, *Diary*, pp. 149–150, 154.

29 Matthews, *Diary*, p. 172.

30 Chapter 10 in this volume; Matthews, *Diary*, pp. 171–172.

31 J.-L. Marais, *Les Societés des Hommes: Histoire d'une Sociabilité du 18e siècle à nos jours* (Vauchrétien: Éditions Iwan Davy, 1986), pp. 44, 109.

32 R. Crego, *Sports and Games of the 18th and 19th Centuries* (London: Greenwood Publishing Group, 2003), p. 163; W.M. Gaugler, *The History of Fencing: Foundations of Modern European Swordplay* (Bangor, ME: Laureate Press, 1998).

33 E. Dunning, 'Sport in space and time: "civilizing processes", trajectories of state formation and the development of modern sport', in O. Weiss and W. Schulz (eds.), *Sport in Space and Time* (Vienna: Vienna University Press, 1995), p. 23; also E. Dunning, *Sport Matters* (London: Routledge, 1999), p. 53; A. Hofmann, 'Sheep, shepherd and the stubble field', in G. Pfister (ed.), *Games of the Past – Sports for the Future?* (Sankt Augustin: Academis Verlag, 2004), p. 100; also Pfister, *Games of the Past*, pp. 103, 111.

34 Holt, *Sport and the British*, pp. 1–12.

35 Behringer, 'Arena and Pall Mall', p. 331.

36 Pfister, *Games of the Past*, p. 88.

37 E. Dunning and G. Curry, 'Football', in Dunning et al., *Sports Histories*, p. 36; G. Jarvie (ed.), *Sport in the Making of Celtic Cultures* (London: Leicester University Press, 1999), pp. 15, 42, 58; D. Miles (ed.), *The Description of Pembrokeshire by George Owen of Henllys* (Landysul, Wales: Gomer, 1994), p. 208; W.J. Baker, *Sports in the Western World*, 2nd edn (Chicago: University of Illinois Press 1988), pp. 46–47, 63.

38 Pfister, *Games of the Past*, pp. 46, 63, 89.

39 P. Kärkkäinen, 'Voimainkoetuksia ja kisailuja', in T. Pyykkönen (ed.), *Suomi uskoi urheiluun* (Helsinki: Liikuntatieteellinen seura, 1992), pp. 19–39. For the apparent absence of organised sport in Sweden as well see M. Hellspong, 'A timeless excitement: Swedish agrarian society and sport in the pre-industrial era', in H. Meinander and J.A. Mangan (eds.), *The Nordic World: Sport in Society* (London: Frank Cass, 1998), p. 15.

40 Pfister, *Games of the Past*, pp. 90, 96; R. van Uytven, 'Scenes de la Vie Sociale dans les Villes des Pays-Bas du XIVe et XVIe siècles', in *Actes du Colloque 'Sociabilité urbaine en Europe du Nord-Ouest'* (Douai: Lefebvre-L'évêque, 1983), p. 17.

41 Behringer, 'Arena and Pall Mall', p. 332.

42 P. Clark, 'Politics, the city and the popular drinking house in early modern Europe', in S. Ehrenpreis et al. (eds.), *Wege der Neuzeit: Festschrift für Heinz Schilling* (Berlin: Duncker and Humblot, 2007), pp. 621–623.

43 B. Kümin, *Drinking Matters: Public House and Exchange in Early Modern Central Europe* (Basingstoke: Palgrave Macmillan, 2007), especially chapters 3, 4 and 6; J. Chartres, 'The eighteenth-century English inn: a transient "golden age"', in B. Kümin and B.A. Tlusty (eds.), *The World of the Tavern* (Aldershot: Ashgate, 2002), pp. 205–226, and also other chapters in this volume; P. Clark, *The English Alehouse: A Social History 1200–1830* (London: Longman, 1983), pp. 153–154; A. Everitt, 'The English Urban Inn 1560–1760', in A. Everitt (ed.), *Perspectives in English Urban History* (London: Macmillan, 1973), pp. 114–117.

44 After David Teniers the Younger, *Series of Peasants* (1625), bowling match outside a tavern, British Museum, Prints Dept., 1997, 0928, 14.64; after A.J. van Ostade, *La Foire Hollandaise*, British Museum, Prints Dept., 1898, 0215.25; A.J. van Ostade, *The Pall Mall Court*, Rijksmuseum, Amsterdam; H. Averkamp, *Ice Landscape* (early 17th century).

45 J. Huizinga, *Homo Ludens* (Amsterdam: Pantheon, 1939).

46 Kümin, *Drinking Matters*, p. 127; Marais, *Les Societés des Hommes*, pp. 44, 109.

47 Information kindly provided by Professor Dag Lindström, Uppsala University.

48 Clark, *European Cities and Towns*, pp. 123–128; also E.A. Wrigley, 'Urban growth and agricultural change: England and the continent in the early modern period', in P. Borsay (ed.), *The Eighteenth Century Town: A Reader in English Urban History 1688–1820* (Harlow: Longman, 1990), chapter 2.

49 P. Clark (ed.), *Cambridge Urban History of Britain: II* (Cambridge: Cambridge University Press, 2000), chapters 14–15, 19–24.

50 T. Devine, 'Scotland', in Clark (ed.), *Cambridge Urban History*, p. 158; P. Borsay and L. Proudfoot (eds.), *Provincial Towns in Early Modern England and Ireland* (Oxford: Oxford University Press, 2002), chapters 1, 4 and 5.

51 Clark, *European Cities and Towns*, p. 229.

52 R.M. Wiles, *'Freshest Advices': Early Provincial Newspapers in England* (Columbus, Ohio: Ohio State University Press, 1965); Clark, *British Clubs*, pp. 172–175; Borsay, 'Town and turf', p. 53.

53 M. Schneider and J. Hemels, *De Nederlandse Krant van 1618–1978* (Baarn: Het Wereldvenster, 1978), pp. 46–77, 85–120 (I thank Dr Boudien de Vries for her advice here). T.C.W. Blanning, *The Culture of Power and the Power of Culture* (Oxford: Oxford University Press, 2002), pp. 157–161. For the critical relationship of sport and the media in the modern period see A. Bernstein and N. Blain (eds.), *Sport., Media, Culture in Global and Local Dimensions* (London: Frank Cass, 2003).

54 J. Innes and N. Rogers, 'Politics and government 1700–1840', in Clark (ed.), *Cambridge Urban History*, pp. 543–548, 551–555; Borsay, *English Urban Renaissance*, p. 279. For sport and militarisation in the late nineteenth century see Meinander, *Towards a Bourgeois Manhood*, p. 83; also Holt, *Sport and the British*, p. 94.

55 N. Elias and E. Dunning, *Quest for Excitement: Sport and Leisure in the Civilizing Process* (Oxford: Wiley Blackwell, 1986), p. 30.

56 G. Rudé, *Hanoverian London 1714–1808* (London: Secker and Warburg, 1971), pp. 38, 48; also L. Stone, 'The residential development of the West End of London in the seventeenth century', in B. Malament (ed.), *After the Reformation* (Manchester: Manchester University Press, 1980), pp. 173–182; Borsay, *English Urban Renaissance*, p. 29; F.-J. Ruggiu, *Les elites et les villes moyennes en France et en Angleterre (XVVe-XVIIIe siècles)* (Paris: L'Harmattan for the Université des Sciences Humaines de Strasbourg: 1997); Clark, *European Cities and Towns*, pp. 131–132, 142–143; Wigglesworth, *Evolution*, pp. 31–32.

57 Lowerson, *Sport and the English Middle Classes*; Meinander, *Towards a Bourgeois Manhood*.

58 Clark, *English Alehouse*, chapters 9–11; Clark, *British Clubs*, pp. 161–165; Chartres, 'The eighteenth-century English inn', pp. 223–224.

59 Kümin, *Drinking Matters*, pp. 87–91; Clark, 'Politics, the city and the popular drinking house', pp. 635–636; N. Wraxall, *A Tour round the Baltic thro' the Northern Countries of Europe* (London: T. Cadell and W. Davies, 1807); Brydon, *Tour Through Sicily*, vol. I, pp. 75, 96–97.

60 Wim Lagae, *Sports Sponsorship and Marketing Communications: A European Perspective* (Harlow: Financial Times/Prentice Hall, 2005); 'Heineken Brand to sponsor UEFA Champions League', www.heinekeninternational.com (accessed 25 May 2005); Wigglesworth, *Evolution*, pp. 136, 140.

61 Clark, *European Cities and Towns*, pp. 193–194; M. Prak et al. (eds.), *Craft Guilds in the Early Modern Low Countries* (Aldershot: Ashgate, 2006); M. van der Heijden et al. (eds.), *Serving the Urban Community: The Rise of Public Facilities in the Low Countries* (Amsterdam: Askant Academic Pulbishers, 2009).

62 R. Hutton, *The Rise and Fall of Merry England: The Ritual Year 1400–1700* (Oxford: Oxford University Press, 1994); Clark, *British Clubs*, pp. 184–187.

63 *Archery Plate 2*, British Museum, Prints Dept., C, 2.2005 (female archers, 1792); Borsay, *English Urban Renaissance*, p. 245; Clark, *British Clubs*, pp. 202–204.

64 For example, see Z.C. von Uffenbach, *London in 1710*, trans. and ed. W.H. Quarrell and M. Mare (London: Faber and Faber, 1934), pp. 48–49 (I am grateful to Professor Peter Borsay for this reference). Clark, *British Clubs*, p. 5; P. Clark, 'Spaces, circuits and short-circuits in the "European Enlightenment"', *De Achttiende Eeuw*, 43 (2011), p. 370.

65 For competitions and modern sports see Holt, *Sport and the British*, pp. 185, 218, 224, 273–275; for sportsmen as national heroes see, for example, J. Huntington-Whiteley, *The Book of British Sporting Heroes* (London: National Portrait Gallery, 1998). See also numerous websites on national sporting heroes. For the international mobility of eighteenth-century musicians see, for instance, S. McVeigh, *Concert Life in London from Mozart to Haydn* (Cambridge: Cambridge University Press, 1993), pp. 80–84, 173, 187–189, 198–200.

II

Processes of selection and adaptation: actors and structures

5

Georgian Bath:
a transnational culture

PETER BORSAY

One of the most striking features of elite leisure and culture in the eighteenth century is the ease with which ideas and forms flow across geographic boundaries. Indeed, it often seems in the period that fashionable pastimes and practices define themselves in relation to an 'international' cultural system, associated with the Enlightenment, which deliberately eschewed the local and parochial, stigmatising it as boorish and uncivilised. In this context, the transnational perspective takes on a particular significance. To be fashionable in England was to be foreign. Among the principal engines of cultural exchange, circulating models of pleasure and taste around the system, were cities and towns. This was in part due to their function as places of economic exchange and social intercourse, but is also reflected the widespread view that towns were the wellsprings of civilisation. In this chapter I want to explore the extent – and limits – of the role of urban centres as the engines of a transnational culture by focusing on one provincial town in Georgian England, Bath. No claim can be made that Bath was typical of the multifarious urban centres in eighteenth-century Britain. In many respects, as we shall see, it was quite exceptional. But it did stand for a new class of urban centres, spas and seaside resorts, which focused on the provision of health and leisure, and often looked to Bath as their model. Moreover, the processes of cultural transfer underway in Bath did exemplify, if normally on a much diminished scale, the forces of change to be seen in hundreds of smaller towns, whose character was being reshaped by transnational flows of culture.

In the late seventeenth century, Bath would not have looked a particularly promising candidate for a city about to become a conduit for international leisure. Its physical fabric was old-fashioned, medieval and early modern in origin, largely Gothic or vernacular in style, and reflected little of the changes underway in the more advanced towns. It was also a small city. There were scarcely 3,000 people in 1700, and they were largely packed into the houses located

94 Processes of selection and adaptation

within the medieval walled town or in the small suburban extensions serving the poor. But it would be wrong to give the impression that it was down-at-heel. Despite the decline, although not disappearance, of its once flourishing textile industry, late Stuart Bath wore an air of modest affluence and had begun to display the first signs of its future golden age. The source of this prosperity was its spa. The springs at Bath had a very long history of usage, and from the late sixteenth century they were undergoing modernisation to cater for an emerging elite market in health. However, it was the late seventeenth century that saw this market take off, with the proliferation of small spas and, critically, the first signs of the health function of spas becoming a platform for the provision of leisure services. During the eighteenth century, Bath became the leading spa and tourist resort in Britain (outside the three metropolitan capitals), as a lucrative and large-scale leisure industry emerged around watering places. By 1800 Bath had a population of more than 30,000 and was among the largest ten towns in England.[1] However, it was not just demographic growth that created the conditions that 'internationalised' Bath's culture. Crucial was the nature of that growth (and the market that underpinned it) with its focus upon the expanding surplus wealth and increasingly sophisticated recreational needs of a prosperous elite. The concentration of a high proportion of the nation's leaders, many of whom had acquired a taste for the high culture of Continental Europe during extended 'Grand Tours', in the Somerset spa during the season proved a honey-pot for entrepreneurs to invest in facilities and services that drew much of their inspiration from outside rather than inside the boundaries of Britain.[2]

This chapter will begin by exploring how cultural ideas from outside Britain influenced the development of Bath's fashionable leisure scene in a variety of fields from material goods to forms of behaviour. The chapter will then exam-ine the vectors through which cultural transmission took place. At the same time there will also be need to consider factors and agencies that may have inhibited the flow of 'foreign' ideas or subjected them to processes of adapta-tion and re-export, so that there was a genuine two-way flow of culture. One potential area of resistance was the strength of national sentiment, and there will be an examination of the concepts of 'national' and 'transnational', and of the entangled relationship between them in Bath.

Foreign influences

How moulded was Bath's emerging fashionable leisure culture by influences from outside Britain? The best direct answer to this question is to identify

Figure 5.1 Thomas Rowlandson, *Comforts of Bath: The Concert*, 1798. Yale Center for British Art, Paul Mellon Collection.

in detail where these influences were at work, and this will be done focusing on recreations and the arts, consumables, behaviour, literature and language. But before doing this, two caveats need to registered. First, no claim is being made that Bath was utterly in thrall to Continental taste, and that it simply mimicked patterns of recreational consumption created in Europe. Bath possessed its own indigenous culture, it could be a creative force in its own right, and much – probably most – of the leisure being developed in the city can be traced to other British sources. Moreover, it could be argued that despite the city's leisure industry often tipping its cap at French and Italian models, this was essentially a superficial exercise, manifested in surface cultural features, more a matter of gesture than substance. Second, there is a need to distinguish between direct and indirect sources of influence. There are those instances where it is possible to trace an unmediated transnational influence at work, such as the presence of a musician trained in Rome or the sale of consumer goods sourced in Paris. But more common, although in many respects no less an example of cultural transmission, is a product or practice whose links to their continental origins may be via a complex chain of intermediaries, many of which may be located in Britain.

Visitors came to Bath to be entertained, and theatre was an essential part of the framework created to do this. Despite the curbs on performance introduced by the Licensing Act of 1737, the city enjoyed a continuous provision of

96 Processes of selection and adaptation

theatre throughout the eighteenth century, reaching the height of its reputation in the 1790s and early 1800s, a period when melodrama, a form derived from French and German sources – a point alluded to in Chapter 3 in this volume – came to dominate programming on the Bath stage.[3] Language was a potential bar to the direct importation of foreign drama (although of course there was no reason why texts should not be translated). Language was, however, no serious hindrance to the performance of music, particularly of an instrumental nature. Arguably it was for this reason that Bath's flourishing musical scene, not to mention that in Britain as a whole, was able to draw so much upon non-native composers, performers, teachers and impresarios. Foreign-born, internationally renowned composers such as Handel and Haydn feature prominently on the spa's concert programmes (both visited the city, Handel for his health in 1745 and 1751, Haydn in 1794).[4] A German compatriot of Handel, who like him settled in Britain, was William Herschel. Initially an oboist in the Hanoverian Guard, he arrived in Bath in 1766 to be the resident organist at the newly opened Octagon Chapel (the organ was built by the Swiss John Snetzler) in 1766, and stayed until 1782, during which time he played in the Assembly Room orchestra, performed as soloist on occasions, taught, composed and from 1776 was director of the New Assembly Rooms band (and therefore effectively controller of public concerts in the spa).[5] Herschel was succeeded in this last capacity in 1777, initially, it would appear, by a combination of the Flemish violinist Franz Lamotte and the Italian castrato Venanzio Rauzzini, before in 1780 the latter – a prolific composer and renowned teacher, as well as performer and impresario – took 'complete control of the city's professional music making' until his death in 1810.[6] The success of figures such as Herschel and Rauzzini, and the presence in Bath of many of the stars of the European concert circuit – such as the Italian violinists Francesco Geminiani (1721) and Giovanni Viotti (1794–1795), the Afro-Polish child prodigy violinist George Bridgetower (1789), the German soprano Gertrude Mora (c. 1796), and the Italian castratos Giusto Fernando Tenducci (1781) and Nicolo Grimaldi (stage name Nicolini, c. 1721) – showed not only the pulling power of Britain and Bath, but also the extent to which Bath's musical scene became internationalised in the eighteenth century.[7] Foreign was fashionable. In 'Jack Dilettante', Christopher Anstey's *New Bath Guide* of 1766 satirised the slavish pursuit of continental glitz; 'He has Taste, without doubt, and a delicate Ear,/ No vile Oratorios ever could bear;/But talks of the Op'ras and his Signiora,/ Cries *Bravo, Benissimo, Bravo, Encora!*'[8] There were, of course, many valued British performers at Bath, but several of those had travelled and been trained abroad; such was the case with the soprano Nancy Storace and Thomas Linley, father (vocalist, harpsichordist, composer and impresario) and son. Thomas Junior, a violinist, was described in 1776 by Charles Burney as 'a Charming Performer, and of a Good School, having been under Nardini, Tartini's best Scholar, in Italy, a considerable time'.[9] Teaching provided an important supplementary source of income for many musicians, and for those from Europe their foreign origins were seen as a valuable selling point, strengthening their role as a conduit for transnational taste. In 1784 The *Bath Chronicle* advertised the services of 'MADEMOISELLE DENIS, just arrived at Bath ... teaches the HARP; [and] has had the honour of teaching some of the first personages in France', four years later it informed its readers that Mr Colson 'belonging to the New Rooms Concert, a native of Versailles, and formerly a student of the Royal Conservatoire at Naples ... teaches the Viola d'Amour, the Musical Glasses, and Violin', and in 1792 it declared Rauzzini 'the first master for teaching in the universe'.[10]

The capacity to perform music, at an amateur level, was seen as an important social accomplishment for gentlemen, and especially ladies. It was part of a wider suite of skills by which the elite, and those who wished to join their ranks, expressed their refinement and status. Dancing was another of these social skills, vitally important in the context of the growth of private balls and public assemblies in the period.[11] French taste and practice was seen as a model to follow. For much of the eighteenth century, balls at the Bath Assembly Rooms were divided between English country dances and French minuets. In 1785, François La Rochefoucauld, a French tourist in Bath, recorded that there were two balls a week in each of the Lower and Upper Rooms, 'and there one dances one dance *à l'anglaise*, another *à la française*'.[12] From the late 1760s, a new dance craze was introduced into Bath from Paris, the cotillion, a more formalised version of the English country dance. By 1784, the Lower and Upper Rooms were both mounting a dress ball and a cotillion ball each week, for which subscription tickets were issued, and in 1789 it was reported in the *Bath Chronicle* that at the neighbouring cathedral town of Wells 'it being the ton at present in Paris among the *belle monde* to explode the dancing of minuets, that formal dance was disposed with'.[13] As in the case of music, foreign teachers were an important conduit for the new fashions in dance. French dancing masters (and some mistresses) abounded in Bath, to offer their services on an individual basis or to the many schools for young ladies to be found in the spa.[14] In 1787, Monsieur Michael advertised that he 'has lately been to Paris and London, to see the newest stile; and as his Children (his Pupils) are engaged to dance the season at the Theatre-Royal in Bath and Bristol, he flatters himself that their proficiency will recommend him to his profession – He will attend Abroad, at Boarding-Schools, or at his Lodgings.'[15]

One area where teaching was fundamental if the necessary skills were to be mastered was language. The high level of demand in eighteenth-century Bath for learning foreign languages, particularly French and Italian, was indicative not only of their practical value in allowing those suitably proficient an unmediated entrée into what were considered high status cultures, but also of the sheer kudos associated with speaking these languages in public. The presence of a foreign language teacher, especially of French, was a requirement for the many private schools in Bath.[16] Some saw a total immersion in French culture as a strong selling point. In 1784 Miss Adelaide Goguel, 'a native of Paris', advertised that she

> has taken a House in New King-street, No. 2, Bath, where she will open a BOARDING and DAY SCHOOL ... where Young Ladies will be taught the French Language, grammatically, Point Lace, all sorts of French needle-work, Tambour, Embroidery, French vocal and Instrumental Music; and nothing will be spoken but the French language in the School.[17]

It is clear from an advert in the same year that the capacity to teach French was also an important asset in those pursuing the position of a governess: 'WANTS a PLACE, as Governess to Young Ladies in a private family, a FRENCH GENTLEWOMAN, who has received a good education; she can teach the French Language perfectly, also dancing in the most fashionable taste.'[18] What seems a particularly important attribute for a teacher was being a native speaker and some acquaintance with European centres of fashionable culture. *The Improved Bath Guide* of 1812 lists seven 'teachers of the French and Italian languages', most with foreign sounding surnames such as Belzons, Cheubini, Graux and Le Boucher.[19] One advert in the *Bath Chronicle* of 1784 offered the services as a governess of 'a Young Woman, who is a Native of France, has resided some years at Paris, and Speaks the French language with the greatest purity', and another of the same year of

> Mr. A. R. lately arrived from Paris [who] ... teaches the Latin, French, and Italian languages, without tiring his pupils [who] ... acquire ... the true delicacy of pronunciation of the French language which is used by the first nobility at the Court of Versailles, and likewise that of the Italian which is used by the first nobility in Rome.[20]

Foreign language teachers resident in Britain, because of their high degree of mobility and pedagogic role, were especially important vectors for the transmission of cultural ideas across national boundaries. However, their influence ultimately depended upon the perceived value of the product they traded in. Language allowed direct access to cultures that were considered the acme of taste and learning. In the 1780s among the items available to subscribers to Hazard's circulating library was the *Journal de Paris* and 'books in all languages', while in January 1788 two subscription series of 'French readings', each of four separate sessions, were arranged in the Lower Rooms, which included works such as Moliere's comedy *Les Précieuses Ridicules*.[21] Command of foreign languages also allowed those with the requisite ability to show off their linguistic skills in public and gain the social cachet associated with this. Bath would appear to have provided good opportunities to do this, particularly as the French Revolution encouraged wealthy aristocrats and gentry to flee their native country. As early as November 1789, Dr Borzaccini, a 'Professor of the Italian and French languages' in Bath, was informing the city's inhabitants how fortunate they were to have his services – which included not only teaching but also the preparation of French and Italian grammars involving mixtures of Bath, Bristol and London printers and booksellers – since 'BY the great resort of Foreigners to this kingdom, the knowledge of the French language becomes every day more necessary'.[22]

Eighteenth-century Britain has been seen as undergoing a 'consumer revolution', supported by a widening web of international commerce.[23] In a city with good links to international ports such as London and Bristol, and increasingly well provisioned with luxury shops, the consumption of material goods became an important channel for accessing foreign fashions and tastes. One focal point was food and drink. French and Iberian wines were available from the city's wine merchants, importing through locations such as Bristol, Southampton and the Channel Islands.[24] How far wine, for those who imbibed it, carried connotations of its European origins is hard to say. A sense of the exotic was almost certainly attached to a drinking craze that swept across Britain from the later seventeenth century and drew its raw materials from Asia, the consumption of tea and coffee, a subject addressed in this volume in Chapter 8 by Cengiz Kırlı. By 1784 more than a third (672) of the shopkeepers in Bath and Bristol were registered tea dealers.[25] Tea and coffee drinking became an important part of a wider set of social rituals, associated with public and private sociability at Bath. The Cornish vicar John Penrose describes several occasions on which he took tea while staying at the spa, on one – after a particularly sumptuous dinner at a friend's:

> [We] drank Tea in the Dining-Room. Coffee out of very large white china cups, Tea out of very large Dishes, next kin to Basons of a Rummer fashion. The Coffee Jug plain upon a square salver ... the Tea urn plain except a Chinese Border round the Bottom, which stood on a Mahogony Table. The Tea and Coffee cups, etc. upon a silver Tea-table or Waiter ... which costs £44.19.0 at 7s.8d. per ounce. The price of the Tea Urn about 30 guineas.[26]

What emphasised the 'Oriental' aspects of tea and coffee drinking, and the potential for cultural transfer, was the elaborate tableware that accompanied drinking, and was clearly a part of a process of conspicuous consumption. As Rachel Kennedy and Trevor Fawcett have shown, Bath possessed a range of tradesmen supplying Chinese porcelain in the eighteenth century, and this had a knock-on effect in generating the demand on which to build a European and British-based industry.[27] In 1792 there was an auction 'at the Exhibition-Room in Bond-Street' Bath that included 'a Superb Assortment of FRENCH PORCELAIN, lately imported from *Paris*; Consisting of elegant Vases, flower stands, table and desert services, tea and coffee sets, &c. likewise a variety of japan'd tea-trays and Waiters'.[28]

A feature article in the *Bath Chronicle* in 1787 set out in minute detail the 'NEW FASHIONS AT PARIS' in clothing and hair styles; 'THE present ton consists of plain muslin caraco or robe, the skirt of which is pinked in points ... They dress their hair in large curls in two ranks, and behind have the *chignon* plat turned up, chiefly with flaxen powder.'[29] This was the sort of knowledge about fashion that visitors to Bath craved for, and it is clear from adverts in the newspaper that in the choice and purchase of accessories that adorned the body – textiles, clothing, millinery, jewellery, cosmetics and coiffures – Continental and particularly French origins and design carried a considerable cachet. Bath shops and tradesmen were in this sense a conveyor belt for the latest ideas in European taste. Several Huguenot craftsmen and traders, such as goldsmiths and jewellers, operated businesses in Bath.[30] Adverts for hats and hair make persistent reference to Paris; 'Ann Perrin, French Milliner, from Paris, sells all sorts of millinery, at her warehouse ... in Stall-street', Minchins in the Circus has 'received a CASE of MILLINERY from PARIS ... which for elegance far exceeds any of the kind seen in the kingdom', the milliner Splisburg on the Lower Walks 'has engaged a Person from one of the first Houses in Paris, to enable her ... to merit the attention of the Public',

Mather the 'Ladies hair-dresser and Perfumer' on the corner of Bond Street has 'lately been at Paris, and imported a large assortment of the choicest Perfumery and every fashionable requisite for hair-dressing' and – for those in need of some genuine creativity – there was 'NEWLY-INVENTED FALSE HAIR, by N. MACKINNON, Ladies Hair-Dresser and Perfumer, from Paris, that will dress any form which the Fashion may alter, last long, and never shrink'.[31]

One expensive article of self-fashioning that many visitors commissioned while in Bath was a portrait. Mostly the painters appear to be British, although in 1784 Andrew Rymsdyk, 'Painter in Miniature', offered to provide 'PORTRAITS in small, accurately drawn at two Guineas each', in 1807 the Finnish artist Jacob Spornberg prepared silhouettes, in 'Etruscan profile' (a process that he had invented) of Mr and Mrs Lybbe Powys during their visit to the spa, and Spornberg was among the artists listed in *The Improved Bath Guide* of 1812, which also included the French miniaturist Madame Chacheré Beaurepaire, who had emigrated to England around 1800, and split her time between studios in London and Gay Street Bath.[32] Simply because an artist was of foreign origins does not necessarily mean that he or she imported a foreign style of painting. Conversely, just because an artist was British did not isolate him or her from foreign influences. This was impossible in the world of eighteenth century art where European masters set the standards, and the well-off residents and visitors to Bath would have been fully conversant with the great tradition of Western European painting through their participation in the Grand Tour and building their own collections (when part of the 'Capital Collection' of Dr Rice Charlton, a leading Bath physician, was auctioned in the city in 1788, it included works attributed to Titian, Rubens, Veronese, Rembrandt and Correggio).[33] William Hoare, one of the principal portraitists in Georgian Bath, was trained in the London studio of the Italian artist Giuseppe Grisoni, before in 1728 accompanying him on visit to Italy that led to a nine-year stay in Rome, during which he became closely acquainted with the works of the old masters. Hoare settled in Bath in about 1738 (although he also undertook a tour of France and the Netherlands in 1749), and using the newly fashionable pastel medium and drawing on the technique of the Venetian pastelist Rosalba Carriera, a favourite of Grand Tourists, Hoare established a hugely successful business among the visitors to Bath.[34] Thomas Gainsborough also operated a thriving portrait practice in Bath between about 1760 and 1774. Although he never left England to train abroad, he was well-acquainted with the work of the European masters and knew what his market in Bath

102 Processes of selection and adaptation

wanted. In 1774 Mrs Delany went 'to see Mr Gainsborough's pictures ... they may be called what Mr. Webb unjustly says of Rubens – they are "*splendid impositions*" '.[35]

The fact that British artists often acted as a conduit for European influences demonstrates the indirect manner in which cultural ideas crossed national boundaries. In no way was this clearer at Bath than in the case of architecture. Few of those who designed or built eighteenth-century Bath were from outside Britain. The architects most associated with the building of the Georgian city, John Wood father and son, were natives of Bath, and never travelled abroad. Yet the classical style in which the eighteenth-century city was almost wholly built was derived from a European tradition originating in Greece and Rome, and 'rediscovered' during the Renaissance. It was a debt, and aspiration, that John Wood acknowledged when in the first edition of his history and guide to Bath, published in 1742–1743, he mused on the progress in the city's architecture, as it first started to absorb the influences of baroque classicism, in the two or so decades before his 'arrival' in the mid-1720s:

> In the Progress of these Improvements Thatch'd Coverings were exchang'd to such as were Tiled; low and obscure Lights were turn'd into elegant Sash-Windows; the Houses were rais'd to five or more Stories in Height; and every one was lavish in Ornaments to adorn the Outsides of them, even to Profuseness: So that only Order and Proportion was wanted to make BATH, sixteen Years ago, vie with the famous City of *Vicenza* in *Italy*, when in the highest Pitch of Glory, by the excellent Art of the celebrated *Andrea Palladio*, the *Vincentin* Architect.[36]

It was Wood's contribution, as he portrayed it, which – through adopting the fashionable Palladian-style architecture, publicised in works like Nicholas Dubois' and Giacomo Leoni's translation and redrawing of Palladio's sixteenth-century *I Quattro libri dell'architettura*, and Colen Campbell's *Vitruvius Britannicus* (both published in 1715) – introduced 'order and proportion' to the spa's provincial classical architecture and raised it to the level of Palladio's Vicenza.[37] In his 1725 plans for Bath, Wood referred explicitly to making

> a grand Place of Assembly, to be called the *Royal Forum* of *Bath*; another Place, no less magnificent, for the Exhibition of Sports, to be called the *Grand Circus*; and a third Place, of equal State with either of the former, for the Practice of medicinal Exercises, to be called the *Imperial Gymnasium* of the City, from a Work of that Kind, taking its Rise at first in *Bath*, during the Time of the *Roman* Emperors.[38]

Although these plans as laid out in 1725 were never to be realised, their Roman models are clear enough, and elements of them were to surface in the

Parades (c. 1740–1748) and the Circus (1754–1767) – the last of which any person who had taken the Grand Tour to Rome would have recognised as modelled, at least superficially, on the Colosseum.[39] The result of the work of the Woods and others was to create what to some visitors seemed like a foreign city. As Katherine Plymley confided in her diary in 1794:

> I am extremely struck with the beauty & singularity of Bath. Passing through Queens square up Gay Street to the Circus & Crescent [all designed by the Woods], I am ready to suspect that I am not in England. … the streets remind me of views I have seen of the inside of towns in Italy & Flanders.[40]

Comparisons with the Imperial City were perhaps taken a little far when one writer suggested in c. 1800 that the Adamesque 'town-hall', or Guildhall as it is known, designed by Thomas Baldwin and built 1775–1778, 'is a magnificent structure, bearing some resemblance to the Vatican at Rome'.[41]

Vectors of transmission

In the eighteenth century, Bath was a fast-growing city whose rapidly developing cultural and leisured life – theatrical, musical, educational, consumer, artistic and architectural – drew heavily upon Continental European models. How did these models travel to Bath? What were the vectors of transmission? People were by far the most important agents of cultural transfer. The most effective were groups who we have already identified, such as performers, teachers and impresarios, especially those from overseas. The dynamic nature of the British economy, its creation of more and more people possessing surplus wealth, and the development of an increasingly commercialised leisure industry on the back of this, turned Britain and its resorts into a honeypot for overseas talent. The parallels with the modern football Premiership in England are all too obvious. Money talked. But we should not forget the role of travellers and tourists, who moved in both directions. The British who went on the European Grand Tour, targeting particularly Paris and Rome, brought back ideas and developed aspirations that a resort like Bath, with its high concentration of the nation's elite, was expected to satisfy.[42] Hence the demand for perfumers from Paris, castratos from Italy and an architecture that mimicked the classical models seen in Rome. Visitors to Bath were in regular communication with relatives abroad. While staying in the spa in 1758 and 1760, the Warwickshire country gentleman George Lucy, himself a grand tourist, received a letter 'from Mr Lucy at Rome and another from my Italian master at Naples informing me of his being in St James's prison for debt', heard from Mrs Bright that she 'had a letter from her son at Venice', and reported that 'Mrs Wright hath had a letter from her son, they are well, and upon their travels to Rome'.[43] Between about 1770 and 1774, Lady Miller and her husband vacated their villa outside Bath (at Batheaston) and lived in France, during which they undertook a one-year tour of Italy. There they purchased an antique Etruscan vase that, on their return, became the centrepiece of Lady Miller's famous Bath literary salon, itself based on the *conversazioni* (or artistic gatherings) she had encountered while in Italy.[44]

Tourists from Europe also visited Bath. How many is difficult to calculate. Barbeau, in his important scholarly history of eighteenth-century Bath, claims that the spa – comparing it to its German counterparts like Baden-Baden – 'was no international rendezvous, and although foreigners occasionally visited it, it never offered the spectacle of a little cosmopolitan world'.[45] That may be a bit harsh, and comparisons with the more centrally placed European spas inappropriate. Whatever the difficulties in undertaking the hundred or so mile journey from London – and these were easing in the eighteenth century with improved roads, vehicles and services[46] – a significant number of foreigners made the trip to Bath. One poem of 1748 could declare: 'Now from all Parts the Company resort,/Sailing, like Vessels, to this neutral Port:/ Bath, Lisbon-like, for ever will admit/Those of all Nations for her Benefit.'[47] It is clear from the extensive accounts of Bath in the travel diaries of those visiting from abroad – such as the German Count Frederick Kielmansegge (visited 28 October–1 November 1761) or the son of a French duke, François de la Rochefoucauld (5–7 April 1785) – that Bath was very much on the tourist circuit for those visiting Britain.[48] Unsurprisingly it was the presence of distinguished foreigners that attracted attention and left a record. John Penrose noted 'the Sardinian Envoy' in the Pump Room in 1766, and in the following year reported that 'the news mentions several French Noblemen of high Distinction, as being in Bath last week'.[49] On 24 May 1787, the *Bath Chronicle* reported that a party of 12 French dignitaries, including the 'the Duke de Polignac, Master of the Horse to the Queen of France' and 'the Duchess of Polignac, Governess of the French King's children', 'attended by a grand retinue, visited Stowe and Blenheim, previous to their arrival in this city for the benefit of the waters', and on 21 June that 'the French Ambassador, the Duke and Duchess of Polignac, and the other noble foreigners in their suite, took leave of the city on Saturday last', suggesting about a month's stay.[50] A sign that those operating the leisure facilities at Bath recognised the social cachet and value of overseas visitors was a small addition

Georgian Bath: a transnational culture **105**

in 1780 (not there in the regulations of 1769), to one of the rules governing behaviour in the 'old' or Lower Assembly Rooms: 'That a certain row of seats be set apart at the upper end of the room, for Peeresses, and Ladies of the first distinction in precedence, *or foreigners of fashion*' (my italics).[51] The French Revolution boosted the foreign contingent in Bath, as royalists and clergy fled the political turmoil.[52] Choosing Bath as a refuge was a perhaps an indication that the spa was already familiar territory for the French aristocracy. As early as December 1789, letters from Bath carry hints of the flight underway, with the news that 'a party of French Ladies and Gentlemen left Bath yesterday, & bespoke 32 horses at each stage', and 'last night I went to the Ball because we have a number of grand Foreigners here and I wish'd to take a peep at their faces'.[53] In 1793, funeral sermons were preached at several of the Bath churches on the news of Louis XVI's death, 'the Catholic Chapel was hung with black, and solemn mass was said; at which all the French refuge Clergy now in Bath assisted'.[54] Bath seems generally to have taken a sympathetic approach to the plight of the émigrés,[55] some becoming teachers,[56] other adding to the crowds using the public facilities; as Caroline Powys recorded in her diary in 1797, 'the pump room was very full of Company many Emigrants there, and one among them with large Gold Earrings, to us in England this appear'd extraordinary, but I believe common in France'.[57] Whether foreigners ever formed a significant proportion of the visitors and residents in Bath, and whether they had a measureable impact on the cultural life of the city, is difficult to say. However, given the general kudos attached to European and particularly French fashions and taste it is likely that the presence of well-dressed members of the French elite, with their retinues, would have given a further boost – if that was needed – to the appeal of foreign cultural models. Anna Cradock's account of the visit to Bath of the French dignitaries in 1797, referred to earlier, gives some impression of the electrifying impact that foreign notables could have on the company, providing models of behaviour for the polite and vulgar alike:

> About 9 the French Ambassador, la Duchesses de Polignac, la Duchesse de Guise etc. etc. came to the ball. Two of the French ladies very handsome; they danced after tea. The stare of the company at them made me ashamed of the vulgarity of the English company, or rather dressed mob who crowded round the dancers so they could scarce move. ... The French gentlemen and ladies appeared easy and behaved with the politeness belonging to that nation.[58]

If people – teachers, tradesmen, performers, artists and visitors – were the principal vectors for transmitting foreign fashions, the role of the media should

Figure 5.2 Thomas Rowlandson, *Comforts of Bath: The Ball*, 1798. Yale Center for British Art, Paul Mellon Collection.

not be overlooked. Bath visitors enjoyed access to a rich print culture. In 1778 there were five circulating libraries and three local weekly newspapers in the resort, and by 1819 nine libraries and four newspapers.[59] The libraries could carry a substantial stock of foreign literature. A catalogue of Samuel Hazard's library in 1796 includes 288 'Libri Classici' and 189 'Livres François Italien etc.'.[60] The spa's circulating libraries and coffeehouses also carried copies of the national, and even international press.[61] Local publications might include translations of foreign literature. *The Bristol and Bath Magazine* in 1782 contained 'a very remarkable Story related at large, in a *French* work, entitled *Causes Celebre*' and 'A SONNET in Prose, from the Italian Language'.[62] As we have seen, the advertisements in the Bath newspapers were an important channel for information about foreign fashions, including where they could be purchased in the city. What, however, is also clear from these adverts, and complicates the whole issue of transnational cultural flows, is that many of these products were sourced through London. The metropolis supplied many of the shops in Bath. In April 1784, Messrs Smith in the Abbey Church Yard reported that they had 'just received from their Warehouse in London, an elegant Assortment of FANCY and PLAIN SILKS suitable for the Summer Season ... N.B. A large assortment of Black Silks ... fabricated on the Italian principle, REMARKABLY CHEAP'.[63] It was common practice for London businesses trading in luxury items and services, with European associations, to open a temporary outlet in Bath during the season. In 1784 'BULL, Hair-Dresser, (from Vere-street, Cavendish-Square, London)' declared himself to be 'at Mr. Elliott's Green-street, Bath, for the Season. Ballroom Curls and Genuine Perfumery from Paris'; in 1787, Coombs of 'Vaudey & Spratt's, Milliners in London', operating from the premises of Mr Dawson in Northgate Street, sold 'Gulmar Muffs and Dresses, with a variety of Fashionable Articles just arrived from Paris'; in the same year, Spilsbury, from Neis and Sivrac of Dover Street, London, and based in Bath on the Lower Walks, declared herself 'just arrived from Town with the Newest and most Elegant MILLINERY she could possible procure, for the ensuing Season ... she has engaged a Person from one of the First Houses in Paris, to enable her ... to merit the attention of the Public'; and in the following year, another milliner, Payne, of Dover Street, London, who had taken apartments in the Abbey Church Yard, begged 'leave to inform the Ladies, that she is returned from Paris'.[64]

Alongside London's role as a commercial intermediary between Bath and Europe, it also mediated at a broad cultural level between Europe – and, with the expansion in formal and informal empire, the world – and the Somerset spa. Many of the British performers and artists (such as William Hoare and Thomas Gainsborough) who worked in Bath were trained or spent some of their formative early years in London, exposed to the multiplicity of influences that flowed into the capital from abroad. There were close connections between London and provincial theatre, and in the early nineteenth century visits to Bath from actors and designers based in the metropolis were a common occurrence, and was probably responsible for introducing the craze for melodrama that originated in France and Germany.[65] Immediately prior (1725–1727) to his permanent re-settlement in Bath John Wood (1704–1754) was living on Oxford Street in London, at the hub of the metropolis's West End expansion, and was one of the principal builders on the adjacent Cavendish-Harley estate, with its square and terraces. Close by he could also see the beginnings of building work on the Grosvenor estate, where the first serious effort was being made, since the publication of the translation of Palladio's *Four Books* and *Vitruvius Britannicus* (1715), to apply the newly fashionable Palladian style to a large-scale urban development. Plans were drawn up to apply the palatial façade of the Palladian country house to one side of Grosvenor Square, but these were never executed. However, it was this idea – seemingly brought from London – that Wood introduced into his first large-scale project in Bath, Queen Square. It was the first implementation of a concept that was to prove hugely influential in urban planning.[66] In London, Wood would also have had

108 Processes of selection and adaptation

access to the early seventeenth-century urban buildings (the Queen's House Greenwich, the Banqueting House Whitehall, Covent Garden – the first urban square in Britain) of Inigo Jones, the first to introduce a purer form of classicism, what we now call Palladianism, into Britain.[67]

Resistance, adaptation and nationalism

If London's role as a cultural entrepôt complicates the model of the simple flow of one nation's culture to another, the picture is further problematised by the response of Bath itself and the entangled issue of nationalism. Bath was not a mere sponge absorbing indiscriminately all and every cultural influence that crossed its path. Just as there were forces facilitating the transmission of culture, so there were those that resisted it. Bath was an independent political and economic community, with its own civic traditions and local interests. Exposure to outside forces might compromise these. One problem that it and many other towns in Britain faced was how far it should exercise its traditional rights to exclude non-freemen from plying their trade in the town. Potentially this could exclude 'foreign' craftsmen, performers, and businessmen from operating in Bath, and bringing with them external cultural influences. In the mid-eighteenth-century the Corporation prosecuted, among others, the perfumers George Duperré and Italian De Coppa for trading in the city without being freemen. In truth, the focus of attack was primarily on British interlopers. Moreover, this was effectively the Corporation's last stand on the matter, as attempts to impose the freemen monopoly were eventually abandoned.[68] It became clear that Bath's long-term growth and success depended upon an open, flexible economy, capable of attracting the sorts of services and products that the fashionable visitors required. What that openness would not have easily spread to was poor migrants, British or foreign, who might be a financial burden on the city, a factor that could affect itinerant entertainers.

To think in terms of local resistance to external influences might, however, be misleading. More typically the response was one of adaptation. The welcome given to Herschel and Rauzzini was one that required them to adapt their musical skills to the specific needs of the social and recreational programme of the spa – servicing the chapels, Pump Room and Assembly Rooms, and the daily and weekly round into which these institutions fitted. Architecture provides another example. The Palladianism that John Wood brought to the spa may have reflected developments in London, but it was the specific social requirements and landscape of Bath that determined the forms that it took. Wood succeeded in introducing the palatial façade to the city's multi-unit residential buildings because it served the social aspirations for a mixture of sociability and elitism of the city's tight-knit high-status clientele. Wood first applied the palatial faced concept to Queen Square, but it was not squares that became the trademark building type in Bath, but the crescent. It was a form, prefigured by Wood in the Circus but brought to maturity by his son in the Royal Crescent and spread around the city by later builders, that accommodated the palatial face but applied it to an open terrace format. The driving force behind the introduction of the crescent was the steeply rising landscape surrounding Bath, unsuitable for the construction of squares, and the opportunity to service the growing demand, stimulated by the picturesque and Romantic movements, for views and engagement with nature.[69]

Bath pioneered the development of the urban crescent. It subsequently spread throughout British towns, and indeed was exported overseas.[70] This highlights Bath's creativity in the process of cultural transfer, and the fact that towns are rarely end-points in the transnational exchange of cultural forms, but rather engines of change and movement themselves, as ideas are imported, adapted and remodelled, before being re-exported. The crescent was a building form widely adopted in Britain's developing network of spas and seaside resorts, where the emphasis on capturing views of nature was fundamental to their appeal. But it was not just physical forms that the watering places took from Bath, but a whole style of living. The Somerset spa knitted together a range of health and recreational facilities (drinking and bathing services, assembly rooms, walks and pleasure gardens, theatres, circulating libraries, etc.) within a tightly organised social programme (the daily, weekly and seasonal round), that provided a blueprint for the development of resorts well into the nineteenth century. At the heart of this was the notion of a new form of social behaviour, promoted by the Master of Ceremonies at Bath, Richard 'Beau' Nash, and disseminated originally to London (reversing the general cultural flow), and from there to the rest of the country. As Nash's eighteenth-century biographer Oliver Goldsmith claimed:

> [Nash] was the first who diffused a desire of society and an easiness of address among a whole people, who were formerly censured by foreigners for a reservedness of behaviour and an awkward timidity in their first approaches. He first taught a familiar intercourse among strangers at Bath and Tunbridge, which still subsists among them. That ease and open access first acquired there, our gentry brought back to the metropolis, and thus the whole kingdom by degrees became more refined by lessons originally derived from him.[71]

110   Processes of selection and adaptation

Goldsmith does not define the 'whole kingdom', although it is likely that he would have included the entirety of the British Isles. However, in the eighteenth century Britain was still very much a nation in the making (Scotland had only joined the Union in 1707, and Ireland was not to do so until 1801), so that it is problematic whether cultural inputs from the various 'nations' of Britain were inter- or intra-national. Bath received many British visitors from outside England, and one of its early Master of Ceremonies was Welsh by birth (Nash), another was Irish (Derrick) and a further one (Collett) was French. Some of its shops championed Scottish and Irish products and in the 1790s Celtic-type dances – Scottish reels and strathspeys, and Irish jigs – were introduced into the spa's balls.[72] The Irish were a particularly numerous and influential element in Bath. In 1799, Katherine Plymley recorded in her diary that 'Bath was uncommonly full, a great many Irish were there', something also noted by the German Frederick Kielmansegge during his visit in 1761:

> the quantity of Irishmen here, of whom the greater part are Roman Catholics … have been educated out of their own country, in France and the Netherlands, without doubt contributes very much to make this place especially pleasant to foreigners. They are easy of access, and take pleasure in showing civility to strangers; in this they are aided by their French, which they speak more frequently and better than most Englishmen. For these reasons, as well as on account of the prevalence of the social customs of Dublin, which are said to have many advantages, the place was decidedly agreeable.[73]

The role of the Irish in easing the entrance of French-speaking Europeans into Bath society would have enhanced the spa's international connections. But the Irish could also introduce frictions to the smooth operation of the Bath social machine. The bitterly fought contest, which led to a riot in the Assembly Rooms, over who should be elected to the position of Master of Ceremonies after the death of Derrick in 1769 was at least in part fuelled by tensions between Irish ('brave sons of Hibernia') and English members of the company.[74] The assertion of national identity was one of the factors that could obstruct the transnational movement of culture. With Britain at war with France at various points during the eighteenth century, and with the forces of xenophobia simmering away awaiting only an opportunity to surface, this was potentially a serious problem. The response to the French Revolution demonstrated how complicated the situation was. In December, the *Bath Chronicle* carried an item that suggested both the continuing influence of France in shaping fashion, but also its capacity to change radically the nature of what had once stood as the epitome of taste:

> FASHION. The disgusting loads of artificial hair which have so long disfigured our fair countrywomen, begin to disappear. The natural ringlet again flows on the neck; and no woman of fashion is now ashamed of her own hair. This sudden revolution, which originated with French liberty, has deprived many ingenious artists of employment, particularly the *hair weavers*, and the worshipful company of *wig makers* ... The *poissarde* [fish seller] cap is at present the *ton* in the fashionable circles. The *outline* of it was taken from the *Amazons*, who headed the deputation at Versailles [the market women's march on Versailles of October 1789]. ... The French *national cockade* is now universally worn by the Ladies with their morning dresses.[75]

The Revolution was still in its early stages, and there was a good deal of sympathy with its objectives. However, over the longer term, attitudes were to change with the execution of the king and the eventual outbreak of war between Britain and France. Although there were elements among artisan Bath who continued to side with the revolutionaries, the business community, and of course the visitors, turned away from revolutionary France, with often extravagant displays of loyalism. Rauzzini composed and performed patriotic odes and marches, the city was illuminated with loyalist transparencies, entertainments were mounted at the theatre to celebrate military success and the latest fashionable head attire became not a *poissarde* but a 'Nelson Flag'.[76] It is difficult to know how much of this was Francophobia, and how much simple patriotism. As we have seen, the French émigrés appear to have been generally welcomed, and it is unlikely that the broad eighteenth-century appeal of French fashions was seriously dented. In May 1788, the Villa Gardens hosted an entertainment that encapsulated the entangled relationship between nationalism on the one hand and transnational cultural transfer on the other. The centrepiece was to be a representation of 'the glorious Engagement between Admiral Rodney and Count de Grasse, with capture of the Ville de Paris', a celebration of the crowning naval victory of Rodney's career at the Battle of the Saintes in 1782. One would imagine that patriotic sentiment was to the fore. But the same event was also to include a fireworks display by the 'celebrated Italian Artist, Signor JOHN INVETTO, from Milan', and the whole occasion was 'to conclude with three Air Balloons' – a new aeronautical craze that had come straight from France.[77]

Bath exemplifies how, given a conducive location, currents of culture and leisure could flow freely across national boundaries. There is little doubt that European, and particularly French and Italian fashions covering a broad range

Processes of selection and adaptation

of practices and products fascinated the well-off visitors to Bath. This was primarily because these fashions came invested with the social cachet attached to the traditional centres of European high culture from which they derived, and status was among the principal social goods that Bath's clientele required from their visit. However, the model of an unmediated traffic in ideas and practices, from culturally superior to inferior nation, does not represent the more complicated and messy reality that operated in practice. Much of the overseas cultural product came via London, Bath was not a passive recipient but often remodelled what it imported to meet its own local purposes, and in many cases re-exported what was then created. What constituted the nation in Britain and therefore what constituted a transnational process was problematised by the presence of four nations, and the fact that Britain was still a polity in the making. In the eighteenth century xenophobia and the assertion of national identities had the potential to inhibit the flow of cultural ideas. However, at this time it was probably the universalist tendencies of the Enlightenment, and the overriding passion for fashion and the status that accrued, that overrode nascent nationalism and patriotic prejudice.

Notes

1 B.R. Mitchell and P. Deane, *Abstract of British Historical Statistics* (Cambridge: Cambridge University Press, 1962), pp. 24–27.

2 For the history of early modern and eighteenth-century Bath see J. Wroughton, *Stuart Bath: Life in the Forgotten City, 1603–1714* (Bath: Lansdown Press, 2004); S. McIntyre, 'Bath: the rise of a resort town, 1660–1800', in P. Clark (ed.), *Country Towns in Pre-Industrial England* (Leicester: Leicester University Press, 1981), pp. 198–249; R.S. Neale, *Bath: A Social History, 1680–1850, or a Valley of Pleasure, Yet a Sink of Iniquity* (London: Routledge and Kegan Paul, 1981); G. Davis and P. Bonsall, *Bath: A New History* (Keele: Keele University Press, 1996); T. Fawcett and S. Bird, *Bath: History and Guide* (Stroud: Sutton, 1994); P. Borsay, *The Image of Georgian Bath, 1700–2000: Towns, Heritage and History* (Oxford: Oxford University Press, 2000); J. Eglin, *The Imaginary Autocrat: Beau Nash and the Invention of Bath* (London: Profile Books, 2005); P. Hembry, *The English Spa 1560–1815: A Social History* (London: Athlone, 1990). Our understanding of Bath's eighteenth-century history has been greatly enhanced by the work of the History of Bath Research Group and its members, much of which has been published in the issues of *Bath History*, appearing from 1986. I am indebted to them and in particular to Trevor Fawcett, whose research I have drawn on a good deal in this essay.

3 T. Fawcett, *Bath Entertain'd: Amusements, Recreations and Gambling at the 18th Century Spa* (Bath: Ruton, 1998), pp. 80–82; M. Hopkins-Clarke, 'A change of style at the Theatre Royal, 1805–1820', *Bath History*, 4 (1992), 127.

Georgian Bath: a transnational culture **113**

4 K. James, 'Venanzio Rauzzini and the search for musical perfection', *Bath History*, 3 (1990), 111; W. Dean, *The New Grove Handel* (London and Basingstoke: Macmillan, 1982), pp. 61, 68; W. Lowdnes, *They Came to Bath* (Bristol: Redcliffe Press, 1987), p. 45.

5 A.J. Turner, *Science and Music in Eighteenth Century Bath* (Bath: University of Bath, 1977), pp. 21–49.

6 James, 'Rauzzini', p. 94.

7 T. Fawcett, *Voices of Eighteenth-Century Bath: an Anthology* (Bath: Ruton, 1995), pp. 91, 96–97; James, 'Rauzzini', p. 103; S.L. Sloman, 'Artists' picture rooms in eighteenth-century Bath', *Bath History*, 6 (1996), 135; *The Pleasures of Bath* (Bristol, 1721).

8 C. Anstey, *The New Bath Guide*, ed. G. Turner (Bristol: Broadcast Books, 1994), p. 80.

9 A. Barbeau, *Life and Letters at Bath in the Eighteenth Century* (London: William Heinemann, 1904), p. 120; E. Wilson, 'A Shropshire lady in Bath, 1794–1807', *Bath History*, 4 (1992), 107; *The Letters of Charles Burney*. Volume 1, *1751–1784*, ed. A. Ribeiro (Oxford: Clarendon Press, 1991), p. 207; *Oxford Dictionary of National Biography*, online, Thomas Linley elder and younger, Ann Selina Storace (accessed 11 March 2014).

10 *Bath Chronicle*, 4 November 1784, 10 January 1788; James, 'Rauzzini', p. 101.

11 P. Borsay, *The English Urban Renaissance: Culture and Society in the Provincial Town, 1660–1770* (Oxford: Clarendon Press, 1989), pp. 150–162; A. Dain, *Assemblies and Politeness 1660–1840* (unpublished PhD thesis, University of East Anglia, 2001); Audrée-Isabelle Tardif, *A Cultural History of Social Dance among the Upper Ranks in Eighteenth-Century England* (unpublished PhD thesis, University of Cambridge, 2004).

12 Fawcett, *Bath Entertained*, pp. 32–34; N. Scarfe (ed.), *Innocent Espionage: The La Rochefoucauld Brothers Tour of England in 1785* (Woodbridge: Boydell, 1995), pp. 154, 156.

13 T. Fawcett, 'Dance and teachers of dance in eighteenth-century Bath', *Bath History*, 2 (1988), 31–32; R. Cruttwell, *The New Bath Guide: or, Useful Pocket Companion* (Bath, 1784), pp. 22–23; *Bath Chronicle*, 11 June 1789.

14 Fawcett, 'Dance and teachers of dance', pp. 32–37; S. Skedd, 'Women teachers and the expansion of girls' schooling in England, c. 1760–1820', in H. Barker and E. Chalus (eds.), *Gender in Eighteenth-Century England: Roles, Representations and Responsibilities* (London: Longman, 1997), p. 122.

15 *Bath Chronicle*, 11 January 1787.

16 W. Evans, 'An academy for young gentlemen: John Naish and his school in Bath', *Bath History*, 10 (2005), 139–140; T. Fawcett, 'Private schooling in eighteenth-century Bath', *Bath History*, 12 (2011), 66–67, 69, 71–74.

17 *Bath Chronicle*, 22 July 1784.

18 *Bath Chronicle*, 1 January 1784.

19 *The Improved Bath Guide; or, Picture of Bath and Its Environs* (Bath, 1812), p. 129.

20 *Bath Chronicle*, 15 April and 30 December 1784.

Processes of selection and adaptation

21 *Bath Chronicle*, 4 November 1784, 10 January 1788, 1 January 1789.

22 *Bath Chronicle*, 5 November 1789; T. Fawcett, *Georgian Imprints: Printing and Publishing at Bath, 1729–1815* (Bath: Ruton, 2008), pp. 54–55.

23 N. McKendrick, J. Brewer and J.H. Plumb, *The Birth of a Consumer Society: The Commercialization of Eighteenth-Century England* (London: Hutchinson, 1983); M. Berg, *Luxury and Pleasure in Eighteenth-Century Britain* (Oxford: Oxford University Press, 2005).

24 T. Fawcett, *Bath Commercialis'd: Shops, Trade and Market at the 18th-Century Spa* (Bath: Ruton, 2002), pp. 127–130; Fawcett, *Voices*, p. 71.

25 J.E. Wills, 'European consumption and Asian production in the seventeenth and eighteenth centuries', in J. Brewer and R. Porter (eds.), *Consumption and the World of Goods* (London: Routledge, 1993), pp. 142–146; R. Kennedy, *Between Bath and China: Trade and Culture in the West Country 1680–1840* (Bath: Museum of East Asian Art, n.d.); R. Kennedy, 'Taking tea', in M. Snodin and J. Styles (eds.), *Design and the Decorative Arts: Georgian Britain 1714–1837* (London: V&A Publications, 2004), pp. 104–105.

26 J. Penrose, *Letters from Bath 1766–1767 by the Rev. John Penrose*, ed. B. Mitchell and H. Penrose (Gloucester: Sutton, 1983), pp. 38, 75, 96.

27 Kennedy, *Between Bath and China*, pp. 14–16; Fawcett, *Bath Commercialis'd*, pp. 83–85.

28 *Bath Chronicle*, 9 January 1792.

29 *Bath Chronicle*, 27 September 1787.

30 Fawcett, *Bath Commercialis'd*, pp. 45, 104, 117.

31 *Bath Advertiser*, 18 October 1755; *Bath Chronicle*, 29 November 1787, 3 April and 24 April 1788.

32 *Bath Chronicle*, 4 November 1784; S.P. Marks, 'The journals of Mrs Philip Lybbe Powys (1738–1817): a half century of visits to Bath', *Bath History*, 9 (2002), 35; *The Improved Bath Guide*, p. 129; Neil Jeffares, *Dictionary of Pastellists before 1900*, Checheré de Beaurepaire, www.pastellists.com/Articles/Chacere.pdf (accessed 29 September 2013). See also S. Sloman, 'Pickpocketing the rich', in *Pickpocketing the Rich: Portrait Painting in Bath 1720–1800*, exhibition catalogue (Bath: Holburne Museum of Art, 2002), p. 14.

33 Fawcett, *Voices*, p. 119.

34 E. Newby, 'The Hoares of Bath', *Bath History*, 1 (1986), 90–106, 110–111.

35 Mary Granville, *Autobiography and Correspondence of Mary Granville, Mrs Delany, Volume 3*, ed. A. Hall (Cambridge: Cambridge University Press, 2011), p. 605.

36 J. Wood, *An Essay Towards a Description of the City of Bath: In Two Parts*, Part One (Bath, 1742), p. 92.

37 For Wood's debt to Palladio see T. Mowl and B. Earnshaw, *John Wood: Architect of Obsession* (Bath: Millstream Books, 1988), pp. 81, 103, 118, 157–158, 162, 178.

38 J. Wood, *A Description of Bath*, 2nd edn (London, 1765), p. 232.

39 M. Forsyth, *Bath* (New Haven and London: Yale University Press, 2003), pp. 142–145, 209–210.

40 Wilson, 'Shropshire lady in Bath', p. 96.

41 W. Mavor, *The British Tourists: or Traveller's Pocket Companion*, Vol. 6 (London, 1800), p. 273.

42 J. Black, *The British and the Grand Tour* (London: Croom Helm, 1985); R. Sweet, *Cities and the Grand Tour: The British in Italy, c. 1690–1820* (Cambridge: Cambridge University Press, 2012).

43 Warwickshire County Record Office, L6 (Lucy MSS), 1452, George Lucy to Mrs Hayes, 29 December 1758; 1455, George Lucy to Mrs Hayes, 2 March 1760.

44 B. White, 'But who was the Queen of Bath?', *Bath History*, 12 (2011), 50–52; E. Chalus, 'Anna Miller, Catherine Mccaulay and Agnes Witts: Bath hostesses, diarists and travellers', paper delivered to Joseph Wright of Derby: Bath and Beyond study day, the Holburne Museum, Bath, 24 February 2014.

45 A. Barbeau, *Life and Letters at Bath in the Eighteenth Century* (Bath: William Heinemann, 1905), p. 308.

46 McIntrye, 'Bath: the rise of a resort town', pp. 208–210; B.J. Buchanan, 'The great Bath road, 1700–1830', *Bath History*, 4 (1992), 71–94.

47 *Bath: A Poem* (London, 1748), pp. 5–6.

48 Frederick Kielmansegge, *Diary of a Journey to England in the Years 1761–1762*, trans. P. Kielmansegge (London: Longman, 1902), pp. 115–135; Scarfe, *Innocent Espionage*, pp. 151–158.

49 Penrose, *Letters from Bath*, pp. 98, 174.

50 Fawcett, *Voices*, p. 55.

51 R. Cruttwell, *The New Bath Guide: or, Useful Pocket Companion* (Bath, 1770), p. 32 and (1784), p. 23. I owe these references to Rose McCormack.

52 T. Fawcett, 'French émigrés at Bath, 1789–1815', *Somerset Archaeology and History*, 141 (1998), 161–169; P. Corfield, 'Georgian Bath: the magical meeting place', *History Today*, 40 (1990), 32.

53 Sheffield Archives, WWM/F/112/81, Lady C. Watson-Wentworth to Fitzwilliam, 11 December 1789; *Betsy Sheridan's Journal: Letters from Sheridan's Sister, 1784–1786 and 1788–1790*, ed. W. Le Fanu (Oxford: Oxford University Press, 1986), p. 190. I owe these references to Rose McCormack.

54 Fawcett, *Voices*, p. 138.

55 Fawcett, *Voices*, p. 180.

56 Fawcett, 'Private schooling', p. 73.

57 Marks, 'The journals of Mrs Philip Lybbe Powys', p. 40.

58 Durham University Special Collections, Add. MS. 1433, transcript of Anna Francesca Craddock, 'Journal of a tour in England, 1786–1791', 17 May 1787. I would like to thank Rose McCormack for drawing this reference to my attention. It has not been possible to trace the history of the transcript.

59 P. Thicknesse, *The New Prose Bath Guide* (1778), pp. 56–57; T. Fawcett, *Georgian Imprints: Printing and Publishing at Bath, 1729–1815* (Bath: Ruton, 2008), p. 112.

60 P. Kaufmann, 'The community library: a chapter in English social history', *Transactions of the American Philosophical Society*, 57:7 (1967), 13, 17.

61 *Bath Chronicle*, 4 November 1784, 1 January 1789.

62 *The Bristol and Bath Magazine; or, Weekly Miscellany*, vol. 2 (Bristol: T.K. Blagden, 1782), pp. 6–7.

63 Fawcett, *Bath Commercialis'd*, p. 102; *Bath Chronicle*, 8 April 1784.

64 *Bath Chronicle*, 16 December 1784, 11 January 1787, 15 November 1787, 4 December 1788.

65 Hopkins-Clarke, 'A change of style', pp. 125–127.

66 J. Summerson, 'John Wood and the English town planning tradition', in J. Summerson, *Heavenly Mansions* (London: Cresset Press, 1949), pp. 87–97; H.C. Colvin, *A Biographical Dictionary of British Architects 1680–1840*, 3rd edn (New Haven and London: Yale University Press, 1995), pp. 1072–1073; Mowl and Earnshaw, *John Wood*, pp. 13–18, 65–84.

67 J. Summerson, *Inigo Jones* (Harmondsworth: Penguin Books, 1966).

68 Fawcett, *Bath Commercialis'd*, pp. 79–80; McIntrye, 'Bath: the rise of a resort town', p. 236; Neale, *Bath: A Social History*, pp. 64–68, 184.

69 M. Girouard, *The English Town* (New Haven and London: Yale University Press, 1990), pp. 162–170; P. Borsay, 'Town or country? British spas and the urban-rural interface', *Journal of Tourism History*, 4:2 (2012), 169.

70 S. Blackmore and P. Bishop, *Circle, Square and Crescent: An Exhibition for European Architectural Year* (Bath: Holburne of Menstrie Museum, 1975), p. 22. For overseas see Franklin Place, Boston, USA, built 1793–1794, designed by Charles Bullfinch probably drawing on the example of Bath, and demolished 1858; P.S. Goodman, *The Garden Squares of Boston* (Lebanon, NH: University Press of New England, 2003), pp. 27, 31.

71 O. Goldsmith, 'The life of Richard Nash', in A. Friedman (ed.), *Collected Works of Oliver Goldsmith*, Vol. 3 (Oxford: Clarendon Press, 1966), p. 298.

72 Fawcett, *Bath Commercialis'd*, p. 67; Fawcett, *Bath Entertain'd*, p. 34; Fawcett, 'Dance and teachers of dance', p. 32.

73 Wilson, 'Shropshire lady in Bath', p. 109; Kielmansegge, *Diary of a Journey to England*, pp. 126–127.

74 Borsay, *The Image of Georgian Bath*, pp. 43–44; *The Conciliade: Being a Supplement to the Bath Contest* (Bath, 1769), pp. 20–22.

75 *Bath Chronicle*, 24 December 1789.

76 James, 'Rauzzini', pp. 108, 110; H. Arnold, 'Genteel widows of Bath; I – Mrs Margaret Graves and her letters from Bath, 1793–1807', *Bath History*, 7 (1998), 85; Fawcett, *Voices*, pp. 180–181.

77 *Bath Chronicle*, 1 May 1788.

6

Music and opera in Brussels, 1700–1850: a tale of two cities

KOEN BUYENS

Sites of leisure hold the promise of enjoyment and satisfaction, appealing to the individual as consumer. At the same time they represent places where the citizen is able to perceive and assert himself as a self-confident and active member of a political community. Therefore the history of leisure is closely related to the rise of the public sphere and, more specifically, to changes in the cultural forms and flows that shaped the content of that sphere.

This relationship is evident in the field of music, a type of leisure that was both highly sociable in character and that travelled easily across national boundaries. Apart from the emergence of the public concert, it is opera that developed into a pivotal institution of nineteenth-century elite culture. As a powerful medium for the conveyance of ideological and political messages, opera played its part in the long process whereby the dynastic state gave way to the nation-state. The most revealing case for the nation-building capacities of music and opera is the Italian Risorgimento.[1] However, the birth of Belgium as an independent state in 1830 also demonstrates how opera can be a catalyst in the dynamics of revolution. The riots provoked by the performance of Auber's *La Muette de Portici* in the Théâtre de la Monnaie in Brussels are at the heart of Belgian national mythology.[2]

Today, the Belgian nation-state is going through a profound crisis, subject to centrifugal forces that seem hard to keep in check.[3] As the importance of language in defining national identities steadily increased in the course of the nineteenth century,[4] the small bilingual country at the crossroad of the Romanic and Germanic cultural orbits found itself in a problematic position. Whereas multiple languages easily coexisted in the privilege-based society of the *ancien régime*, this changed in the context of the nation-state, with its need for one national language shared by the entire community of its citizens and, following this logic, constituting a *sine qua non* for a genuine public sphere.

Processes of selection and adaptation

In Belgium the linguistic competition between Dutch and French was not on equal terms. Paris was so close geographically that the history of Brussels only makes sense when told as a 'tale of two cities'. In the timespan covered in this chapter, the nature of Brussels' relationship with Paris was deeply affected by the repeated succession of political regimes. Evidently these changes involved all Belgian towns, but for Brussels it often meant a dramatic shift in status and prestige. This gives the history of the Belgian capital a distinctive quality, with flows of cultural forms and patterns of appropriation remarkably shifting in geographical direction and intensity over time, but with Paris as a constant point of reference.

The court as the measure of all music

Brussels' fame in early modern Europe largely rested on its court. The lavishness and exuberance found at the Brussels court of Philip the Good, Duke of Burgundy (1419–1467), had set a new standard for rulers all over Europe. Of equal splendour was the court of Emperor Charles V, but matters changed when his son, Philip II, left the Netherlands in 1559 to head for Spain and settle there for the rest of his life. From then on the Brussels court was the domain of a governor representing the Spanish king. The same less lavish pattern endured once the southern Netherlands had passed into the hands of the Austrian branch of the Habsburg Dynasty under the Treaty of Utrecht (1713).

If the succession of a hereditary ruler inherently engenders discontinuities, this applies even more so to the succession of an appointed governor. Given the size of their landed possessions, the Habsburg rulers were able to recruit from a vast geographical area. As a consequence, the successive governors could differ substantially from each other in terms of background, education and taste.

Generally the splendour of court life depended on four, mostly interrelated, elements: character, ambition, ancestry and financial resources. It was the delegation to Brussels of a prince of the blood that justified high expectations for the arts. The early history of opera in the southern Netherlands illustrates this very well. Brussels owed its first opera performance, Zamponi's *Ulisse nell'isola di Circe*, staged in the magnificent Aula Magna of the Palace of Coudenberg on 24 February 1650, to Archduke Leopold Wilhelm, the youngest son of Emperor Ferdinand II. Leaving Vienna for Brussels in 1647, the new governor found himself in the company of a first-rank ensemble of Italian musicians. When his sovereign, Philip IV of Spain, married in 1649, the staging of *Ulisse*

Music and opera in Brussels, 1700–1850   **119**

allowed Leopold Wilhelm to give Brussels a standing in the world of Italian baroque culture.[5]

The brilliance of Leopold Wilhelm's bold initiative and his focus on Italian culture proved to be short-lived. It was not until the appointment of Maximilian II Emanuel, elector of Bavaria, that opera would establish itself more solidly in Brussels. Maximilian's appointment as governor of the Spanish Netherlands was the result of elaborate diplomatic negotiations and fitted into his strategy to be elected Holy Roman Emperor one day. Court life, of course, had to reflect and support his imperial ambition. During these years, while Louis XIV reached the apogee of his power and glory, Maximilian Emanuel fell under the spell of Versailles. French culture and language were well on the way to acquiring supremacy all over Europe. In fact, the first *tragédie lyrique* by Jean-Baptiste Lully, the Sun King's court composer, had already been performed in Brussels in 1681. When Maximilian Emanuel ordered the building of a public theatre in 1695, the conditions were right for the new genre to thrive. In the Grand Théâtre de la Monnaie, opened in 1700, Lully's *tragédies lyriques* would remain the standard repertoire for more than 20 years.[6]

This enthusiastic adoption of the *tragédie lyrique* may seem surprising from a political point of view. From 1635 onwards, the Spanish Netherlands had been in an almost permanent state of war with France. It was the disastrous bombardment of Brussels by the French marshal de Villeroy in 1695, that had levelled the ground for the construction of Maximilian Emanuel's public theatre in the centre of the city. It would seem that the cosmopolitan character of court culture remained impervious to the workings of the dynastic state, political antagonism and even military ravages. Inspired by classical sources, French court culture, just like the Italian from which it originated, had a claim to universal validity and applicability. For the *tragédies lyriques* performed in Brussels, this meant that only the prologues consisting of allegorical allusions to the deeds and virtues of the French sovereign had to be suppressed, adapted or replaced.[7]

The War of the Spanish Succession (1701–1714) turned out to be a shattering experience for the southern Netherlands, and the Austrian Habsburgs would need years to stabilise their newly acquired possessions after the Treaty of Utrecht (1713). With the appointment of Maria Elisabeth (1725–1741), sister of Emperor Charles VI, as the new governor, the government in Vienna wanted to make a fresh start with the southern Netherlands. Culturally this implied a remodelling of the Brussels court to the Viennese imperial standard. For the staging of opera this resulted in the French *tragédie lyrique* giving way again to Italian opera, in particular the genre of *opera seria*.[8] However, splendour would not be the right word to describe the period. Maria Elisabeth was apparently too inclined to piety and austerity, which occasioned foreign travellers to compare her court to a convent.[9]

The restoration of an Italian-based court culture under Maria Elisabeth was little more than an Indian summer. During the war of the Austrian Succession (1740–1748), the final breakthrough of French fashion in Brussels was accomplished. Furthermore, the five-year occupation of Brussels by the French troops of Marshal Maurice of Saxony was decisive. To make his stay in Brussels more pleasurable, Maurice appointed the well-known Parisian playwright Charles Simon Favart (1710–1792), who settled with his troupe in the Grand Théâtre. There he introduced the new genre of *opéra comique*. It soon conquered the hearts of the audience to such extent that it would dominate the Brussels opera scene until the Revolutionary Era.[10]

Once again, the departure of the French troops did not bring about a wave of anti-French feelings. On the contrary, the French style became more compelling than it had ever been. It would seem that its most dedicated supporter was the new governor himself. Charles Alexander of Lorraine (1741–1780)

Figure 6.1 *View of the Place de la Monnaie in Brussels*. Collection Archive de la Ville de Bruxelles, D 881.

had grown up in Lunéville, seat of the dukes of Lorraine, where Germain Boffrand, a pupil of Mansart, had built an enormous château in the early eighteenth century. In this *Versailles Lorrain* Charles Alexander had all the opportunity he needed to absorb French court culture, albeit with a distinct provincial flavour.[11]

As governor, unlike his predecessor, Charles Alexander saw himself reduced to a merely representative role. Boredom was never far away and patronising the arts was one of his strategies to cope with it. Prince Charles-Joseph de Ligne (1735–1814), the most flamboyant of his courtiers, remembered the place in his memoirs as 'this lovely court, merry, safe, pleasant, naughty, a place of drinking, eating and hunting'.[12] In music the pompous idiom of the Maria Elisabeth period made way to the *style galant*. The governor wanted to hear only music of the latest fashion.[13]

Music, cosmopolitanism and the public sphere

For Brussels, the time of Charles Alexander of Lorraine was one of qualitative change. First of all the physiognomy of the city underwent important transformations.[14] Apart from a new palace for the governor – the old ducal palace had been destroyed in a fire in 1731 – Brussels was embellished with two large squares and a park, all in the French style. They combined to give the city a more open, inviting and cosmopolitan character. These changes emanated from the court, but their influence spread more broadly to include layers of the middle classes in the widening circle of polite society. The lively character of the city was affirmed by foreign visitors. They were struck by the many shops in the centre and, due to the introduction of extensive lighting, the city did not lose its charms after sunset.[15]

These elements can all be interpreted as signs of a vivid and cosmopolitan-oriented urbanity. But did music also follow this pattern? Was music in Brussels becoming part of a larger, emerging public sphere? The answer is not straightforward. In many respects, the court continued to be pivotal to musical activity in the city. The opera house, the city's main musical institution, was privately owned and managed, but functionally it was well integrated into the fabric of the court through a system of patenting and subsidising. The troupe presented itself to its audience as 'Comedians in ordinary to His Royal Highness'. Although *opéra comique* no longer conveyed the message of absolutism as *tragédie lyrique* and *opera seria* had done, the presence of the governor in the opera house was highly symbolic. In the winter season,

Charles Alexander spent several evenings a week there. As the opera house could accommodate 1,200–1,300 individuals, opera was not confined to the elite. At the same time, however, the hierarchical arrangement of the building, with a parterre and different layers of boxes, was conceived to reflect and affirm the established social order.[16]

Similar observations can be made regarding public concerts. Of the three concert societies that left traces of their activities, the Concert Bourgeois was the most dynamic.[17] The society, founded in 1754 and modelled after the Concert Spirituel in Paris, was probably an initiative of Pierre Van Maldere, Charles Alexander's most distinguished court musician. In 1758, Van Maldere was appointed *valet de chambre*, which meant that from then on he was counted among the intimates of the governor. Van Maldere's involvement in the Concert Bourgeois – in 1756 he appears in the sources as director – together with Charles Alexander's frequent and ceremonial attendance of the concerts, indicate how close the ties were between the society and the court.

At the same time, the name of the society leaves no doubt about the participation of 'bourgeois' elements in the concerts. Yet the input of the middle classes was still insufficient for public concerts to be viable as a commercial undertaking. This is clear as soon as factors of size and space enter the picture. The concerts of the Concert Bourgeois took place in a building at Place de Bavière that had formerly served as a meat hall. It had a surface area of just ten by 20 metres, which meant that only a small fraction of the population – about 60,000 inhabitants in the middle of the eighteenth century – could have attended the concerts. Equally revealing is the size and composition of the musical profession in the city. Discounting the singers in the opera house – a highly mobile group – the number of musicians and choristers may be estimated at some 50 individuals. About 30 were members of the governor's court chapel, frequently combining this position with performing at the opera.[18]

These numbers all testify to the court-centred character of the musical landscape at the time. A consumer-driven market for music had not yet developed. Scores and musical instruments remained expensive, affordable only by the well-to-do. This does not mean, however, that there were no early signs of commercialisation. An interesting case is the Brussels Vauxhall. Pleasure gardens, a British cultural import, found their way to the Continent in the second half of the eighteenth century. As Paris had opened a 'Wauxhall' to the public in 1764, Brussels did not want to get left behind. In 1777, Alexandre-Florentin Bultos, director of the opera house at the time, installed a Vauxhall (with the English spelling) in the newly designed Warandepark. One of his main concerns was to

Figure 6.2 François Harrewijn, *Charles de Lorraine*. Bibliothèque royale de Belgique.

remedy the constant threat of the financial collapse of his core business. This was basically due to the tight conditions in the patent granted by the government, and the patent he also needed for the Vauxhall. His scope as a theatrical entrepreneur was therefore restricted.[19]

The politics of language

The French occupation (1745–1749) stimulated the gradual Frenchification of Brussels, as it started to embrace segments of the middle classes. Speaking

French became a necessity for social advancement. The opera house, as the place to be for the fashion-conscious, was probably the main transmitter of French culture and lifestyle. The Austrian government had no inclination at all to counteract the process. French had become the court language of the Austrian Habsburgs and in enthusiasm for *opéra comique* Vienna was second only to Paris. Chancellor of state Kaunitz actively promoted French opera to consolidate Austria's alliance with France.[20]

In the meantime, the large majority of the population in Brussels remained Dutch-speaking. As it suggests a national language, however, the term 'Dutch-speaking' is not accurate and the language should instead be understood as a mosaic of local dialects. These Dutch-Flemish dialects had their own theatrical traditions. From the late Middle Ages onwards, drama in the vernacular had been a business of the chambers of rhetoric, typical exponents of a guild-based urban culture. Brussels, by the end of the Austrian period, had eight *compagnies*, as the chambers were named at the time. Significantly, in two of them, communication was in French. In the Dutch-speaking *compagnies*, translations of French pieces, including *opéras comiques*, grew in importance.[21]

Occasionally the *compagnies* gave Dutch language performances in the opera house.[22] In 1772 Charles Burney, the famous British connoisseur and traveller, attended a Dutch version of two *opéras comiques* by the Belgian-French composer F.-J. Gossec. In his comments, Burney showed surprise at how easily Gossec's Italian-style music might be adapted to any language, 'however rough and barbarous'.[23] It seems improbable that Burney had a particular dislike for Dutch. He would have said the same about any language that fell outside the scope of the cosmopolitan community of the civilised. Language functioned as a clear marker of social status. In line with Burney's observations, the Privy Council in 1772 objected to the idea of regular performances in Dutch in the opera house, as the opera subscribers would see their expensive boxes damaged by those attending the 'amusements of the mob'.[24]

In the *compagnies* there was a growing awareness of the problematic status of Dutch theatre. As early as 1722, J.L. Krafft, a successful Brussels playwright, had denounced the impoliteness of Dutch-speaking players, whom he deemed pretentious and inclined to drunkenness.[25] In 1751, Francis de la Fontaine, an admirer of Voltaire, made a Dutch adaptation of Riccoboni's *Réflexions historiques et critiques sur les différens théâtres de l'Europe* (1738). With regard to the Dutch performances in the Brussels opera house, he complained about the lack of silence, due to an audience that lost itself in drinking and cracking nuts: 'One is constantly hearing an unpleasant noise, mixed with the whistling of youngsters. [...] In this way we show our bestiality [sic] to other nations.' With the Académie Française in mind, de la Fontaine saw the development of Dutch into a civilised language as a *sine qua non* for all cultural advancement in the southern Netherlands.[26]

In 1788, more than a decade after the scarce Dutch language performances in the Brussels opera had disappeared, a remarkable pamphlet came out. The *Verhandeling op d'onacht der moederlyke tael in de Nederlanden* (*Essay on the Disregard of the Native Language in the Netherlands*) was written by Jan Baptist Verlooy, an enlightened lawyer and advocate of the principle of national sovereignty.[27] Lampooning the Gallomania of his co-citizens, Verlooy paid particular attention to theatre and opera: 'Our language has been banished from the theatre', he observed with sadness. Unlike de la Fontaine, Verlooy's stance was markedly political. Shortly before the revolutionary turmoil would seal the fate of the Austrians in the southern Netherlands, he perceived linguistic unity as a prerequisite for political unity.

From a comparative perspective, it is significant that speakers of the Dutch language in its multiple dialects in the southern Netherlands shared in most of the prejudices against the German language, to which Dutch was linguistically intimately related. So one can see clear parallels between the efforts of de la Fontaine and those of Gottsched in Germany or his disciple von Sonnenfels in Austria. Their crusade against the *Hanswurst* in German drama went hand-in-hand with a desire to clean out the Augean stables of German dialects and create a dignified and standardised German language. In the final analysis, these reformers, still troubled by feelings of inferiority, were all driven by the same motive: elevating their native language to the French standard.[28]

In Verlooy's pamphlet, the tone had changed. Although a direct influence is hard to demonstrate, much in it is reminiscent of the thinking of Johann Gottfried Herder. In particular there is the same emphasis on language, in its singularity and individuality, as the beating heart of the nation. In any case, Germany is very present in Verlooy's argument. Stressing the affinity between Dutch and German, he draws a profile of the Netherlander that was made up of the same stereotypes that Herder and his sympathisers used in their understanding of the German *Volksgeist*. In Verlooy's pamphlet this results in a dichotomy, contrasting the freedom-loving, hard-working Netherlander to the slavish, idle and lascivious Frenchman.

Although it has been argued that Verlooy's was not a voice crying in the wilderness, there were few signs of a Dutch renaissance in the southern Netherlands by the end of the Austrian regime. Here, the contrast with Germany was sharp.

126   Processes of selection and adaptation

The Storm-and-Stress movement had, from the late 1760s, raised German literature and drama to unprecedented heights – Goethe's *Werther* appeared in 1774, Schiller's *Die Räuber* premièred in 1781 – and a broad national theatre movement had even forced a breakthrough for German drama at the institutional level. In Brussels, Dutch-language theatre barely succeeded in breaking through the protective cocoon of the time-honoured chambers of rhetoric.

Shifting cultural outlooks: the French and Dutch regimes

In 1792, the French revolutionary armies invaded the southern Netherlands. From the annexation in 1795 until Napoleon's defeat in 1814, the nine Belgian *départements* formed an integral part of France. For Brussels, two factors deeply affected its cultural prospects. The first is language. Whereas the official role of the French language under the Austrians had still been restricted to the court and central administration, Frenchification henceforth became the object of a systematic policy, affecting all branches of administration and education. A second element is the city's diminished political status. The historic court capital was turned into the capital of a *département*. Integrated in the centralistic state, Brussels saw its cultural dependence on Paris reinforced by political integration.

In music, a substantial regression occurred. With the dissolution of the court chapel and the church choirs, the backbone of musical practice in Brussels was broken. Concerts and opera continued, but the outlook of the music scene in the city had become provincial. In this respect the origin of the conservatoire is revealing.[29] When Jean-Baptiste Roucourt obtained permission in 1813 to open a singing school in Brussels, it was under the strict condition that his school should be merely preparatory to the Conservatoire Impérial in Paris. The financial resources available for Roucourt's school, which attracted around 30 students, were very modest. The whole initiative rested upon the idealism of the founder, himself a former pupil of the Conservatoire in Paris. The fame of the Conservatoire, established in 1795, was enormous, but outside Paris, musical education did not get off the ground. As a consequence, talented young people in the Belgian departments often found their way to Paris. As this example already makes clear, this migration would be decisive for the musical future of Belgium.

The Belgian departments were well on the way towards full assimilation with France when Napoleon was defeated. The Vienna Congress (1814–1815) led to a radical shift of direction, as the European powers decided to reunify the northern and southern Netherlands as a strong buffer against French expansionism. The crown of the new kingdom was offered to the Dutch Prince William of Orange-Nassau. Although this was a period of considerable economic expansion, the United Kingdom of the Netherlands did not last, and language proved to be one of the divisive elements. King William's policy of promoting Dutch as the national language was unacceptable to the Frenchified elites in the Belgian provinces.

The position of Brussels under William I was ambivalent. On the one hand, Brussels became a capital and royal residence, albeit alternating annually with The Hague. On the other hand, William's language policy provoked animosity in the Francophile city. Attempts to integrate performances in Dutch at the Théâtre de la Monnaie or to establish a permanent Dutch theatre in the city were stillborn.[30]

William's efforts in favour of a unifying national language were not inspired by Gallophobia. On the contrary, as a monarch and aristocrat he had a clear sense of a linguistic hierarchy, with French at the very top. French was the language of the House of Orange-Nassau, and for reasons of international prestige, William, in spite of his pragmatism and general indifference towards the arts, felt no hesitation in subsidising and stimulating French opera. Actually, his annual subsidies of the Théâtre de la Monnaie added up to 20 times the amount that King Leopold I would spend on opera in the first decade of Belgium's independence![31] Besides, William's patronage of French culture was not restricted to the southern provinces of his kingdom. The northern provinces also shared in the Europe-wide tide of Francophilia. The Hague especially, as royal residence with a corresponding density of aristocrats, diplomats and officers, had since the late seventeenth century developed into a self-aware and persistent nucleus of French culture. The history of French opera as an institution in The Hague, until 1871 subsidised by the king, would only come to an end after World War I.[32]

Independently from opera, public concerts had considerably grown in importance in Brussels by this time. Since the purely instrumental recital had been introduced by Franz Liszt in the late 1830s – on which occasion the virtuoso would have remarked: 'Le concert, c'est moi!'[33] – the human voice remained quintessential in every concert programme. In this way public concerts mirrored to a large extent what was going on in the opera house. Arias were alternated with instrumental pieces, which most of the time were popular overtures, marches and dancing tunes. A single part of a symphony or concerto often appeared on the programme as well, but taken

128 Processes of selection and adaptation

as a whole these concert programmes placed little demands on the audience. Distraction and simple enjoyment were the key aims. Given the substantial involvement of touring singers and virtuosos, it is difficult to draw a clear picture of the repertoire.[34] If general trends may be discerned, Brussels again followed in the wake of the French capital. Under Napoleon's rule, the Brussels audience had already acquainted itself with the symphonies of Haydn, but it would take until the 1820s for them to enjoy fragments of Beethoven's orchestral music.[35]

By the end of the Dutch regime, a central position on the Brussels music scene was held by Charles-Louis Hanssens (1777–1852).[36] Born and trained as a musician in Ghent, Hanssens completed his studies in Paris. Soon after Napoleon's coup, he returned to Ghent. At the head of a French company, he toured in the Batavian Republic, conducting performances in Amsterdam, Utrecht and Rotterdam. In 1825 Hanssens became conductor of the Théâtre de la Monnaie in Brussels. It is significant that William called upon Hanssens, whose orientation towards France was straightforward, to become his musical director in 1827.

The status of Hanssens as the king's favourite in his southern capital, appeared again when he was appointed in the same year inspector of the royal school of music in Brussels. In the long term, William's decision to establish four royal schools of music, equally distributed between the northern (Amsterdam and The Hague) and southern (Brussels and Liège) provinces, was his main achievement in the field of music.[37] In Brussels, the royal initiative amounted to the upgrading of Roucourt's singing school. Here too it proved impossible to impose Dutch as the principal language for teaching. Several of the teachers were French and, as the school committee affirmed, they did not have the slightest grasp of the kingdom's national language. In practice, the schools in Brussels and Liège came under little pressure to change their French orientation, as they enjoyed a large degree of autonomy. In the northern provinces, on the other hand, the decentralist design of higher music education caused resentment. It was feared that a true national musical style would never come about this way.[38]

In search of a Belgian national and cultural identity

The Belgian revolution of 1830 was a complex event. Catholics and liberals joined forces against William I in a coalition known as the 'monstrous alliance'. The revolution was successful, but for William it would take until 1839

Music and opera in Brussels, 1700–1850   **129**

to accept Belgium's independence. So for a period of time the country's viability remained questionable. Yet there were sound reasons for confidence. Belgium was the first country in Continental Europe to industrialise; its railway appeared as early as 1835. As the propertied classes of landowners and industrialists soon managed to canalise the revolutionary forces, the main concern of the new regime was creating stability. Averse to adventures, Belgium strived to be taken seriously by the European powers. The inauguration of King Leopold I on 21 July 1831 was of great symbolic meaning in this respect.[39] Brussels, the hub of the revolution, finally became a national capital in the full sense of the word. With Belgium's economic boom, the capital soon developed into a major financial centre. The prominence of its financial elite, living in a close symbiosis with the political decision-makers, largely determined the city's atmosphere, permeated as it was by a utilitarian and calculating spirit.[40]

These were the circumstances in which the Belgians had to forge a national identity. In government circles, there was an awareness that the arts could contribute substantially to this end. However, the utilitarian mentality meant that there was opposition to spending too liberally on the arts. Parliament shied away from investing public money in anything deemed 'useless'.[41] These negative attitudes were reinforced by moral objections from Catholics. For these reasons, the opera house in Brussels could not look to the government for assistance and remained a municipal theatre.[42] Although the liberal bourgeoisie dominated in the capital, even in Brussels an educated middle class large enough to compensate for the utilitarian spirit of the politico-economic elite did not exist. This was due to the city's longstanding peripheral position, which had culminated in its far-reaching marginalisation in the French period. In addition, the situation of education in Belgium was deplorable. Economically advanced as it was, 40 to 50 per cent of the population were illiterate in the 1840s.[43]

In framing a national identity, the Belgians were faced with the challenge of developing a viable relationship that combined independence and dependence on their big and powerful southern neighbour. The Belgian revolution seemed like a warm embrace of France. The belief was widespread that without France, the conservative European powers would have intervened under the Metternich system. As strong symbols of liberty, the Marseillaise and French tricolour constituted integrating elements in the revolutionary idiom.[44] Yet the will of independence was strong in Belgium, and for the propertied classes France was too heavily tinged with the smell of revolution and upheaval. But culturally, the situation was different. The Belgian elites and, in particular, the liberal bourgeoisie in the cities subscribed to the universal claims of French civilisation. Consequently, only French could qualify to become Belgium's national language. On the national level, the French language should guarantee the country's unity, whereas on the international level, it was seen as the entrance ticket to the civilised world. Given the weakness of the cultural and intellectual strata in society, however, it seemed questionable that Belgium would be able to gain a voice in the Francophone world and not fall into a pattern of feeble imitation.

The establishment of the Brussels Conservatoire Royal in 1832 was a major step forward in the plan to place Belgium on the musical map of Europe. The government's choice of François-Joseph Fétis (1784–1871) as its first director left no room for doubt about the direction taken.[45] More than anyone else Fétis seemed to be in the best position to tune Brussels to Paris. Born in Mons, Fétis was one of those daring young musicians who had found their way to the Paris Conservatoire in the French period. He was appointed as professor of composition in 1821, and five years later he became the librarian of the Conservatoire. In the French capital, Fétis developed into a music critic and scholar of Europe-wide renown.

In 1833 Fétis returned to Brussels, well aware of the challenge ahead of him. Determined to proceed in a systematic way, he had in 1832 already drawn up an elaborate plan for the musical organisation of Belgium.[46] A centralist logic underlay the plan, in which Fétis himself figured as supervisor, not only of the Brussels Conservatoire, but of all musical activity in the country. As it turned out, his realm remained confined to the Conservatoire, and he painfully experienced how narrow the financial constraints were.

Although for Fétis Paris was the shining example, it would be a mistake to write him off as a poor imitator. His cosmopolitanism was sincere.[47] Fétis considered a thorough knowledge of the French, Italian and German musical traditions a prerequisite for every aspiring composer. A transnational approach to music was at the heart of his cultural agenda. Moreover he deepened the historical perspective, making a real effort to promote the re-evaluation of renaissance music. Given the prominence of the Netherlandish School (Josquin, Lassus, etc.) in such a project, in this way Fétis was also promoting the national cause.[48]

A main concern for Fétis was to educate his audience. With regard to public concerts, he regarded the prevailing potpourri-style of programming as unbearably superficial. Therefore, soon after his installation, he set up his own concert series at the conservatoire, with the Beethoven symphonies at the very core of the repertoire. Fétis, in his conservative state of mind, clearly wanted to

Figure 6.3 Caricature of François-Joseph Fétis.

counterpoise French frivolity with German seriousness. The recipe to do so, however, was again provided by Paris itself, where F.-A. Habeneck, with his excellent orchestra, had from the late 1820s made the conservatoire into a mecca for the Beethoven-lover.[49]

How compelling the Parisian example could be was apparent in 1836, when J.-A. Géraldy was appointed singing teacher at the conservatoire. Fétis agreed that Géraldy could continue to reside in Paris; his presence in Brussels was expected for only part of the year, initially for three months, and then from 1842 on a half-yearly basis. The way in which the arrangement was supported in *L'Indépendant*, one of Brussels' leading newspapers and a main source for its music history in the period, is revealing of the relationship that then existed between the two cities:

> We can say this without hurting our pride: Paris is the centre of everything relating to the intellectual life. In Paris are promulgated the decrees on taste, good or bad, that prevail in Europe. All the arts are subject to change, more or less frequently, but more than any other is music exposed to the capricious changes of fashion, both in composition and performance. [...] The repercussions of these revolutions are felt after a certain passage of time wherever Paris is exporting its musical products, but so as to keep oneself informed of the requirements created this way, it is necessary to have frequent contact with the capital [sic]. During the six months that he will spend each year in Paris, Mr Géraldy, one of the singers most looked for in the salons, competing in talent and success with the artists of the Théâtre-Italien and the Opéra, will drink from the source out of which are flowing the ideas applicable in the arts. Returning to his students, he will give them the profit of the fruit gained from his observations.[50]

The appointment of Géraldy attracted considerable attention, given the centrality of opera in the musical landscape. Although Brussels' promotion to capital had given the Théâtre de la Monnaie a new élan and prestige, it continued to function as an extraterritorial French theatre. Not only was the repertoire derived from the main theatres in Paris, in particular the Opéra, but the actual productions also relied on a supply of performers, settings and costumes from the French capital.[51] This was what the public expected, and at the same time it allowed the theatre administration, always pressed financially, to save money. Yet the strong dependence on Paris turned the production of 'national' operas into a problematic undertaking.[52] The singers, often French and internationally mobile, were not keen on learning parts that were of no use in their further career.

The staging posed another problem, as there was no Parisian model to rely on. It resulted in productions that involved a high degree of tinkering and manipulation. When the opera *Louis de Male* by Augustin de Peellaert, a member of the conservatoire school committee, was performed at the Monnaie in 1838, it elicited scornful comments in *L'Indépendant*. According to the columnist, all the actors had dressed on a whim. The prima donna was eye-catching, 'tarted up with a man's wig from the beginning of the fifth century'. A little bit of research would have been useful, he dryly concluded.[53] For the same reason, winners of the Belgian Prix de Rome had little chance to see one of their operas staged at the Monnaie. This is significant, since the *raison d'être* of the award, established by the government in 1840, was precisely to encourage young composers of Belgian nationality.[54]

Growing Flemish resentment

A reaction against the wave of Gallomania was bound to come from the Dutch-speaking Belgians. They represented more than half of the population, but the elites in Flanders had given up Dutch for French as well. The Flemish Movement, coming to the fore from the late 1830s onwards, therefore began among members of the lower middle classes who saw themselves socially and professionally discriminated against in the monolingual Belgian state. Since, for the time being, the right to vote remained out of the reach of the vast majority – by the middle of the century less than 2 per cent of the population went to the polls – the Flemish Movement started as a literary movement, striving for cultural emancipation and recognition of the Dutch language. With the publication of Henri Conscience's *De Leeuw van Vlaenderen* (*The Lion of Flanders*) in 1838, the movement gained momentum. In origin it was not anti-Belgian at all. On the contrary, Dutch, or more precisely, its Flemish variant, was considered essential in defining the Belgian national identity.[55]

In Brussels, unlike Flanders, Belgian independence had ensured that the process of Frenchification was irreversible. Large segments of the middle classes were affected; in the 1840s French was the language of more than one third of its inhabitants. Given their outsider status and feelings of impotence, resentment against French culture among Flemish activists was stronger in the capital than in the provinces.[56]

The music columns that appeared in the short-lived newspaper *Vlaemsch België* (*Flemish Belgium*) are illustrative.[57] The author Domien Sleeckx, a teacher born in Antwerp, showed little mercy for his French-speaking fellow citizens in the Théâtre de la Monnaie, whom he portrayed as thoughtless, dumb parvenus. Especially irritating to him was the reaction to the first performances in 1844 of operas sung in German. It occurred in a context of intensifying relations between Belgium and Prussia, resulting in a trade agreement with the German Customs Union in the same year. However, the audience of La Monnaie seemed less open to the German approaches and Sleeckx felt disgust at the cold reception given to *Die Zauberflöte*, *Fidelio* and *Der Freischütz*.[58]

In Berlin, the world premiere of Weber's *Der Freischütz* at the Schauspielhaus (Playhouse) in 1821 had been not only a tremendous success, but at the same time a truly 'national' event. By then German opera had developed into a real challenge for the Court Theatre, where the Italians, with Gasparo Spontini as the favourite of King William Frederick III, held sway.[59] When Brussels came to hear *Der Freischütz* in 1844, Richard Wagner was putting the finishing

134 Processes of selection and adaptation

touches to his *Tannhäuser*, while Mendelssohn and Schumann had already created the essential part of their musical legacy. Compared to this German waterfall of musical creativity, the Flemish activists had very little to rely on. In literature, Hendrik Conscience had made worthy efforts, but the musical landscape made a sorry sight.

The cultural and intellectual gap, when combined with the outsider status of the Dutch-speaking Belgians, increased the need within the Flemish Movement for a strong ally. Therefore, the music columns in *Vlaemsch België* read like an endless eulogy of German music. Often Sleeckx's words, centring on the notions of purity and authenticity, seem directly borrowed from German sources of nationalist and Romantic inspiration.[60] At a practical level, attempts were made to join in the German musical boom. In 1846 a Flemish-German Choral Federation (Vlaemsch-Duitsch Zangverbond) was established, aiming at a close cooperation between Flemish and German men's choral societies. Three festivals resulted from the initiative. The first took place in Cologne, with 49 societies participating and Mendelssohn among the conductors. Two more festivals took place in Belgium (Brussels and Ghent), but the confederation did not survive the turmoil of 1848 in the German states.[61]

The worship of German music was more than an aesthetic judgement. The ethical component in it was just as strong. As such, the discourse common in the Flemish Movement dovetailed with the language already used by Verlooy in 1788. Significantly, in terms of the complex nature of transnational cultural flows, a permanent trait in this mental scheme of a Germanic-Romanic antagonism was its gender-bias, claiming the superiority of the strong, male German 'culture' over the weakened, effeminate French 'civilisation'. It would be a mistake, however, to identify the Flemish Movement with blind Germanophilia. Sleeckx himself, for example, in a liberal state of mind, had little confidence in Prussian politics.[62] As was the case in the *ancien régime*, the political and the cultural did not necessarily coincide.

In the 1840s, Brussels experienced not only German opera, but also the newer Italian repertoire. Guest performances of an Italian troupe in 1840 made Edouard Fétis, son of François-Joseph and music columnist for *L'Indépendant*, dream about a permanent *opéra italien* in Brussels.[63] Growing up in Paris, he had conceived a passion for Rossini, Bellini and Donizetti at the Théâtre-Italien, the place to be for the connoisseur of sophisticated taste. Stendhal, Delacroix and Chopin were counted among its famous habitués. As a state-subsidised institution, the Théâtre-Italien was fully integrated in the theatrical design of the French capital.[64] For Edouard Fétis, who extolled

Italian opera as 'the enjoyment par excellence of the most enlightened stratum in society', it was clear that Brussels could not lag behind 'nations of which the taste is less sure and less brought to perfection than ours'. The Belgian capital should be ready to take this 'big step on the road to musical civilisation'.[65] In truth, his reveries were unlikely to come true. With the history of the poorly subsidised Théâtre de la Monnaie full of tales of financial woe, the chances of an autonomous Italian theatre establishing itself in Brussels were scant.

Conclusion

By the middle of the nineteenth century, Brussels had grown into a large city; in 1856 it had a population of 236,000 inhabitants.[66] This growth made room for commercial initiatives in the field of theatre and music. Some 20 locations can be traced in the city where music or theatre performances took place on a more than occasional basis.[67] Commercialisation, however, has not been the focus of this chapter. Instead it has aimed at demonstrating that leisure is not ideologically neutral. As such, the Brussels opera house, which has been central to the discussion, has always been a mirror in which the prevailing power relations can be seen reflected and affirmed. In the dynastic state there were the competing models of Italian and French court culture. The outcome depended partly on the governor's background and ambitions, but in the long term the ascendance of France proved decisive. The Sun King's expansionist policy and warfare laid the foundation of France's cultural hegemony in the eighteenth century. Courtly in origin, the French model evolved into a recipe for a fashionable and civilised way of life, embraced by socially aspiring urbanites.

For the Belgians of 1830, this legacy was hard to deal with. The elites in the country felt no hesitation in subscribing to the universalist import of French culture. Yet the nation-state presented a context that differed substantially from the dynastic state and complicated the flow of cultural forms. In a country where more than half of the population spoke Dutch, the unremitting imitation of all that happened in Paris was not likely to result in the creation of a firm national identity. This was sensed in the Flemish Movement, but for its representatives it proved hard not to fall into the same, but this time German, trap. It shows how difficult it can be for a small country with big neighbours to uphold a degree of cultural autonomy, especially if the country in question has failed to impose a unitary national language.

136 Processes of selection and adaptation

Notes

1 T.C.W. Blanning, *The Triumph of Music: The Rise of Composers, Musicians and Their Art* (Cambridge, MA: Belknap Press, 2008), pp. 264–272; D.R.B. Kimbell, *Verdi in the Age of Italian Romanticism* (Cambridge: Cambridge University Press, 1981), pp. 3–22, 445–459, 561–574.

2 T. Verschaffel, '1830. De zangexplosie rondom de Belgische Revolutie', in L.P. Grijp (ed.), *Een muziekgeschiedenis der Nederlanden* (Amsterdam: Amsterdam University Press, 2001), pp. 409–416.

3 T. Judt, 'Is there a Belgium?', in B. Barnard et al., *How Can One Not Be Interested in Belgian History? War, Language and Consensus in Belgium since 1830* (Ghent: Academia Press, 2005), pp. 13–32.

4 E.J. Hobsbawm, *Nations and Nationalism since 1780: Programme, Myth, Reality* (Cambridge: Cambridge University Press, 1992), pp. 102–104.

5 P. Stryckers, '1650. Muziek aan het hof van Leopold Wilhelm en de opkomst van de barok in de Zuidelijke Nederlanden', in Grijp (ed.), *Een muziekgeschiedenis der Nederlanden*, pp. 296–301.

6 H. Liebrecht, *Histoire du théâtre français à Bruxelles au XVIIe et au XVIIIe siècle* (Paris: Librairie ancienne Edouard Champion, 1923), pp. 111–151; M. Couvreur and J.-P. Van Aelbrouck, 'Gio Paolo Bombarda et la création du Grand Théâtre de Bruxelles', in M. Couvreur (ed.), *Le Théâtre de la Monnaie au XVIIIe siècle* (Brussels: GRAM-ULB, 1996), pp. 1–27.

7 Couvreur and Van Aelbrouck, 'Gio Paolo Bombarda', p. 12.

8 J. Isnardon, *Le Théâtre de la Monnaie depuis sa fondation jusqu'à nos jours* (Brussels: Schott Frères, 1890), pp. 18–19.

9 This was the conclusion of the German traveller Baron von Pöllnitz, quoted in R. De Peuter, *Brussel in de achttiende eeuw* (Brussels: VUB Press, 1999), p. 22.

10 B. Van Oostveldt, *The Théâtre de la Monnaie and the Theatre Life in the 18th Century Austrian Netherlands: From a Courtly-Aristocratic to a Civil-Enlightened Discourse?* (Ghent: Academia Press, 2000), pp. 60–80.

11 J. Schouteden-Wery, *Charles de Lorraine et son temps* (Brussels: Dessart, 1943), pp. 69–87.

12 Quoted in Schouteden-Wery, *Charles de Lorraine et son temps*, p. 299.

13 S. Clercx, 'La Chapelle de Charles de Lorraine et l'activité musicale à Bruxelles au XVIIIe siècle', *La Revue Générale*, 73 (1940), pp. 664–677.

14 Y. Leblicq, 'L'Urbanisme', in J. Stengers (ed.), *Bruxelles: la croissance d'une capitale* (Antwerp: Fonds Mercator, 1979), pp. 149–156.

15 R. De Peuter, *Brussel in de achttiende eeuw*, p. 49; E. Stols, 'Regards étrangers sur les Pays-Bas autrichiens', in H. Hasquin (ed.), *La Belgique autrichienne, 1713–1794* (Brussels: Crédit communal, 1987), p. 518.

16 E. Hennaut and M. Campioli, 'La construction du premier théâtre de la Monnaie par les Bezzi et ses transformations jusqu'à la fin du régime autrichien', in Couvreur (ed.), *Le Théâtre de la Monnaie au XVIIIe siècle*, pp. 33–109; M. Galand, 'Relations et liens financiers entre le gouvernement et le théâtre de la Monnaie sous le

régime autrichien', in Couvreur (ed.), *Le Théâtre de la Monnaie au XVIIIe siècle*, pp. 117–131.

17 M. Cornaz, 'Le Concert Bourgeois: une société de concerts publics à Bruxelles durant la seconde moitié du XVIIIe siècle', *Revue Belge de Musicologie*, 53 (1999), pp. 113–136.

18 K. Buyens, 'Henri-Jacques De Croes and the court chapel of Charles of Lorraine', *Revue Belge de Musicologie*, 55 (2001), pp. 165–178, 177.

19 P. De Zuttere, 'La direction des frères Alexandre-Florentin et Herman Bultos (1777–1794)', in Couvreur (ed.), *Le Théâtre de la Monnaie au XVIIIe siècle*, pp. 133–155.

20 B.A. Brown, 'La diffusion et l'influence de l'opéra-comique en Europe au XVIIIe siècle', in P. Vendrix (ed.), *L'Opéra-comique en France au XVIIIe siècle* (Liège: Mardaga, 1992), pp. 302–309.

21 J. Smeyers, 'La littérature néerlandaise à Bruxelles au cours du XVIIIe siècle', in R. Mortier and H. Hasquin (eds.), *Etudes sur le XVIIIe siècle*, Vol. 4 (Brussels: Editions de l'Université de Bruxelles, 1977), pp. 101–116.

22 P. Andriessen, '1768. Nederlandstalige operavoorstellingen in Brussel', in Grijp (ed.), *Een muziekgeschiedenis der Nederlanden*, pp. 355–361.

23 C. Burney, *The Present State of Music in Germany, the Netherlands, and United Provinces*, Vol. 1 (London, 1775), p. 53.

24 Van Oostveldt, *The Théâtre de la Monnaie*, p. 107.

25 K. Langvik-Johannessen and K. Porteman, '1700. Inauguratie van de Muntschouwburg te Brussel', in R.L. Erenstein (ed.), *Een theatergeschiedenis der Nederlanden* (Amsterdam: Amsterdam University Press, 1996), p. 288.

26 Van Oostveldt, *The Théâtre de la Monnaie*, pp. 120–126.

27 J.B.C. Verlooy, *Verhandeling op d'onacht der moederlyke tael in de Nederlanden*, ed. J. Smeyers and J. van den Broeck (The Hague: Nijhoff, 1979); S. Tassier, 'Verlooy, précurseur du mouvement flamand', *Revue de l'Université de Bruxelles* 43:2 (1937–1938), pp. 155–171.

28 T.C.W. Blanning, *The Culture of Power and the Power of Culture: Old Regime Europe 1660–1789* (Oxford: Oxford University Press, 2002), pp. 239–243; P. Burke, *Popular Culture in Early Modern Europe* (London: Ashgate, 2009), pp. 240–241.

29 E. Mailly, *Les Origines du Conservatoire royal de musique de Bruxelles* (Brussels: Hayez, 1879), pp. 5–8.

30 C. De Baere, 'Het Nederlandsch Tooneel te Brussel tijdens de Regeering van Koning Willem I (1815–1830)', *Eigen Schoon en De Brabander* 37:1–3 (1944), pp. 43–5.

31 R. Van der Hoeven, *La Monnaie au XIXe siècle* (Brussels: GRAM-ULB, 2000), p. 37.

32 J.H. Furnée, '"Le Bon Public de La Haye": local governance and the audience in the French Opera in The Hague, 1820–1890', *Urban History*, 40 (2013), pp. 625–645.

33 Letter of Liszt to princess Christina Belgiojoso, 4 June 1839, quoted in A. Rousselin-Lacombe, 'Piano et pianistes', in J.-M. Bailbé et al., *La Musique en France à l'époque romantique (1830–1870)* (Paris: Flammarion, 1991), p. 145.

34 For an elaborate analysis, see S. van Zuylen van Nyevelt, *La vie musicale à Bruxelles: les concerts vocaux et instrumentaux (1789–1833)* (Mémoire de licence, Université Libre de Bruxelles, 1986).

35 H. Vanhulst, 'Orchestres et concerts', in R. Wangermée and P. Mercier (eds.), *La Musique en Wallonie et à Bruxelles*, Vol. 2, *Les XIXe et XXe siècles* (Brussels: La Renaissance du Livre, 1982), pp. 44–45; C. Van den Borren, 'Les premières exécutions d'oeuvres de Beethoven à Bruxelles', *Revue Musicale*, 8 (1927), pp. 98–104.

36 J. Lade, 'Charles-Louis(-Joseph) Hanssens [l'aîné]', in S. Sadie and J. Tyrrell (eds.), *The New Grove Dictionary of Music and Musicians*, Vol. 10 (London: Macmillan, 2001), p. 835.

37 H. Baeck-Schilders, '1826. De bevordering van het muziekonderwijs in Nederland en België', in Grijp (ed.), *Een muziekgeschiedenis der Nederlanden*, pp. 398–402.

38 J. van Gessel, *Een vaderland van goede muziek. Een halve eeuw Maatschappij tot bevordering der toonkunst (1829–1879) en het Nederlandse muziekleven* (PhD dissertation, Universiteit Utrecht, 2001), pp. 54–56.

39 E. Witte, J. Craeybeckx and A. Meynen, *Political History of Belgium From 1830 Onwards* (Brussels: Academic Scientific Publishers, 2009), pp. 19–59.

40 E. Witte, 'The formation of a centre in Belgium: the role of Brussels in the formative state of the Belgian state (1830–1840)', *European History Quarterly*, 19 (1989), pp. 435–468.

41 V. Montens, 'Finances publiques et art en Belgique (1830–1940)', in G. Kurgan-van Hentenryk and V. Montens (eds.), *L'Argent des arts. La Politique artistique des pouvoirs publics en Belgique de 1830 à 1940* (Brussels: Editions de l'Université de Bruxelles, 2001), pp. 9–24.

42 R. Van der Hoeven, *La Monnaie au XIXe siècle*, pp. 9–47.

43 E.J. Hobsbawm, *The Age of Revolution, 1789–1848* (London: Weidenfeld & Nicolson, 1962), p. 136; M. de Vroede, 'Onderwijs en opvoeding in de Zuidelijke Nederlanden 1815-circa 1840', in *Algemene geschiedenis der Nederlanden*, Vol. 11 (Haarlem: Fibula-Van Dishoeck, 1983), pp. 128–144.

44 J. Stengers, *Histoire du sentiment national en Belgique des origines à 1918*, Vol. 1, *Les Racines de la Belgique* (Brussels: Racine, 2000), pp. 214–215.

45 H. Vanhulst, 'Le Conservatoire royal de Musique de Bruxelles: origine et directorat de François-Joseph Fétis (1833–1871)', in A. Bongrain and Y. Gérard (eds.), *Le Conservatoire de Paris. Des Menus-Plaisirs à la Cité de la Musique, 1795–1995* (Paris: Buchet-Chastel, 1995), pp. 201–217.

46 Reproduced in R. Wangermée, *François-Joseph Fétis, musicologue et compositeur: contribution à l'étude du goût musical au XIXe siècle* (Brussels: Palais des Académies, 1951), pp. 178–201.

47 E. Baeck and H. Baeck-Schilders, 'Fétis versus Benoit: een conflict over kosmopolitisme en nationalisme in het Belgisch muziekleven', *Revue Belge de Musicologie*, 62 (2008), 231–250.

48 R. Wangermée, 'Fétis et la Belgique', *Revue Belge de Musicologie*, 62 (2008), 181–183.

49 H. Vanhulst, 'Orchestres et concerts', pp. 45–47.

50 'Variétés musicales', *Indépendant*, 25 August 1842.

51 Van der Hoeven, *La Monnaie au XIXe siècle*, pp. 127–275.

52 Van der Hoeven, *La Monnaie au XIXe siècle*, pp. 277–297.

53 'Théâtre Royal', *Indépendant*, 17 November 1838.

54 M. Cornaz, 'François-Joseph Fétis et le Prix de Rome', *Revue Belge de Musicologie*, 62 (2008), pp. 112–114.

55 Witte, Craeybeckx and Meynen, *Political History of Belgium from 1830 Onwards*, pp. 56–59.

56 E. Gubin, 'L'emploi des langues au XIXe siècle. Les débuts du mouvement flamand', in Stengers (ed.), *Bruxelles: la croissance d'une capitale*, pp. 235–245.

57 E. De Bens, *Vlaemsch België: het eerste Vlaamsgezinde dagblad* (Ghent: Story, 1968).

58 D. Sleeckx, 'Kunst- en Letternieuws', *Vlaemsch België*, 2 and 8 August 1844.

59 Blanning, *The Triumph of Music*, pp. 140–143.

60 On German music journalism, see C. Applegate, *Bach in Berlin: Nation and Culture in Mendelssohn's Revival of the St. Matthew Passion* (Ithaca and London: Cornell University Press, 2005), pp. 80–124.

61 H. von der Dunk, *Der deutsche Vormärz und Belgien 1830/48* (Wiesbaden: F. Steiner, 1966), pp. 259–289 and 317–330; J. Dewilde, 'Vlaemsch-Duitsch Zangverbond', in *Nieuwe Encyclopedie van de Vlaamse Beweging*, Vol. 3 (Tielt: Lannoo, 1998), pp. 3501–3502.

62 H. von der Dunk, *Der deutsche Vormärz und Belgien 1830/48*, p. 314.

63 P. Becquart, 'Fétis, Edouard', in *Nouvelle Biographie Nationale*, Vol. 5 (Brussels: Palais des Académies, 1999), pp. 151–153.

64 N. Wild, 'Le spectacle lyrique au temps du Grand Opéra', in *La Musique en France à l'époque romantique* (Paris: Flammarion, 1991), pp. 41–48; J.H. Johnson, *Listening in Paris: A Cultural History* (Berkeley: University of California Press, 1995), pp. 182–196.

65 E. Fétis, 'Théâtre Royal. Représentation de la troupe italienne', *Indépendant*, 28 April 1840.

66 J. Kruithof, 'De samenstelling der Brusselse bevolking in 1842. Proeve tot opbouw der sociale stratifikatie', *Tijdschrift voor Sociale Wetenschappen*, 3 (1956), p. 164.

67 Number based on L. Renieu, *Histoire des théâtres de Bruxelles depuis leur origine jusqu'à ce jour*, 2 vols (Paris: Duchartre & Van Buggenhoudt, 1928).

7

Leisure culture, entrepreneurs and urban space: Swedish towns in a European perspective, eighteenth–nineteenth centuries

DAG LINDSTRÖM

In 1805, no fewer than 327 prominent citizens purchased shares in the newly founded Assembly and Theatre House Company in the small town of Linköping. The shareholders represented a mix of old and new elites, including the archbishop of Sweden, the bishop of Linköping, local nobility, officers, officials, distinguished burghers and manufacturers. The list of subscribers also included the names of several women. Most of the shareholders lived in the town, others in the near country districts, and some in other towns such as Norrköping and Stockholm.[1]

The Linköping Assembly and Theatre House (Assemblé- och spektakelhuset) opened its doors in 1806. The main event for the opening evening was a Swedish comedy in three acts. The venue offered a number of different entertainments. Theatre companies performed regularly during the season, and from time to time the theatre was also used by other artists, such as the tightrope walker Mrs Price, an invisible girl and a Danish magician. A restaurateur and a pastry cook rented premises in the house. Public amateur concerts were performed and private dinner parties were arranged. The building was also frequently used for public dance evenings called *assembléer*. A typical *assemblé* evening started with one hour of conversation and tea drinking followed by one hour of musical entertainment, after which the evening ended with one hour of dancing.[2]

The initiators had proclaimed that they wanted not only to offer pleasure, but also to promote a refined and moral social life (*förädlad och sedlig sällskapslevnad*), where all respectable people, and even the less wealthy, could take part. It was also important that the establishment kept certain standards so as not to let the house degenerate into a simple tavern or a gathering place for people of bad repute. The board was obliged to vouch for good order at the dance evenings and to guarantee that only decent people were admitted. The initiators also emphasised that no one should be deterred from attending the evening arrangements for economic reasons. Because of this, women were explicitly requested not to arrive in clothing that was too expensive. Class and class difference were of obvious importance here, but these were expressed not in terms of money or titles, but in more discrete terms relating to decency and good behaviour. The Assembly and Theatre House was also explicitly established as an arena for both men and women. It was, however, equally obvious that men were expected to take the initiative in discussions, gatherings and dance evenings, while women were expected to be passive and to wait for the men to ask them for a dance.[3]

The Assembly and Theatre House was a novelty in the urban leisure landscape of Linköping, a rather small yet significant cathedral city and centre of the regional government of the province of Östergötland in the south-east of Sweden. The wooden building soon became a popular venue for the town's entertainment and leisure activities, and remained the town's main theatre house for almost a century until its demolition in 1901. The Assembly and Theatre House Company was an economic success as well, as for many years the shareholders could enjoy an annual return of 10 per cent on their investments.[4]

The establishment of the Linköping Assembly and Theatre House offers a good illustration of how many Swedish provincial towns in the late eighteenth and early nineteenth centuries introduced new sites for urban leisure activities. Many of these new leisure activities first developed in the capital. In late eighteenth-century Stockholm, going to the theatre and spending free time in parks and gardens were well-known amusements, and cafés and restaurants soon added new options for those who had time and money to spend. In some cases, however, provincial towns appropriated and adapted innovative forms of leisure directly from foreign examples.

Figure 7.1 Assemblé och spektakelhuset, Linköping, 1900. Photograph by Didrik von Essen. Didrik von Essens fotosamling, DvE13, Östergötlands museum, Linköping.

This chapter considers the national and transnational rise and development of three closely related new leisure practices and their impact on urban space in eighteenth- and nineteenth-century Sweden: 1. public entertainments and theatres, concert halls and other establishments for public performances; 2. public parks and other recreation areas; and 3. restaurants, cafés and similar catering services. These new activities and establishments obviously reflected international trends, but how can the actual mechanisms of selection, appropriation and adaptation as they were introduced in the Swedish urban environment be understood? How significant was the impact of individual entrepreneurs? And how important was the capital? Was the new urban leisure landscape primarily diffused via Stockholm, or did the provincial towns import most of these innovative practices and cultural models directly from abroad?

The examples in this chapter have been picked mainly from Stockholm and from Linköping and Norrköping in the province of Östergötland – two significant provincial towns that represent two very different types of towns, making them excellently suited for a comparative approach. In 1800, Stockholm had about 75,000 inhabitants, representing more than a quarter of the total urban population of Sweden at that time. Stockholm was the capital, had a leading position as a seaport, and was a leading centre for early Swedish industry. In 1750, Linköping had only about 1,800 inhabitants, rising to 2,680 in 1800 and 5,240 in 1850. However, the town was more important than its size may indicate. It was the seat of the regional government, a cathedral city, a centre for culture and education, and a town often visited by the local nobility who liked to spend part of the year there. Norrköping, in turn, was one of the most important centres for manufacture in early modern Sweden. Around 1750, the town had about 6,000 inhabitants, increasing to about 9,000 in 1800 and almost 17,000 in 1850. With a large proportion of workers and poor people, its social and economic structure was quite different from Linköping.

Theatres

In the seventeenth century, the Swedish government actively tried to develop both the capital and the royal court in order to match its imperial ambitions. Attracting foreign actors was one of many measures introduced to enhance the glory of the Swedish kingdom. From the 1640s, numerous international theatrical companies visited the capital: most of them came from Germany and the Netherlands, but some of them travelled all the way from France and Italy. It did not take long before the Swedish government also took the initiative to establish the first permanent theatre buildings in the capital.

From 1667 until 1689, the so-called Lion's Den (Lejonkulan), a building close to the royal castle where two lions had formerly been kept, regularly functioned as a semi-public court theatre. It was frequented by several foreign groups as well as by Swedish amateur groups. The first public theatre house in Stockholm was established in 1699 when the Jeu de paume building (Stora Bollhuset), also close to the royal castle, was reconstructed into a permanent theatre. Several French and German groups gave regular public performances there while visiting Stockholm.[5]

Until the 1730s, professional theatre in Sweden depended solely on visiting foreign groups. Even the first professional Swedish theatrical company, Swenska Comedien, established in 1737, was heavily influenced by French examples. The first director, Charles Langlois, was a French actor and silk trader, who had arrived in Stockholm with a French theatre group in the 1720s. The Swedish company did not succeed in pleasing the court very much.

Processes of selection and adaptation

Its performances were regarded as inferior, and the court continued to engage foreign actors, dancers and opera singers.[6] In fact, none of the groups performing at Stora Bollhuset had any long-term success. After a couple of years, even the less privileged audience usually failed to turn up. Contemporary eye-witnesses often described the evenings at the theatre as rather noisy and rowdy. Unable to support themselves in the capital alone, most theatre companies had to travel in the provinces. Especially from the mid-eighteenth century, most provincial towns profited from regular performances of travelling theatre companies.[7]

In the eighteenth century, several Swedish kings, particularly Gustav III (1771–1792), took a deep personal interest in theatre and opera. In the 1750s, new theatres were built at two of the royal residences outside Stockholm, Ulriksdal and Drottningholm, and in 1782 the first permanent opera house in Stockholm was finished, built in a square close to the castle. Together with other buildings and a statue of Gustavus Adolphus it formed an impressive manifestation of royal power and royal promotion of culture. In 1781, Gustav III recruited a new French theatre group, which included one of France's most famous actors, Jacques Marie Boutet de Monvel, who stayed in Stockholm until 1787. At first they performed only at the court, but after some years they also performed publically at Stora Bollhuset. In 1787, the king also initiated and financed a Swedish theatre company, Kungliga Svenska Dramatiska Theatern. After Gustav III's death in 1793, Stora Bollhuset was pulled down, but in the very same year Stockholm received a new theatre house, built in the seventeenth-century Makalös palace at Kungsträdgården, which functioned until it was destroyed in a fire in 1825.[8]

In addition to the theatres primarily funded by royal patronage, Stockholm also saw the rise of some privately funded theatres. In the 1750s, Petter Stenborg, a member of the first Swedish theatre group, organised a new Swedish theatre company, which toured mainly in the provinces and only performed in Stockholm from time to time. From the 1770s, however, the company took a more permanent residence in the capital. After being denied permission to perform at Stora Bollhuset in 1772, the company began to use the royal pavilion in a former royal garden (Humlegården), which by that time had become a public park. From 1773, the pavilion was used regularly as a theatre. Stenborg offered a wide programme, including plays by Molière and Holberg, but also pantomimes and marionette and acrobatic performances. The company also frequently staged comical parodies of the more elevated plays performed at the royal theatres. Although the theatre in Humlegården was only available during the summer season, the Stenborg group managed to perform about 50 times a year. From 1780, the group also played in one of the inns in Stockholm (Eriksberg), and in 1784 they were able to move into a new theatre house Nya Swenska Theatern at Munkbron in the old town. At that time, the repertoire moved towards French *opéra comique*. The quality of their performances increased and the theatre became very popular, until, in 1798, the government introduced a theatre monopoly in Stockholm, granting only the Royal Opera and the Royal Dramatic Theatre the right to perform in the capital. For the Stenberg group this was a severe blow: the actors had to return to an ambulant existence and in 1809 the group was finally dissolved.[9] However the royal monopoly did not hinder another theatre entrepreneur to build a theatre house at Djurgården in 1801 (see below).[10]

In the course of the eighteenth century, theatre began to develop into one of the major amusements for the Swedish urban population. Norrköping appeared as one of the more important sites in the development of Swedish theatre outside the capital. Several German theatre groups had already visited Norrköping in the 1720s and the 1730s, and several Swedish companies were active in the 1750s, 1760s and 1770s. Carl Gottfried Seurling, born in Germany, became the leading theatre manager outside Stockholm. His group visited Norrköping many times and his actors usually stayed there for several months. In 1776, the visit caused extensive debate in one of the local newspapers, *Norrköpings Weko Tidningar*, lasting for at least two months and covering some 20 pages. Just as elsewhere in Europe, most of the performances started with a longer and more serious play usually followed by a short comedy. The debate reveals that some spectators (or the majority according to one participant in the debate) preferred the shorter and simpler burlesque comedies, while the more sophisticated audience was deeply moved by, for example, the tragic tale of Romeo and Juliet. Several participants in the debate emphasised the importance of virtue and reason, and argued that theatre could and should improve morals and education. To their disappointment, however, a huge part of the audience just wanted a good laugh and did not understand how to appreciate a 'beautiful tragedy'.[11] In the late eighteenth century, Sweden clearly not only appropriated foreign theatre genres and acting styles, but also foreign theatre debates.

Norrköping was one of the first provincial towns to build a theatre house. The first one, Egges tater, was built by the German restaurateur Johan Ulric Egge in 1762. The building, located close to Egge's inn and a garden, was small (18 by seven metres) and far from spectacular. At Egge's, the audience could go to theatre, listen to music, watch acrobats and trained bears, and view wax-works, and they could also have a beer and drink liquor. Later the public could also visit a reading-room.[12] In the early 1790s, a second theatre house was established, Dahlbergska teatern, in an old drying house for tobacco. For some time, two separate theatre groups were simultaneously active in Norrköping. Dahlberg's theatre became something of a permanent stage with ensembles staying for the whole season with a regular programme, and with an organised system for ticket subscriptions.[13]

At the end of the eighteenth century, both Egge's and Dahlberg's theatres were replaced by a new theatre house, as they were both considered insufficient for the growing and more demanding audience. In 1794, newspapers were already suggesting that Norrköping needed a new theatre house with a larger and more comfortable auditorium. Presumably, this would also honour the town, and promote education and good manners among the youth. In January 1798, the new theatre house, Saltängsteatern, was established, organised as a company with shareholders. The initiative came from John Swartzs, a member of one of the leading industrial families in Norrköping. After his studies at Uppsala, he had served at the Swedish embassies in London, Constantinople and Paris, where he actively experienced the latest novelties in theatrical cul-ture and enterprise. Taking several other initiatives to embellish and modernise Norrköping, Swartzs successfully attracted several leading industrial families in Norrköping onto the board of the new theatre. However, this did not prevent the theatre from experiencing severe economic difficulties soon after, and in 1813 his theatre was taken over by the Hedvig Church (often referred to as the German Church), with another manufacturer, Johan Arosenius, as the new leading man.[14]

In Linköping, theatre had become a common and popular attraction from at least the 1790s. The local newspaper, *Linköpings Bladet* (1794–1851), fre-quently informed its readers about plays performed in the city. This is no sur-prise, as the first editor, Didric Gabriel Björn, was a former actor who also translated and adapted many plays into Swedish. Unfortunately, the archives do not reveal much about the origins of the local theatre culture. Court records from 1697 mention the performance of a comedy and, in 1737, the prohib-ition of comedies during Advent by the governor. In 1739, a visiting German theatre company, led by Johan Fredrik Darmstädter, failed to attract spectators to their plays. Fortunately for him, Darmstädter combined theatre and den-tal care, obviously earning some money from the latter activity. The intense theatre activities in the 1790s appear to be something rather new. At that time, different theatre groups visited the city and some of them stayed for quite a long time, offering a large number of different plays and using a riding house in the courtyard as a theatre. In 1798, the rise of Linköping's theatre scene was severely impeded when its bishop managed to persuade the king to prohibit comedies and other plays in towns with academies and schools. For a while, theatre companies had to perform outside the town. In 1805, however, one theatre group received the right to perform in Linköping again, on condition that they only played outside the school seasons. From that time onwards, the new assembly and theatre house also welcomed other theatre groups, such as the earlier mentioned Stenborg Company from Stockholm. However, theatre performances were still forbidden during the school season. Only in 1825 did the board of the Assembly and Theatre House Company manage to convince the king and the governor to expand the performing period to run from 10 December to 10 February. Arguing that theatre would corrupt the city's youth, the cathedral chapter, the school board and the governor rejected any further extension of the theatre season until the second half of the nineteenth century.[15]

Concerts and balls

By the mid-eighteenth century, the upper and middle classes in Stockholm started to embrace the performance of music in their private homes, while at the same time public concerts began to develop into regular pleasure events. Lacking any purpose-built formal concert hall until the end of the nineteenth century, most concerts took place in churches, the great hall at the House of Nobility (Riddarhuset), the Bourse (Börshuset), and the Orangery in Kungsträdgården (King's Garden).[16] In Norrköping, the first concerts dated from the 1760s and were often held in private homes, even though they were announced in the newspapers as public arrangements for those willing to buy tickets. In the 1780s, many concerts took place in the Town Hall, as well as in churches and, at the end of the century, in one of the theatres. At least a hundred concerts are known from the period 1762–1800, indicating a very active local musical scene. In 1803, a musical society was established, giving three to four concerts annually in the Town Hall.[17] Linköping's Assembly and Theatre House was also used also for musical concerts, but from 1823 onwards public concerts were also held on annual basis in St Lars Church, attracting an audience of as many as 900–1,000 people, many of them travelling to Linköping for these specific events.[18]

Linköping's Assembly and Theatre House was not only designed to offer theatre and musical concerts. One of the main objectives was to house so-called *assembleer*, a popular form of public dance party, comparable to the assemblies in Georgian English towns. Tickets were on sale and tea or other refreshments were often included in the price. In Stockholm, public dances and masquerades had been organised at inns and at the Town Hall on Södermalm from at least the mid-eighteenth century. Public *assembleer* became popular in Stockholm from at least the 1770s, often held at Börshuset. From the 1790s onwards, the former orangery in Kungsträdgården was used as a dance hall, now called the Vauxhall – copied from the London example. In the summer on Thursdays and Sundays, the Vauxhall was open between 5pm and 9pm. Before the dance began there was a concert of brass instruments. The ticket price was modest and ladies enjoyed free admission. The dances at the Vauxhall were considered to be more relaxed than the *assembleer* at Börshuset. At the turn of the century, *assembleer* also became popular in many other Swedish towns[19] and before the Linköping Assembly and Theatre House was built, they had been organised in private homes.

During the last decades of the eighteenth century, *assembleer* also became popular in Norrköping. There was, of course, a long tradition of popular dances, but public balls seems to have been introduced here in 1760, when a French dance teacher arranged a series of balls, without official permission, and local authorities decided not to enforce any restrictions as long as the balls did not lead to abuses of any kind. The first known *assemblé* in Norrköping took place in 1779. Contrary to Linköping, where they started in private houses, *assembleer* in Norrköping were organised in the Town Hall. The assemblies on Friday evenings were for men only, but on Tuesdays women were allowed as well. Men could buy tickets and then bring an 'honourable' lady on Tuesday evenings when dances were organised. Tea, coffee and tobacco were offered to the guests. During the nineteenth century, balls, dance evenings and even masquerades continued to be very popular and the Town Hall continued to be a common place for these occasions, giving several dance teachers, often Frenchmen, a decent living.[20]

Cafés and restaurants

Drinking and even dining for pleasure in polite public settings started to develop during the eighteenth century. The introduction of modern grand cafés and restaurants took place only in the second half of the nineteenth century,

Leisure culture, entrepreneurs and urban space **149**

coinciding with the development of modern hotel businesses and larger enter-tainment halls. However, by the end of the eighteenth century a well-to-do clientele could enjoy coffee, drinks, pastries and even dinners in much fancier premises than the traditional drinking-houses. Again, many of these innova-tions had foreign origins. How did these new practices and institutions find their way into Swedish towns?[21]

Inns (*gästgiverier*), where travellers could seek lodging and possibly have something to eat and to drink, had existed in Swedish towns since the Middle Ages. In 1344, royal authorities explicitly prescribed that each town should have at least two inns that could provide both beer and food, followed by more detailed regulations in the next centuries. In the seventeenth and eighteenth centuries, foreign and Swedish travellers usually argued that Swedish inns had very poor standards. Beds were not always available and sometimes guests had to sleep on the floor. Food was commonly identified as mediocre at best. Meals were served not in a dining room, but in the kitchen, and travellers often dined together with the innkeeper's family.[22] Obviously, these inns had little in com-mon with hotels and restaurants of the kind introduced in the eighteenth and nineteenth centuries.

In eighteenth-century Swedish towns, the number of drinking houses (*krog*) was impressive. At the end of the century Stockholm had no fewer than about 700 public places to have a drink.[23] Norrköping had about 40 in the 1750s,[24] while in Linköping the number of drinking houses increased from 28 in 1778 to 48 in 1785. Most drinking houses were located in private homes and many of the keepers were people of poor circumstances, who could receive some extra income from serving beer and possibly simple food. Their reputation usu-ally was rather poor. One of the places in Linköping was called Lilla Helfwete (Little Hell) and when it closed down in 1797, a local newspaper hailed this as a victory for enlightenment and morality. The county governor repeatedly expressed his concerns about excessive drinking habits and tried to convince the town authorities that honourable burghers should avoid visiting these places. The moral campaigns against the drinking houses seem to have had some con-siderable success. In 1804, the number of *krogs* in Linköping had decreased to 21 and in the 1840s there were no more than about ten of them left.[25]

The first coffeehouses were introduced in Stockholm in the late seventeenth century. In 1758, there were already 22 coffeehouses in the capital and in 1788 the number had increased to 45. These premises were often run by immigrants, especially by Frenchmen and Walloons. In contrast to the drinking houses, which were usually situated in cellars or on the ground floor, most coffeehouses were originally found on the first or second floors.[26] Coffeehouses in Stockholm also sometimes offered performances. In 1734, the German-Hungarian acrobat Johannes Grigg performed several times at the Herr Lehmann Coffe-Hauß.[27]

Outside the capital, coffeehouses had little success. Gothenburg, the second largest town in Sweden, had only a few of them. In Linköping, coffeehouses are mentioned only occasionally in the sources. In the late eighteenth and the early nineteenth centuries, coffee drinking was even prohibited on several occasions. Although these restrictions were not very efficient, they obviously hampered the establishment of coffeehouses in the provincial towns.[28]

At the end of the eighteenth century, coffeehouses in Stockholm also faced competition from premises of somewhat higher standards: confectioners who began to serve coffee, tea, chocolate, liqueur, and other drinks together with pastries. In the early nineteenth century, many of these more elegant cafés were known as *schweizeri*, clearly denoting their Swiss origins. Until 1766, Swiss confectioners held a leading position in Venice, but after a dispute with the authorities many of them emigrated to Berlin and northern Germany. Some of them moved on and established their businesses in Stockholm. By the early nineteenth century, the existing coffeehouses had become somewhat tarnished, and the *schweizeri* represented something more neat and tidy, suitable for the more well established urban middle class. In the 1830s, the concept of *konditori* (from German *Konditorei*) also became more popular. A *konditori* served pastries and confectionary, as well as coffee, tea, chocolate and possibly even wine, liqueur and Swedish punch. At this time the concept of the *schweizeri* gradually changed, the name often just used to indicate a respectable place where alcoholic drinks and maybe simple food was served. In the 1830s, the French concept of the café also found its way into Swedish towns. The coffeehouse gradually became outdated, both as a term and as a specific type of establishment. In Stockholm cafés became fashionable and many of them took French names, even though many of the owners were Germans. Several of the cafés opened in connection with restaurants, and many offered musical entertainment as well.[29]

In the late eighteenth and early nineteenth centuries, inns and restaurants of somewhat higher quality appeared in many Swedish provincial towns. Guests no longer had to eat in the kitchen together with the innkeeper's family. Instead they could sit more comfortably in a special dining room. In 1797, one of the better restaurants in Linköping was established in the local inn (*gästgivaregården*). Foreign visitors nevertheless differed greatly in their assessments of this establishment. According to Charles Colville Frankland, an

English captain who visited Linköping in 1830, this was 'a bad inn, full of fleas and vermin', and staff were 'uncivil and inhospitable'. However, according to Theodor von Wedderkop, a German visitor in 1840s, who delivered an extensive description of the building, its facilities and the food served in the restaurant, the establishment was well comparable to Der weisse Schwan in Frankfurt or Das Hotel zum Erbprinzen in Oldeburg. In the early nineteenth century, at least two inns in the countryside close to Linköping had become popular for weekend trips among the town burghers. From 1806, there was also a restaurant in the Assembly and Theatre House.[30] In Stockholm there were of course a larger number of better inns. Many of them were located in the outskirts of the capital, and quite a few of them (for example at Djurgården, see below) had become popular for visits at the weekends. Several inns also provided musical entertainment and organised dances.

In the eighteenth century, the number of rooms to rent was small, even in the bigger towns, and their standard was very poor. Many travellers, especially the more well-to-do, choose to sleep in private homes if they needed to stay overnight. In Linköping, the more distinguished travellers often stayed in the governor's palace. The first 'modern' hotels in Sweden were established in Gothenburg and in Malmö, starting with the opening of Hotell Göta källare in Gothenburg in 1812, with 56 rooms and a restaurant with a billiard table. In Stockholm, the first hotel (Hotel Garni) opened only in 1832, as a rather small but exclusive enterprise. A larger hotel (Hotel Rydberg) opened in the Swedish capital only in 1857, and from 1859 was run by a Régis Cadier, a French chef educated in Paris, who also ran a *schweizeri* and a restaurant. This restaurant, called Trois Frères Provençaux and serving French cuisine, was more or less the first high-class restaurant in Sweden. Several other French style restaurants soon followed in the capital. In 1872, Cadier opened a second hotel in Stockholm, the Grand Hôtel. Both Linköping and Norrköping got their first hotels in the 1850s. In Linköping the leading men of the town decided that there was a need to build a proper hotel, and in 1852 the Stora Hotellet opened in the main market square. In 1857, Norrköping also got its Stora Hotellet, with 30 rooms, a café and a billiard hall.[31]

Parks and promenades

Public parks and promenades were not very common in Swedish towns before the mid-nineteenth century. Nevertheless, in some towns it had been possible to visit parks for walking and amusement in the eighteenth and early nineteenth centuries. These parks were basically of three different types: royal parks and gardens that were opened for public visitors; private gardens opened up for public visitors; and (in the nineteenth century) parks built by gardening societies. All of these different types found their origins abroad.

At the end of the eighteenth century, several royal parks and gardens in Stockholm began to be adapted into venues for public pleasure and recreation. By 1763 at the latest, the public was admitted into Kungsträdgården (King's Garden), originally laid out as a royal kitchen garden in the fifteenth century but gradually transformed into a baroque pleasure garden. At first admission was certainly restricted. Visitors were expected to be people of rank, and servants and children were not allowed to enter the park at all. At the end of the eighteenth century, however, the old royal orangery to the northern end of the park was changed into a dance hall with service on the premises, and was referred to as the Vauxhall (*Vauxhallen*) from at least the 1790s. According to some upper-class informants, the dances at the Vauxhall mostly attracted people of lower rank. When in the early nineteenth century the surrounding walls were pulled down, the park became a popular public pleasure garden. Although the king soon turned most of Kungsträdgården into a military drill-ground with the Vauxhall used as an arsenal, the park avenues, first on the west side and later also on the east side, turned into popular promenades for the Stockholm upper classes. In 1825, a Professor Mosander started to serve water in the arsenal, responding to the increasing popularity of health resorts and spas among wealthy families. Kungsträdgården now offered an opportunity for those who could not afford to stay at a spa or those who did not want to wait for the summer season to enjoy their mineral water. The avenues at Kungsträdgården remained the favourite promenades for the upper classes until the end of the nineteenth century, when Strandvägen was completed and became the most fashionable avenue in the capital.[32]

When in the seventeenth century Kungsträdgården was changed from a kitchen garden into a pleasure garden, a new royal kitchen garden, known as Humlegården, was built further north in Stockholm. In the mid-eighteenth century, this park also opened its gates to the public, yet with the same restrictions concerning servants and children. In the late eighteenth century, subsequent regulations also prohibited the entry of beggars and poorly dressed people. As the wall surrounding Humlegården was pulled down in the early nineteenth century, the park became quite popular among common people in Stockholm. Besides the theatre in the former royal pavilion, already mentioned and established in 1773, the park also offered other pleasures, such as

Leisure culture, entrepreneurs and urban space **153**

a restaurant, a dance-pavilion, a zoo and an amusement park. However, in the course of the nineteenth century, Humlegården received a negative reputation as a rather bad and dangerous place. It never really challenged Kungsträdgården as the prime venue for walking for the upper classes.[33]

In addition to Kungsträdgården and Humlegården, three other royal parks in the outskirts of Stockholm became popular public leisure areas in the late eighteenth and early nineteenth centuries. In the 1780s, King Gustav III had established a park at Haga, just north of Stockholm, according to the ideals of the English landscape parks, which became a popular picnic area in the early nineteenth century.[34] The royal garden at Drottningholm, west of Stockholm, had opened for public visitors by the 1790s, and became one of the major destinations when regular steamship traffic started round 1820.[35] The most popular leisure attraction, however, was the former royal game park at Djurgården. In the seventeenth century, the southern part of the park had already been used during the summer season as a recreation area. In the eighteenth century it was transformed into Stockholm's main pleasure and recreation area, with several popular inns, followed later on by popular cafés, as well as a theatre house, built in 1801, a Vauxhall dance hall and, from 1831, a permanent circus building established by a French circus manager. In 1850 an amusement park was added to the scenery. In the course of time, the southern part of Djurgården developed into a more distinguished area, while the northern part attracted the common people.[36]

Public parks built on the initiative of the municipal authorities were not very common in Sweden prior to the mid-nineteenth century. According to Catharina Nolin, early communal parks were usually found in towns with a strong middle-class. The argument was often that any town with self-esteem needed a park, which would make the town more beautiful and more pleasant to live in.[37] In Stockholm the first communal park was built in 1832. It was the small garden Strömparterren at one of the bridges close to the royal castle and the royal opera house. A second communal public park, Berzelii park, was built in the 1850s.[38]

More important was a public garden established by a private group of elite citizens. In 1832, the Swedish Garden Society was founded in Stockholm, initiated by members of the aristocracy and the bourgeoisie, and supported by the king. In 1838, the society began to build a larger garden close to Drottninggatan, one of the main streets in Stockholm. The garden was planned according to English and French models and visitors had to pay a small entrance fee. Two pavilions with a *schweizeri* and a café were added and

Figure 7.2 Strömparterren, Stockholm, 1841. Lithography by Fritz von Dardel, Stockholms Stadsmuseum, Stockholm.

the garden soon became a popular meeting place. The brothers August and Wilhelm Davidsson, who ran the establishment, also arranged skating and fireworks in the winter and theatre and concerts in the summer. In 1845, Wilhelm Davidsson suggested building an amusement park in a new part of the garden. Harlad Conrad Stilling, who had designed the well-known amusement park Tivoli in Copenhagen, was engaged in the project, but in the end the board of the society rejected the proposal. The garden was moved to Djurgården in 1861, where it gradually lost popularity. In 1911 the Stockholm Garden Society was finally dissolved.[39]

During the nineteenth century, the idea to establish public gardens for recreation was also introduced in Linköping and Norrköping. In Linköping, the physician Johan August Åman opened the first public garden in the 1820s. Originally his idea was to let his patients take walks for their health in his private garden. In 1826, he bought a piece of land just outside the town, where he built a large public garden decorated with flower beds and lots of fruit trees. This garden also became the location for many dinner parties and musical entertainments. In 1851 the garden was sold and in 1855 it was turned into a private garden no longer open to the public.[40]

Of increasing importance in Linköping was the Werner Garden (Wernerska trädgården). Originally a private garden dating from the late seventeenth century, it was rearranged in a more grandiose style by the German physician Henrik Werner in in the 1830s, and after his death in 1849 it was changed into a public leisure area. In the park, a *schweizeri* offered coffee, tea, chocolate, lemonade, cakes and ice creams, soon followed by musical entertainments and attractions such as 'stereoscopic pictures', humourists, tightrope walkers, fire-eaters and dancers. In 1864, the garden was purchased by Anders Peter Andersson, who transformed it into the leading entertainment and leisure institution in the town, an attraction far beyond what one would have expected to find in a town of Linköping's size. It had a theatre, an inn, a circus area, a music pavilion and meeting rooms. When Andersson bought the Werener Garden, he already owned a hotel, a restaurant and a wine and liquor store. He also leased the whole Assembly and Theatre House, which he then bought in 1874. From 1884, he even controlled liquor licensing in Linköping. At that time, Andersson more or less monopolised the local leisure market. He visited Stockholm frequently, and he also made several journeys through Europe. Obviously his establishments in Linköping were inspired by what he saw in Stockholm and in Germany.[41]

While the Werner Garden replaced the Åman Garden as a place for entertainment and consumption, it did not offer an environment for promenades and outdoor recreation. This was one of the principal aims of the garden society in Linköping, founded in 1859 after several years of discussion. The goal of the society, established by leading members of the city's upper classes, was to offer a park for promenades and recreation, but also to promote gardening and to organise a nursery where trees and plants could be purchased at a moderate cost. The city's governor acted as vice-president and played an active role when it came to providing suitable land for the park.[42] Together with the earlier-mentioned Swedish Garden Society, founded in Stockholm, and the Garden Society of Gothenburg, founded in 1843, Linköping's garden society was one of the most important and most successful garden societies in Sweden to organise a large public park. With the London Horticultural Society and the Garten-Verein in Berlin as obvious sources of inspiration, the garden societies in Swedish towns were part of an international trend. Leading members of the societies both in Stockholm and Gothenburg had visited Berlin and its Garten-Verein.[43] And Carl Ferdinand Liepe, born in Berlin and educated in Germany, first became manager of the Gothenburg garden and later planned the garden of the Linköping Horticulture Society. In 1859, another German

Processes of selection and adaptation

gardener, Christian Fredrik Kroné, was appointed as manager, after his earlier engagement as gardener at the Garden Society of Gothenburg.[44]

Outside Norrköping, the health spa at Himmelstalund developed into a leisure area similar to the Stockholm Djurgården. In 1708, the water in this spa was officially recognised as having health-giving properties. A tavern opened in 1733, and later on *assemblé* were regularly organised on Sundays during the summer season. Acrobats, runners, air-balloons and other attractions were added to the amusements, and Himmelstalund became so popular that in 1839 two 'omnibus' lines were organised.[45] In the early 1840s, the confectioner P.U. Öhman turned Strömsholmen, a small island close to the town, into a popular leisure area with an inn and a skittle ground, where large parties with fireworks and outdoor theatre performances were held.[46] In the 1850s, Erik Schwarz, a leading industrialist in Norrköping, finally took the initiative to embellish the city with a system of avenues and public parks, financed by the municipal government and explicitly intended to make the town not only more beautiful and pleasant, but also to promote good moral standards among the population.[47]

Conclusion

The main elements of the new leisure culture that emerged during the eighteenth and early nineteenth centuries are very similar in Stockholm, Norrköping and Linköping: in all these cities, we find the establishment of theatres, public dances and concerts, restaurants, cafés, hotels, public gardens and amusement parks. It is quite obvious that Stockholm in many ways had a leading role in the development of this new urban leisure culture in Sweden. But the developments in provincial towns like Norrköping and Linköping were not just imitations of what took place in the capital.

In all three cities, the development towards a 'modern' landscape of urban leisure culture followed different chronologies. In Stockholm, the process of change can be traced at least back to the early eighteenth century, but it was from the mid-eighteenth century that it really took off. In Norrköping, we see a more gradual process throughout the whole eighteenth century. In Linköping, however, there are very few obvious signs before the decades around 1800, when the new urban leisure culture exploded.

All of these new leisure activities contributed to the creation of new urban spaces, including the introduction of new uses for old spaces and the attribution of new meanings to them. In Stockholm especially there are numerous examples of former royal spaces transformed into public leisure spaces.

Some of them developed into social arenas for the rising urban middle class, whereas other areas attracted rather more common people. In these processes, old social barriers were deconstructed, as when royal gardens were made public and even the walls surrounding them were pulled down. But other examples illustrate how new barriers – sometimes physical, but often economic, social and cultural– were put up. Many of the new leisure spaces were accessible only to those able to pay a fee. Sometimes unwanted people, especially of lower rank, were simply not permitted to enter, as illustrated by the regulations of the Assembly and Theatre House in Linköping.

Leading contemporaries frequently claimed that establishing new public parks, theatres, restaurants, etc. would not only enhance urban wellbeing, but were in fact necessary elements for any self-respecting city and urban elite. Promoting culture, education, elegance, and decent behaviour as important ingredients for the design and control of urban space, male members of the middle and upper classes, who most explicitly formulated the ideals of a new urban polite leisure culture, refashioned their cities, themselves and their social inferiors.

Private entrepreneurs – many of foreign descent – played crucial roles in all of these urban transformations. Many of them, like Johan Ulric Egge in Norrköping and Régis Cadier in Stockholm, were involved in the development of different leisure activities at the same time, sometimes by organising different activities in the same building or space, as shown in the examples of the Assembly and Theatre House in Linköping and the various pleasure parks. International influences and international connections were extremely important. Many of the leading entrepreneurs, theatre and circus performers, as well as the owners of restaurants and cafés, were of foreign (mainly Continental) origin. Moreover, many Swedish entrepreneurs had spent time abroad. Taken together the international influences were strong, and they were Continental (German and French) rather than British. To some extent, local authorities supported the emergence of all of these new leisure activities. At the same time, there are also examples of state authorities and the Church taking actions against the new trends. The ambiguous attitudes expressed by the Linköping bishops offer an illustrative example.

The patterns of adaption and the introduction of the new leisure activities differed quite a lot between the three cities described. Compared to those in Stockholm and Linköping, private initiatives and entrepreneurs in Norrköping seem to have been even more important, even if these initiatives sometimes included public financing. In Linköping, the old elite – the regional nobility, the Church, officers and public officials – had played a prominent role,

Processes of selection and adaptation

while royal connections were of particular significance in the capital. Although Stockholm clearly played a leading role in many of the developments, it would be a misleading oversimplification to view the development in the provincial towns simply as an example of cultural diffusion from the capital. Both in Norrköping and Linköping, private entrepreneurs and members of the local elite modelled their new leisure facilities to examples seen in the capital, but often also copied them directly from abroad.

Notes

1 Folke Lindberg, *Linköpings historia 2. 1567–1862* (Uppsala: Sahlströms, 1946), pp. 557–559; Linköpings stiftsbibliotek, Linköping, Handskriftssamlingen, E 47.

2 Lindberg, *Linköpings historia 2*, pp. 557–559. Obviously Mrs Price is identical with Hanne Price, married to James Price. The couple lived in Copenhagen and arranged acrobatic performances in both Denmark and Sweden in the late eighteenth and early nineteenth centuries. Per Arne Wåhlberg, *Cirkus i Sverige. Bidrag till vårt lands kulturhistoria* (Stockholm: Carlsson, 1992), p. 22.

3 Lindberg, *Linköpings historia 2*, p. 558.

4 Lindberg, *Linköpings historia 2*, pp. 557–559.

5 Lennart Breitholtz, 'Fransk och nationell teater', in Gösta Berg (ed.), *Det glada Sverige. Våra fester och högtider genom tiderna 2* (Stockholm: Natur och kultur, 1947); Gunilla Dahlberg, 'Hovens och komedianternas teater', in Sven Åke Heed (ed.), *Ny Svensk teaterhistoria 1. Teater före 1800* (Hedemora: Gidlund, 2007), pp. 139–163.

6 Marie-Christine Skuncke, 'Frihetstidens teaterliv i Stockholm', in Sven Åke Heed (ed.), *Ny Svensk teaterhistoria 1. Teater före 1800* (Hedemora: Gidlund, 2007), pp. 165–187.

7 Breitholtz, 'Fransk och nationell teater', pp. 946–948, 954–966, 968–972, 978–984.

8 Breitholtz, 'Fransk och nationell teater', p. 986; Marie-Christine Skuncke, 'Gustaviansk teater', in Sven Åke Heed (ed.), *Ny Svensk teaterhistoria 1. Teater före 1800* (Hedemora: Gidlund, 2007); Ingeborg Nordin Hennel and Ulla-Britta Lagerroth, 'Nystart på Arsenalen', in Ulla-Britta Lagerroth and Ingeborg Nordin Hennel (eds.), *Ny Svensk teaterhistoria 2. 1800-talets teater* (Hedemora: Gidlund, 2007), pp. 13–28.

9 Johan Flodmark, *Stenborgska skådebanorna. Bidrag till Stockholms teaterhistoria* (Stockholm: Norstedt, 1893); Breitholtz, 'Fransk och nationell teater', pp. 980–984, 1009–1018; Lennart Hedwall, 'Stenborgs teater och det svenska sångspelet', in Leif Jonsson and Anna Ivarsdotter-Johnson (eds.), *Musiken i Sverige 2. Frihetstiden och gustaviansk tid. 1720–1810* (Stockholm: Fischer, 1993).

10 Dag Nordmark, 'På Djurgårdsteatern', in Ulla-Britta Lagerroth and Ingeborg Nordin Hennel (eds.), *Ny Svensk teaterhistoria 2. 1800-talets teater* (Hedemora: Gidlund, 2007).

11 Arthur Nordén, *Norrköpings äldre teatrar. 1700-talets teatrar* (Norrköping: Norrköpings Tidningar, 1955), pp. 26–58; Viggo Loos, 'Kulturen i Norrköping. 1719-1800-talets mitt', in Björn Helmfrid and Salomon Kraft (eds.), *Norrköpings historia 4* (Norrköping: Norrköpings stad, 1968), pp. 118–120; Dag Nordmark, 'Teater utanför Stockholm', in Sven Åke Heed (ed.), *Ny svensk teaterhistoria 1* (Hedemora: Gidlunds, 2007), pp. 218–234.

12 Nordén, *Norrköpings äldre teatrar*, pp. 64–139; Loos, 'Kulturen i Norrköping', pp. 36, 120–126; Nordmark, 'Teater utanför Stockholm', pp. 224–234.

13 Nordén, *Norrköpings äldre teatrar*, pp. 140–156; Loos, 'Kulturen i Norrköping', p. 224; Nordmark, 'Teater utanför Stockholm', p. 225.

14 Arthur Nordén, *Norrköpings äldre teatrar. Saltängsteatern 1798–1850* (Norrköping: Norrköpings Tidningar, 1957); Loos, 'Kulturen i Norrköping', pp. 126–130; Nordmark, 'Teater utanför Stockholm'. Until the end of the eighteenth century theatre houses were built also in several other Swedish provincial towns like Gothenburg, Karlskrona, Gävle and Udevalla.

15 Lindberg, *Linköpings historia 2*, pp. 535–538, 553–559.

16 Göran Axel-Nilsson, 'Frihetstidens borgarnöjen', in Gösta Berg (ed.), *Det glada Sverige. Våra fester och högtider genom tiderna 2* (Stockholm: Norstedt, 1947), pp. 1090–1092; Leif Jonsson, 'Mellan konsert och sallong', in Leif Jonsson and Anna Ivarsdotter-Johnson (eds.), *Musiken i Sverige 2. Frihetstiden och gustaviansk tid. 1720–1810* (Stockholm: Fischer, 1993), pp. 399–406.

17 Loos, 'Kulturen i Norrköping', pp. 61–70. In the early nineteenth century, musical societies were organised in many Swedish towns, but in many cases they didn't really start to perform public musical concerts until the later nineteenth century. Leif Jonsson and Martin Tegen, 'Musiklivet privat och offentligt', in Leif Jonsson and Martin Tegen (eds.), *Musiken i Sverige 3. Den nationella identiteten. 1810–1920* (Stockholm: Fischer, 1992), pp. 118–123.

18 Sven Hellström (ed.), *Linköpings historia 4. Tiden 1863–1910* (Linköping: Sahlströms, 1978), p. 328.

19 Axel-Nilsson, 'Frihetstidens borgarnöjen', pp. 1084–1090; Olof Ehnmark, 'Bellmanstidens nöjesliv', in Gösta Berg (ed.), *Det glada Sverige. Våra fester och högtider genom tiderna 2* (Stockholm: Norstedt, 1947), pp. 1187–1191; Jonsson, 'Mellan konsert och sallong', p. 404.

20 Loos, 'Kulturen i Norrköping', pp. 34–36, 41.

21 Mats Rehnberg, *Stora krogboken. Bilder ur restauranglivets kulturhistoria* (Stockholm: Wahlström och Widstrand, 1987), pp. 143–188.

22 Lars Levander, *Landsväg, krog och marknad* (Stockholm: Åhlén & Söner, 1935), pp. 100–138; Per Hartmann, *Hotellens kulturhistoria i Västerlandet* (Stockholm: Mimer, 1983), pp. 47–56; Rehnberg, *Stora krogboken*, pp. 129–140.

23 Ehnmark, 'Bellmanstidens nöjesliv', pp. 1138–1146; Rehnberg, *Stora krogboken*, p. 37.

24 Loos, 'Kulturen i Norrköping', p. 36.

25 Thord Lindell, *Hantverk och manufaktur i Linköping* (Linköping: 1940), p. 68; Lindberg *Linköpings historia 2*, pp. 549–552.

160 Processes of selection and adaptation

26 Ehnmark, 'Bellmanstidens nöjesliv', p. 1139; Rehnberg, *Stora krogboken*, p. 109.
27 Dahlberg, 'Hovens och komedianternas teater', p. 163.
28 Ehnmark, 'Bellmanstidens nöjesliv', p. 1139; Rehnberg, *Stora krogboken*, p. 112; Lindberg, *Linköpings historia 2*, p. 552.
29 Rehnberg, *Stora krogboken*, pp. 109–126.
30 Lindberg, *Linköpings historia 2*, pp. 549–552.
31 Hartmann, *Hotellens kulturhistoria i Västerlandet*, pp. 92–104, 156–159, 166–172; Staffan Tjerneld, *Stockholmsliv. Hur vi bott, arbetat och roat oss under 100 år. Första delen. Norr om Strömmen* (Stockholm: Norstedt, 1996), pp. 128–130.
32 Mats Rehnberg, '1700-talet dansar', in Gösta Berg (ed.), *Det glada Sverige. Våra fester och högtider genom tiderna 2* (Stockholm: Norstedt, 1947), pp. 864–867; Tjerneld, *Stockholmsliv*, pp. 115–123: Bertil Asker, *Stockholms tekniska historia 2. Stockholms Parker. Innerstaden* (Stockholm: Liber, 1986), pp. 37–43; Catharina Nolin, *Till stadsbornas nytta och förlustelse. Den offentliga parken i Sverige under 1800-talet* (Stockholm: Byggförlaget, 1999), pp. 36, 62.
33 Breitholtz, 'Fransk och nationell teater', pp. 1008–1016; Asker, *Stockholms tekniska historia 2*, pp. 30–34; Nolin, *Till stadsbornas nytta och förlustelse*, p. 36.
34 Tjerneld, *Stockholmsliv*, p. 432.
35 Nolin, *Till stadsbornas nytta och förlustelse*, p. 39.
36 Rehnberg, *Stora krogboken*, p. 56; Tjerneld, *Stockholmsliv*, pp. 589–619; Wåhlberg, *Cirkus i Sverige*, pp. 25–36; Nolin, *Till stadsbornas nytta och förlustelse*, pp. 37–39.
37 Nolin, *Till stadsbornas nytta och förlustelse*, p. 159.
38 Nolin, *Till stadsbornas nytta och förlustelse*, pp. 137–144.
39 Catharina Nolin, 'Svenska trädgårdsföreningen, 1832–1911', *Bebyggelsehistorisk tidskrift*, 31:2 (1996), 149–162.
40 Arvid Kugelberg, *Gamla Linköpingsgårdar 2* (Linköping: Östgöta Correspondenten, 1949), pp. 119–122; Inga Wallenquist, *Trädgårdar i Östergötland. En skön historia* (Linköping: Östergötlands länsmuseums förlag, 2004), pp. 127–129.
41 Kugelberg, *Gamla Linköpingsgårdar 2*, pp. 196–206; Ove Hassler, *Det legendariska Linköping. Bonn på Druvan och andra Linköpingsporträtt* (Linköping: Östgöta Correspondenten, 1977), pp. 7–35.
42 Inga Wallenquist, *En park i staden. 150 år med Linköpings Trädgårdsförenings Park* (Linköping: Linköpings kommuns förlag, 2009), pp. 37–41.
43 Nolin, *Till stadsbornas nytta och förlustelse*, pp. 41–47.
44 Wallenquist, *En park i staden*, pp. 44–49.
45 Nordén *Norrköpings äldre teatrar. Saltängsteatern 1798–1850*; Loos, 'Kulturen i Norrköping', pp. 38–40.
46 Loos, 'Kulturen i Norrköping', p. 42; Viggo Loos, 'Kulturen i Norrköping från 1800-talets mitt till 1914', in Björn Helmfrid and Salomon Kraft (eds.), *Norrköpings historia 5. Tiden 1870–1914* (Norrköping: Norrköpings stad, 1972), p. 44.
47 Nolin, *Till stadsbornas nytta och förlustelse*, pp. 153–159.

8

Coffeehouses: leisure and sociability in Ottoman Istanbul

CENGIZ KIRLI

When coffee was first introduced in the Middle East is unclear. Although the earliest mention of coffee goes back to the sixteenth century, it is usually believed that it was already known as a beverage in the mid-fifteenth century.[1] There is, however, a general agreement in all the legends and stories regarding the origins of coffee drinking in the Islamic lands that the use of coffee began in Yemen, and that its original use is connected to Sufi orders, the adherents of an inner, mystical dimension of Islam.[2] The members of these heterodox Muslim confraternities consumed coffee during their communal worship, usually held at night. Anything that would create mental excitement and keep them awake was seen as an aid to devotion, and due to coffee's physiological properties, it was quickly adopted as the appropriate drink.[3] Its non-alcoholic character seemed to be tailor-made for a culture that prohibited alcoholic consumption.

Much of what we know about the introduction of coffee and coffeehouses to Istanbul, the capital of the Ottoman Empire, has come down to us through seventeenth-century authors. According to Peçevi, an early seventeenth-century Ottoman chronicler, coffee and coffeehouses were introduced to the Ottoman capital in 1554 by two men, Hakam from Aleppo and Shams from Damascus, each of whom opened a coffeehouse in the Tahtakale district of Istanbul.[4]

Coffee and coffeehouses enjoyed phenomenal success immediately after their introduction in Istanbul and the rest of the empire. Contemporary chronicles suggest that until the end of the sixteenth century around 50 coffeehouses were opened in Istanbul, and their number dramatically increased in subsequent years. By the first half of the seventeenth century there were approximately 600 coffeehouses in Istanbul.[5] The figures given here, however conceivable they may have been, are impressionistic rather than based on reliable statistics. The first and only reliable official figures for the number of coffeehouses in Istanbul can be derived from a survey on shops and the overall workforce conducted in the 1790s. According to the survey, 1,654 coffeehouses filled the narrow streets of Istanbul, approximately one in every eight shops, and three times as many as grocery stores in a city with perhaps 300,000–400,000 inhabitants. As many European travellers who passed through the capital observed with astonishment, Istanbul looked like a 'big coffeehouse'.[6] If one also takes into consideration 1,046 barber shops – the next most frequent workplaces that functioned, hairdressing apart, very much like coffeehouses as places for intimate sociability – that impression appears to be more than accurate. In the 1840s there were as many as 2,500 coffeehouses in Istanbul. Other major urban centres of the empire such as Cairo, Aleppo and Damascus probably experienced similar levels of density in coffeehouse businesses.[7]

In Istanbul from the sixteenth until the nineteenth century, Ottoman coffeehouses fulfilled a broad range of social, cultural, economic and political functions. What were their main characteristics and how did these differ from coffeehouses in West and Central Europe, which clearly built on the Ottoman example but developed themselves in different ways? And, how did European leisure culture enter the Ottoman coffeehouse in its turn?

Coffeehouses in Europe and the Ottoman Empire: a diverging tradition?

Coffee and coffeehouses did not have a foothold in Europe until the second half of the seventeenth century, although Europeans, as is evident in travel accounts and medical treatises, had certainly been aware of this hot and exotic drink with a bitter taste, the rituals that surround it and the coffeehouses where it was primarily consumed since at least the late sixteenth century. Italian merchants introduced coffee beans to southern Europe in the early seventeenth century, but those who played the leading role in spreading coffee and coffeehouses to Western Europe were the Greeks and Armenians, who were presumably former Ottoman subjects living in Ottoman lands and intimately familiar with the success story of coffee and the coffeehouses there. The first coffeehouse was opened in Oxford in 1650 and two years later in London by a Greek servant to a Levant company merchant.[8] In the 1660s, the first coffeehouses appeared in Amsterdam, and Armenians received licences to open coffeehouses in Paris in the 1670s and in Vienna in the 1680s.

By the early eighteenth century, coffee was known everywhere and there was hardly any big town across Europe without at least one coffeehouse.

Major European capitals abounded with them. Struggling in the early decades following their introduction, London coffeehouses were ubiquitous by the eighteenth century. By 1734, 551 licensed coffeehouses in addition to a significant number of unlicensed ones had carved out an alternative place of public sociability in London, even though their numbers were far from overthrowing the dominance of alehouses and taverns. Cafés in Paris, however, seemed to have enjoyed an even more extraordinary success than their counterparts in London. Paris had approximately 3,000 cafés in 1789, which soared to 4,500 by the middle of the nineteenth century, to 22,000 in 1870 and 30,000 in the late 1890s, although by the second half of the century many of such cafés were no longer primarily focused on coffee.[9] By the nineteenth century, coffee had established itself as the most prominent drink, dwarfing its past and recent rivals such as chocolate and tea, respectively, and the coffeehouse as the most ubiquitous place of sociability in large parts of Europe and the Middle East.

How did coffee achieve this astonishing success in Europe? This is, in fact, part of a larger question of the diffusion and assimilation of foreign exotic 'soft drugs' such as tobacco, chocolate and tea in the early modern world in the age of early globalisation. It is impossible to systematically chart here the diffusion and the reasons for appropriation of coffee in Europe, much less for other substances, although the vast literature that exists has immensely contributed to a better understanding of the intricacies of cultural transfer in the early modern world. Historians have now largely moved away from the biological essentialism that emphasises the tastiness of chocolate, addictiveness of tobacco and the medicinal properties of coffee or the economic determinism that highlights increasing commercialisation in the age of mercantilism as the primary cause for the diffusion and appropriation of these substances, toward cultural functionalism that gives primacy to the social context in which they were appropriated by local cultures.[10]

The triumph of coffee and coffeehouses was not achieved easily. It took almost a century for the European lower classes to acquire the taste of the bitter drink and to accept the coffeehouse as an important centre of urban sociability. Europe imported the drink and its institution with the full knowledge of their 'Turkish' origin and without any attempt to disassociate the cultural meanings that surrounded its consumption, and precisely because of this, coffee deserves a different treatment from other 'soft drugs'. Unlike these exotic colonial products, it was a cultural import from the Ottoman Empire.

Scholarly views vary on the question of whether the 'Turkish' imprint on coffee and coffeehouses supported or impeded their reception in Europe.

164 Processes of selection and adaptation

Writing on English coffeehouses, Brian Cowan, for example, argues that the success of coffee and coffeehouses in England is all the more astounding because it happened despite the negative image associated with the Turks and their customs. Arguing that the Ottoman Empire was viewed by contemporary Europeans as the embodiment of the antichrist, projecting repugnance, fear and despotism, he places his entire emphasis, along the lines of cultural functionalism, on what he calls the 'virtuosi' (those among the elite in post-Restoration England interested in fashionable culture), the subjective motivations of British consumers towards 'limitless curiosity' and the changing conceptions of erudition and sociability.[11] Other scholars, however, take the opposite tack and argue that the success of coffee and coffeehouses in Europe was achieved not despite but because of the Ottoman imprint on them. Calling the period 1650–1750 the golden age of turquerie, 'the pan-European interest in and the emulation of Ottoman culture',[12] Bevilacqua and Pfeifer list an impressive array of Ottoman cultural practices and institutions, from coffee drinking to music, from dress and decoration to plays and novels that were enthusiastically appropriated by Europeans.[13] This was a period that was marked by increasing trade and intensified diplomatic contact between Ottomans and Europeans that caused more Europeans to live in the Ottoman lands, making them the agents of an intense cultural transfer between the two. This was also a period in which European anxiety and fear towards the Ottoman Empire was waning due to the increasing wealth and self-confidence of Europeans and the declining fortunes and military prowess of the Ottomans. However exotic the European representation of foreign substances, artefacts and cultural practices, including those of the Ottomans, may have been, the Ottoman Empire was neither the colonial Americas nor China. The Ottomans were familiar strangers, a liminal oddity in the collective psyche of Europeans, which they knew intimately and much earlier than any other foreign culture. In European minds, then, the Ottomans were tamed, largely, if not entirely domesticised in the seventeenth and eighteenth centuries, which paved the way for appreciating and admiring a foreign yet familiar civilisation and its customs. The intensified contact and cultural transfer cut both ways. As Bevilacqua and Pfeifer pointedly argued, the European influence on the Ottoman Empire in the eighteenth century from courtly etiquette to printing and architecture was not merely Westernisation of the empire, but 'an expression of pan-European elite culture' that manifested itself in new forms of consumption and sociability in which coffee and coffeehouses takes the centre stage.[14]

As happens to all cultural practices and institutions on the move, coffee and coffeehouses were given distinct identities whenever they were appropriated by local cultures. European coffeehouses were not carbon copies of their Ottoman counterparts; they were different and diverse from their internal decoration and seating arrangements to their menus they served to their customers. Coffee and tobacco were common to all, but Ottoman coffeehouses never served meals or alcoholic drinks as English and French coffeehouses did. A more important difference was the absence of women in Ottoman coffeehouses; not even prostitutes looking for customers were allowed. Coffeehouses have always remained an exclusively adult male gathering place, from the owner to the servants to the customers. Coffeehouse clientele avoided mingling sexes and ages, turning the coffeehouse into a male- and adult-dominated refuge. It was a space imbued with male values, reinforcing the idea of manhood in the spirit of male sociability. When a young man gazed through the window of a coffeehouse, he was an aspiring to adulthood, and his admission to the institution was a communally recognised transition to adult life. This does not necessarily mean that the English and French coffeehouses were public places where women were active participants. They were just as masculine spaces in many respects as Ottoman coffeehouses, with political conversations and business transactions that were considered to be manly activities. Women were usually banished behind the counters serving food and drinks in the eighteenth century. However, in the absence of written or unwritten rules that prohibited women's entry into coffeehouses, some women occasionally went to coffeehouses even though they ran the risk of being asked to leave by male customers. But women's participation in coffeehouse life dramatically improved in the nineteenth century as more women became coffeehouse proprietors and then customers, a change that did not occur in Ottoman coffeehouses until the arrival of cafés in the twentieth century.[15]

Despite these striking differences, Ottoman and European coffeehouses were similar in several respects, two of which are worth mentioning at this stage. The first one was the class composition of early coffeehouse clientele and its change in the following century. The early coffeehouse clientele both in the Ottoman Empire and in Europe were men of the upper classes. Eager to experiment with new forms of taste, erudition and sociability, as Peçevi noted, the Ottoman 'gentlemen of leisure, wits and literary men seeking distraction and amusement' went to coffeehouses where 'some would read books, some play chess or backgammon, and some poets read their poems to their companions'.[16] The class structure of coffeehouse frequenters and their intellectual exchange followed the same pattern in early European coffeehouses in the second half of the seventeenth century.

Figure 8.1 Interior of a large coffeehouse at the square of Tophane at the end of the eighteenth century. Antoine Ignace Melling, *Voyage pittoresque de Constantinople et des rives du Bosphore*, Paris 1819.

The second common feature was the hostile reception of coffeehouses by the authorities. No sooner did coffee and coffeehouses appear in Istanbul than religious and political controversy surrounded them, which culminated in the closing of all coffeehouses in Istanbul in 1568, followed by further clampdowns in the late sixteenth and the seventeenth centuries. The close association of coffee with the Sufi orders provided the ground for an unfavourable attitude towards coffee until the end of the sixteenth century, and 'vice', 'vigilance' and 'debauchery' were the terms associated with coffeehouses. In addition, there were attempts to introduce high taxes on coffee to prevent coffee drinking and to drive coffeehouses out of business. However, this was to no avail, as the following writ of the finance minister to the Sultan in 1697 illustrates:

> Although all coffeehouses are currently closed, the people from high to vile are so addicted [to this drink] that they settle for dry bread once a day, but are not satisfied without drinking a few cups of coffee every day; so much so that even if the tax levied on coffee was a gold *lira*, nobody would mind.[17]

Similarly, Charles II's attempt to suppress coffeehouses in England was abandoned on the advice of the secretary of state who argued for the importance of excise duties on coffee.[18] The political will to suppress the new sociability formed around the coffeehouse was there, but no cash-strapped polity suffering from the financial crisis of the long seventeenth century could afford to ignore the benefits of taxing the most important drink of the new consumer revolution.

What made coffeehouses the target of governmental attention and a subject of official suppression that continued well into the eighteenth century were several interrelated factors, which included financial crises coupled with population growth, uncontrolled migration into cities that manifested itself in increased social fluidity and the gradual disintegration of existing hierarchical structures, and urban unrest mobilised around new forms of sociability. In Ottoman political discourse, as in Europe, the coffeehouse came to be a metaphor for urban disorder, the culprit of society's problems, 'a house of evil acts', mobilising malcontents and representing social breakdown, where 'villains assemble and indulge in debauchery and perdition'.[19]

But most importantly, rumour – and especially political rumour, which was perceived to be a tool for stimulating political malcontent – was seen by the authorities as more alarming than anything else. Popular political discourse or, as the authorities called it in Ottoman parlance, '*devlet sohbeti*', stood out as the prime reason in the justifications for suppressing coffeehouses. While its ambiguous and anonymous characteristics made it a powerful agent in the web of social communication, its capacity to mobilise dissent also made it an object for the state to control and suppress.[20] In the eyes of the state, its uncontrollable nature made it a formidable threat against the social order both in the Ottoman Empire and in Europe. To justify the suppression of coffeehouses in the 1660s, the Earl of Clarendon said that coffeehouses allowed 'the foulest imputations [to be] laid upon the government', and that 'people generally believed that those houses had a charter of privilege to speak what they would, without being in danger to be called into question'.[21] Similarly, in France the secretary of state wrote to the chief of the Paris police in 1685:

> The King has been informed that, in several places in Paris where coffee is served, there are assemblies of all sorts of people, and especially foreigners. Upon which His Majesty ordered me to ask whether you do not think it would be appropriate to prevent them from assembling in the future.[22]

In the wake of the continuous anti-coffeehouse discourse of the Ottoman ruling elite the social status of the coffeehouse significantly decreased as 'men of manners', who at earlier times constituted an important segment of the coffeehouse clientele, retreated from it.[23] Increasingly in the late seventeenth, and

168 Processes of selection and adaptation

entirely in the eighteenth century, the coffeehouse clientele was dominated by the lower orders and the coffeehouse was turned into a place where 'a crowd of good-for-nothings was forever meeting'.[24] Put differently, the real decline in coffeehouses' social status happened in the eighteenth century as their political significance increased.

Patrons and clients

Who, then, were the proprietors and patrons of coffeehouses that the Ottoman ruling elite so despised? Most of the 1,654 coffeehouses that existed in the capital of the Ottoman Empire at the end of the eighteenth century were small-scale enterprises. While 53 per cent of them were run only by one person, 41 per cent were operated by two people. There was hardly any neighbourhood in Istanbul without at least one coffeehouse and usually they had more than one. Coffeehouses run by three and more people were exceptional and almost always located at the centre of the town where passers-by would stop to have a cup of coffee.

As for the owners, coffeehouses were predominantly Muslim establishments: 95 per cent of coffeehouse owners were Muslim, while only 2 per cent were Greek, 2.5 per cent Armenian and less than 1 per cent Jewish.[25] In a city where Muslims constituted barely half of the population at the end of the eighteenth century, the near monopoly of Muslims in coffeehouse businesses is striking.[26] More importantly about 42 per cent of these Muslim coffeehouse owners were members of the Janissary corps. Once the elite troops of the sultan, they eventually turned into rebels as from the late sixteenth century their salaries declined due to financial crises and high inflation, added to which there was less war booty available as military defeats were becoming more commonplace.[27] This was the time when the corps was increasingly engaged in mercantile activities and especially in coffeehouse business. The overwhelming presence of janissaries in coffeehouse business is worth emphasising because, from the seventeenth century onwards, virtually every insurrection in Istanbul was led by the janissaries – half of the sultans, including the executions of two of them, between the seventeenth and the early nineteenth centuries were deposed by janissary-led urban crowds, often using coffeehouses as headquarters during times of uprisings. The janissary revolt of Patrona Halil in 1730, for example, which resulted in the dethronement of Ahmet III (ruled 1703–1730), was sparked off in the coffeehouse of one of the rebel leaders.[28] Similarly, Mustafa Ağa, a prominent leader of the Kabakçı Mustafa revolt in 1807, which forced

Selim III (ruled 1789–1807) to abdicate, was running a coffeehouse in the Atpazarı district of Istanbul. Already notorious, coffeehouses in early modern Istanbul had become even more suspect in the eyes of the authorities with the large presence of janissaries in them who had made and unmade sultans with their power to mobilise the urban crowd.

The janissary presence in coffeehouses was so prevalent that when Sultan Mahmud II (ruled 1808–1839) abolished the corps and massacred thousands of janissaries in 1826, all coffeehouses in Istanbul and elsewhere were closed down, the first wholesale closing in nearly two centuries, as a measure to prevent the sheltering of the remnants of janissaries. Those who managed to survive the massacre disguised their identity, but still many of them could easily be spotted due to the official emblem of their mess that was carved out on the walls of their coffeehouses. Weeks after the massacre, for example, in the town of Izmit adjacent to Istanbul, Sofuoğlu Mehmet, a former janissary who was running a coffeehouse in the neighbourhood of Gazi Baba, could not escape being executed, apparently because he did not do a good job of hiding the axe, the emblem of his forty-sixth mess, with lime mortar.[29]

Commenting on the coffeehouse clientele in Istanbul, Thévenot, a seventeenth-century French traveller, said 'all Men are free to go to these Houses, without any distinction of Religion or Quality'.[30] Why men went to coffeehouses, who went and who conversed with whom are not simple questions to answer. Yet they are crucial in determining the extent and the limits of coffeehouse sociability and in understanding the functioning of Ottoman society in general, for coffeehouses were the most appropriate sites to observe the spirit of sociability among the Istanbul populace.

The evidence from the mid-nineteenth century, which was no doubt true for the early modern period as well, confirms Thévenot's observation about confessional heterogeneity of the coffeehouse clientele.[31] Muslims went to coffeehouses more often than other religious groups, largely because taverns, the rival institution of sociability, served alcoholic drinks and were legally available only to non-Muslims. Although the ban on consumption of alcohol by Muslims was frequently violated, coffeehouses obviously catered to larger segments of the Muslim population who shied away from taverns for religious or legal reasons. Yet non-Muslims were frequently part of coffeehouse sociability in the company of Muslims.

As for the occupational profile of coffeehouse frequenters, the most numerous groups consisted of artisans and shopkeepers. They went to coffeehouses not only for pleasure or sociability, but for business purposes as well. Some coffeehouses located at the centre of Istanbul were frequented almost exclusively by people from different trades and professions as well as people seeking jobs.[32] Parallel to the guilds, in which different commercial activities were carried out in different organisations, certain coffeehouses evolved into meeting places for people from the same occupations. In other words, people from different professions went to different coffeehouses and in most cases such coffeehouses functioned like professional clubs.[33]

The second most numerous group were merchants. Most of them were foreigners from various countries such as England, Russia, France, Venice, Genoa and Tuscany. We frequently find them in coffeehouses in Galata, the most important port of the city, conversing about prices, custom duties and the political situation in the Mediterranean. They were usually in the company of Muslim and non-Muslim local partners, money-lenders and brokers of Ottoman subjects, conversing with clerks and messengers of European embassies in Istanbul, and exchanging information about the latest economic and political situation in their home countries and the Ottoman Empire. Most of the inns where transients and recent migrants stayed housed a coffeehouse that provided not only accommodation for their customers but also a coffeehouse where tradesmen from the provinces would spend considerable time and meet with their fellow tradesmen to strike deals and exchange information. They also met with their fellow townsmen residing in Istanbul to provide news about their towns to the latter who usually kept their ties with their hometowns through these transient merchants.

After merchants, civil servants formed the next largest category of coffeehouse-goers. They consisted largely of clerks and government officers of low to middle range who went to coffeehouses often. Members of the higher level bureaucracy and military shied away from sipping their coffee in coffeehouses, whose notoriety in the eyes of the urban elites never relented, so that such groups hardly ever dared to go to these disreputable places. Yet, in rendering coffeehouse-going dishonourable, wealth did not necessarily translate into status. The presence of brokers, middlemen and money-lenders, who must have had considerable wealth, as well as of some provincial notables and tax-collectors who had a recognised status among the inhabitants of the provinces they served, is illustrative of this point. Put differently, however disreputable the coffeehouse may have been in the eyes of prestigious urban elites, it seems to have been a usual practice for wealthier segments of the population, who had accrued their riches not through government service but through commercial means, to frequent them.

Among coffeehouse clientele we also find such religious figures as prayer heads (*imam*) and callers for prayer (*müezzin*). Not only did they go, a number of them also owned coffeehouses. Charles MacFarlane, an English traveller, expressed his astonishment when he witnessed religious figures visiting coffeehouses and smoking a water pipe there.[34] He was surprised, no doubt, to observe a member of the *ulema*, who was supposed to set an example to the Muslim community, engaging in such a disreputable act as going to the coffeehouse. The best place in the coffeehouse would be reserved for the *imam* of the neighbourhood mosque and, upon his arrival coffeehouse clientele would ask him questions about religious matters.[35] Their presence in the coffeehouse was probably not limited to religious matters. As respected members of the community, they would wield their authority on social and political matters concerning their community in an everyday and profane environment, which would render the message more effectively than the consecrated atmosphere of the mosque.[36] When the headman of the neighbourhood (*muhtar*), who also frequented coffeehouses, is added to this equation, we can imagine how a coffeehouse could become a neighbourhood assembly and how a mundane conversation could quickly turn into a social forum.

What both early European travellers such as Thevénot and later ones such as Nerval observed with a certain astonishment, regarding the heterogeneity of coffeehouse clientele in terms of socio-professional and confessional distinctions, is to a large extent supported by Ottoman evidence. Doubtlessly, such surprise ensued from the stricter gap between public sites of upper-class sociability, such as salons, and public places of lower-class sociability, such as pubs. Although coffeehouses, with their heterogeneous clientele, appeared to the European gaze as places where social distinctions would collapse, it would be mistaken to assume that existing differences dissolved once people of varying classes stepped into the same coffeehouse.

Sociability and politics

Coffeehouses in Istanbul were places where Istanbul men met, exchanged information, played games, smoked tobacco, told stories[37] and conversed outside the home, fashioning a semi-private spirit in this public setting. Sometimes a temporary home of new migrants or displaced people, it was also a second home for the city's indigenous population, so much so that men did not hesitate to make their nightly visit in their pyjamas.[38] When the chief of a janissary

172 Processes of selection and adaptation

regiment sent a messenger to summon a certain Emin Ağa to his office in 1812, the first place that the messenger looked to find him was not his house but the coffeehouse in his neighbourhood.[39]

The coffeehouse was indeed an extension of home, the street and the market, resisting the easy and convenient distinction between the 'public' and the 'private' that has proved a pivotal ingredient of the debate on the emergence of the public sphere in early modern Europe.[40] The primary characteristic of coffeehouse life was intimacy, not anonymity, where every patron in all likelihood knew the others and was almost always aware of the presence of outsiders. In February 1813, when a high state official, dressed as a poor dervish to disguise his identity, walked into a coffeehouse in Istanbul in the hope of prying into subversive political conversation, the customers immediately sensed his intention. Although they did not know who he was, they turned the conversation into a forum to voice their expectations and sufferings to imperial ears, lacing the content with praise and prayer for the sultan.[41]

This 'second home' around the corner was also a setting for various theatrical performances in Ottoman Istanbul. The development and spread of these forms of theatre coincided in time with the introduction and spread of coffeehouses.[42] Especially during Ramadan, the month when Muslims fast from dawn to sunset, coffeehouses were crowded in evening hours, and all sorts of entertainment flourished. Among these theatrical performances, shadow theatre (*Karagöz*) is particularly important in understanding the social atmosphere prevailing in coffeehouses.

In shadow theatre, a single puppeteer provides the dialogue and speaks – using a distinctive form of delivery – for the characters behind the screen. There is no fixed text or script. The plays are essentially the same but precisely because of the fact that the puppeteer, by and large, improvises the dialogue according to the mood of the audience, the performance of a play one night is not the same as that of the very same play on another. In other words, the scripts of *Karagöz* plays are socially derived texts, representing a common experience shared by the puppeteer as the actor and the coffeehouse customers as the audience. Since the script is multi-vocal and socially derived, there is no real distinction between the puppeteer and the spectators. The curtain separating the puppeteer and the audience remains symbolic. Everybody is a participant, and the puppets are the medium through which experience of real social life was dramatised and expressed.

Much of the play consists of the conversation, which is based on speech play, between the two main characters, Karagöz and Hacivat. Hacivat is a respected

Figure 8.2 Karagöz (right) and Hacivat (left).

man of the neighbourhood. He is articulate, educated, cultured, mannered and compromising, yet selfish, insidious and insincere. He expresses himself in a polished Ottoman language, with plenty of Arabic and Persian words. Karagöz, on the other hand, is ignorant, uneducated, rude, coarse, naïve, simple, sincere and immoral. He is also greedy, liar, subversive and incurably unsuccessful. From the depiction of the two main characters, it is obvious to everyone that Hacivat symbolises Ottoman high culture, a man of the ruling class. Karagöz, on the other hand, represents Ottoman commoners. The dialogue, which consists exclusively of quarrelling and argument between Karagöz and Hacivat, is therefore the imaginary and staged confrontation between the ruling class and the people.

It is impossible to detach the content of shadow theatre from politics.[43] European travellers who attended several performances often point to the criticism directed at high-level bureaucrats, the grand vizier and even the sultan.[44] The critical-political aspect of shadow theatre, however, cannot be reduced simply to overt political satire. Even when there is no political theme or figure, the performance has a covert political content in the sense of its subversive character, expressing itself symbolically in the deliberate violation of officially held cultural norms, values and linguistic codes through double entendre, puns and wordplay.

With the elements of laughter, irony, humour and satire and their manifestation in popular festive forms, where a utopian dream of community, freedom and equality was manifested and hierarchical relations temporarily suspended and norms and prohibitions were transgressed, *Karagöz* plays were truly carnivalesque performances.[45] In the atmosphere of the informally organised social life of the coffeehouse, shadow theatre produced an avenue through which the populace conveyed their everyday experiences, challenged official normative codes, subverted meanings, and safely voiced the unspoken. Sometimes overtly, but mostly in a hidden and disguised fashion, shadow theatre envisioned the triumph of the simple, the modest and the ignorant. The humpback, fool hero of the performance, Karagöz, was the embodiment of popular fervour that was directed against Hacivat, the dominant, the insidious and the mannered; that is, the embodiment of the elite culture of the state. In other words, the whole performance was not merely a theatrical spectacle but rather a dramatisation of social life. To the extent that the script was derived from the everyday experiences of the audience, the play produced an alternative reality that was shaped according the desires of the populace in which Karagöz beats and trashes Hacivat every night.

Coffeehouses were the centres of commerce where merchants struck deals, ship-captains arranged their next load and brokers looked for potential customers. Practitioners of different professions and trade frequented particular coffeehouses in which employers found new labourers, and labourers found new employers. They were the nodal points of migration networks where new immigrants found temporary and even sometimes permanent shelter, and established contacts in setting up a new life in Istanbul. Coffeehouses were also the centres of political opposition, in the form of violent janissary rebellions or of subversive shadow theatre. Above all, they were the primary place where people gathered to talk; that is to exchange news, information and opinions. The well-known couplet captures the heart of coffeehouse going: 'The hearth desires neither coffee nor coffeehouse/The hearth desires conversation, coffee is an excuse.'

Coffeehouses: leisure and sociability in Ottoman Istanbul   **175**

The coffeehouse was at the centre of this dense oral information network. Displaying unending appetite, the people were curious about everything, but particularly about affairs of state. Officially they had no voice in the business of government, and in fact they were not even permitted to talk about it. However, this did not prevent them from offering opinions about the conduct of the government. Despite this the state did not openly suppress coffeehouses in the nineteenth century to prevent insolent talk as it previously had, but continued to monitor them very closely, as evidenced by several hundred spy reports in the archives of the 1840s, signifying that the notoriety of coffeehouses remained a fixture of Ottoman polity.[46]

'Europe' in the Istanbul coffeehouse

Stationed in coffeehouses and other public places, informers listened intently to people's mundane conversations carried out in a dozen languages – Turkish, Greek, Armenian, Arabic, Rumanian, Bulgarian, Russian, Italian, English, French, Serbian and Persian – and submitted them to the authorities as the manifestations of public opinion. Reading these spy reports with their impressive array of topics is similar to perusing a newspaper published at the time. In addition to conversations on the new tax system, corruption of high officials, rebellions in the Balkans and North Africa, or rising prices – the kinds of topics that had an immediate and profound effect on the wellbeing of the general population – the spy reports contain coffeehouse conversations that reveal a surprisingly impressive interest in political developments in Europe. In the absence of newspapers, except for *Takvim-i Vekayi*, the official newspaper, or a widely literate public, most of the information about Europe was gathered from clerks and translators working in various European embassies, from sailors who recently arrived from European ports, or from Europeans living in Istanbul, and every single piece of news was hastily disseminated in the various coffeehouses. While the political developments among the European Great Powers, such as pro-republic rebellions against the King Louis-Philippe I in France, the Chartist movement in England or the assassination attempts on the French king or the Russian czar, Nikola I, were discussed at length, even events that took place in countries less consequential to Ottoman international politics – such as revolutionary insurgency against Queen Maria II in Portugal or the rebellions against the rule of Espartero in Spain – were subjects of conversation in the Istanbul coffeehouses. The official visits of European kings

176 Processes of selection and adaptation

and princes to other countries were carefully observed with an eye to their possible effects in shaping international politics. The Opium War between Britain and China that was taking place far away from the Ottomans was followed as eagerly as the invasion of Algeria by France.[47]

Ottoman coffeehouses present one of the most powerful images on the cartography of the European imagination regarding 'the Orient'. Almost every European traveller's account of Istanbul includes a vivid description of coffeehouses and their clientele. After reading one of these accounts, the reader is left with images of despairing 'Orientals' smoking their tobacco and sitting idly in a gloomy coffeehouse trapped in one of the unending narrow streets of Istanbul, invoking the picture of the temple of the numbed, neither alive nor yet dead 'Orientals' waiting for the almost stagnant time of 'the Orient' to pass. These spy reports and the conversations therein are a powerful reminder that, far from being inhibitors of change, coffeehouses were located at the centre of a dense international network of information, and were the agents of cultural exchange. It was this international and intercultural context that bred coffeehouse life as much as local social and political change. And it was in the coffeehouse, more than anywhere else, that the pervasive experience of modernity in the nineteenth century was negotiated, interpreted and contested.

Monitored and chastised by the authorities, and frowned upon by European travellers, Ottoman coffeehouses did not find any more appreciation among Ottoman intellectuals in the nineteenth century. Ebuziyya Tevfik, the publisher and a contributor to the magazine *Mecmua-i Ebuziyya*, compared Istanbul coffeehouses with London coffeehouses in the following way:

> London coffeehouses were meeting places of cultured and enlightened people, whereas Istanbul coffeehouses were the seat of the ignorant and evil. While the former contributed to the progress of their country through the intellect of their frequenters, the latter were the means to carry out the evil intentions of some malicious people to endanger the safety of the country by disturbing the order of society.[48]

Writing in 1914, Ebuziyya Tevfik was stating the prevalent view of middle-class Ottoman intellectuals on neighbourhood coffeehouses. Similarly, Mehmet Akif (Ersoy), the renowned poet of the Turkish national anthem, expressed his views about neighbourhood coffeehouses in the following verse: 'The murderer of the Orient is the neighbourhood coffeehouse/it is exactly the equivalent of those old gambling dens.' The coffeehouse in Berlin,

Coffeehouses: leisure and sociability in Ottoman Istanbul **177**

however, inspired him to write: 'This coffeehouse ... Is it like that? But, it is really great!/Space within space ... A source of light.'[49]

Caught between the condescension of imposed Westernisation and the humiliation of internalised Orientalism, middle-class Ottoman intellectuals were, in fact, crying for the reform of popular culture embodied in coffee-houses. The 'literary coffeehouse' (*kıraathane*), the first of which was opened in 1861 in Istanbul, was a mix of the European café, a literary salon and a men's social club.[50] It was an attempt on the part of Ottoman intellectuals to provide an alternative institution to neighbourhood coffeehouses, one that would reform, educate and rescue the frequenters of the latter through a stock of around 40 newspapers published in major European languages.[51] The Ottoman coffeehouse that was exported to Europe two centuries ago was now imported back in a completely new form and without a local content, and thus never became an integral part of urban fabric and an alternative place of public sociability, except for a tiny group of intellectuals. As the number of traditional neighbourhood coffeehouses flourished as a result of migration and population increase, there were only a handful of literary coffeehouses at the end of the century.

The profound ambivalence towards the coffeehouse hardly ever faded throughout its long existence in the Ottoman society. It was a place of igno-rance and idleness for intellectuals, a site of subversion and debauchery for the state, and the source of the powerful conviction that it was the culprit responsible for society's problems, whatever those problems may be: sometimes defined as social chaos, and sometimes as underdevelopment. Yet, it was also a space always crowded by ordinary men. The coffeehouse's openness to news and ideas from all over Europe provided the customers with the intellectual material with which to critique Ottoman politics. Throughout its long history the coffeehouse remained a strong metaphor for the encounter between elite culture and popular culture. Behind these contradictory attitudes and deep ambivalence lay the long history of the coffeehouse where state and society encountered, contested, negotiated and in the historical process shaped and transformed each other. 'In large part,' as Stallybrass and White have argued, 'the history of political struggle has been the history of the attempts to control significant sites of assembly and spaces of discourse.'[52] In other words, in the long history of coffeehouses lay the history of power and resistance. The con-tinuous attempt on the part of the state to control this most important space of popular political discourse was met with evasion, subversion, and resistance by the populace.

Notes

1 Ralph S. Hattox, *Coffee and Coffeehouses: The Origins of a Social Beverage in the Medieval Near East* (Seattle: University of Washington Press, 1985), pp. 18–19.

2 There are also assumptions that attribute the origins of coffee to Ethiopia around the tenth and eleventh centuries. It was then introduced to Southwestern Arabia in the thirteenth and fourteenth centuries where its cultivation spread and the preparation of a hot beverage with roasted seeds began. See Massimo Montanari, *The Culture of Food* (Cambridge: Blackwell, 1994), p. 124; Rudi Matthee, 'Exotic substances: the introduction and global spread of tobacco, coffee, cocoa, tea, and distilled liquor, sixteenth to eighteenth centuries', in Roy Porter and Mikulas Teich (eds.), *Drugs and Narcotics in History* (Cambridge: Cambridge University Press, 1995), p. 27.

3 Ayşe Saraçgil, 'L'opposition au café dans l'Empire ottoman', in Hélène Desmet-Grégoire and François Georgeon (eds.), *Cafés d'Orient revisités* (Paris: CNRS Ethnologie, 1997), pp. 29–30.

4 İbrahim Peçevi, *Tarih-i Peçevi*, Vol. 1 (Istanbul: Matbaa-ı Amire, 1866), p. 363.

5 Mouradgea d'Ohsson, *Tableau général de l'empire ottoman*, Vol. 4 (Paris, 1788), p. 76.

6 François Georgeon, 'Les cafés à İstanbul à la fin de l'Empire ottoman', in Desmet-Grégoire and Georgeon (eds.), *Cafés d'Orient revisités*, pp. 39–78.

7 Alan Mikhail, 'The heart's desire: gender, urban space and the Ottoman coffee house', in Dana Sajdi (ed.), *Ottoman Tulips, Ottoman Coffee: Leisure and Lifestyle in the Eighteenth Century* (London and New York: Tauris Academic Studies, 2007), pp. 133–170; Dana Sajdi, *The Barber of Damascus: Nouveau Literacy in the Eighteenth-Century Ottoman Levant* (Stanford: Stanford University Press, 2013).

8 Brian Cowan, *The Social Life of Coffee: The Emergence of the British Coffeehouse* (New Haven: Yale University Press, 2005), p. 94.

9 W. Scott Haine, *The World of the Paris Café: Sociability among the French Working Class, 1789–1914* (Baltimore: Johns Hopkins University Press, 1996), pp. 3–4.

10 The literature is too exhaustive to list here. Some prominent examples are Wolfgang Schivelbusch, *Tastes of Paradise: A Social History of Spices, Stimulants, and Intoxicants* (New York: Pantheon Books, 1992); Marcy Norton, *Sacred Gifts, Profane Pleasures: A History of Tobacco and Chocolate in the Atlantic World* (Ithaca: Cornell University Press, 2008); Jordan Goodman, Paul E. Lovejoy and Andrew Sherratt (eds.), *Consuming Habits: Drugs in History and Anthropology* (London and New York: Routledge, 1995).

11 Cowan, *The Social Life of Coffee*, p. 6.

12 Alexander Bevilacqua and Helen Pfeifer, 'Turquerie: culture in motion, 1650–1750', *Past and Present*, 221 (2013), 75.

13 Bevilacqua and Pfeifer, 'Turquerie: culture', for coffee and coffeehouses, pp. 94–98.

14 Bevilacqua and Pfeifer, 'Turquerie: culture', p. 115.

15 Haine, *The World of the Paris Café*, p. 185.

16 Peçevi, *Tarih-i Peçevi*, p. 364. The English translation belongs to C. van Arendonk, 'Kahwa', in *Encyclopaedia of Islam*, new edition, Vol. 4 (Leiden: Brill, 1978), p. 451.

17 Prime Ministry's Ottoman Archives, Istanbul (hereafter PMOA) Cevdet-Maliye, 1955, undated.

18 Cowan, *The Social Life of Coffee*, p. 195.

19 26 Zilkade 975/23 May 1568, quoted in Ahmed Refik, *Onuncu Asr-ı Hicride Istanbul Hayatı* (Istanbul: Enderun Kitabevi, 1983), p. 141.

20 Discussing how powerful rumour was in the dissemination of news and in what ways it became an instrument in French rural uprisings in 1789, Lefebvre pointed out, 'for the government and the aristocracy, this means of transmission was a great deal more dangerous than freedom of the press'; Georges Lefebvre, *The Great Fear of 1789: Rural Panic in Revolutionary France*, trans. Joan White (New York: Panthon Books, 1973), p. 70.

21 Cowan, *The Social Life of Coffee*, p. 194.

22 Quoted in Jean Leclant, 'Coffee and cafés in Paris, 1644–1693', in Robert Foster and Orset Ranum (eds.), *Food and Drink in History: Selections from the Annales, ESC*, Vol. 5, trans. Elborg Forster and Patricia M. Ranum (Baltimore: John Hopkins University Press, 1979), p. 91.

23 Mustafa Naima, *Tarih-i Naima*, Vol. 3 (Istanbul: Tabhane-yi Amire, 1863), p. 161.

24 Naima, *Tarih-i Naima*, p. 162. Translation belongs to Lewis V. Thomas, *A Study of Naima* (New York: New York University Press, 1972), p. 95.

25 The terms 'Greek' and 'Armenian' refer not to ethnicity but to officially recognised religious affiliation. Here, Greeks refer to all Orthodox Christians, and Armenians to those who were members of the Armenian Gregorian Church irrespective of their ethnicity.

26 Despite the fact there are no reliable statistics regarding the confessional distribution of Istanbul in the late eighteenth century, some mid-nineteenth-century figures might give an idea. Muslims constituted 47.91 per cent, Greeks 21.39 per cent, Armenians 22.43 per cent, Catholics 2.4 per cent and finally Jews 5.87 per cent. See Cem Behar, *The Population of the Ottoman Empire* (Ankara: SIS Press, 1996), pp. 22, 70.

27 Ali Çaksu, 'Janissary coffee houses in late eighteenth-century Istanbul', in Sajdi (ed.) *Ottoman Tulips*, pp. 117–32.

28 Ariel Salzmann, 'The age of tulips: confluence and conflict in early modern consumer culture (1550–1730)', in Donald Quataert (ed.), *Consumption Studies and the History of the Ottoman Empire: An Introduction* (Albany: State University of New York Press, 2000), p. 96.

29 (PMOA) HH, 19334, (1241/1825–1826). For the follow-up documents of this case, and decrees issued to close Janissary coffeehouses in Anatolia, see HH 19334 A, 19334B, 19334 C, 17335, 17335 C, 17335 D, all dated 1241 (1825–1826).

30 Jean de Thévenot, *The Travels of Monsieur de Thévenot into Levant*, translated by Archibald Lowell, 3 parts (London: H. Clark, 1687), Part I, p. 34.

31 The data on the profile of coffeehouse clientele is gathered from a set of spy reports prepared in the 1840s. For a collection of these reports, see Cengiz Kırlı, *Sultan ve Kamuoyu: Osmanlı Modernleşme Sürecinde "Havadis Jurnalleri" (1840–1844)* (Istanbul: İş Bankası Kültür Yayınları, 2009).

Processes of selection and adaptation

32 Ekrem Işın, *Istanbul'da Gündelik Hayat* (Istanbul: İletişim Yayınları, 1995), p. 244; Abdülaziz Bey, *Osmanlı Adet, Merasim ve Tabirleri: Toplum Hayatı*, 2 vols, ed. Kazım Arısan and Duygu Arısan Günay (Istanbul: Tarih Vakfı Yurt Yayınları, 1995), Vol. 1, pp. 301–302.

33 In Europe, too, coffeehouses functioned as commercial centres. Similar to the case of coffeehouses in Istanbul, each group of tradesmen had its favourite coffeehouse. The role the coffeehouses played in the economic history of Europe is very significant. For an interesting story of the evolution of Lloyd's coffeehouse at the end of the seventeenth century in London to the famous Lloyd's Insurance Company, see Aytoun Ellis, *The Penny Universities: A History of the Coffee-Houses* (London: Secker & Warburg, 1956), pp. 117–122.

34 Cited in Georgeon, 'Les cafés à İstanbul à la fin de l'Empire ottoman', p. 42.

35 Georgeon, 'Les cafés à İstanbul à la fin de l'Empire ottoman', p. 42.

36 As Georgeon underlines, the symbiotic relationship between the Muslim community and religious leaders had been paralleled in the non-Muslim communities of Istanbul as well. For example, in Balat, which was predominantly inhabited by the Jews, coffeehouse owners were also community leaders. Georgeon, 'Les cafés à İstanbul à la fin de l'Empire ottoman' p. 42; M.C. Varol, *Balat, faubourg juif d'Istanbul* (Istanbul: ISIS Press, 1989), p. 8.

37 Cyrus Adler and Allan Ramsay, *Told in the Coffee House: Turkish Tales* (New York: Macmillan, 1898).

38 Salah Birsel, *Kahveler Kitabı* (Istanbul: Koza Yayınları, 1975), p. 67.

39 Cabi Efendi, *Cabi Tarihi: Tarih-i Sultan Selim-i Salis ve Mahmud-ı Sani*, ed. Mehmet Ali Beyhan (Ankara: Türk Tarih Kurumu, 2003), p. 1021.

40 Mikhail, 'The heart's desire', pp. 135–136.

41 Cabi Efendi, *Cabi Tarihi*, pp. 1152–1153.

42 Andreas Tietze, *The Turkish Shadow Theater and the Puppet Collection of the L.A. Mayer Memorial Collection* (Berlin: Gebr. Mann Verlag, 1977), p. 19.

43 Metin And, *A History of Theater and Popular Entertainment in Turkey* (Ankara: Forum Yayınları, 1963), p. 38.

44 See for a comprehensive list of travellers who mentioned political satire in the shadow theatre, Metin And, *Geleneksel Türk Tiyatrosu* (Istanbul: Inkilap Yayınları, 1985), pp. 293–296.

45 Further, just as the shadow theatre had degraded official, elite culture in the form of comic dialogues between *Karagöz* and *Hacivat*, similar representation of dualities were paralleled in medieval and early modern Europe, too. Such was the case, for instance, of King Solomon and the clown Morolf, where the former's sententious pronouncements are contrasted to mocking expressions and degraded to the bodily level of food, drink and sexual life: Edward Muir, *Ritual in Early Modern Europe* (Cambridge: Cambridge University Press, 1997), p. 20.

46 Cengiz Kırlı, 'Surveillance and constituting the public in the Ottoman Empire', in Seteney Shami (ed.), *Publics, Politics and Participation: Locating the Public Sphere in the Middle East and North Africa* (New York: SSRC, 2009), pp. 282–305; Cengiz Kırlı, 'Coffeehouses: public opinion in the nineteenth century Ottoman Empire',

in Armando Salvatore and Dale F. Eickelman (eds.), *Public Islam and the Common Good* (Leiden: Brill, 2004), pp. 75–97.

47 Kırlı, *Sultan ve Kamuoyu*, pp. 79–80.

48 Ebuziyya Tevfik, 'Kahvehaneler', *Mecmua-i Ebuziyya*, 129 (1914), 16.

49 Birsel, *Kahveler Kitabı*, p. 86.

50 Benjamin C. Fortna, *Learning to Read in the Late Ottoman Empire and the Early Turkish Republic* (New York: Palgrave Macmillan, 2011), p. 162.

51 Uygur Kocabaşoğlu, 'İlk Kıraathane'nin Açılışı', *Tarih ve Toplum*, 1 (1984), 377–379.

52 Peter Stallybrass and Allon White, *The Politics and Poetics of Transgression* (London: Methuen, 1986), p. 80.

III

Towards an 'entangled history' of urban leisure culture

9

The rules of leisure in eighteenth-century Paris and London

LAURENT TURCOT

In a manuscript drafted in around 1781, but not published during his lifetime, Louis-Sébastien Mercier highlighted that to understand Paris fully it was necessary to adopt a cross-Channel perspective:

> Only one nation can challenge [French] power and has staked all her strength and reputation on resisting and opposing French influence: England. Neighbour and rival, inevitably London furnishes the pendant to the portrait I have painted – the comparison suggests itself. The two capitals are so close and so different, yet bear so strong a resemblance to each other that my study of Paris would be incomplete were I not to consider some aspects of the other.[1]

Mercier's comments serve to introduce the comparative histories of these two cities. The object of the present chapter is to study the distinctions but also the links between Paris and London, with especial reference to what I will refer to as the 'culture of leisure', a phenomenon formalised during the eighteenth century. Recent research by Robert and Isabelle Tombs, Jonathan Conlin, François-Joseph Ruggiu, Renaud Morieux and others has shown the multifaceted advantages of comparative histories of eighteenth-century France and Britain.[2] Meanwhile, the comparative study of Paris and London, as capital cities and global metropolises, has been advanced by the work of scholars such as Karen Newman and Vanessa Harding.[3] In adopting an approach based on the theme of cultural transfer, it becomes clear that these two cities, despite their lack of a common political history, possessed numerous links that allow us to understand how far each was defined by reference to the other. In particular, it is possible to observe the extent to which mutual emulation contributed to transformations in the social realities of both cities.

Rather than a straightforward case of comparative history, the history of leisure in Paris and in London allows the analysis of forms of social interaction that developed between the two cities, because the sources analysed here highlight the importance of considering both points of reference, with Parisians comparing themselves to Londoners and vice versa. In this way, what is at stake is not just the juxtaposition of two case studies, but rather two models whose development involved mutual observation and emulation, with some degree of self-definition by reference to one another. That which was typical of London in terms of social behaviour in the eighteenth century might, according to many writers, be in marked contradistinction to the French model; in this way, forms of interaction could involve resistance to cultural exchange as well as impetuses for it.

In the closing decades of the eighteenth century, these connections seemed more numerous and more striking to contemporaries than ever before. As shown in the chapters by Clarisse Coulomb and Peter Clark in this volume, the two preceding centuries had certainly seen British and French travellers document national contrasts with verve and *esprit*.[4] But, arguably, a new impulse was also making itself felt. Observers still sized each other up from opposite sides of the Channel, but the aim was no longer merely to present, for those curious about such things, a catalogue of strange facts, amusing anecdotes and descriptions of monuments. Rather, alongside continued attempts to describe particular national characteristics with ever greater accuracy, some writers at least were also seeking to emphasise similarities and areas for potential mutual emulation and improvement. John Andrews's *A Comparative View of the French and English Nations* and John Moore's *A View of Society and Manners in France, Switzerland and Germany* are two British examples of this new approach.[5] In France, Pidansat de Mairobert and Jean-Jacques Rutlidge were engaged in similar endeavours.[6] Arguably, then, London and Paris were moving closer, so much so that Mercier seemed willing at least to toy with the idea that Paris and London might represent the same city. At one point Mercier described London as 'another, much vaster Paris, with different inhabitants', located north of Paris. When discussing the flood of French exiles to London that resulted from the Revocation of the Edict of Nantes, Mercier proposed: 'This would surely make London Paris?' Mercier's question was well judged, since the eighteenth century saw a flowering of cultural exchange between London and Paris: and this can be well observed through a focus on the history of leisure.

This chapter, then, focuses on the theme of leisure so as to compare Paris and London, and to examine how far parallels can be drawn out between these

The rules of leisure in eighteenth-century Paris and London   **187**

two societies, and the extent to which this in turn points to a wider European culture of leisure transcending particular nations. This European culture of leisure encompassed regional differences, of greater and lesser extent, which both informed and transformed the matrix of conduct in urban space. In some degree, leisure might indeed be seen as one facet of the larger dynamic, noted by Stéphane Van Damme, by which 'The London/Paris couple plays a central role in fixing of a set [of] national character types within the philosophical discourse of the Enlightenment'.[7]

Whether in London or in Paris, polite social norms were marked by a considerable degree of similarity, in that the two cities were traversed in significant ways by a shared culture. When London launched the fashion for Vauxhall-style pleasure gardens, haste was made in Paris to take up the challenge by creating 'Waux-hall' variations on the theme. Similarly, the French dancing master had become a stock figure in London by the second half of the eighteenth century: and, although acerbically caricatured in many visual representations as effeminate and mannered, the dancing master nonetheless remained a key point of reference for various prescriptive accounts – such as the work of Chesterfield – concerned with fostering French-style elegance.[8] These cultural exchanges involved more than just representations, but also contributed to changes in the reality of leisure practices by giving form to new patterns of comportment.

Leisure culture is understood here as comprising sites such as the theatres, coffeehouses, promenades and pleasure gardens. These new spaces were made possible by the commercialisation of leisure activities. The socio-cultural frameworks in which such pastimes blossomed in London and Paris reveals the social dimension of interactions between individuals. Leisure implies personal performances as part of a larger whole: in order to be part of the assemblage that is formed by a group or crowd, it is necessary to be aware of, and to be able to put precisely into action, a particular way of being in public. How do these ways of conducting oneself within a given gathering take shape? A key aim of this chapter is to identify the normative meaning of pleasure during the eighteenth century. By 'normative meaning', I refer to the different forms of injunction, or rules – formal or informal – discussed here as 'prescriptions', which came to frame the activities of members of the crowd within leisured spaces. The notion of cultural transfer encompasses a spectrum of different degrees of receptivity to, and assimilation of, elements originating elsewhere.[9] This critical approach, accordingly, is well suited to the analysis of the cultural markers that permitted the mutual influence of London and Paris upon one another by a form of

Towards an 'entangled history' of urban leisure culture

civilising emulation that tended to the reform and improvement of the behaviour of the public present in places of leisure.

I propose to focus on two main kinds of source, which are highly divergent, and whose aims and functions are, moreover, diametrically opposed: on the one hand, treatises concerned with civility; and on the other hand, judicial archives. A key element to emerge from these sources is the trope of social mixing in the spaces of leisure. Numerous historians have cast leisure activities as a key prism for investigating the spaces where different social groups encountered and intermixed with one another, with some scholars going so far as to see in this the premises of a democratic society. I argue that this is in fact a false idea: instead, I propose that, although the different social classes certainly saw one another, they did not intermix directly: there was to this extent a respect for the differences of class.

I set out to show how the analysis of these two distinctive sets of sources reveals the boundaries of what was considered appropriate behaviour in fashionable leisure spaces. In the case of the conduct literature, what is at stake is a normative ideal to be attained, without completely submitting to the notion of dissolving oneself in a crowd. In the case of the judicial and police records, a measure of confirmation of these themes may be observed by arrests and other policing measures undertaken in leisure spaces. Social segregation was the order of the day, and these spaces were in reality firmly anchored in the logic of social hierarchy. As Hannah Greig has shown in a recent article on the original London Vauxhall Gardens, the idea of social mixing was more imagined than it was experienced.[10] Comparing the cases of Paris and London can only reinforce this conclusion. However, it is not enough to invalidate the thesis of social mixing, it is also necessary to seek to understand how socially different people could live side-by-side in the same spaces and enjoy the same diversions. The argument I develop here is that the gradual elaboration and imposition of prescriptions – social and judicial – can be conceived of as a body of rules structured around different social categories.

While the lower social orders were to be given more polish, they were not to be rendered equal to the higher social groups; rather, they were merely to be made more capable of sharing the same spaces as their social superiors. In this process, the different social orders did not mix as such: instead, they were in proximity to one another but did not merge; and a better understanding of this ensemble of individuals is enabled by studying the processes of social polishing involved. The injunctions for proper or improved patterns of behaviour were concerned less with an ideal of greater equality, and more with furnishing a

Figure 9.1 Reinier Vinkeles, *The Tuileries in Paris*, 1770. Collection Rijksmuseum Amsterdam.

precondition for successful involvement in a given spectacle; in other words, prescriptions sought to foster appropriate conditions in order to make an event agreeable to the public. This transformation was underway entirely within the contemporary matrix of inequality based upon social distinction, and was distilled within social space. A series of different historical actors – such as the police, the judicial authorities or the writers of conduct literature – were engaged in maintaining and enforcing these social prescriptions.

This is not intended to be a study of the civilising process or of the disciplining of behaviour, or indeed of the constitution of a public sphere.[11] This research can best be situated, instead, at the intersection of each of these conceptual programmes, and connected by a simple point of reference: the ways by which a diverse public came to gather in order to take part in a social performance. On the one hand, this encompassed the behaviour of the elite, where processes of self-distinction continued, but as part of an ensemble whose social diversity was far wider; and, on the other hand, it involved wider social groups, which gained access to assemblies where they might come alongside the elite, and where a system of police or justice was present in order to ensure respect for rules of social cohabitation so that everyone present might profit from a given event. With these transformations in social norms and behaviour, it was possible for a new form of assemblage to emerge: the commercialised leisure of an inegalitarian society.

Fixing norms: the normative literature

Conduct literature has long been a major source for historians studying the construction of behaviour in public spaces. Some have even gone so far as to treat these sources as reflecting the social reality of a given period. It would be straightforward to point to the weaknesses of such an approach; but it would also be reductive to consider these treatises as having no truth to them. Arguably, it is possible to use them in a more limited sense: in that, rather than providing a simple reflection of social practices, these sources instead permit an understanding of how a society saw or idealised itself.

In Britain, the events of 1688 fostered political and cultural changes that would make 'politeness' a lodestone in defining social relations.[12] Politeness was supposed to provide individuals with a means to live alongside one another in order to enable social intercourse. At the same time that the influence of politeness was becoming more ascendant, at the end of the seventeenth century, the cityscape of London was undergoing profound shifts, especially with the reconstruction of the city after the Great Fire of 1666.[13] Socially, the capital became ever more established as the centre for a wide spectrum of members of the elite, the middling sort and those engaged with trade; the London population surged, and with it the opportunities for business, and the built environment was itself extended and enriched. With the court no longer the centre of attention, the centre of gravity turned towards the city itself, and it was there that politeness came, in some measure, to establish its headquarters.[14] In France at the same period a broadly comparable movement was underway.[15] Versailles increasingly ceded ground to Paris as the country's primary cultural centre; and the city itself grew and became denser.[16] Rather than a great fire, the symbol of this renewal came with the increasing re-centring of elite cultural life on Paris, reversing the forced exile to Versailles under Louis XIV. Thereafter it would be in the space of Paris that social norms were increasingly defined.

In the French case, at least, there has often been a tendency to consider the second half of the seventeenth century as a period of social constraint and of obligation, with courtiers obliged to bend to protocol, at the risk otherwise of consigning themselves to irrelevance at a period when royal power was at its zenith. Against this, traditional historiography has opposed the transformations that supposedly drove the eighteenth century: liberty, sincerity and authenticity. Accordingly, historians have discussed the notion of a return to intimacy (or '*revanche de l'intimité*'), and some have pushed this idea as far as the invention of feelings.[17] The idea of a degree of abandonment of the constraints of civility or courtliness seems to have become largely accepted.

Let us consider briefly the statistics on the publication of conduct treatises. For the period 1600–1800, a total of around 435 French treatises have been identified, and 563 in the case of Britain.[18] Production of treatises of civility was not in decline during the eighteenth century, but rather maintained its vigour (although it was not necessarily the case that an increase in the volume of output corresponded to a growth in the readership of each publication). Moreover, the contents of the conduct books were themselves changing. In the first place, there was an ever greater specificity in terms of sites of leisure, sustained by an editorial presentation that separated this theme into distinctive chapters. Second, there was a greater attention to – and greater elaboration of – rules for conduct in the spaces of leisure.

A few examples will suffice to substantiate this. The output of Antoine de Courtin may be taken as the most marked example of the precepts of civility. Of the 33 chapters of his *Nouveau Traité de la civilité* (1671) – of which an English translation was published in London in 1703 – five are concerned, more or less, with leisure. On closer inspection, moreover, it becomes clear that the majority of the chapters are in some measure concerned with feelings or attitudes to be adopted. On the subject of dance, for example, Courtin took care to stress that one should know, in the words of the English translation, 'the Rules observ'd in dancing, especially in the Place where you are (for in all Places the Rules are not the same)'. When walking with someone of a higher social rank, precedence must be observed:

> If two Noblemen be in discourse with a private Ge[n]tleman, and do put him in the middle, that they might both hear him the better; as often as he comes at the end of the Alley, he must turn towards that Lord that is the greater of the two. If the Lord be equal, at the one end of the Alley he must turn to one, and at the other to the other, observing still to quit the middle place when his story is done.[19]

At the turn of the eighteenth century, Jean-Baptiste De la Salle produced a synthesis of the courtly model of social distinction.[20] The fifth chapter of his *Règles de la bienséance et de la civilité chrétienne* (1703) is dedicated to the

192   Towards an 'entangled history' of urban leisure culture

question of entertainments ('Des divertissements'), with five subsections considered: recreation and laughter, the promenade, gaming, singing and diversions that are not permitted. De la Salle attempted, like Antoine de Courtin before him, to restrain the good Christian as far as possible from frequenting places that were seen as insalubrious for the soul. But he recognised that this would be difficult; for, despite the preaching and entreaties of ecclesiastical spokesmen, he acknowledged the existence of a series of practices that, in the fashionable world, were deemed acceptable entertainments, and that he could only seek to place within strict frameworks so that the soul should not be tainted by sin.[21] His *Règles* can be seen as an expression of this particular moment at the turn of the century where a series of dynamics intersected: in the first place, entertainments were taken to be part of the everyday experience of the man of the world; second, they were the object of increasingly close attention on the part of authors of conduct literature; and third, men of the Church set out stringent rules in a bid to limit, as far as possible, the kinds of entertainment involved.

From the beginning of the eighteenth century, a series of shifts in these texts become notable. For one thing, there is a marked insistence on urban space, its function, its utility and its different locales, notably those concerned with leisure. In 1730, Dupuy La Chapelle, in his *Instruction d'un père à son fils*, divided his treatise into 29 chapters, and among them entries can be noted on 'Des spectacles' and 'Des plaisirs'. These elements are relatively established, since this kind of division was already in place in the work of De la Salle. However, Dupuy La Chapelle goes further in specifying particular kinds of activities and diversions; indeed, he even goes so far as to celebrate the merits of all varieties of entertainments, advising his readers to take both reason and religion as a guide in the conduct of their pleasures.[22]

Pleasure was becoming a useful component of man's activities. The Abbé Prévost, in his *Élémens de politesse et de bienséance* (1767), shows to what degree leisure had become an object of specific attention, and especially how it was by this point the focus of a particular code of conduct.[23] Prévost's account gives attention to the rules to be observed at public spectacles such as the theatre, when undertaking a promenade, when at a ball, when gaming, during musical concerts or while playing different games. Detailed directions are given, for example, in the case of the garden walk: with stipulations not to laugh, or to take the fruit or flowers ornamenting the paths.[24] At the theatre, meanwhile, one should beware of sinning against civility in becoming carried away with enthusiasm ('prenez garde de ne pas pécher contre la civilité en vous emportant d'admiration'). Later in the text, it is stated that if participating in a game

The rules of leisure in eighteenth-century Paris and London   **193**

involving exercise, such as *la paume*, *boules* or billiards, one should be careful to avoid adopting 'ridiculous' and 'grotesque' bodily postures.[25] What might be seen as remarkable here is that the code of conduct is no longer merely intended for marking out social distinctions, but rather for the provision of rules of good living applicable to all.

In Britain, a comparable and extensive normative literature existed on the figure of the 'gentleman'. The British context, however, did not favour such fine-grained and precise definitions as could be found in the French civility treatises. Anna Bryson has maintained that civility was a foreign notion that was only very haltingly adapted to the British context.[26] This context needs to be taken into consideration, since the British court did not possess a dominance as considerable as that exercised by the court Louis XIV over the elite in France. As Jacques Carré has written, with reference to what he describes as a 'crisis of courtesy', 'after the first English Revolution, this courtly model was almost fatally discredited in Britain'.[27]

Even so, civility treatises flourished: and this is demonstrated in part by translations of the work of Antoine de Courtin, among others. These translations offer a clear sign of the cultural transfers underway between France and Britain, and they also show an interest on the part of a section of the British public in learning the rules of French-style civility. Some, perhaps, got to know these better so that they might undertake a Grand Tour, or other cross-Channel travel; but it would also appear that ideas about civility in some measure went beyond supposedly national characteristics to form, through a community of readers, something of a shared model.

Surveying original English-language works also makes it possible to track significant differences in emphasis. In *The Gentleman's Library, Containing Rules for Conduct in All Parts of Life* (1715), leisure is presented as a necessity: '*Pleasure* and *Recreation*, of one kind or other, are absolutely necessary to relieve our Minds and Bodies from too constant *Attention* and *Labour*.'[28] The theatre appears here as the quintessence of entertainment, with it being noted that 'the Stage might be made a perpetual Source of the most Noble and Useful Entertainment, were it under *proper Regulations*'.[29] In a later text, *The Man of Manners* (1737?), the reader is presented with a veritable guidebook on the art of pleasing in public right from the first pages, notably with its 'Rules for Walking the Streets, or other Publick Places', where it is proposed: 'If we walk in the *Park*, or any other *Publick Place*, with a Superior, we are always to observe to give him the upper Hand; and if three or more be in Company, we are to take care to place him in the Middle.'[30] Women should stay in the position that they have been allotted; and 'Persons of Figure, when they choose to amble the Publick Streets, should always appear in a Dress suitable to their Dignity; not only for the sake of the Way, and to prevent Insults; but to preserve the Respect due to great Personages'.[31] Later in the text, note is taken of 'Rules to be observ'd at Play', which are spelt out in detail, notably with the precept that '*Giggling* and talking to any Stander-by, with other unnecessary Interruptions, should be avoided'.[32] Also, for the theatre, 'the Gentlemen in the Pit, will all sit with their Hats off, and not suffer any young Coxcomb (dress'd like a Footman) to be leaning on his Stick, and playing Monkey's Tricks betwixt the Acts'.[33] Considerations follow regarding the etiquette to be observed in coffeehouses and in public gardens.

Other treatises were even more specific, such as that of François Nivelon, a figure who exemplifies the continued influence of French models in Britain. That Nivelon was French and that his work was published in English shows how France, even if criticised by many, remained a key model. A dancing master, Nivelon's *The Rudiments of Genteel Behavior* (1737) set forth a veritable grammar of the body, enlivened by engravings, in order that readers might comport themselves decently in public space. All of this was presented in order to 'describe the true Way to make Courtsie'.[34] If a number of dancing positions can be recognised, this was done in order to demonstrate how to move oneself appropriately and, notably, how to make respectful gestures.

Also remarkable are treatises aimed specifically at women, in which there is no hesitation in reproving certain kinds of diversion and encouraging others. In *The Lady's Delight, or Accomplish'd Female Instructor* (c. 1740) it is stated that 'Recreations and Pleasures, are undoubtedly lawful, if we abuse them not by Irregularity'. A rule is outlined: 'Recreations there are of many other kinds, which may be suited, as the Place and Humour of the Company requires.'[35] The tendency towards the elaboration of specific dedicated chapters regarding aspects of leisure is evident, with certain texts going so far as to itemise chapters for the theatre, the promenade or Vauxhall.

It may appear convenient simply to sweep away these texts, by insisting on the normative quality of this literature, suggesting that this type of work had no role to play in reality; such an approach points instead towards studying literary aesthetics, or the study of shifts in terminology. But it is necessary to go beyond this first stage of analysis in order to reinvest these sources with their fuller dimensions. It is by setting these sources alongside others that the full interest of these texts emerges. As a first step, it is possible to take stock of the carrying over of these rules and precepts into other forms of literature.

Many types of text pick up on these rules in some measure. However, arguably diaries provide an especially full reflection of the role of such rules in everyday life. The recent studies of Hannah Greig on the fashionable world in London in the second half of the eighteenth century provide abundant support for this. The rules of conduct manuals seem to have corresponded in some measure to the behaviour of some members of the elite. In particular, it seems clear that what was at stake was not merely taking part in a series of fashionable diversions, but doing so according to precepts and in appropriate company. Benjamin Heller has highlighted the same type of behaviour in his study of diaries that reveal the variety of practices underway at Bartholomew Fair.[36] For eighteenth-century Paris, comparable kinds of references may be found, although maintaining a private journal was a far less common practice in Paris than in London. While a number of daily chronicles can be cited, as well as some autobiographical memoirs and recollections, private diaries as such are less well-known.[37]

One thing can be confirmed here: there were clear injunctions to behave decently in the spaces of leisure. The idea was not to attain equality, but rather to distinguish oneself in order to be able to be recognised by those who belonged to the same social class. This was all the more true of the ever more multifaceted crowds that were to be found assembled in such spaces, notably newly enriched groups seeking to deploy their fortunes in order to obtain social advancement.

Did historical actors, then, seek to dissolve themselves into the mass when they went to the theatre, to a promenade or Vauxhall? It seems clear that they did not: and yet, the fact of having different codes for different social groups does not obviate, as Lawrence Klein has highlighted, the possibility of having a 'shared social experience', which nevertheless respected those codes:

In addition to decent clothing and spare change, participation in the polite spaces of London required an ability to act somewhat politely... [T]he reason that politeness was being purveyed in these books to plebeian readers was that participating in a polite social milieu was an opportunity offered to middling Londoners in this period.[38]

This train of analysis leads us, then, to focus on specific attitudes and forms of behaviour. Conduct literature, among other source material, enables an understanding of the increasing complexity of the leisure spaces of Paris and London during the eighteenth century. The process was not unique to either city, but rather took place in both cities simultaneously.

Policing leisure

In France the genealogy of the concept of 'police' can be related to the idea of the policing of manners (*moeurs*). In 1667, Louis XIV established the Lieutenance générale de police, which reformed the magistrature, and whose remit was wide-ranging, including responsibilities relating to religion and morality, health and sanitation, road construction and street cleaning, public order and security, food regulation, arts and sciences, trade and manufactures, domestic servants and poor relief.[39] To a Parisian, the police became a standing point of reference for government authority, supported by a network of spies. Louis-Sébastien Mercier found the freedoms he encountered in London remarkable, given that the situation for the Parisian was:

> Spies are all about him. Two citizens cannot whisper, without a third craning his neck to hear what the conversation is about. The Lieutenant de Police commands a regiment of ears, differing from a regiment of soldiers only in that each of its soldiers changes his uniform daily and completely. In the twinkling of an eye he can and does metamorphose himself.[40]

Mercier's account was as much prescriptive as descriptive: but rather than rendering his account less informative, this aspect surely renders it all the more interesting to us today. In depicting London, Mercier presents a vision of a utopian city, a model of what in France at this period was called '*la ville policée*'. To some extent, Mercier's London was thus a projection of the philosophe imagination: not so much a rounded portrait of the British capital as a reflection of what Paris might become. British commentators also found the concept of 'police' useful, even if they sometimes struggled to translate it into English: 'We are accused by the French, and perhaps but too justly, of having no word in our language', Walpole wrote in one 1756 number of his periodical *The World*, 'which answers to the word police, which therefore we have been obliged to adopt, not having, as they say, the thing.'[41] Despite the establishment of the Bow Street Runners, 'police' had yet to come to denote a citywide force of uniformed peace officers under a central command structure, although Patrick Colquhoun's *Treatise on the Police of the Metropolis* (1796, first drafted 1792) did result in the creation of the Thames River Police, the first force in Britain to carry that name.

How, then, was the policing of behaviour in leisure spaces to be undertaken? The Paris police comprised many branches, each directed at particular areas of jurisdiction and having distinctive identities and quirks; this made practice at least as important as theory in the treatises concerned with matters of policing and justice. Moreover, by making reference only to treatises, such as those of Delamare, Jousse or even Lemaire, no indication is ever found of a dedicated department focused on leisure spaces: but in effect this did gradually come to be formed, apparently as a pragmatic response to the practices of policing. Regulations aimed at maintaining public morality at Paris were very numerous, but for the most part these involved very general rules that do not specify how a police agent was to act in the particular context of leisure. Whether the focus is on theatres, promenades, coffeehouses or Vauxhalls, what largely emerges are different forms of improvisation aimed at controlling behaviour, with the desired outcome being that all participants in leisure activities should be permitted to take advantage, in due measure, of the pleasures available. The guiding principle seems to have been that public spectacles were not to be interrupted, be it on the stage, in a room or in an exterior space; this was particularly evident in the policing of officially endorsed theatre sites such as the Comédie-Française, the Comédie-Italienne and the Opéra.

Similarly, on the Champs-Élysées, numerous individuals were arrested for failing to respect the promenade (*ne respectent pas la promenade*), or for reasons threatening its tranquillity (*pour le calme de la promenade*).[42] For example, on one occasion in 1778, the watchman responsible, Ferdinand de Federici, was obliged to play the role of bodyguard following the appearance on the promenade of the Princesse de Lamballe. As Federici wrote in his report the following day, the idiotic populace (*la populace imbecille*) had followed the princess, who

Figure 9.2 *Première vue des boulevards prise de la porte Saint-Antoine*, c. 1750. © Musée Carnavalet, Roger-Viollet, no. 46120–1.

was at the promenade with a lady companion, and he had therefore intervened in order to shield her from the crowd; not long after the departure of the princess, a similar scene then played out around the promenade of another high society figure, Madame de Boulogne, leading Federici to note that it seemed as if all of Paris had been in the Champs-Élysées.[43]

On the Paris boulevards, a site for promenading and the location of popular theatres, such as those of Nicolet and Audinot, the *Bureau de Ville* created in 1736 a guard of 40 men, split into eight squads. Eight bodies of Guards were also raised in the city.[44] In this way, provision was made at regular intervals for police groups whose function was to maintain order. The spaces for promenading were especially closely watched. In 1755, the number of soldiers present in the Guard on the gates of Saint-Antoine and Saint-Honoré was increased in order to ensure a night-time presence.[45] In this area there were theatres, cabarets, roving drinks-sellers and traders of all sorts; the aim of the police was to manage this rolling entertainment event, which unfurled daily from the start of the afternoon and finished when the various shows ended in the early hours of the next morning.

A study of police commissaire records highlights what were considered inappropriate forms of behaviour and how they were punished. Cases of drunkenness were numerous: in 1784, for instance, a groom named François Galand was reported as having misbehaved in seeking entry to Nicolet's while in a state of drunkenness.[46] Inebriation was sometimes the reason given in records of arrest.[47] Alcohol could also be one of the explaining factors for other quarrels, such as an incident in 1769 involving Michel Du Chatellier and François Sganzin, who placed themselves on the balcony in such a way as to block the view of other spectators.[48] Similarly, there was the case of Joseph Villedien Tullelier, who was found to have urinated in his seat at Nicolet's, with his urine falling onto the spectators in the boxes below.[49] The majority of the arrests, however, apparently related to lack of respect accorded to the performance at hand. Some spectators found themselves in trouble for talking back to the performers on stage: François Louis Corgere and Henry Lacour Charron both allowed themselves to make ripostes to the dialogue being acted out.[50] Pierre Martin Jolivet, for his part, displeased by the play being performed, went rather further: he was reported to have caused commotion and uproar in the playhouses on the boulevards for several days, lashing out at and injuring actors and actresses as well as private spectators.[51] Several people having complained about his behaviour to the Guard, he was quickly removed so that performances might continue in peace.

The rules of leisure in eighteenth-century Paris and London **199**

For the theatres with an official privilege, a dedicated section of the police known as the '*police des spectacles*' was gradually developed. This involved members of the Guard, spies and *exempts* who were tasked with informing the lieutenant de police what was done, seen and heard at such performances. In the first half of the eighteenth century, one or two brigades formed of seven to 14 men were assigned to the two Comédie theatres; at the Opéra, 40 musketeers were deployed, half of them inside and half outside the theatre. From 1717 to 1765, 73 police interventions are recorded, comprising a total of 94 arrested spectators. In the majority of these cases, the concern was to avoid overcrowding, which, as the archives show, risked causing problems and even riots. Accordingly, the authorities took the opportunity to arrest those who were considered as responsible for causing tumults, as well as those who abused the actors in the course of reciting their parts, or who insulted ladies in the boxes, or who shoved the spectators in the parterre in order to make a passage through the crowd; none of these actions were tolerable, and they had to be rapidly stopped. The idea was always to make an example of the malefactor and to show the crowd the determination of the police agents present in the auditorium. This tendency to foreground the agents of the police became more and more widespread during the second half of the century. The fairs of St-Laurent, St-Germain and St-Ovide were also policed, sometimes by private enterprise.[52]

The case of Paris is very well documented for understanding how the police gradually moulded a public worthy of frequenting the same diversions as those higher in the social scale. By a relatively simple technique, which consisted in making an example out of an individual who went beyond the acceptable limits, an attempt was made to establish the parameters of appropriate public conduct. The other main approach was that of ensuring that there was a conspicuous police presence, tasked with arresting and bringing before the commissaire those who failed to conform.

The case of London is substantially less well documented, or rather is documented through very different sources. As J.M. Beattie has underlined: 'In the City of London, many of the activities we would summarise as "policing" were carried out by a variety of officials and by private citizens.'[53] A more French-style form of police could be said to have emerged with the Bow Street Runners.[54] Studies of them have allowed historians to gain a sense of everyday delinquency, but in the specific case of leisure, the Bow Street Runners have left little trace, except in certain occasional references in the Old Bailey material. Elaine A. Reynolds has highlighted, however, the existence of another distinct form of law enforcement in the form of the parish paid watchmen, who were tasked with ensuring security by arresting those accused of crimes. This body became increasingly structured from mid-century, and saw its prominence grow.[55] The constables also began to extend their influence into poorer districts: at the end of the 1770s, a night watch was established in Southwark, and in 1774, a Night Watch Act provided the legal framework to enhance crime prevention and detection. The resulting picture is far from the specialisation of functions observable in the case of Paris, and far too from the richly documented arrests there. Despite this, a number of historians have for several years sought to understand the London police machinery, such as it was, and to outline its distinctive and less centralised characteristics.

What then of the role of places of leisure in London? Records exist for some of the rules promulgated in order to frame acceptable behaviour in given locales, such as public gardens. Orders were made in 1703 relating to park management, included stipulations prohibiting coaches and carriages, excluding hogs and dogs, and confining pedestrians to the gravel walks. As Alison O'Byrne has remarked, 'the regulations were designed both to prevent damage and maintain a certain amount of decorum by attempting to exclude the lower sorts'.[56] In order to ensure respect for the rules, officers were empowered 'to send a corporal and soldiers when necessary to assist the keepers in enforcing these regulations and bringing offenders before a Justice of the Peace'.[57]

How then were certain forms of conduct prescribed through the processes of justice? While the sources are somewhat patchy, study of the Old Bailey papers makes it possible to present a pendant of sorts to the case of Paris during the same period. Robert Shoemaker has had occasion to flag up some of the limitations of these sources, which are often inaccurate or abbreviated.[58] More recently, Benjamin Heller has sought to bring out the potential of these documents by considering them with reference to what they can reveal about leisure activities. His conclusions allow some support for the idea of social prescriptions, but with several major nuances. In the first instance, Heller's emphasis is on plebeian recreation mentioned in the context of a trial. Accordingly, an overrepresentation of drinking can be found, with, for example, a near total absence of coffeehouses and bookshops.[59]

Heller's analysis of plebeian activities recoded in testimony at the Old Bailey (see Table 9.1) allows note to be taken of the diversity of practices, but also of the paucity of many of the respective activities involved. Indeed, it is difficult to draw general conclusions from the small number of cases recorded. The quantitative aspect here needs to be put into perspective, but perhaps drawing out particular cases offers a useful means of fathoming larger patterns of

The rules of leisure in eighteenth-century Paris and London **201**

Table 9.1. Plebeian activities recorded at the Old Bailey

	1760	1790	1810
Alcohol (domestic)	1	3	1
Animal sports	2		
Assemblies and shows	2		
Club (generally in pubs)	1		3
Coffeehouse	2	2	1
Dining out	2	4	3
Drinking (pubs)	28	22	22
Fairs	2	1	3
Gambling	2		
Meals (domestic)	1	1	2
Bagnio/New Hummums		2	
Prostitutes	5	2	4
Pub games		2	1
Public events	2	1	3
Singing (pubs)	1		
Smoking (pubs)	1	1	1
Tea and pleasure gardens	3		
Tea drinking (domestic)	1	1	2
Theatre	2	1	8
To see the king/prince regent		1	1
Visiting		1	1
Walking	2	2	1
Watching sport	1	1	1
Window shopping	1		
Other		2	2

everyday practice. Most of the cases are concerned with theft, but in working through the documentation, more varied information can also be traced. Two spaces in particular, public gardens and theatres, allow us to understand social practices a little better.

From the nine sessions studied in the Old Bailey documents by Heller between 1760 and 1810, around 58 cases record a 'park' or a 'garden', notably St James's Park or Hyde Park. The cases highlight above all the cohabitation of different social classes, but this does not appear to have posed problems in

Figure 9.3 Thomas Rowlandson, *An Audience Watching a Play at Drury Lane Theatre*, c.1785. Yale Center for British Art, Paul Mellon Collection.

and of itself. Also notable are cases of arrest for sexual liaisons, gambling and drinking. Heller remarks that 'the language used to describe trips to the parks in company also suggest that working Londoners did not expect to see people they knew – a major difference from polite walkers but recalling the casual relationships that developed in public houses'.[60] In this way, the same activity for different social classes did not necessarily occasion the same codes, norms or expectations. For example, the case of Thomas Gray, in 1769, also allows us to understand a little better the diversity of practices in the park: in this case the accused, who was charged with theft, declared that he had gone to the park to meet 'a gentleman', while a witness, a butcher, recounts having seen him as he 'was carrying some meat through the Park'.[61]

In the case of the theatre, David Worrall has insisted on the important place of skilled and artisanal groups in the audience.[62] A more detailed study of the Old Bailey proceedings supports this. Many of the documents, mostly of thefts, emerge out of events in the pit, notably at Drury Lane and the other principal theatres. The pit was recognised as being the place where young men gathered, and the witnesses at the Old Bailey noted that the working people 'went to the theatre singly or in groups of two of three, just as propertied society did'.[63] The idea of reinforcing social networks was not a prerogative of the aristocracy alone, and leisure was a key forum for this, as well as for the

The rules of leisure in eighteenth-century Paris and London   **203**

creation of new links. One of the attractions of the theatre was the possibility of creating 'short-term communities within the pits and galleries of London's public venues'.[64]

Arguably, then, this does not amount to the same degree or depth of information as that available from the Paris sources on arrests, which permit an understanding of how justice came to give the lead to behavioural practices. But what the Old Bailey documents do suggest is the formalisation of behaviour in leisure spaces. There were conditions both of individual performance and of collective performance by crowds assembled for an event in common, and the two were inextricably linked. Heller notes that the 'evidence indicates that a certain amount of social mixing went on, but it does not seem to have involved polite society infiltrating working pleasure spaces for amusement'.[65] Moreover, the information contained in the Old Bailey papers, even if it does not permit the same kinds of analysis as the Paris sources with regards to the framing of policing, does nevertheless allow us to highlight the norms and forms adopted by ordinary people in leisure spaces.

Conclusion

The idea that individuals shift between the role of actor and that of spectator provides a useful prism for studies of leisure practices. However, scholars should also not lose sight of the several contextual factors, which may have been more salient than often supposed and constituted a heavy brake on patterns of behaviour. The societies discussed here were fundamentally unequal, and the reproduction of social habitus found its confirmation in the variety of forms of distinction evident in leisure practices and their policing. In particular, those who were paying for their entertainments did not seek to participate in scandals, but rather expected peaceable leisure practices that took place according to appropriate forms and norms.

The historiography on the definition of social behaviour in public space in eighteenth-century Britain and France is particularly rich. Both feature close reference to conduct literature, and highlight the transformations underway around the beginning of the century. In the British case, studies have focused on politeness, and its implications for rethinking social norms; while studies of France have highlighted a return to intimacy (*revanche de l'intimité*), a dynamic associated with a rejection of constraint in favour of sincerity of sentiments, and yet in which social distinction continued to be expressed.[66] In both cases, meanwhile, a concern with the reform of manners in order to

204 Towards an 'entangled history' of urban leisure culture

limit public disorder may be observed, and especially a desire to provide a framework in which urban behaviour might be standardised and defined, in a context in which the crowd was an increasingly important factor. This, then, can be viewed in terms of the imposition of the forms and norms of civil society. The authors of conduct literature highlighted as much, and agents of the police and of justice sought to have these ideals honoured. Arguably, just as Pierre Bourdieu affirmed that distinction is only possible through conformity, access to and participation in leisure spaces were only available with appropriate qualifications in terms of respect for elite social classes.

A remarkable aspect of Paris and London in the context of eighteenth-century leisure practices is the tendency by which a range of interventions took place in both cities with a view to framing social comportment; so too is that the behavioural patterns involved were in many ways becoming more alike. Naturally, London commentators tended to regard the kinds of behaviour available to them as being distinctive to London. In this way, Samuel Johnson could affirm, 'Why, Sir, you find no man, at all intellectual, who is willing to leave London. No, Sir, when a man is tired of London, he is tired of life; for there is in London all that life can afford.'[67] On the other side of the Channel, Parisian commentators can be quoted along the same lines, such as Louis-Sébastien Mercier's remarks in the opening lines of his *Tableau de Paris*, in which he summarises the interest and attractive force of Paris: 'Anyone in Paris who knows how to understand things has no need to leave the limits of its walls to learn about people from other parts of the world.'[68] In both these cases, there is a sense of there being no need to look beyond their own city, even if such commentators might also regard their neighbouring and competing counterpart across the Channel as offering a significant example of otherness. As numerous historians have argued, notions of Britishness were developed in contradistinction with French characteristics and vice versa.[69] In reality, the two cities were also involved in larger cultural exchanges and affinities tending to transcend national character. Leisure practices offer, in this respect, a key to investigating the wider new forms of urban culture developing at this period. Shared models for behaviour meant that, by the second half of the eighteenth century, Paris or London would be increasingly familiar to those visiting them for the first time. Such parallels were put in place over the course of the century through what has been described here as a form of civilising emulation: whether in a theatre or in public space, appearance and deportment became common points of reference, as did the notion that all participants should be able to enjoy a given entertainment. Those who did not conform risked societal sanction because of

The rules of leisure in eighteenth-century Paris and London   **205**

their failure to behave correctly, and if they went further in disrespecting the rules, they might be removed by the police and judicial authorities: the key consideration was that the show should go on.

To some extent, London and Paris were coming to share in a common culture that went beyond the bounds of national frameworks, and in which leisure practices can be seen as a key aspect of developing urban life. Civilising emulation, as it has been termed here, had a part to play in this process. More than seeing and being seen, this was a matter of enjoying the performance within certain imposed frameworks and prescriptions. Accordingly, the core of the new injunctions or prescriptions for leisure during the eighteenth century can be linked to the simple idea of the enjoyment of the spectacle, whatever it might be, but in terms of particular modes appropriate to given participants' social standing, and in order to maintain the bonds of sociability.

Translated by Simon Macdonald.

Notes

1 Louis-Sébastien Mercier, *Neighbours and Rivals: Paris and London (c.1780)*, trans. Jonathan Conlin and Laurent Turcot (forthcoming).
2 Robert Tombs and Isabelle Tombs, *That Sweet Enemy: the French and the British from the Sun King to the Present* (London: William Heinemann, 2006); Jonathan Conlin, *Tales of Two Cities: Paris, London and the Making of the Modern City, 1700–1900* (London: Atlantic Books, 2013); François-Joseph Ruggiu, *L'individu et la famille dans les sociétés urbaines anglaise et française: 1720–1780* (Paris: PUPS, 2007); Leora Auslander, *Des révolutions culturelles: la politique du quotidien en Grande-Bretagne, en Amérique et en France, XVIIe–XIXe siècle* (Toulouse: Presses Universitaires du Mirail, 2010); Renaud Morieux, *Une mer pour deux royaumes: La Manche, frontière franco-anglaise XVIIe–XVIIIe* (Rennes: Presses Universitaires de Rennes, 2007); Stephen Conway, *Britain, Ireland, and Continental Europe in the Eighteenth Century: Similarities, Connections, Identities* (Oxford: Oxford University Press, 2011).
3 Karen Newman, *Cultural Capitals: Early Modern London and Paris* (Princeton: Princeton University Press, 2007); Vanessa Harding, *The Dead and the Living in London and Paris, 1500–1670* (Cambridge: Cambridge University Press, 2002).
4 See Chapters 4 and 10 of this volume; see also Gilles Chaubaud, ,Pour une histoire comparée des guides imprimés à l'époque moderne', in *Les guides imprimés du XVIe au XXe siècle. Villes, paysages, voyages. Actes du colloque de Paris de décembre 1998* (Paris: Belin, 2000), pp. 641–649; Claire Hancock, *Paris et Londres au XIXe siècle: Représentations dans les guides et récits de voyage* (Paris: Éditions du CNRS, 2003); Laurent Turcot, 'Entre promenades et jardins publics: Les loisirs parisiens et londoniens au XVIIIe siècle', *Revue belge de philologie et d'histoire*, 87 (2009),

645–663; Jonathan Conlin, 'Vauxhall on the boulevard: pleasure gardens in London and Paris, 1764–1784', *Urban History*, 35:1 (2008), 24–47.

5 John Andrews, *A Comparative View of the French and English Nations in Their Manners, Politics and Literature* (London: Longman, 1785); John Moore, *A View of Society and Manners in France, Switzerland and Germany* (London, 1780).

6 Mathieu-François Pidansat de Mairobert, *L'Espion anglois, ou correspondance secrète entre milord All'eye et milord All'ear* (London: J. Adamson, 1779); Jean-Jacques Rutlidge, *Essai sur le caractère et les mœurs des François comparées à celles des Anglois* (London, 1776); Raymonde Monnier (ed.), *Paris et Londres en Miroir, extraits du Babillard de Jean-Jacques Rutlidge* (Saint-Étienne: Publications de l'Université de Saint-Étienne, 2010). See also, Ange Goudar, *L'Espion français à Londres, ou observations critiques sur l'Angleterre et sur les Anglais* (London, 1779).

7 Stéphane Van Damme, 'Measuring the scientific greatness: the recognition of Paris in European Enlightenment', *Les Dossiers du Grihl*, http://dossiersgrihl.revues.org/772, 27 June 2007 (accessed 16 July 2010).

8 John Goodman, 'Altar against altar: the Colisée, Vauxhall utopianism and symbolic politics in Paris', *Art History*, 15 (1992), 434–469; Gilles-Antoine Langlois. ' "Les charmes de l'égalité": éléments pour une urbanistique des loisirs publics à Paris de Louis XV à Louis-Philippe', *Histoire Urbaine*, 1:1 (2000), 7–24; Conlin, 'Vauxhall on the boulevard', pp. 24–47.

9 Michael Werner and Bénédicte Zimmermann (eds.), *De la comparaison à l'histoire croisée* (Paris: Seuil, 2004); Michael Werner, 'Les usages de l'échelle dans la recherche sur les transferts culturels', *Cahiers d'études germaniques*, 28 (1995), 39–53. See also Gesa Stedman, *Cultural Exchange in Seventeenth-century France and England* (Aldershot: Ashgate, 2013).

10 Hannah Greig, ' "All together and all distinct": public sociability and social exclusivity in London's pleasure gardens, c.1740–1800', *Journal of British Studies*, 51:1 (2012), 50–75.

11 Xavier Rousseau, Bernard Dauven and Aude Musin, 'Civilisation des mœurs et/ou disciplinarisation sociale? Les sociétés urbaines face à la violence en Europe (1300–1800)', in Laurent Mucchielli and Pieter Spierenburg (eds.), *Histoire de l'homicide en Europe de la fin du Moyen Âge à nos jours* (Paris: La Découverte, 2009), pp. 273–321; Diane Roussel, *Violences et passions dans le Paris de la Renaissance* (Seyssel: Champ Vallon, 2012), p. 16; Brian Cowan, 'Publicity and privacy in the history of the British coffeehouse', *History Compass*, 5:4 (2007), 1180–1213; Brian Cowan, 'What was masculine about the public sphere? Gender and the coffeehouse milieu in post-Restoration England', *History Workshop Journal*, 51 (2001), 127–157; Brian Cowan, 'The rise of the coffeehouse reconsidered', *Historical Journal*, 47:1 (2004), 21–46.

12 Lawrence Klein, *Shaftesbury and the Culture of Politeness: Moral Discourse and Cultural Politics in Early Eighteenth-century England* (Cambridge: Cambridge University Press, 1994); Anna Bryson, *From Courtesy to Civility: Changing Codes of Conduct in Early Modern England* (Oxford: Clarendon Press, 1998); Paul Langford, *A Polite and Commercial People: England, 1727–1783* (Oxford: Oxford University Press, 1998); Philip Carter, *Men and the Emergence of Polite Society: Britain, 1660–1800*

(Harlow: Longman, 2001); Amanda Vickery, *The Gentleman's Daughter: Women's Lives in Georgian England* (New Haven: Yale University Press, 1998); Lawrence Klein, 'Liberty, manners, and politeness in early eighteenth century', *Historical Journal*, 32:3 (1989), 583–605.

13 Miles Ogborn, *Spaces of Modernity: London's Geographies, 1680–1780* (New York and London: Guildford Press, 1998); Elizabeth McKellar, *The Birth of Modern London: The Development and Design of the City 1660–1720* (Manchester: Manchester University Press, 1999).

14 Lawrence Klein, 'Politeness and the interpretation of the British eighteenth century', *Historical Journal*, 45:4 (2002), 869–898.

15 Maurice Magendie, *La politesse mondaine et les théories de l'honnêteté en France au XVIIe siècle, de 1600 à 1660* (Paris: Slatkine Reprints, 1993); Roger Chartier 'Distinction et divulgation: La civilité et ses livres', in *Lectures et lecteurs dans la France d'Ancien Régime* (Paris: Seuil, 1987); Emmanuel Bury, *Littérature et politesse: L'Invention de l'honnête homme (1580–1750)* (Paris: PUF, 1996).

16 Jean-Louis Harouel, *L'Embellissement des villes: L'Urbanisme français au XVIIIe siècle* (Paris: Picard Éditeur, 1993); Michel Le Moël and Sophie Descat (eds.), *L'urbanisme parisien au siècle des Lumières* (Paris: Action artistique de la ville de Paris, 1999).

17 Jacques Revel, 'Les usages de la civilité', in Roger Chartier (ed.), *Histoire de la vie privée*, Vol. 3, *De la Renaissance aux Lumières* (Paris: Seuil, 1999), p. 202.

18 Alain Montandon (ed.), *Bibliographie des traités de savoir-vivre en Europe du Moyen Age à nos jours* (Clermond-Ferrand: Université Blaise-Pascal, 1995).

19 Antoine de Courtin, *Nouveau traité de la civilité qui se pratique en France parmi les honnestes gens* (Paris: H. Josset, 1671); for the English translation, see *The Rules of Civility; or, the Maxims of Genteel Behaviour, as They are Practis'd and Observ'd by Persons of Quality, upon Several Occasions. Newly Done Out of the Twelfth Edition in French* (London, 1703).

20 Jean-Baptiste De La Salle, *Règles de la bienséance et de la civilité chrétienne* (Troyes-Reims, 1703).

21 De La Salle, *Règles de la bienséance*, p. 183.

22 N. Dupuy La Chapelle, *Instruction d'un père à son fils sur la manière de se conduire dans le monde* (Paris: Jacques Estienne, 1730), p. 427.

23 See also Barthélémy-Claude Graillard de Graville, *L'ami des filles* (Paris: Dufour, 1762), pp. 119–121, 125, 139, 135–138.

24 Antoine François D'Exiles Prévost, *Élémens de politesse et de bienséance, ou la civilité* (Paris: Duchesne, 1767).

25 Prévost, *Élémens de politesse et de bienséance*, pp. 82–89.

26 Anna Bryson, *From Courtesy to Civility: Changing Codes of Conduct in Early Modern England* (Oxford: Clarendon Press, 1998), p. 277.

27 Jacques Carré, 'Introduction', in Jacques Carré (ed.), *The Crisis of Courtesy: Studies in the Conduct-Book in Britain, 1600–1900* (New York: Brill, 1994), p. 3.

28 *The Gentleman's Library, Containing Rules for Conduct in All Parts of Life* (London, 1715), p. 183.

29 *The Gentleman's Library, Containing Rules for Conduct*, p. 186.

30 *The Man of Manners: or, Plebeian Polish'd* (London: J. Roberts, n.d. [1737?]), p. 1.

31 *The Man of Manners*, pp. 4–5.

32 *The Man of Manners*, p. 35.

33 *The Man of Manners*, p. 43.

34 François Nivelon, *The Rudiments of Genteel Behavior* (n.p., 1737).

35 *The Lady's Delight, or Accomplish'd Female Instructor* (London: James Hodges, n.d. [1740?]).

36 Benjamin Heller, 'The "mene peuple" and the polite spectator: the individual in the crowd at eighteenth-century London fairs', *Past and Present*, 208 (2010), 131–157.

37 See Laurent Turcot (ed.), *L'ordinaire parisien des Lumières* (Paris: Hermann, 2013).

38 Lawrence Klein, 'Politeness for plebes: consumption and social identity in early eighteenth-century England', in Ann Bermingham and John Brewer (eds.), *The Consumption of Culture, 1600–1800: Image, Object, Text* (London and New York: Routlege, 1995), p. 375.

39 For a discussion of Parisian police see Vincent Milliot, *Un policier des Lumières* (Seyssel: Champ Vallon, 2011).

40 Louis-Sébastien Mercier, *Panorama of Paris, Selections from 'Tableau de Paris'*, trans. Jeremy D. Popkin (Philadelphia: Pennsylvania State University Press, 1999), p. 36.

41 *The World*, 189, 12 August 1756.

42 Archives Nationales, Paris (hereafter AN), O^1 1589, f. 462, 3–10 September 1787.

43 AN O^1 1589, f. 99, 24–31 April 1779.

44 AN H^2 2021. See also Alan Williams, *The Police of Paris, 1718–1789* (Baton Rouge and London: Louisiana State University Press, 1979), pp. 70–75; and Jean Chagniot, *Paris et l'armée au XVIIIe siècle: Étude politique et sociale* (Paris: Economica, 1985), pp. 117–157.

45 AN H^2 1941^1, 10 July 1755.

46 AN Y 14479, 5 November 1784.

47 AN Y 14474, 30 June 1779.

48 AN Y 14464, 5 June 1769.

49 AN Y 16022, 21 December 1786.

50 AN Y 16022, 8 July 1780; AN Y 16022, 5 September 1784.

51 AN Y 14456, 15 May 1761.

52 AN Y 12227, Foire St-Ovide (1773–1775), 6 September 1774.

53 J.M. Beattie, *Policing and Punishment in London, 1660–1750: Urban Crime and the Limits of Terror* (Oxford: Oxford University Press, 2001), p. 77.

54 David J. Cox, *A Certain Share of Low Cunning: A History of the Bow Street Runners, 1792–1839* (London: Willan Publishing, 2010).

55 Elaine A. Reynolds, *Before the Bobbies: The Night Watch and Police Reform in Metropolitan London, 1720–1830* (Stanford: Stanford University Press, 1998), p. 29; Joanna Innes, *Inferior Politics: Social Problems and Social Policies in Eighteenth-Century Britain* (Oxford: Oxford University Press, 2009).

56 Alison O'Byrne, *Walking, Rambling and Promenading in Eighteenth-century London: a Literary and Cultural History* (PhD dissertation, University of York, 2003), p. 149.

57 Robert Pentland Mahaffy (ed.), *Calendar of State Papers, Domestic Series, of the Reign of Queen Anne*, 2 vols (London: 1916), Vol. 1, p. 723.

58 Robert Shoemaker, 'The Old Bailey proceedings and the representation of crime and criminal justice in eighteenth-century London', *Journal of British Studies*, 47 (2008), 565.

59 Benjamin Heller, *Leisure and Pleasure in London Society, 1760–1820: An Agent-Centred Account* (DPhil dissertation, University of Oxford, 2009), p. 247. The table is reproduced by kind permission of Dr Heller.

60 Heller, *Leisure and Pleasure*, p. 262.

61 Old Bailey Proceedings Online (OBP) (www.oldbaileyonline.org, 18.2.2014), 28 June 1769, trial of Thomas Gray and James Waldin (t17690628-30).

62 David Worrall, *Theatric Revolution: Drama, Censorship, and Romantic Period Subcultures 1773–1832* (Oxford: Oxford University Press, 2008), pp. 227–229.

63 Heller, *Leisure and Pleasure*, p. 267.

64 Heller, *Leisure and Pleasure*, p. 266.

65 Heller, *Leisure and Pleasure*, p. 270.

66 Revel, 'Les usages de la civilité', p. 202.

67 James Boswell, *The Life of Samuel Johnson, LLD* (London: Routledge, 1859) p. 120.

68 Mercier, *Panorama of Paris*, p. 29.

69 Linda Colley affirms that Britons 'defined themselves as Prostestants struggling for survival against the world's foremost Catholic power. They defined themselves against the French as they imagined them to be, superstitious, militarist, decadent and unfree.' Linda Colley, *Britons: Forging the Nation 1707–1837* (New Haven: Yale University Press, 1992), p. 6. See also: Anthony Smith, 'The origins of nations', *Ethnic and Racial Studies*, 12 (1989), 340–367; Carol Watts, *The Cultural Work of Empire* (Toronto: Toronto University Press, 2007); P.J. Marshall, *The Making and Unmaking of Empires: Britain, India and America c.1750–1783* (Oxford: Oxford University Press, 2005); David A. Bell, *The Cult of the Nation in France: Inventing Nationalism, 1680–1800* (Cambridge, MA: Harvard University Press, 2001).

10

City of pleasure or *ville des plaisirs*? Urban leisure culture exchanges between England and France through travel writing (1700–1820)

CLARISSE COULOMB

In 1698, the Englishman Martin Lister went to Paris as a medical attendant to the Earl of Portland, who was negotiating with the French about the Spanish succession. Lister transformed the notes that he took on his journey into a travel memoir, entitled *A Journey to Paris in the Year 1698.*[1] The same year, the French Huguenot Maximilien Misson published his *Memoires et observations faites par un voyageur en Angleterre.*[2] Lister's *Journey* became a bestseller, which went through numerous editions. In 1719, Misson's *Memoires* appeared in an English translation, a proof of success for a travel diary.[3]

Indeed, despite the wars that divided the two countries for almost 45 years during this period, the so-called long eighteenth century was a time of reciprocal fascination between England and France. If travels across the whole of Europe were common, the ones between these rival nations were the most numerous; France was the major destination for British travellers and vice versa.[4] The French Revolution and the Napoleonic Wars affected this mutual tourism badly. It was not until after Waterloo in 1815 that tourism between the two countries revived, and experienced a new era with the dawn of the railway revolution around 1820.

In recent decades, Josephine Grieder and Robin Eagles have rightly emphasised that travellers were the main vehicles for Anglomania in France and Francophilia in England.[5] Cross-Channel cultural exchanges during the

City of pleasure or *ville des plaisirs?* **211**

long eighteenth century have been well researched.[6] However, even though Peter Borsay argued that entertainment 'regularly acted as vehicles for foreign influences', an 'entangled history' of urban leisure culture between France and Britain still remains to be written.[7] This chapter will analyse, through the eyes of the travellers, the reciprocal perceptions and mutual influences in leisure patterns in France and Britain during the long eighteenth century.

My analysis is essentially based on the abundant travel literature, letters and memoirs of those travellers who actually visited the other country.[8] These sources serve a dual purpose: first, they provide a lot of information on the development of urban entertainments and the ways in which they were perceived by foreign tourists. 'It's deplorable,' a certain John Andrews lamented, 'that most of the travellers going to France have hardly other grounds for doing it than those they would have to go to Bath, Tunbridge or Scarborough. They are only seeking frivolous entertainments.'[9] According to Andrews, travellers no longer stressed education as the prime motive for the Grand Tour, but increasingly sought enjoyment and amusement.[10] This recreational tourism was an urban tourism: tourists travelled as rapidly as possible between major cities where the range of new forms of entertainment was immense. The growing concentration of the elite and the new middle-class in towns had changed the urban landscape.[11] The enlightened city served increasingly as a socio-cultural centre, designed for spending time and money on new distractions.

A second reason to study travel accounts is that travellers were not only witnesses of the birth of the leisure town, but also formed the key players in this major urban transformation. Tourists were agents of cultural transmission. They acted as 'importers' of foreign entertainments in two ways: first, when they went back home, they influenced their compatriots, either by publishing an account of their travels, in which they had advice to offer based on their experiences, or by adopting new attitudes. Second, the presence of tourists strongly affected the development of urban leisure culture in the cities they visited. This chapter not only aims to see the changing leisure landscape through the eyes of contemporaries, but also to analyse processes of transfer through imitation, translation or adaptation. How were leisure practices transmitted and how were they experienced by the men and women who created and practised them?

It is important to note that these processes of cultural transfer were asymmetrical. Since the 1690s, leisure had become an urban industry in England. London was in the vanguard of change regarding the leisure business, but this new industry rapidly spread to the provincial towns.[12] At the end of the seventeenth century, none of the English upper-class pastimes pleased French travellers very much.[13] However, in the eighteenth century, surprise and disdain gradually gave way to admiration and imitation. While French towns started to imitate new English leisure activities, Paris built a new reputation as a town of festivities, pleasures and entertainment, even to such extent that many contemporaries started to contrast merry France with the duller England. How can this development be explained? As I will show in this chapter, changing patterns and perceptions of class, gender and nation offer crucial ingredients to better understand this development.

Social distinctions

In the seventeenth and eighteenth centuries, French aristocratic and upper middle-class travellers were often surprised at how Englishmen amused themselves in urban public and semi-public spaces, which was in many ways strikingly different from what they were used to in their own country. One thing that struck them most was the social composition of the public gathering together for commercial entertainments: on the one hand, they were surprised by the high numbers of idlers and their extremely luxurious life style that dominated the new leisure towns; on the other hand, they were amazed by the social heterogeneity of the audience and the rise of a mass consumer culture affecting the social hierarchy. Neither of these observations pleased them very much.

'There are here shows of which we don't have any idea', Madame du Bocage observed after her visit to England in 1764.[14] French travellers were impressed by the commercial pleasure gardens that offered, for a few shillings, 'illuminations, concerts and everything one could want'.[15] They were amazed by the luxurious assembly rooms funded by subscription and stunned by the illustrious promenades and shopping streets and the sidewalks unknown in Paris. In 1779, the Abbé Coyer noted that 'one doesn't merely walk, one strolls while feasting one's eyes on a continual spectacle, the display of the wealth of the world in the prominent windows so attractive to the buyer'.[16] To their great surprise, even the provincial towns were equipped with a recreational infrastructure. The Marquis de Bombelles thought York a pleasant town thanks to 'an auditorium, fortifications, fine walks and very long, wide, streets'.[17]

From the end of the seventeenth century, French travellers were fascinated by the rise of spa towns, in particular by Bath. However, they often experienced the modern spa towns with mixed feelings, where the search for pleasure and the presence of idlers was too dominant. According to Misson, visitors rushed 'without caring about Baths nor waters to drink, but only to enjoy themselves with good company. There is Music and Games, Promenades, Balls and perpetual small Fairs.'[18] French travellers were particularly sensitive to the idea that the idle rich seemed to be more numerous than in France, and commercial entertainment promoted the expansion of a new leisure class. The Abbé Coyer, a member of the Royal Society, remarked: 'The wealthier and larger the town, the more people it contains who are looking for relaxation at the end of the day, and also the more idle people there are who think only of enjoying their fortune. Pleasure is becoming a necessity for all.'[19] A few years later, the Marquis de Bombelles described the Ranelagh pleasure garden in London as a 'temple of Pleasure' and 'a sanctuary for the idle who are proportionally more numerous in London than anywhere else'.[20]

A major critique of British commercial entertainment was the cult of financial excess, especially with regard to gambling. In the late seventeenth century, Maximilien Misson reported enthusiastically about the new and 'extremely convenient' London coffeehouses: 'You have all manner of news there; You have a good fire, which you may sit by as long as you please; You have a dish of coffee; You meet your friends for the transaction of business, and all for a penny, if you don't care to spend more.'[21] But he found the betting on sport in coffeehouses appalling, especially when he learned that not only horseracing but also boxing and cockfighting were popular because they afforded an opportunity to gamble. In the late eighteenth century, the Abbé Coyer was still shocked by the spectacle of wrestlers 'motivated by money, challenges and public admiration'. According to him 'luxury is excessive in gaming and betting'.[22]

Figure 10.1 Joseph Highmore (attr.), *The Coffee House Politicians*, c. 1725 or after 1750. Yale Center for British Art, Paul Mellon Collection.

Many French travellers looked down upon the enthusiastic adoption of commercial entertainment by the British leisure classes as a sign of a lack of elegant taste and a preference for superficial mass culture. In 1784, the Marquis de Bombelles wrote that Bath was born out of the 'need felt by the idle to be amongst a crowd', explaining that 'the Englishman, more desirous to enjoy himself than ingenious in the means to get the true pleasures of a good society, goes where the crowd gathers and attaches much importance to the life of Cabaret'.[23] Count Ferri de Saint-Constant criticised the way British upper middle classes followed the crowd to join the elite culture of distinction in the spas:

> It can only be the most ridiculous fashion or the most imperious need to move elsewhere which provokes an Englishman, the father of a family, the owner of a superb garden and a clean and comfortable abode as well as horses, animals etc., to leave his home and to go and shut himself up in a small house with only two or three front windows, in full sunlight, surrounded by other houses, situated on bare sand and where his family is uncomfortably housed, for the sake of showing off his horse and carriage on an elegant promenade and seeing his name in the gazette.[24]

For many French travellers, one of the most shocking features of English commercial entertainment was the increasing blurring of social boundaries between aristocratic, bourgeois and sometimes even lower-class audiences. 'Society at Ranelagh Gardens', Count Ferri de Saint-Constant remarked disdainfully, is made up 'of people of taste, the rich and those who imitate them'.[25] P.J. Grosley, a barrister and an academic, in 1774 reported in a neutral tone that the pleasures of Vauxhall united 'all ranks and conditions'.[26] Joseph Raby, however, was appalled that the Vauxhall gardens erased existing class hierarchies and the lower classes seemed to dominate the scene, comparing the site with a *guinguette*, a suburban tavern for working people.[27] Even elitist leisure venues such as the theatre were available to the general public: Grosley was shocked by the large working-class audience, which was undisciplined and riotous.[28] Similarly, the historian P.-N. Chantreau explained that London's public dances strikingly differed from the *bal de l'opéra de Paris*: 'The populace takes part in them in a most disagreeable manner, particularly for the women.'[29]

The commercial nature of urban entertainments made it difficult to exclude audiences from middle- and lower-class backgrounds. At the same time, the increasing professionalisation of leisure promoted the social status and power of leisure entrepreneurs. The Marquis de Bombelles was frustrated by the master of ceremonies of Bath: 'The English, so fanatical about liberty, so licentious

City of pleasure or *ville des plaisirs?* **215**

at the theatre, like sheep obey a *polisson* who after misconducting himself elsewhere comes seeking a job which every other man of good society would decline.'[30] Leisure had been democratised as well as commercialised[31] and, for French travellers, this meant conflict and subversion.

Despite all of their critical remarks, French travellers played an important role in the enthusiastic appropriation of English models of leisure culture in French cities in the second half of the eighteenth century: either indirectly, by distributing information on commercial entertainment on the other side of the Channel, or directly, by taking concrete initiatives to establish 'English' recreational institutions in French urban contexts. 'I had not been in Paris for fifteen years: when I arrived, I thought I had come to London', said the astonished Charles de Peyssonel in 1782.[32] Many English travellers were surprised too to find so many 'English' leisure innovations in the French capital and provincial cities. However, many of them quickly recognised a fundamental difference: the French cosmopolitan aristocracy ensured that the new leisure amenities they had imported from England remained socially much more exclusive.

In 1766, Horace Walpole excitedly reported that he had just attended his first true horserace, not at Hounslow near his home, nor at Newmarket where he had been several times, but in the Plaine des Sablons, near Paris.[33] The first horserace in France was established by Lord Forbes and the Count de Lauraguais; both were familiar with the races at Newmarket.[34] Since 1775, the Count d'Artois, the youngest brother of Louis XVI, regularly organised horse races too.[35] In July 1765, a group of Englishmen living in Toulouse held a horserace just outside the city gates, a spectacle never witnessed before.[36] By the late 1760s, Paris already had a dozen 'Wauxhalls', modelled on the Vauxhall Pleasure Garden of London but not so vast.[37] In 1785, the Duc de Chartres, the king's cousin who often travelled to England, cut down some trees in the garden of the Palais-Royal to establish, according to the British aristocrat Hester Piozzi, 'a sort of Vauxhall, with tents, fountains, shops, full of frippery, brilliant at once and worthless, to attract them [customers]'.[38]

Interestingly, the demands and expectations of aristocratic English tourists also played an important role in the innovation of French leisure culture, especially in the development of health resorts. In 1783, Joseph Cradock made an excursion to Bagnères-de-Luchon in the Pyrenees and noted that 'several of our English nobility were then in the neighbourhood ... and there were often balls, concerts, and various diversions'.[39] Initially, French spas took a long time to equip themselves to equal the English model.[40] Arthur Young, during his stay in the same resort in 1787, complained about the baths which he found to be 'horrible holes' and about the 'very little variety' of the social life. But change was underway, because the States of Languedoc were 'building a large and handsome bathing house, to contain various separate cells, with baths, and a large common room, with two arcades to walk in, free from sun and rain'.[41] On the coast, French towns seemed to take on the air of English seaside resorts. Coquebert de Montbret indicated that 'there are English-like sea baths at Boulogne'.[42] Although not yet French territory, Nice was the most famous example: its popularity was due less to Tobias Smolett's *Letters to Nice from Nice*, than to Captain Harvey, third Count of Bristol, who had served in Nice and want back there between 1752 and 1758.[43] When Arthur Young visited the town in September 1789, he was struck by the new buildings 'an unequivocal proof that the place is flourishing; owing very much to the resort of foreigners, principally English, who pass the winter here, for the benefit and pleasure of the climate'.[44]

Apart from the climate, what were the reasons for English aristocrats giving preference to French leisure towns? One explanation might be that they soon discovered that the French versions of English leisure venues were socially often much more exclusive: 'I found no greater alteration in Paris, after ten years' absence from it, than the prodigious difference of expense', Philip Thicknesse remarked in 1777, pointing out that many Parisian entertainments were primarily aimed at the upper class.[45] Sir John Paul described Frascati's garden in Paris as 'an entertainment somewhat like our Vauxhall, but on a smaller and far more elegant scale'.[46] During his stay in 1771, Horace Walpole criticised the new attraction, the Colisée, near the Champs-Élysées, which was 'a most gaudy Ranelagh, gilt, painted, and becupided like an opera'.[47] However, it was, according to John Andrews, 'frequented by the better sort'.[48] Similarly, Lady Knight, living in Toulouse in 1777, was amazed by the exclusive social composition of theatre audiences, resulting from the high ticket prices: 'We have been to the Comedy, which is a large elegant house and was as much filled as a London theatre when Garrick acts, but more than two-thirds were gentlemen.'[49] This was a great contrast to the populist audiences of English theatres. Grosley even recorded that Garrick, after his sojourn in Paris, was tempted to raise Drury Lane's prices in order to put them 'on the same footing as those in Paris'.[50] Horace Walpole saw the high prices not only in theatres but also in the Wauxhalls as an explanation for the failure of Parisian pleasure gardens: 'There are few nabobs and nabobesses in this country, and ... the middling and common people are not much richer than Job.'[51] The mixing of social classes was

City of pleasure or *ville des plaisirs?* **217**

the basis of their success, but for many Parisian aristocrats this price seemed too high.

Nevertheless, the commercialisation of leisure culture in French cities also stimulated an increasing mixing of social classes. According to some historians, the eighteenth century witnessed the decline of traditional recreation, as the French elite turned to exclusive urban leisure in imitation of England.[52] Yet English travellers were fascinated by the heterogeneous audience composition of the popular *théâtres de foire* of St-Germain and St-Laurent, including people of high society.[53] In 1785, Mrs Cradock, seeing the Place Royale in Toulouse full of popular shows with puppets and dancing monkeys, was surprised 'as this seemed to charm the audience, many members of which belonged to the high society'. Within five months, she learned that 'it is good form' to stroll the fairs and observed that even a café at St-Laurent's fair was 'filled up with the most varied public from the petit bourgeois to the great seigneur'.[54]

In the second half of the eighteenth century, the boulevards that encircled Paris were another space for plebeian entertainments very attractive to aristocratic tourists from across the Channel. The Duchess of Northumberland, arriving in Paris on 9 May 1770, went the next evening to the Old Boulevard: here she observed 'the confusion of Riches & poverty, hotels & hovels, pure air & stinks, people of all sorts & conditions'; she saw also 'puppet shews, raree shews, monsters, dancing dogs & ... crowds incredible'.[55] Minor amusements, confined to seasonal fairgrounds in the first half of the century, now settled on the northern boulevards in between fair seasons.[56] According to John Andrews, 'the most essential advantage that Paris enjoys over London' was the promenades and, above all, the boulevards where 'all those exhibitions, in short, that serve to entertain the vulgar, are in a manner concentrated here. There are also some attempts at elegant pastimes, such as rooms with vocal and instrumental music.'[57] Indeed, after 1784, the Opéra's proprietary concerns in the boulevard encouraged an explosion of popular spectacles, often copied from England. To these the Cirque olympique belonged, a horse show of Sieur Astley, and the Waux-Hall d'été.[58] These new-established spectacles filled the social-cultural gap between the royal theatres of the elite and the popular amusements of the people.[59] Here, Arthur Young attended the farce, among the prostitutes.[60] According to Hester Piozzi, the boulevards had become 'a sort of Sadlers Wells'.[61]

For Madame Roland, the French boulevards were more attractive than their English equivalents.[62] In England, French tourists looked down upon elite participation in plebeian sports, like boxing matches.[63] But they did not despise popular theatre, such as Sadler's Wells, or fairs like St Bartholomew's, which

218 Towards an 'entangled history' of urban leisure culture

were, as in France, leading centres of entertainment.[64] As Peter Borsay noted, English elites were withdrawing from their participation in traditional culture and were turning to the exclusive but expanding world of fashionable urban leisure.[65] The French delay in the adoption of some of these new forms of commercial leisure allowed their traditional recreations to continue into the nineteenth century.[66]

Gendered leisure towns

Lady Holland, while on an extended stay in Paris during the year 1763, wrote to her sister: 'Upon the whole I think every woman past thirty that really lives a Paris life among the French, and understands the language, and who like conversation better than cards, will prefer Paris to London.'[67] For English women, the salon society of Paris hosted by distinguished ladies was a revelation.[68] Most of the Englishmen also eulogised the conversation of women. Thanks to Anglomania, the English were welcomed, as Horace Walpole was by Madame du Deffand. The prominent role of women in the salons was a feature of elite sociability in France.[69] *Salonnières* were praised for their social skills, and their ability to maintain *politesse* and harmony, even across several social categories.[70] Sir Philip Thicknesse, being introduced to the Princess de Beauvau, a 'lady of the first quality', was 'agreeably surprized [sic] with the easy and familiar conversation of one of the most agreeable women in the world.'[71]

Many English tourists – men and women – were delighted by French sociability, mainly represented by the salons. Although the notion that the Enlightenment salons were part of a 'bourgeois' Republic of Letters is misguided, as philosophers were mainly welcomed because they conformed to aristocratic norms, many English travellers were surprised by their social openness, especially to 'bourgeois' philosophers.[72] It was, however, the social importance of women in these exclusive social gatherings and their leading role in discussing literature, philosophy and the arts that struck them most, as this greatly differed from what they were used to in England, where the new commercial entertainments generated more gender-defined spaces, while French sociability remained mixed.[73]

According to various English tourists, leisure time in France was structured by women. Indeed, the fact that dinner was taken at about one o'clock, much earlier than in England, provided more spare time, to the utter despair of Arthur Young: 'What is a man good for after his silk breeches and stockings are on, his hat under his arms ... Can he clamber the rocks to mineralize? Can he farm with the peasant and the ploughman? He is in order for the conversation of the ladies.'[74] Public entertainments followed at five and continued till eight, when the elite guests returned to the public walks before supper. Such recreations seemed to grant sexual licence. Lord Chesterfield advised his son to 'frequent La Foire St-Laurent, which I see is now open; you will improve more by going there with your mistress, than by staying at home and reading Euclid with your geometry master. Adieu. "*divertissez-vous, il n'y a rien de tel.*" '[75] Philip Thickenesse was more critical of mixed socialising: 'No wonder then if there is but little virtue to be found amongst women who … exhibited at these suppers, mixed with both sexes and spend the remainder of the night in revelling and riot either at their own houses or at some public nocturnal rendez-vous.' He called Paris this 'city of love and folly'.[76]

While English travellers were often astonished by the mixing of genders in French urban culture, French tourists in England, in turn, observed with surprise and disapproval the existence of exclusively men's leisure cultures such as sport, coffeehouses and clubs. Georges-Louis Lesage did not understand why gentlemen enjoyed sports, regarding them as incompatible with a polite people: 'It is true that they enjoy seeing Gladiators fighting, seeing Bulls being torn to pieces by dogs & watching cockfighting, & at the Carnival they like to throw sticks at Cocks, but this is less through cruelty than through coarseness.'[77]

French travellers also denounced the frequent drunkenness of English gentlemen. According to the Abbé Le Blanc, Englishmen 'prefer the pleasure of drinking the health of beauties in a tavern to that of talking with them at a soirée', which had 'given rise to all those societies whose meetings are held in a drinking house'.[78] And, indeed, male predominance probably owed a good deal to the origin of many such associations in drinking houses, from which women were conventionally excluded.[79] The clubs, in particular, seemed a source of gender division: were they the cause, or the consequence, of the secluded life of English women?[80] Manon Roland, a follower of Jean-Jacques Rousseau, noted that in England,

> The two sexes live much more separately than in France … The men come together to form what are called clubs … The women thus normally remain on their own; they meet together, play very little, take walks and are in no way distracted from caring for their families.[81]

In the same period, Lacoste considered that the English home was 'a sanctuary for good manners, but at the same time a place of vapid boredom',[82] from which the men escaped by going to their club. The separation by gender seemed to ensure virtue, but also dullness.

French tourists, used to the social importance of women, agreed that this was the reason for the tiresomeness of English pleasures. They underlined the absurdity of the conventions that allowed women to sit at a table in a cake shop, but not to go into a café.[83] But even in England one could not speak of two separate leisure spheres, as some commercial entertainments were, of course, mixed. As for Bath, French visitors noticed mischievously that the new entertainments that were more popular among women, such as the pleasure gardens, attracted people from various classes. Raby put it crudely: Vauxhall was not a 'decent place' and 'there is no shortage of girls'.[84] For Bombelles, Ranelagh was the 'temple of pleasure' but also of 'libertinism'.[85] Indeed, many pleasure gardens were spaces of erotic delights,[86] but some French travellers even credited the taste of English women for shopping to their desire to meet men.[87] And it is true that such meetings were a response to the restrictions of dominant modes of polite masculinity.[88]

French travellers claimed that there was no English equivalent of the salon, as *raouts* could not be considered a substitute. The crowd made conversation impossible, so this was replaced by card games, and they were also socially exclusive. The Comtesse de Boigne, who lived as a French émigré in Britain for many years, was surprised by a duchess who did not speak to most of her guests and she confessed that as a Frenchwoman, her social instincts were irritated by the snobbish English system of social gradation.[89]

Indeed the silent English women surprised Continental visitors. In 1725, the Swiss Béat de Muralt described three female leisure activities: the walk, comedy and concerts 'where they go to be seen'.[90] He noticed that, although dining was a mixed social activity, following custom, women would retire leaving the men to drink and converse.[91] Grosley, nearly 50 years later, pointed out the lack of mixed conversation: 'The only thing that unites both sexes is play. If they meet only to chat and converse, the women, generally speaking, place themselves near the door, and leave the upper end of the apartment and the conversation to the men.'[92] The contrast between sociability and taciturn women provided numerous *traits d'esprit*: the Baron d'Holbach compared the silent women parading in Vauxhall gardens to Egyptians processing around the mausoleum of Osiris; the Marquis de Bombelles wrote that the women sitting at a ball at Bath looked like 'the Fathers at the Council of Constance'. Assembly rooms, public gardens and theatres had not encouraged, as they had in France, relations of easy informality between the sexes.

Figure 10.2 James Caldwall, *The Cotillion Dance*, 1771. Yale Center for British Art, Paul Mellon Collection.

In the eighteenth century, there were numerous attempts to import the idea of the salon into England.[93] Mrs Montagu, Mrs Ord, Mrs Vesey and others set up *bureaux d'esprit* in imitation of those they had seen in France. According to Nathaniel William Wraxall, they 'entertained the *litterati* of both sexes', but he admitted that these 'blue-stocking assemblies' were more or less failures.[94] In the end, French influence was mainly reduced to worldly entertainments: *faro* and *quinze* then *charades* became the latest thing in *bon ton*.[95] French dances, such as *cotillon*, were also fashionable.

While some Englishwomen tried to appropriate the French model of the mixed salon, some French gentlemen attempted to import the model of the male-only club to Paris. In 1750, Lord Chesterfield described for his son 'les Milords anglais' in Paris who spent their time in 'English' coffeehouses and taverns.[96] In Paris, the so-called 'macaronis' congregated in cafés, joined by Continental acquaintances, such as Fox's equestrian partner the Duc de Lauzun, engaging in excessive gambling and riotous behaviour.[97] The Marquis de Bombelles, who had appreciated the clubs in London, had himself accepted into the first French club, *Club de Paris*, established in 1782 on the English model.[98] According to the Abbé Coyer, many of these clubs failed due to their

Towards an 'entangled history' of urban leisure culture

exclusion of women.[99] During the Restoration, however, aristocratic *anglomanes*, such as the Duc de Guiche, again tried to establish several exclusive, and male, circles.[100]

By the late eighteenth century, English ladies who travelled often became used to leisure practices that were forbidden at home. Mrs Cradock, visiting the Saint-Germain fair in Spring 1784, noticed cabarets 'where I was surprised to see ladies of the society; but apparently it is admitted'. In October 1785, she went cautiously to the café at the Palais-Royal to see a procession:

> M. Cradock came in first and, seeing some ladies, urged me to follow him. ...
> I first remarked one who seemed to belong to the high society. She entered alone,
> while her footman waited for her at the door, she asked for coffee, read the newspaper, paid and left, without any of the 20 persons being present being surprised
> by her manners.[101]

Even if in England women could and did enter the metropolitan coffee-houses, they could never join the company there and feel entirely 'at home' with the men.[102] Helen Maria Williams explained that 'women, as well as men, are admitted to these coffee-houses; for the English Idea of finding ease, comfort, or festivity, in societies where women are excluded never enters into the imagination of a Frenchman'.[103] According to Helen Maria Williams, the Paris Lycée, established in 1785 on the model of London clubs, differed admitting by both men and women to its public lectures. She commented: 'I regret we have no such institution in London.'[104] In 1770, London intellectuals founded the Coterie, a club whose fundamental regulation was that men should elect the women and vice versa. On the list of its original members are found the names of Fox, Fitzpatrick, Walpole and several French people, but the club was short-lived.[105]

English women attended some Paris entertainments with a shiver of excitement. Hester Piozzi enjoyed one performance on the boulevards depicting a mock altercation between men with muskets and women with clyster pipes: 'The ladies conquered & were much applauded, so much for French Delicacy.'[106] Like Hester Piozzi, Lady Montagu was horrified by the '*grossierete* of their harlequin' at the St Laurence fair.[107] At the fairs, everyone participated in derisive laughter at the behaviour of civil society; derisive humour was expressed in erotic posturing and grotesque grimacing, insulting language or song and bodily imagery associated with eating and defecation.[108] Indeed, destabilisation and danger assumed a great role within tourism: they allowed the traveller to combine a frisson of excitement with a self-congratulatory awareness of having survived.[109]

National identities

No opera, no comedies, no concerts in London on Sunday; playing cards is so expressly forbidden that only the upper class and the gentlemen gamble on that day. The rest of the nation goes to sermons, inns or houses of ill repute.[110]

As early as 1732, Voltaire, in his *Lettres angloises*, had ridiculed the puritanism of English leisure culture. Descriptions of deserted and bleak cities on Sundays are a *topos* of travel accounts in England.[111] Voltaire's remark is significant in showing that the elite had a more permissive attitude. Indeed, Georgiana, Duchess of Devonshire, confessed: 'I am not at all pleas'd with the manner I have spent this Day, for after Dinner I really forgot it was Sunday & proposed playing a whist.'[112]

French travellers also wondered about the lack of distractions in London in the summer season.[113] In England, the calendar of parliament governed the recreational life of the elite and the towns came to life and emptied according to the rhythm of the sessions.[114] In French parliament towns, the holidays of the law courts traditionally also caused the departure of the nobility to the countryside and the end of the shows, but this phenomenon seemed to be less significant, especially in the capital. In 1777, John Mitford wrote: 'Paris is always gay. In the winter it has only the gaieties of a town. In summer it has some of those of the country. Operas, plays, balls and entertainments of various kinds are perpetual resources for the idle.'[115] In September 1787, Arthur Young reported:

[A]t this time of the year, and for many weeks past, Paris is, comparatively speaking, empty. ... This remarkable revolution in French manners was certainly one of the best customs they had taken from England; and its introduction was effected all the more easily, being assisted by the magic of Rousseau's writings.[116]

Nevertheless, in the next summer James Brogden found the city

very gay, four play houses open every night and the opera three times a week ... nothing can be more gay than the *tout ensemble* of this place [Palais-Royal], as it is the fashionable promenade of Paris it is filled with company every day, about 2 o'clock and again in the evening.[117]

The differences between English and French urban leisure culture laid less in their diversity than in their rhythms, which were more intense in France. Horace Walpole complained that his old friend, Madame du Deffand, was killing him: 'If we return by one in the morning from suppers in the country, she proposes driving to the *Boulevard* or to the *Foire St Ovide*, because it is too early to go to bed.'[118] Travellers were often surprised by the nightlife: Hester Piozzi noted about tradesmen: 'He goes to the Boulevards every nights, treats his wife with a glass of lemonade or ice and holds up his babies by turns to hear the jokes of *Jean Pottage*.'[119] The bordelais merchants went to the theatre every day, according to Arthur Young.[120] For her part, Helen Maria Williams wondered:

> Is it a proof of the superior refinement of the French that they are fonder of theatrical amusements than the English? Or does it arise from that love of gaiety and pleasure, which is so much more prevalent in the French than the English character? A London tradesman, when the business of the day is over, sits down contentedly with his wife and children, and reads the newspaper. But a bourgeois in Paris usually concludes the day at one of the spectacles and this without injuring his circumstances.[121]

Many travellers explained the diverging urban leisure cultures in terms of national differences: the private sphere of virtuous English civil society was contrasted to the frivolous public sphere of French society. However, this social opposition also had, a clear political connotation. In 1771, Grosley remarked that 'the great difference between London and Paris is in the activity of the police'. Twelve years later, Andrews agreed: 'In the article of pleasure and recreation, you will observe a material difference between the police of Paris and that of London.'[122] In the eyes of travellers, the politics of leisure could be summarised by the opposition between the despotism of the French monarchy and the disorderly freedom of that of the British.

Philip Thickenesse attributed the use of gesture by Frenchmen in their conversation to their fear of the Bastille, which prevented them from speaking frankly.[123] English travellers were convinced that they were being watched by 'those multitude of spies, commissioned by the lieutenant of the police in Paris, that swarm around coffee-houses and other places of public resort ... the emissaries of the grand vizir'.[124] According to them, the French were the slaves of a despotic monarch. Nevertheless, the French police were sometimes praised. On 1 December 1783, Hester Piozzi went with Mr and Mrs Cradock to see the first ascent in a hydrogen balloon and praised the organisation in spite of the crowd: 'Such are among the few comforts that result from a despotic government.'[125]

Many English travellers were surprised by the permissiveness of the Parisian authorities towards the local entertainment industry:

> What must be thought of a state, who tolerate and allow booths theatres, coffee-houses, and all sorts of public spectacles, to be exhibited and opened during the whole night and that too within the walls of the capital city! At this

City of pleasure or ville des plaisirs? **225**

time there is a theatrical entertainment upon the boulevards at Paris, which is
frequented by people of the first distinction, the doors of which are not opened
till after twelve o'clock at night![126]

John Andrews explained that this tolerance by the government demonstrated its commitment to avoiding the wrath of the people and stated that
one despotic maxim is 'to provide as amply as possible for the entertainment of
people of all conditions'.[127] Despotism could be a good thing, particularly for
the younger members of the English noblesse bored by the dullness of George
III's court.[128]

According to John Andrews, the only power wielded by French aristocrats
was social: 'Though composing a large body, they do not give themselves much
concern about anything that is not conducive to pleasure and amusement.'[129]
Frenchmen were both enslaved and emasculated: dancing was the leisure pursuit which best symbolised French identity: 'Happy People! says Sterne who
can lay down all your cares together, and dance and sing and sport away
the weights of grievance, which bow down the spirit of other nations to the
earth.'[130] As Diana Donald has noted, one of the French stereotypes of the
1770s and 1780s was a dancing master.[131] French dances were highly fashionable and England swarmed with dancing masters from the Continent.[132]
As Andrews noted, 'the best dancers are usually far from being remarkable for
their intellectual merit'.[133]

According to Andrews, this typical French frivolity explained their failure to enjoy English sociability. 'We find their coffee-houses, and other
resorts of that nature, plentifully provided with these elderly orators', but
they did not talk about politics for fear of the government, and above all,
because they were coxcombs.[134] In Moulins, the capital of the province of
Bourbonnois, Arthur Young noted: 'I went to the coffee-house of Madame
Bourgeau, the best in the town, where I found near twenty tables set for
company, but, as to a newspaper, I might as well have demanded an ele-
phant.' And he concluded: 'Could such a people as this ever have made a
revolution, or become free?'[135]

French travellers did not share this point of view. Politics did not mix well
with leisure and sociability, as the tiresomeness of London coffeehouses demonstrated to them:

Within you will find a dreary silence; and the occupation of those who go there
is simply to read the voluminous publications of the day, or to talk tediously
about politics in low voices; which gives these places a truly lugubrious air.[136]

226 Towards an 'entangled history' of urban leisure culture

For some philosophers, however, the English commercialisation of leisure created a new society based on equality. The Abbé Prévost remarked: 'What a lesson to see a lord or two, a baronet, a shoemaker, a tailor, a wine-merchant and a few others of the same stamp poring over the same newspapers. Truly the coffee houses ... are the seats of English liberty.'[137] According to Ferri de Saint-Constant, the English King was a consumer like any other: '[T]he King himself pays each time he attends a show; the box he sits in is magnificently decorated, but it is only ever hired for one show, and the following day anyone who wants to may use it.'[138] The Abbé Coyer compared Beau Nash to the leader of a republic and marvelled at the pavements where all social classes walked together.[139] The Marquis de Bombelles, staying in York in September 1784, remarked that notices, instead of forbidding the use of wooden clogs, asked those wearing them not to walk in the main street, which showed 'the consideration that citizens of standing have and indeed should have for the lower classes'.[140] In France, public gardens were simply forbidden to 'people in rags' and those 'in livery', the great majority of people.

But the corollary of this liberty was that there was no police control. Pierre Jean Grosley, reported in 1765 that 'The police leave shows well alone'. Disturbances often occurred: 'Such are, in London, the effects of the lack of police at shows; but it is part of the freedom of this nation & it is easy to imagine the opportunity this provides for talk.'[141] Grosley was a lawyer who belonged to the 'patriotic' party that demanded more freedom in France. The Comte de Bombelles, on the other hand, who was part of the court nobility, was more critical. He attended a theatrical performance in which 'the public were diverted by the indecent shouts and the singing of a drunken man in the third row of boxes who was calling down and talking to the people in the stalls. That is what they call freedom.'[142] Indeed, in France, since the beginning of the century, the Gardes Françaises, soldiers with bayonets, had policed the theatres.[143]

Conclusion

In his 1753 play, *The Englishman in Paris,* the dramatist and actor Samuel Foote, who had spent a considerable period in Paris, made fun of Frenchified British travellers through the character of the Francophile Luke Lappelle, who complained, 'there's a roughness, a bourgoisy about our barbarians, that is not at all to my taste'.[144] French fashions influenced provincial Britain largely through the nobility, the group that most regularly visited London and travelled abroad for pleasure. English middle-class audiences did not always appreciate aristocratic Francophiles in their attempts to appropriate French leisure culture from across the Channel. When the Duchess of Bedford tried to establish a Comédie Française in London, she had to give up the idea in the face of general hostility: 'Let them imitate the Duke of ***, who travels from London to Paris whenever there is a new play.'[145] In the course of the eighteenth century, 'to visit France or England was to visit the national enemy'.[146] Tourism and cultural transfer posed the threat of political ambivalence. Fascination was mixed with blame. Due to the appropriation of English leisure models in France, we witness on the one hand a very strong convergence in urban culture. On the other hand, national models of leisure retained and even strengthened their distinctive character. To some extent, the French *joie de vivre* reinforced the puritanical values of English travellers, while the French, unanimous in their rejection of a male and bleak England, did not think of too radically changing the ways they enjoyed their leisure time.[147]

Notes

1 M. Lister, *A Journey to Paris in the Year 1698* (London, 1698; 2nd and 3rd edns, 1699).

2 M. Misson, *Mémoires et observations faites par un voyageur en Angleterre* (La Haye, 1698).

3 *M. Misson's Memoirs and Observations in his Travels over England*, trans. J. Ozell (London, 1719). A.M. Roos argues that Lister's journey was translated into French, A.M. Roos, *Web of Nature: Martin Lister (1639–1712), the First Arachnologist* (Leiden: Brill, 2011), p. 381.

4 R. Morieux, *Une mer pour deux royaumes: la Manche, frontière franco-anglaise, XVIIe-XVIIIe siècles* (Rennes: Presses Universitaires de Rennes, 2008).

5 J. Grieder, *Anglomania in France 1740–1789: Fact, Fiction and Political Discourse* (Geneva: Droz, 1985); R. Eagles, *Francophilia in English Society, 1748–1815* (London: Basingstoke, Macmillan, 2000). See also C.H. Lockitt, *The Relations of French & English Society, 1763–1793* (New York: Longman, 1920).

6 Most recent studies are C. Jones and D. Wahrman (eds.), *The Age of Cultural Revolutions: Britain and France, 1750–1820* (Berkeley and Los Angeles: University of California Press, 2002); F. Ogée (ed.), *Better in France? The Circulation of Ideas between Britain and the Continent in the Eighteenth Century* (Lewisburg: Bucknell University Press, 2005); C. Charle, J. Vincent and J. Winter (eds.), *Anglo-French Attitudes: Comparisons and Transfers between English and French Intellectuals since the Eighteenth Century* (Manchester: Manchester University Press, 2007); K. Hardesty Doig and D. Medlin (eds.), *British-French Exchanges in the Eighteenth Century* (Newcastle: Cambridge Scholars Publishing, 2007); S. Audidière,

S. Burrows, E. Dziembowski and A. Thomson (eds.), *Transferts Culturels: Studies on Franco–British Intellectual and Cultural Exchange in the Long Eighteenth Century* (Oxford: Voltaire Foundation, 2010).

7 J.K. Walton and J. Walvin, *Leisure in Britain, 1780–1939* (Manchester: Manchester University Press, 1983); P. Borsay, *A History of Leisure: The British Experience since 1500* (London: Basingstoke, 2006); A. Corbin (ed.), *L'Avènement des loisirs, 1850–1960* (Paris: Aubier, 1995).

8 C. Maxwell, *The English Traveller in France, 1698–1815* (London: Routledge, 1932); J. Lough, *France on the Eve of Revolution: British Travellers' Observations 1763–1788* (London-Sydney: Croom Helm, 1987); P. Gerbod, *Les voyageurs français à la découverte des îles britanniques du XVIIIe siècle à nos jours* (Paris: L'Harmattan, 1995); J. Black, *France and The Grand Tour* (Basingstoke: MacMillan, 2003); J. Gury (ed.), *Le Voyage Outre-Manche: Anthologie des voyageurs français de Voltaire à Mac Orlan du XVIIIe au XXe siècle* (Paris: Robert Laffont, 1999); M. Sacquin-Moulin, *Les voyageurs français en Angleterre et les voyageurs anglais en France de 1750 à 1789* (unpublished thesis, Thèse de l'Ecole Nationale des Chartes, 1977).

9 J. Andrews, *Letters to a Young Gentleman on his Setting out for France. Containing a Survey of Paris* (London: J. Walter, 1784; 2nd edn, 1787), p. 530.

10 Black, *France and the Grand Tour*, pp. 119–120.

11 P. Borsay, *The English Urban Renaissance: Culture and Society in the provincial town, 1660–1770* (Oxford: Clarendon Press, 1989); P. Clark and R.A. Houston, 'Culture and leisure, 1700–1840', in P. Clark (ed.), *The Cambridge Urban History of Britain*, Vol. 2, *1540–1840* (Cambridge: Cambridge University Press, 2000), pp. 575–613; P. Borsay, 'Londres entre 1660 et 1800: une culture spécifique?', in J. Carré (ed.), *Londres, 1700–1900: Naissance d'une capitale culturelle* (Paris: Presses universitaires Paris-Sorbonne, 2010), pp. 85–110; J. Csergo, 'Extension et mutation du loisir citadin: Paris XIXe siècle-début XXe siècle', in A. Corbin (ed.), *L'Avénement des loisirs, 1850–1960* (Paris: Flammarion, 1995), pp. 119–169; F.-J. Ruggiu, *Les élites et les villes moyennes en France et en Angleterre, XVIIe-XVIIIe siècle* (Paris: L'Harmattan, 1997); A. Corbin, 'Les loisirs et la ville', *Histoire Urbaine*, 1 (2000); C. Charle (ed.), *Capitales européennes et rayonnement culturel, XVIIIe-XXe siècle* (Paris: Ed. rue d'Ulm, 2004).

12 J.H. Plumb, *The Commercialization of Leisure in Eighteenth-Century England* (Reading: University of Reading Press, 1973); J. Brewer, N. McKendrick and J.H. Plumb, *The Birth of Consumer Society: The Commercialization of Eighteenth-century England* (London: Hutchinson, 1983); J. Brewer and R. Porter (eds.), *Consumption and the World of Goods* (London: Routledge & Kegan Paul, 1993); J. Brewer and A. Bermingham (eds.), *The Consumption of Culture, 1600–1800: Image, Object, Text* (London: Routledge, 1995); J. Stobart, A. Hann and V. Morgan, *Spaces of Consumption: Leisure and Shopping in the English Town, c. 1680–1830* (London: Routledge, 2007).

13 G. Ascoli Georges, *La Grande-Bretagne devant l'opinion française au XVIIe siècle* (Paris: 1930); G. Bonno, *La culture et la civilisation britanniques devant l'opinion française de la paix d'Utrecht aux Lettres philosophiques* (Philadelphia: Transactions of the American Philosophical Society, 1948).

14 *Lettres sur l'Angleterre, la Hollande et l'Italie, in Recueil des œuvres de madame du Bocage*, Vol. 3 (Lyon: Frères Perisse, 1764), p. 22.

15 *Lettres sur l'Angleterre, la Hollande et l'Italie*, p. 22.

16 G.-F. Coyer, *Nouvelles observations sur l'Angleterre par un voyageur* (Paris: Veuve Duchesne, 1779), p. 16–17.

17 M. de Bombelles, *Journal de voyage en Grande-Bretagne et en Irlande, 1784*, ed. J. Gury (Oxford: Voltaire foundation, 1989), p. 151.

18 Misson, *Mémoires et observations*, pp. 25, 409.

19 Coyer, *Nouvelles observations*, p. 81.

20 De Bombelles, *Journal de voyage*, p. 314.

21 *M. Misson's Memoirs*, pp. 39–40.

22 Coyer, *Nouvelles observations*, pp. 88, 236.

23 De Bombelles, *Journal de voyage*, p. 291.

24 J.-L. Ferri de Saint-Constant, *Londres et les Anglais* (Paris: Fain Jeune, 1804), p. 278.

25 Ferri de Saint-Constant, *Londres*, p. 135.

26 P.J. Grosley, *Londres. Ouvrage d'un François* (Neuchâtel: Société typographique, 1774), p. 222.

27 J. Raby, *Journal d'un voyage à Bordeaux, à Londres et en Hollande, 1775*, ed. F. Weil (Paris: Champion, 2004), p. 405; Ferri de Saint-Constant, *Londres*, I, and XII, p. 134.

28 M. Baer, *Theatre and Disorder in Late Georgian London* (Oxford: Clarendon Press, 1992), p. 43.

29 P.-N. Chantreau, *Voyage dans les trois royaumes d'Angleterre*, Vol. 2 (Paris: Briand, 1792), p. 103. R.T. Semmes argues that the success of public balls at the opera house in Paris provided the model for the masquerade's Haymarket theatre after 1716; R. Templar Semmes, *The Bals Publics at the Paris Opéra in the Eighteenth Century* (New-York: Pendragon Press, 2004).

30 De Bombelles, *Journal de voyage*, p. 293.

31 J. Black, *Culture and Society in Britain, 1600–1800* (Manchester: Manchester University Press, 1997), p. 23.

32 Quoted by J. Grieder, *Anglomania*, p. 20.

33 Letter to William Cole, 28 February 1766.

34 N. de Blomac, 'Les hippodromes, centres d'événements-attraction', in Charle (ed.), *Capitales européennes*, pp. 133–140.

35 A. Martin-Fugier, *La vie élégante ou la formation du tout Paris, 1815–1848* (Paris: Seuil, 1993), p. 333.

36 R.A. Schneider, *Public Life in Toulouse, 1463–1789* (Ithaca, NY: Cornell University Press, 1989), p. 354.

37 G. Langlois, 'Ephémères vauxhalls', in B. de Andia and G. Rideau (eds.), *Paris et ses théâtres: Architecture et décors* (Paris: CID, 1998); G. Langlois, 'Les charmes de l'égalité: Éléments pour une urbanistique des loisirs publics à Paris, de Louis XV à Louis-Philippe', *Histoire Urbaine*, 1 (2000), 7–24.

38 H. Lynch-Piozzi, *Observations and Reflections Made in the Course of a Journey through France, Italy and Germany*, Vol. 1 (London: T. Cadell, 1789), p. 13.

39 Quoted by J. Lough, *France on the Eve of Revolution: British Traveller's Observations, 1763–1788* (London: Crook Helm, 1987), p. 437.

40 D.P. Mackaman, *Leisure Settings: Bourgeois Culture, Medicine and the Spa in Modern France* (Chicago and London: University of Chicago Press, 1998).

41 A. Young, *Travels in France during the years 1787, 1788 & 1789*, (Dublin, 1793), Vol. 1, p. 51; W.B. Brockliss, 'The development of the spa in seventeenth-century France', in R. Porter (ed.), *The Medical History of Waters and Spas* (London: Welcome Institute, 1990), pp. 14–47.

42 C.-E. Coquebert de Montbret, *Voyage de Paris à Dublin à travers la Normandie et l'Angleterre en 1789*, ed. I. Laboulais-Lesage (Saint-Etienne: Publications de l'université de Saint-Etienne, 1995), p. 100.

43 M. Boyer, *L'hiver dans le Midi: L'Invention de la Côte d'Azur* (Paris: éd. de l'Aube, 2002), p. 124.

44 Young, *Travels in France*, p. 436.

45 Philip Thicknesse, *A Year's Journey through France and Part of Spain* (Dublin: Williams, 1777), Vol. 2, p. 150.

46 Quoted by Maxwell, *The English Traveller*, p. 221.

47 Letter to H.S. Conway, 31 July 1771.

48 Andrews, *Letters to a Young Gentleman*, p. 553.

49 *Lady Knight's Letters from France and Italy, 1776–1795*, ed. Lady Eliott-Drake (London: Arthur, 1905), p. 11.

50 Baer, *Theatre and Disorder*, p. 49.

51 Letter to H.S. Conway, 30–31 July 1771.

52 R.A. Schneider, *Public Life in Toulouse, 1463–1789: From Municipal Republic to Cosmopolitan City* (Ithaca, NY: Cornell University Press, 1989), p. 357. Robert Isherwood argues against the view that a clear split emerged in the eighteenth century between popular and elite culture, for it is clear that fairs were frequented by all classes; R.M. Isherwood, *Farce and Fantasy: Popular Entertainment in Eighteenth-Century Paris* (Oxford: Oxford University Press, 1986).

53 *Voyage de Lister à Paris en 1698* (Paris: Société des Bibliophiles, 1878), p. 151. Isherwood, *Farce and Fantasy*, p. 24.

54 A.-F. Cradock, *Journal de Madame Cradock. Voyage en France (1783–1786)*, ed. O. Delphin-Balleyguier (Paris: Perrin, 1896), p. 6; see R.M. Isherwood, 'Entertainment in the Parisian fairs in the eighteenth century', *Journal of Modern History*, 53 (1981), 24–47, 30–31.

55 B. Dolan, *Ladies of the Grand Tour: British Women in Pursuit of Enlightenment and Adventure in Eighteenth-Century Europe* (New York: HarperCollins, 2001), p. 166.

56 M. Root-Bernstein, *Boulevard Theatre and Revolution in Eighteenth-Century Paris* (Ann Arbor: UMI Research Press, 1984), pp. 41–42.

57 Andrews, *Letters to a Young Gentleman*, pp. 502–505.

58 Root-Bernstein, *Boulevard Theatre*, p. 42.

59 Root-Bernstein, *Boulevard Theatre*, p. 41.

60 *Travels in France*, p. 196.

61 Quoted by F.W. Hemmings, *Theatre and State in France, 1760–1905* (Cambridge: Cambridge University Press, 1994), p. 27.

Madame Roland, 'Voyage en Angleterre', *Œuvres de J. M. Ph. Roland* (Paris: Bidault, 1800), Vol. 3., p. 23. In Marylebone Gardens, in 1776, a representation of the Boulevards of Paris was contrived, see W. Wroth, *The London Pleasure Gardens of the Eighteenth Century* (London, 1896), p. 33–34.

63 Grosley, *Londres*, pp. 81–82; R.W. Malcolmson, *Popular Recreations in English Society, 1700–1850* (Cambridge: Cambridge University Press, 1979), p. 42.

64 P. Burke, *Popular Culture in Early Modern Europe* (Burlington: Ashgate Publishing, 2009), p. 158–159.

65 P. Borsay, 'The rise of the promenade: the social and cultural use of space in the English provincial towns, c. 1660–1800', *British Journal of Eighteenth-Century Studies*, 9 (1986), pp. 125–139.

66 Martin-Fugier, *La vie élégante*, p. 308.

67 Quoted by S. Tillyard, *Aristocrats: Caroline, Emily, Louisa and Sarah Lennox, 1740–1832* (London: Chatto & Windus, 1994), p. 167.

68 Eagles, *Francophilia*, p. 5.

69 C. Lougee, *Le Paradis des femmes: Women Salons and Social Stratification in Seventeenth-Century France* (Princeton: Princeton University Press, 1976).

70 A. Lilti, 'The kingdom of *politesse*: salons and the republic of letters in eighteenth-century Paris', *Republics of Letters: A Journal for the Study of Knowledge, Politics, and the Arts*, 1 (2009).

71 P. Thicknesse, *Observations on the Customs and Manners of the French Nation: In a Series of Letters* (London: R. Davis, 1766), p. 87.

72 Eagles, *Francophilia*, p. 128. Cf. Lilti, 'The kingdom of *politesse*'.

73 J. Andrews, *Remarks on the French and English Ladies in a Series of Letters* (London: Longman and Robinson, 1783), pp. 17–18.

74 *Travels* (Dublin: 1793), Vol. 1, p. 53; Eagles, *Francophilia*, p. 135.

75 *Chesterfield's Letters to his Son, 1746–1771* (London: Echo Library, 2007), p. 383.

76 P. Thicknesse, *Useful Hints to Those Who Make the Tour of France in a Series of Letters Written from that Kingdom* (London: R. Davis, 1768), pp. 51, 158.

77 G.L. Lesage, *Remarques sur l'Angleterre faites par un voyageur dans les années 1710 & 1711* (Amsterdam: Frish & Bohm, 1715), pp. 130–131.

78 J.-B. Le Blanc, *Lettres d'un François* (La Haye: Jean Neaulme, 1745), p. 44.

79 Clark and Houston, 'Culture and leisure', p. 589.

80 Quoted by Lockitt, *The Relations*, p. 32.

81 Madame Roland, 'Voyage en Angleterre', p. 242.

82 La Coste de, *Voyage philosophique d'Angleterre fait en 1783 et 1784*, quoted by J. Gury, *Voyage d'Outre-Manche*, p. 806.

83 Defauconpret, *Une année à Londres* (1819) quoted by J. Gury, *Voyage d'Outre-Manche*, p. 174.

84 Raby, *Journal*, p. 405.

85 De Bombelles, *Journal de voyage*, p. 314.

86 K. Harvey, 'Spaces of erotic delights', in M. Ogborn and C.W. Withers (eds.), *Georgian Geographies: Essays on Space, Place and Landscape in the Eighteenth Century* (Manchester: Manchester University Press), p. 146; see also M. Ogborn, *Spaces of Modernity: London's Geographies, 1680–1780* (London: Guilford Press, 1998), p. 116.

87 Ferri de Saint-Constant, *Londres*, p. 27.

88 Harvey, 'Spaces of erotic delights', p. 146.

89 *Memoirs of the comtesse de Boigne, 1781–1814*, ed. C. Nicoullaud (London: Heinemann, 1907–1913), p. 145.

90 B.L. de Muralt, *Lettres sur les Anglois et les François et sur les voiages* (1726), p. 69.

91 De Muralt, *Lettres sur les Anglois*, p. 41.

92 N. Wraxhall, *A Tour Through the Western, Southern and Interior Provinces of France* (Rotterdam, 1777), quoted by Lockitt, *The Relations*, p. 34.

93 M. Cohen, *Fashioning Masculinity: National Identity and Language in the Eighteenth Century* (New York: Routledge, 2002), p. 33.

94 Quoted by Lockitt, *The Relations*, p. 110.

95 Eagles, *Francophilia*, p. 161.

96 *Chesterfield's Letters*, pp. 271–273.

97 Eagles, *Francophilia*, p. 157. Black, *Grand Tour*, p. 28.

98 De Bombelles, *Journal de voyage*, p. 92.

99 Coyer, *Nouvelles observations*, p. 256.

100 Martin-Fugier, *La vie élégante*, p. 338; M. Agulhon, *Le cercle dans la France bourgeoise* (Paris: A. Colin, 1977).

101 Cradock, *Journal*, pp. 318–319.

102 B. Cowan, *The Social Life of Coffee: The Emergence of the British Coffeehouse* (New Haven: Yale University Press, 2005), p. 254.

103 H.M. Williams, *Letters from France* (London: Robinson, 1796), p. 80.

104 Quoted by D. Kennedy, *Helen Maria Williams and the Age of Revolution* (Lewisburg: Bucknell University Press, 2002), p. 83.

105 Lockitt, *The Relations*, pp. 110–111.

106 *The French Journals of Mrs Thrale and Doctor Johnson* (London: Haskell House, 1973), p. 124.

107 *The Letters and Works of Lady Mary Wortley Montagu* (London: Heney, 1861), Vol. 1, p. 395.

108 Isherwood, *Farce*, p. 27.

109 B. Hagglund, *Tourists and Travellers: Women's Non-Fictional Writing About Scotland, 1770–1830* (Bristol: Channel View Publications, 2009), pp. 65–66; C. Chard, *Pleasure and Guilt on the Grand Tour: Travel and Imaginative Geography, 1600–1830* (Manchester: Manchester University Press, 1999), p. 213.

110 Voltaire, *Philosophical Letters or Letters regarding the English Nation*, ed. J. Leigh and P.L. Steiner (London: Hackett Publishing, 2007), p. 19.

111 A.J.B. Defaucompret, *Quinze jours à Londres à la fin de 1815* (Paris, 1816), quoted by J. Gury, *Voyage outre-manche*, p. 237: 'What happened in London tonight? The town seems deserted – You have then forgotten that it is Sunday?'. Cf. P. Borsay, *History of Leisure*, p. 206; A. Cabantous, *Le dimanche, une histoire: Europe occidentale, 1600–1830* (Paris: Seuil, 2013).

112 Eagles, *Francophilia*, p. 157.

113 Raby, *Journal*, p. 399.

114 Borsay, *History of Leisure*, p. 204.

City of pleasure or *ville des plaisirs?* **233**

115 Quoted by Black, *France*, p. 25.
116 A. Young, *Travels in France* (London: Richardson, 1792), p. 57. Although Rousseau was far from being an Anglophile, he spoke out against the artificiality of French urban society, and he especially condemned the rage for theatre in the summer season.
117 Quoted by Black, *France*, p. 25.
118 Letter to George Montagu, 7 September 1769.
119 Lynch-Piozzi, *Observations and Reflections*, p. 13.
120 Young, *Travels*, p. 157.
121 Williams, *Letters from France*, p. 79.
122 Andrews, *Letters to a Young Gentleman*, p. 500.
123 Thicknesse, *Observations*, p. 70.
124 Andrews, *A Comparative View*, p. 44.
125 Lynch-Piozzi, *Observations and Reflections*, pp. 22–23.
126 P. Thicknesse, *Useful Hints to Those Who Make the Tour of France in a Series of Letters Written from that Kingdom* (London: R. Davis, 1768), p. 65.
127 Andrews, *A Comparative View*, pp. 482–483.
128 Eagles, *Francophilia*, p. 162.
129 Andrews, *A Comparative View*, p. 68. Cf. Cohen, *Fashioning Masculinity*, p. 50.
130 F.W. Blagdon, *Paris as it Was and as it is or a Sketch of the French Capital*, Vol. 1 (London: Baldwin, 1803), p. 344: '*Vive la danse ! Vive la danse* seems now to prevail here universally over *Vive l'amour* [...] When the Prussians were at Châlons, the Austrians at Valenciennes and Robespierre in the Convention, they danced.'
131 D. Donald, *The Age of Caricature: Satirical Prints in the Reign of George III* (New Haven and London: Yale University Press, 1996).
132 Eagles, *Francophilia*, p. 166; Borsay, *History of Leisure*, p. 169.
133 Andrews, *A Comparative View*, p. 206.
134 Andrews, *A Comparative View*, p. 322.
135 Young, *Travels*, I, p. 327. See J. Lough, *France*, p. 428.
136 *Voyage philosophique d'Angleterre fait en 1783* quoted by J. Gury, *Voyage d'Outre-Manche*, p. 807.
137 Quoted by Ogée, *Better in France?*, p. 32, note 19.
138 Ferri de Saint-Constant, *Londres*, I, p. 141.
139 Coyer, *Nouvelles observations,* pp. 17, 100.
140 De Bombelles, *Journal de voyage*, p. 152.
141 Grosley, *Londres*, p. 78.
142 De Bombelles, *Journal de voyage*, p. 255.
143 J.S. Ravel, *The Contested Parterre: Public Theater and French Political Culture, 1680–1791* (Ithaca, New York: Cornell University Press, 1999), p. 133.
144 Black, *France*, p. 185.
145 Chantreau, *Voyage dans les trois royaumes*, Vol. 2, pp. 107–110.
146 J. Black, *Italy and the Grand Tour* (New Haven: Yale University Press, 2003), p. 5.
147 H. Levenstein, *Seductive Journey: American Tourists in France from Jefferson to the Jazz Age* (Chicago: University of Chicago Press, 1998).

11

The role of inland spas as sites of transnational cultural exchange in the production of European leisure culture (1750–1870)

JILL STEWARD

Baths and spas have a long history as leisure settings. In the ancient world, luxurious Roman baths offered a model of what a leisure resort might aspire to, as embellished with gardens, promenades, gymnasiums, libraries and museums, they constituted 'a microcosm of many of the things that make life attractive'[1]. For this reason, they attracted plenty of customers uninterested in their health, serviced by motley collections of shopkeepers, pimps and peddlers. Centuries later, many of the water sources used by the Romans were still used for bathing and some had evolved into important centres of resort life. By the 1580s, however, of the spas in France, Germany and Italy visited by Michel de Montaigne hoping to find relief for his gallstones, only Baden in Switzerland possessed the kind of permanent facilities able to cater for relatively large numbers of people with spaces for walking and bedrooms with private bath cubicles for the better-off.[2] Exemption from sumptuary laws created a resort atmosphere accentuated by mixed bathing, licentious behaviour, the presence of ladies of easy virtue and itinerant bands of entertainers.

Eighteenth- and nineteenth-century spa resorts have often been conceptualised as examples of heterotopic or liminal spaces;[3] however, they should not be seen in isolation, but treated as one of several different types of resort and leisure settings differentiated from each other by virtue of their location, function and the social profile of their users. A distinguishing feature of the spas and the basis of their claim to distinction was their reputation as places of healing and

The role of inland spas as sites of transnational cultural exchange **235**

as therapeutic environments at a time when conventional medicine had little to offer and therapy could be combined with amusement; indeed, many physicians considered the latter to be an important element in the cure.

In the centuries following Montaigne's tour of the spas, the development of the spa trade was indebted, in the first instance, to princely ambition and the lifestyles and recreational practices of the European courts and high aristocracy and, secondly, to the cultural interests, social practices and ambitions of the lower nobility and bourgeois classes for whom the spas represented a way of mingling with fashionable high society and of directly accessing examples of transnational cultural trends that they might otherwise have discovered only by hearsay or through print culture. The cosmopolitan life of the leading resorts brought together people from many different social and cultural networks in settings designed to facilitate social intercourse and forms of social display: it provided them with useful information about fashionable new tastes and modes of consumption informing everything from manners and fashion to garden design, literature and music. Finally, it is important to remember that, in addition to the sophisticated international resorts frequented by the *mondaine* world, there were also many smaller 'watering places' with a relatively mixed clientele contributing to the diffusion of cultural trends. Moreover, the aristocratic and bourgeois classes were not themselves internally coherent and the keenly registered distinctions between the practices of different social groups influenced and gave meaning to lifestyle choices involving leisure activities and consumption patterns, including those represented by recreational travel.[4]

Just as important as the medical and social dimensions of the spa trade was its economic function. The leading European spas were important commercial ventures, creating centres of local employment and sources of revenue, operating in an increasingly competitive marketplace that in the course of the nineteenth century gradually expanded to accommodate new kinds of settings for leisure tourism. Consequently, the spas were forced to make themselves attractive to potential customers who, thanks to better communications, a vastly expanded print culture and growing prosperity, were becoming increasingly mobile and well-informed, and whose behaviour, expectations, tastes and requirements were shaped by their habitual practices and experience of leisure settings elsewhere. The more exclusive spas, catering for a wealthy, sophisticated and cosmopolitan clientele, were particularly receptive to new ideas and models of development evolved within an international context, the influence of which was marked in changes to the built environment, the installation of new leisure amenities, and redesigned parks and gardens.

236   Towards an 'entangled history' of urban leisure culture

The spa trade of Continental Europe was geographically extensive but its development was neither spatially nor chronologically uniform since both nature and extent were mediated by geographical location and the structure of landownership, by political events and the extent of modernisation in particular regions, transport routes and the availability of capital. Just as important were the ambitions and attitudes of the key agents in its instigation, the owners, administrators and municipal authorities as well as the social profile and the recreational practices, tastes and behaviours of customers. An overview of some of the principal features of spa development during the period in question provides some indication of the way in which both spa authorities and customers were influenced by transnational shifts of direction across a number of fields – enlightened science and medicine, commerce, education, administration and aesthetics – mediated by the growth of print culture.

This chapter focuses on the spas of Continental Europe and their role as cultural vectors in the period from 1750 to 1870 when they functioned as important sites for the reception and transmission of the transnational trends that played a part in the production of European leisure culture. It covers three phases: the first, from the mid-eighteenth century to the beginning of the French Revolutionary wars, was a period of revival and recovery after decades of decline and stagnation: the second, from the 1790s to the 1840s, was one of rapid growth and expansion made possible by major innovations in transport and communications. The final phase, from 1850 to 1870, marks a period of transition and the start of a massive new burst of development stimulated by the rapid expansion of recreational and health tourism, culminating in the following decades (outside the scope of this chapter) in a so-called 'golden age' that lasted until the outbreak of the First World War.

The making of the spas: 1750–1790

Not until the seventeenth century did the European spas begin to recover from the effects of decades of warfare and economic stagnation and their fortunes begin to improve as peace, together with enlightened interest in the medical and commercial benefits of mineral waters, combined with cameralist policies, encouraged absolutist monarchs, landowners, spa doctors and local entrepreneurs to take an interest in their commercial exploitation. In Britain, particularly in and around London, the use of wells and springs gave rise to a variety of leisure settings so that, by 1700, an expanding network of resort towns, which included a number of spas, serviced the leisure needs of the local aristocracy and gentry. In these sociable settings, fluid and loosely assembled groups could meet in public and semi-public spaces to enjoy card games, evening parties, dancing and music.[5] Foreigners were much impressed by this recreational culture and its social codes, which were informed by the concepts of civility, sociability and politeness exemplified by the social codes regulating life in the West Country spa of Bath.[6] Foreign visitors to that city were struck by its array of pump-rooms and bath houses, assembly rooms, wide paved streets, shops, libraries, balls, concerts and pleasure gardens, a reason why the city was described by the *Guide-Joanne* (1854) as 'l'Eden que des milliers de touristes français s'apprêtent a visiter' ('the Eden that thousands of French tourists are getting ready to visit') and considered an important influence on spa development elsewhere.[7]

Not all spas had a resort function. In the eighteenth century, French spas were more fashionable than at the time of Mme de Sévigné's visit to Vichy in 1676 but were still dogged by their reputation as 'courts of last appeal' for the chronically sick.[8] This was because a key factor making for a spa resort was the existence of an aristocratic leisure class that engaged in *villégiature/villeggietura* (country holiday) a practice that, although common in Britain, Germany, Italy and Central Europe, had not yet reached Paris. Outside France, the most important resorts were the spa towns of Spa in the Ardennes, Carlsbad in Bohemia, Aachen/Aix-le-Chapelle and Baden near Vienna. Aachen and Spa were particularly celebrated for their amusements: cosmopolitan Spa attracted many wealthy Britons whose influence was clearly visible in 'le boulevard des Anglais' and 'le quarter de Balmoral'.[9] Carlsbad and Teplitz were popular with German and Russian royalty and princes, Austrian aristocrats and high bureaucrats, while Baden near Vienna served as the court spa of the Habsburg family. In all these places the relative informality of spa life was instrumental in the formation of cultural networks and cosmopolitan habits of thought among the visitors, who included many distinguished artists, writers and musicians in search of patronage.

As well as spa towns (governed by the municipal authorities), there were princely spas founded on estate land: these were the product of courtly leisure practices and the interests and ambitions of their aristocratic owners whose exposure to enlightened ideas, cosmopolitan lifestyles and aesthetic tastes was evident in the planning and styling of the built environment and the design of their gardens. Across Germany and Central Europe, cultural capital acquired through extensive and expensive travel abroad, foreign contacts and membership of cultural networks was expended in competitive displays of conspicuous

238   Towards an 'entangled history' of urban leisure culture

consumption that created magnificent palaces, elaborately laid-out grounds (*Lustgarten*) and summer residences incorporating elements of the latest architectural and gardening fashions: spectacular examples were Wörlitz in Anhalt-Dessau and the Wilhelmshöhe in Kassel. In a number of these places, mineral springs on estate land were exploited to create small but profitable spas set amid parks and pleasure gardens, usually styled in the formal French manner, where family, friends, landless nobility and high bureaucrats socialised in the summer months, bathed, drank the waters and generally amused themselves with dancing, theatricals, music and promenading.

A short-lived example was Kuks/Kukus in Bohemia founded by Count Francis Anton Sporck (1692–1722). Sporck was an example of a 'cultural innovator' and a man with social and cultural ambitions. Habsburg Bohemia was not a society in which freedom of thought was encouraged and the count, a member of the lesser nobility whose family had risen rapidly to become one of the wealthiest in Bohemia, was a highly cultivated and ambitious man of independent ideas who had made the Grand Tour and spent time at Versailles and in England. On discovering his springs had medicinal value (1694), he took advice from the doctors at Carlsbad and decided to make them profitable and impress his neighbours by creating a rival establishment.[10] The baroque-styled complex incorporated features he had admired on his travels included a residence, baths and chapel and a house for philosophers incorporating a library and printing press (a feature that, in the political and religious context of the day, led to accusations concerning subversive texts and heretical tracts)[11] as well as a theatre, two hostelries, a racecourse, a casino and a dovecote, the whole ensemble set amid promenades and pleasure gardens adorned with mazes, fountains, a hermitage and a great deal of sculpture.[12] Enlightened philanthropic elements included a bath for the poor, a home for wounded veterans and a hospital. Until the count's death, the spa sustained a lively, if brief cultural life. More resilient, if less complete versions of these aristocratic 'ideal' worlds included Luhatschowitz in Moravia, Postyèn in Hungary, Schwalbach, Kissingen and Wildbad in Germany and Luxeiul and Plombières in the Vosges. In Austria, influenced by cameralist principles, the Habsburg Empress Maria Theresa commissioned a survey of all the mineral springs in her territories (1777) and founded the spa of Herkulesbad in the Banat for the use of officers stationed on the military frontier.[13] In Italy, another Habsburg, the Grand Duke of Tuscany restored the decaying Renaissance spa of Montecatini (1765–1790), later to become Italy's leading spa resort, by draining the unhealthy marshland and personally designing an orderly townscape echoing

The role of inland spas as sites of transnational cultural exchange **239**

that of Bath, which was based on two central axes converging on a central piazza, like the forum of an ancient city.[14]

Initially, this phase of spa development was heavily influenced by places seen on the Grand Tour but, as the spas developed, their design was increasingly shaped by reference to and competition with their perceived rivals. The primary requirements of any spa were facilities for bathing and drinking as well as lodgings, spaces for conversing and dining and for entertainment and for walking. But equally important were the effects of transnational shifts in attitudes and the diffusion of the codes of 'polite' behaviour creating changes in sensibility that impacted on bathing practices, social conduct and attempts to regulate spa life, all of which necessitated changes to the built environment. In early modern spa towns, the presence of prostitutes combined with mixed bathing in varying states of undress encouraged their reputation for immorality and licentiousness, something that became increasingly unacceptable as 'polite society' became sensitised to matters of hygiene, morality and decency.[15] In this respect, foreign visitors to Bath in the decades following the reign of Beau Nash, such as Joanna Schopenhauer from Weimar, used to the more relaxed ways of the German spas,[16] were deeply impressed by the enforcement of the strict codes regulating social behaviour and the daily routine in which decorum was promoted by the inclusion of private tubs and dressing rooms in the design for the new and exclusive Hot Bath (1778) and the remodelled and colonnaded Cross Bath (1783).

In Continental Europe, spa authorities were also encouraged by the spread of these new behavioural codes to impose restrictions on 'impolite' behaviour and to invest in new facilities as they recognised the desire for greater privacy but, since these cost money to build, they were also dearer to use, opening the way to greater exclusivity and profitability. In many places, better understanding of the properties of their waters led doctors to try and restrict access to the waters for medical reasons (and thereby also increasing their fees): the baths frequented by a purely local clientele and the lower orders remained relatively unmodernised. In places patronised by the social elites, the rapid spread of the new fashion for drinking required the introduction of new building types, examples of which were the Italianate arcades in Aachen (1694), covered wells, pump rooms and colonnades, such as the Hot Spring Colonnade in Carlsbad (1826) where the open-air atrium and columned hall were built to accommodate the growing numbers of guests.[17]

The widespread enlightened enthusiasm for the ancient world and neoclassical styles of architecture, originating in the Grand Tour, also impacted on spa design across Europe, as the appropriation of models utilising the new styles became standard practice. Direct and indirect influences included the fashionable neoclassical and Palladian buildings of Georgian England, exemplified by iconic developments in Bath, such as John Wood the elder's Queen's Square (1728–1736), and John Wood the younger's Assembly Rooms (1769–1771) and Royal Crescent (1765–1775), whose Palladian façade opened down onto the green spaces beyond, giving it the character of an English country house. The influence of Bath was evident in the spatial organisation of a number of Continental spas, including Montecatini in Italy, Franzenbad in Bohemia, Bad Pyrmont in northern Germany and the seaside resort of Putbus on Rügen Island on the Baltic coast (founded in 1810).[18] Skalník, one of the architects working on the new spa colony of Marienbad (1818–1823) was known to have visited Britain before he drew up his plans.[19] Spa designers were also inspired by the many small structures with Palladian motifs informed by antique and Renaissance models found dotted around the new English landscape parks, which were often visited by foreign tourists and were praised for their natural and poetic form by C.L. Hirschfeld in his influential *Theorie de Gartenkunst* (1779–1850).[20] Architects, charged with designing new covered spaces for walking and drinking, found the allusive classical forms of these buildings extremely useful as models for the temples, pavilions and *gloriettes* used to shelter the mineral springs, as in Bad Pyrmont and Bad Kissingen, as well as for the open colonnades used to facilitate access, as in the Leopoldine Terme in Montecatini (1775–1780), and the first Baltic seaside resort at Bad Doberan (founded in 1793).[21]

The easy sociability of spa life, assisted in the more cosmopolitan spas by the widespread use of French among the elite visitors, was considered an important element in the therapeutic process as relative strangers were brought together at baths and springs, at mealtimes and on the promenades in ways that were less subject to the rather rigid rules of etiquette and hierarchy to which they were accustomed. Appropriate spaces and settings were required for this kind of social intercourse: medical and social functions were increasingly housed in separate buildings, the conception of which was often derived from urban models originating in England. In Carlsbad, for example, the 'Sprudelhalle' (1774–1777) was modelled on English assembly rooms in the Palladian style: in Germany (and Harrogate) these establishments came to be known as the *Kursalon/Kursaal/Konversationshaus*.[22] In Spa, British influence created private clubs or 'casinos' to accommodate various amusements, including gambling: one of these was known as the 'Wauxhall' (1770),[23] a variant of the term

'Vauxhall' originating with the London pleasure garden (formerly the Spring Garden) and often used abroad to refer to similar establishments or places of amusement,[24] such as the Coliseum on the Champs-Élyseés in Paris, or to urban pleasure gardens. A plan for a similar project in Aix-les-Bains was only realised in 1824 when it became an essential element of the spa's attraction.[25]

Many of the recreational activities comprising spa life replicated those practised in leisure settings elsewhere, including different kinds of walking practices,[26] such as urban promenading or pleasurable walking in green spaces.[27] The importance of the spaces given over to walking was spelt out in Hirschfeld's *Theorie* where he discussed the spa park at Wilhelmsbad in Hanau, declaring that ideally 'ein Garten bei Gesundsbrunnen' ('a garden near a healing spring') should: 'bequeme und mannichfaltige Spaziergänge haben, die zur Bewegung in der freyen Luft anreizen' (' have comfortable and varied walks for movement in the fresh air') and 'viele Plätze zur Versammlung, zu gesellschaftlichen Belustigungen ('many meeting places for sociable amusements') as well as 'zur Ruhe im Schatten' ('quiet shady places').[28] Spa promenades fulfilled all these functions, including the creation of continuous and spatially open systems facilitating the movement and exercise that played an increasingly important element in the new drinking regimens instituted by reforming spa physicians, such as Dr Becher of Carlsbad, who incorporated walking into the ritual of 'taking the waters'.

In many early modern spas, the promenade usually linked the springs to the town or princely residence, replicating areas used for walking in semi-private courtly pleasure gardens, and in towns and cities where walking and 'taking the air' for pleasure and health was increasingly popular with the lesser nobility and the urban bourgeoisie. Not surprisingly then, the promenades were among the first items to be considered when a spa was developed or modernised and were specifically designed to accommodate these kinds of activities. In newly laid-out court spas, the positioning of the promenades was usually dependent on their location within a formal geometrical structure of the kind commonly used in neo-baroque pleasure gardens as, for example, those in the prince-bishopric of Bad Brückenau (1747–1751) that, in a tribute to French taste, had been modelled on the Maison de Plaisance of the Chateau de Marly built by Louis XIV where the promenades were laid out in the form of two axes linking two small pavilions.[29] In early modern Aachen, the leading German spa town of the period, new covered arcades were built to accommodate walking situated along the main promenade used by both riders and pedestrians. In the spa town of Carlsbad, the promenade was created by building stone banks

Figure 11.1 E. Whymper, *The Baths at Leukerbad*, c. 1860, in S. Green (ed.), *Swiss Pictures drawn with Pen and Pencil* (London: Religious Tract Society, 1891, revised edn, p. 96). Collection of author.

along the river and the walk lined with chestnut trees, giving it urban feel by emulating a standard feature of French and Italian cities, while simultaneously referencing the kind of views opening out from the promenade at Bad Ems and the seaside walks at Naples.[30]

Like their courtly and urban counterparts, spa promenades constituted important settings for gossiping, matchmaking and the transmission of cultural influences and tastes as walkers took note of the displays of fashion and manners that played such an important role in the self-fashioning of aristocratic and bourgeois society.[31] In Paris, for example, foreign visitors enjoyed observing the capital's 'polite society' walking in the Luxembourg gardens and the tree-lined terrace of the Tuilleries.[32] In Berlin they joined the strollers in the Tiergarten, which was opened to the public in 1649 and then transformed into a French-style garden from the 1740s. Elsewhere in Europe, as the quality of life improved after the end of the Seven Years' War (1756–1763), people could be seen walking on the old fortifications of towns and cities, such as Karlsruhe, Mannheim, Frankfurt, Hannover, Weimar and Vienna. In the last of these,

Joseph II ordered the Prater (previously a royal hunting ground) to be opened to the public in 1766, and the landscaping of the Glacis (a broad circular corridor surrounding the old city, later the location of the Ringstrasse, 1859–1872), transforming them into open public spaces devoted to walking, coffeehouses and popular amusements.[33] Similarly, the tree-lined Hauptalle (1688) linking the castle to the springs in Count Waldeck's hugely successful Bad Pyrmont, was lined by typically urban leisure amenities – the ballroom, theatre and concert halls, a casino (1724–1732), coffeehouse (1770) and expensive shops, making it into the centre of spa life.

The pleasure of walking in public parks and spaces was accompanied by a feeling for the natural world, to be seen, for example, in the growing interest in landscape gardening, so that another feature of spa design intended to appeal to the tastes and interests of customers were the garden areas, used for pleasurable walking. Interest in garden design was not confined to well-travelled aristocrats: widespread bourgeois interest was stimulated by exposure to an expanded print culture as access to books, journals and printed images contributed to the dissemination of information about new aesthetic tastes and fashionable trends.[34] Print culture was a major factor in the growth of domestic tourism, encouraging people to see for themselves by visiting aristocratic gardens in the locality, such as Neuwaldegg in the Wienerwald outside Vienna,[35] which offered them direct access to architectural features and horticultural styles imported from elsewhere. In some cities this could also be done by visiting examples of the public gardens advocated by Hirschfeld, such as the Volksgarten in Munich laid out in the picturesque English style (1789), which became regularly used to update princely gardens and spa parks all over northern Europe.

The practice of local tourism by the urban carriage trade helped to lay the foundations of recreational travel to places further afield, including the spas. Recreational outings to noteworthy monuments and landscapes in the neighbourhood of large towns and cities turned them into popular leisure settings, one example of which was the much admired landscape park of Ermonville (1766), where Rousseau was buried, which was popular with the Parisian carriage trade. At nearby Montmorency/Enghien, the discovery of a warm sulphur spring in 1755 led to its transformation into a lakeside spa resort.[36] In Vienna, the enterprising owner of a hot spring in the outlying village of Heiligenstadt built a public bathhouse: tubs were set up in wooden huts (1781) and the site adorned with a flower garden and a lake, making it into an attractive addition to the semi-public spaces where the middling orders mingled with each other and

Towards an 'entangled history' of urban leisure culture

observed and participated in the fashionable culture of the locality.[37] Health concerns made the production of bottled mineral waters highly profitable and they were often sold in urban parks: in Vienna a mineral water establishment on the Glacis (1810) evolved into a centre for popular amusements.[38] These were excellent examples of the way that entrepreneurial initiatives succeeded in linking the popular respect for healing waters and local leisure practices, anticipating the subsequent popularity of the spas with the urban bourgeoisie.

In the spas themselves, the company was still drawn primarily from the ranks of the wealthier members of the higher and lower nobility, although it was gradually becoming more mixed as the wealthy urban bourgeoisie grew more adventurous. Spa culture played a particularly important role in social life in Germany, a country without a capital city and a central court society.[39] Spas outside the immediate locality offered people better opportunities for mixing with social superiors or interesting people from outside their usual social networks. A summer in Carlsbad in 1795, for example, brought the Jewish Meyer sisters from Prussian Berlin into contact with J.W. Goethe, with whom they subsequently corresponded.[40] The spas also functioned as marriage markets and sites for romantic encounters,[41] as Goethe's own history demonstrates. A visit to a popular resort with an international clientele enabled visitors to engage in first-hand observation of current metropolitan trends and practices, which they had previously only been able to access through print, thus providing useful cultural models for emulation. In any case, the amusements on offer – concerts and music-making, conversation, reading, dancing, going to plays, games of hazard, shopping, walking, outings to local monuments and beauty spots – were identical with the kind of leisure pastimes that were shaping the way that members of the urban bourgeoisie perceived and defined themselves.[42] Moreover, in some spas conversation and access to foreign publications in libraries and bookshops could sometimes provide visitors with political information difficult to access at home, where strict censorship was often applied. Spa visits therefore became something to aspire to: for people who needed advice on where to go and what to wear, periodical magazines, such as *Das Journal des Luxus und der Moden* (1747–1822) provided useful information and reviews of major and minor German spas.[43]

The making of resort culture: 1790s–1840s

The period covering the Revolutionary wars and up to the Second Empire saw the spa trade undergoing further change and development, as old spas

The role of inland spas as sites of transnational cultural exchange **245**

were rediscovered and new settlements founded. Urban dwellers developed a growing taste for country life as a persistent strain of anti-urbanism supported the creation of rural resort areas. The British fashion for sea-bathing began to spread, encouraged by the writings of travellers such as the German philosopher G.C. Lichtenberg, whose visit to England in the mid-1770s took him to the seaside resorts of Deal and Margate, the pure breezes of which he compared favourably with the close air of the promenades in the inland spas.[44] In the next century, the development of seaside resorts was to create important new settings for recreational tourism that provided serious competition for the inland spa trade.[45] All these developments were contingent upon improvements in transport. Better roads, railways and steamships dramatically improved the accessibility of some places to the detriment of others, such as Spa. Wiesbaden in particular, benefited from the Taunusbahn (1839) linking it to the important commercial centre of Frankfurt, which was now joined by rail to other major cities in Germany, so that the building of the Mainz–Neckar railway in 1846, connecting it to the Rhine traffic, made it easily accessible by the wealthy British travellers with whom the Rhineland spas were becoming increasingly popular. By contrast, the French spas did not feel the benefit of the railways until the 1850s and even then transport and communications in much of the interior remained poor, rendering it relatively inaccessible.[46] This was also true of many other parts of Europe, where commercialised health tourism remained relatively undeveloped until the last quarter of the century.

In the 1790s many ruling families continued to support the spa trade through intervention and patronage. Political events also played a part. In France, links with England and the efforts of interested enlightened intendants to stimulate commercial exploitation of the waters led to some improvements as in Vichy,[47] and in Luchon in France where plans to introduce something along the lines of the Cross Bath in Bath were dashed by the Revolution.[48] In Vichy, sequestration and state ownership adversely affected investment and renovation by an alliance of spa doctors and financiers during the Restoration period, although it did have access to state funds (unlike Aix-les-Bains, which was seized from Savoy in 1792, nationalised, then returned to Sardinia in 1820); their use, however, was hindered by bureaucracy.[49] Innovation in both spas was therefore dependent upon alliances of local interests and although a certain amount was achieved and visitor numbers steadily increased, both were handicapped by lack of capital and the overwhelming popularity of foreign rivals with French pleasure-seekers faced with the ongoing difficulties of travel in *La France profonde*.

246   Towards an 'entangled history' of urban leisure culture

As the origins of Maria Theresa's spa of Herkulesbad demonstrated, development was sometimes an offshoot of warfare and imperialism since the military required both therapy and entertainment. Teplitz in Bohemia, for example, contained the Austrian military baths built in 1807 and in the 1820s a form of spa culture evolved in the Russian borderlands of the northern Caucasus.[50] Aachen, in decline after the Revolution, revived with the arrival of the French army. Napoleon, no doubt mindful of the city's links with Charlemagne, stayed there with his family and paid for improvements to the town. The Napoleon family were enthusiastic spa goers. His sister revived the spa of La Villa at Lucca in Italy by linking the town to the new baths, lifting the sumptuary laws and transforming the place into a court spa. Subsequently, it functioned as a site of *villeggietura* for the expatriate British community.[51] Montecatini, destined to become Italy's most popular spa, was returned to public administration after Napoleon suppressed the religious order that controlled it.[52] In Germany, the Congress of Ratstatt (1797–1799) made Baden-Baden visible and began its rise to social eminence, assisted by a visit from the Prussian queen and crucially, the support of the elector and state funds, something that was lacking in Bad Pyrmont as it began to decline.[53] Aachen, the site of a major post-war congress (1818) was acquired by Prussia in the post-Napoleonic settlement: it benefited from new developments and, despite the fact that gambling was forbidden in Prussian territory, was allowed to maintain its all-important casino, although Prussian officers and local townsfolk were barred. However, in the face of competition from Baden-Baden and Wiesbaden, the city never succeeded in regaining its former social status.

In the following decades new spa settlements, such as Marienbad in western Bohemia (1808), were founded: growing competition forced established spas to innovate as they adapted to shifts in medical theory and practice, growing numbers and fashionable taste. New building types were developed as bathing and drinking began to take place in separate drinking halls and bathhouses, a clear differentiation of the functions. In Baden-Baden, where the Badense government appointed a Spa Commission (1805) to develop the place, a new Trinkhalle (1822) and steam baths were built,[54] while, in the new Badischer Hof hotel, greater privacy was afforded to visitors by the provision of separate bathing cubicles.[55] Social interaction was catered for by innovations such as Frederick Weinbrunner's Konversationshaus (1821–1824) with its large main hall and separate rooms for other functions, such as reading, music-making, gambling and eating.[56] Architects happily borrowed from elsewhere. Weinbrenner, an influential town planner as well as an architect,

The role of inland spas as sites of transnational cultural exchange   **247**

was heavily influenced by English Palladianism after a stay in Berlin where neoclassical architecture flourished.[57] Joseph Esch, the director of the Building Administration in Carlsbad, touring in search of new ideas for the rebuilding of the neo-baroque hot spring colonnade, visited Baden near Vienna, rebuilt after a devastating fire by Joseph Kornhauser (1813–1814) in the neoclassical Biedermeier style originating in France. Esch subsequently adopted the same style for the new colonnades (1826), which he extended out on both sides to facilitate socialising. He drew further inspiration from the neoclassical forms used by the French architects Boullée and Ledoux for the dome over the spring.[58] A similar form was used for the Elisenbrunnen in Aachen (1822–1827) as part of an attempt to counteract competition from Wiesbaden and Baden-Baden.

In the early decades of the nineteenth century, recreational tourism became increasingly popular with the bourgeoisie and, as the wealthy began to travel further afield, the spas benefited from the new reverence for nature and landscape that accompanied the paradigm shift in attitudes generated by the spread of philosophical ideas and aesthetic tastes emanating from Britain and Germany, reinforced by Rousseau's writings and the circulation of artistic and literary images of picturesque and sublime scenery. The ground for these had been well laid by popular health manuals, such as Samuel-Auguste Tissot's *Avis au peuple* (*Advice to the People*, 1761) and C.W. Hufeland's *Makrobiotica* (1797), which advised readers of the moral and physical wholesomeness of 'natural' lifestyles embracing exercise and 'moderation in all things' and attacking defective and excessive urban lifestyles, the effects of which were supposedly remedied by a spa cure.[59] The new taste for nature was expressed in the country villas of the wealthier bourgeoisie, found in spa towns, such as Carlsbad where they lined the promenade, in Baden near Vienna, and in *maisons de champagne* appearing around Paris in the 1820s and 1830s.[60] The less well-off enjoyed recreational excursions in the local countryside: Berliners admired the view from the neighbouring hills, visiting the beer gardens and inns of Kreuzberg, where smoking (forbidden in the city) was allowed, and an ill-fated Tivoli that, for a brief period, offered roller-coaster rides, while the Viennese visited the Kahlenberg and the inns of Nussdorf. Travel literature encouraged journeys further field. The multi-volumed *Voyages pittoresques* (1820–1878), for example, helped to open up *La France profunde* to tourists by informing them about places that were previously inaccessible and unknown.[61] Austrian travel books surveying the sights and monuments of the national territories, many of which were still unknown to inhabitants of the monarchy, performed a similar function (one reason why they escaped the heavy censorship). One of the recorded sights along the Danube was the picturesque military spa of Herkulesbad that, thanks to the new steamships on the Danube, became an attraction for river tourists.

The spas did their utmost to capitalise on their natural assets of waters, good air and beautiful scenery as towns and cities became increasingly industrialised, polluted and overcrowded. Adjustments to the design of the promenades and parks helped to meet the expectations of the visitors. Early modern spa gardens were formal, bounded spaces, but in the eighteenth century this began to change as spa design was adjusted to accord with new tastes. In some places, techniques derived from landscape painting had been applied to the design of promenades and vistas, as in Bad Ems and Luchon, where the Grand Alleé opened onto a distant view of the Pyrenees, linking the promenade to the magnificent landscape beyond. The eighteenth-century feeling for the picturesque was evident in the continued and widespread admiration for the English landscape style.[62] This became widely used by spa designers as a device for giving a 'natural' feel to the parks and gardens, for example, in the Lichtentaler Allée (1850–1870) in Baden-Baden, where it simultaneously masked the increasingly urban nature of the facilities while emphasising the contrast with the polluted, industrialised and noisy urban environments, so often cited as a source of physical and moral danger to health. In Teplitz and in Aachen there were particular problems: in the latter visitors could see 'huge chimneys starting up on all sides, and the clouds of smoke', forcing the authorities to build new spa quarters away from the old town.[63] As part of the attempt to deal with its problems the city also built a new public garden in the English style (1851–1853) designed by P.J. Lenné, who also designed gardens for a number of other spas.

The arrival of the railways and steamships made an enormous difference to recreational tourism: the cost of travel, however, remained expensive, accentuating the differences between places that were accessible, such as Wiesbaden, which was increasingly popular with people from Frankfurt, and those that remained relatively distant or difficult of access, such as the elite spa of Baden-Baden, which became more exclusive. Improvements in local transport, particularly the building of the railways, meant that spas, hitherto accessible only to the carriage trade, were transformed. On a visit to Vienna in 1843 the German traveller J.G. Kohl noted that the numbers visiting Baden on a Sunday could not be less than

> twelve thousand … smokers, drinkers and cooks, many to the baths … Life in Baden has undergone a great change of later years. Formerly the emperor Francis

The role of inland spas as sites of transnational cultural exchange **249**

lived here in the summer, and, like king Frederick William at Teplitz, assembled much of the great world around his person. Both places have lost by the development of the two sovereigns, nevertheless, now that the railroad brings, daily, thousands into the neighbourhood, and inundates it with smokers, drinkers and cooks, the pleasures of the arenas have become of infinitely more consequence than those of the saloons. The baths will be great gainers. They are now within the reach of many whereas before they were unattainable.[64]

A consequence of the taste for country walks meant that the town was now incorporated into what became a new type of resort area since excursionists not only used the baths, but also strolled in the picturesque hinterland enjoying the 'wild, woody and rocky valleys' of the Helenthal, carefully landscaped by their owners. Kohl noted that Prince Lichtenstein's father had adorned the summits of his estate 'with pavilions and summerhouses, built a magnificent seat in the neighbourhood, and abandoned the picturesque old ruins to the curiosity of the public'. So popular was area that:

> Coffee house civilisation has put to flight the nymphs and dryads of the woods. The caves of the fauns have been fitted up for the sale of beer and wine (*Heurigen*), and where formerly a solitary lover of nature could scarcely force his way, the population of a whole quarter of the city are now gadding about in merry crowds.[65]

By mid-century, the extension of the railway network and increased prosperity encouraged the wealthier members of the bourgeoisie to visit spas further from home, including places in the country and by the sea.[66] John Murray's *Handbook* (1840) advised British readers that 'with the Germans an excursion to a watering place is essential to existence, and the necessity of such a visit is confined to no one class in particular, but pervades all, from emperors and princes, down to tradesmen and citizens wives'.[67] By 1845, the train enabled Berliners to reach the scenery and good air of the Harz Mountains and 'Saxon Switzerland' in Silesia, areas that then began to exploit their therapeutic assets of climate and altitude as they gradually became home to a number of small spas and air resorts (*Luftorte*), private clinics and sanatoria.[68] The expansion of the spa trade also created greater diversity in their social profiles, more competition and increasing specialisation of function. Murray advised his readers:

> Carlsbad, Teplitz and Brückenau are the resort of emperors and kings; Baden and Ems of grand dukes, princes, and high nobility. Wiesbaden is a sort of Margate, whither the overflowing population of Frankfurt repairs on Sunday afternoon; while the other baths like Schlangenbad, Kissingen, are frequented

250 Towards an 'entangled history' of urban leisure culture

by those whose business is to be cured, and who are strenuously endeavouring by a few weeks of abstinence and exercise, to revive themselves from the effects of over eating and drinking.[69]

Even in the quieter, medicalised spas guests had to be entertained with, for example, donkey rides around the park and out into the local countryside to view 'picturesque' ruins and 'romantic' beauty spots.[70] The widespread use and appreciation of these aesthetic terms by nineteenth-century tourists was an abiding legacy of the impact of Grand Tourism and British and German philosophy on the shaping and framing of pan-European travel experiences and perceptions of place. In the alpine spa of Pfëffers in Switzerland, for example, British tourists with a taste for sublime horror were able to tremble before the sight of a dark hole down into which bathers were formerly lowered by rope and where they remained for a week at a time, immersed in warm water and illuminated solely by a few hours of daylight. John Murray's *Handbook* (1840) noted that modern safety improvements had nearly ruined the experience of the nearby chasms and raging torrents, although 'had Dante and Virgil known of this spot, they would certainly have conducted their heroes through it to the jaws of the inferno'.[71] In Leukerbad, a popular spectacle enjoyed by tourists was the communal bathing that took place in baths surrounded by public galleries (a balneological practice largely discontinued elsewhere) and where the bathers stayed immersed in the water for up to eight hours at a time with only little floating trays containing refreshments and pastimes to lessen the tedium (see Figure 11.1).[72] As late as the 1860s Edward Whymper noted:

> men, women and children, attired in bathing-gowns, chatting, drinking and playing at chess in the water. The company did not seem to be perfectly sure whether it was decorous in such a situation and in such attire for elderly men to chase young females from one corner to another, but it was unanimous in howling at the advent of a stranger who remained covered.[73]

Modernisation and redevelopment of the principle spa buildings was a costly business. Lavish development was only possible in places with access to considerable sources of external capital, municipal cooperation, entrepreneurial drive and the ability to attract wealthy customers to pay for it. All these were available in the Rhineland spas, where initiatives intended to attract tourists and replenish princely coffers generated important new developments. The exclusive Badisher Hof in Baden-Baden was a former monastery, which in 1807–1808 was converted by a pair of publishers from Tubingen. Neoclassical styling imported from France referenced contemporary taste, as did the

Figure 11.2 J. Watter, *City People on the Alm: Sunny Days*, 1874, in H. Schmid and K. Steiler, *The Bavarian Highlands and the Salzkammergut with an Account of the Habits and Manners of Hunters, Poachers and Peasantry of these Districts* (London: Mills and Boon, 1874). Courtesy of the Literary and Philosophical Society: Newcastle upon Tyne.

up-to-date facilities, which include a new bathhouse with private baths, modelled on those in Bath, and two communal ones using water pumped directly from the springs. A converted church provided a space for dancing, music and gambling: adjacent green spaces were attractively laid out and included English-style parkland. The place was widely admired and copied as, for example, in the Imperial Grand Hotel in Aix-les-Bains (1858).[74] After it was sold on for a large profit in 1830, the hotel was rebuilt, and again in 1858. By this time Baden-Baden was rapidly evolving into a really grand spa, its luxury hotels, theatres, expensive shops, casinos, gardens, race course and shooting facilities providing a model for resort development elsewhere. Success and expansion changed the nature of sociability as growing numbers of visitors encouraged the introduction of forms of social exclusion as, for example, in the serving of a later and more expensive dinner in addition to the customary *table d'hote*, where everyone ate together.[75]

The key to Baden-Baden's international popularity was its gambling casino. Where permitted, gambling represented one of the principal attractions of a

Towards an 'entangled history' of urban leisure culture

leisure resort. Under the *ancien régime* it was customary for states to exercise a monopoly over gaming, although in Bath, Paris, Spa and Carlsbad a great deal of gambling was carried on in an ad hoc and often under-the-counter way.[76] Modern gambling casinos appeared in Paris, but when Louis Philippe banned gambling in France in 1827 (excluding Aix-les-Bains), French entrepreneurs moved to Germany, where they negotiated with rulers sorely in need of money and set about transforming the fortunes of the Rhineland spas by establishing luxurious casinos dedicated to gambling. The first to arrive was Anton Chabert who acquired a monopoly over wagering in Baden-Baden where he established his casino in the Konversationshaus in 1822. In the 1830s he was outbid by Jacques Bénazet, who had been an overseer of gambling in the Palais Royal in Paris. As Baden-Baden became the elite destination of choice for gambling, the profits financed a number of improvements, including a railway extension (1843), racecourse and gas lighting. Chabert took over the concessions in Hesse-Nassau, including Bad Ems and Wiesbaden, which rapidly changed from a centre of healing into a pleasure resort. Bad Homburg, where the Landgrave had serious debts, underwent a similar transformation when the casino operated by the Blanc brothers, also from Paris, transformed the place into a resort town. The French ban on gambling meant that the domestic spas could not hope to compete with their German neighbours as leisure resorts.

Spa resorts represented a major source of employment, attracting not only foreign visitors but also workers from abroad: much of this labour was seasonal for, as Murray observed:

> all the machinery of amusement is to be found here – all the artists and artificers that contribute to all the follies and enjoyments of indulgence – actors from Vienna -gaming table keepers and cooks from Paris – money-lenders from Frankfurt – singers from Berlin- shopkeepers, *voituriers*, pastry-cooks, mountebanks, dancing masters, donkey lenders, blacklegs, mistresses, lacqueys – all bustling and contriving in their essential vocations to reap the short harvest of profit which the season affords.[77]

The spas provided employment for many different kinds of cultural workers, including musicians, performers and composers.[78] Music was an important feature of spa life, providing a background for promenading. It was also increasingly valued as a means of soothing the 'nervous' and cheering people made gloomy by illness or the sight of sufferers. In Germany and Austria it was paid for by the *Kur*-tax. Regular concerts and operatic events provided entertainment: Aachen, Baden-Baden and Carlsbad all had serious musical

The role of inland spas as sites of transnational cultural exchange **253**

reputations and drew many of their visitors from foreign cities boasting a rich musical life. Writers and composers found the spas pleasant places to work in during the summer since they provided proximity to others in their field and useful opportunities to meet influential and wealthy patrons. Beethoven frequently spent the summer in a spa, particularly in Baden near Vienna where he enjoyed solitary walks. Writers also benefited from the social intercourse offered by the relatively relaxed atmosphere as well as finding their fellow visitors useful sources of material.

The making of the leisure resorts: 1850–1870

The extension of railway networks continued to open up the more remote parts of the continent to commercial activity and recreational tourism: improved access to scenic rural areas with mineral springs, particularly in France, encouraged tourism and local entrepreneurial initiatives while also contributing the decline of old resorts like Spa. As rural tourism increased in northern Germany, established spas were faced with new competitors along the coastal resorts of the North Sea and the Baltic, and in the Harz Mountains as the air resorts became increasing attractive to people with pulmonary disorders. The French also began to visit alpine resorts and the seaside. In Austria, health tourism was still dominated by the traditional spas such as Bad Ischl, now the summer residence of the royal family, but many wealthy Viennese bourgeoisie also spent the *Sommerfrische* (summer holidays) in the lakeside resorts of the Salzkammergut or Carinthia[79] (see Figure 11.2). Resort development was greatly assisted by the availability of joint-stock capital, which facilitated private investment in the railways and in recreational tourism, a good example of which was the privately owned Southern Railway Company responsible for the route across the Eastern Alps (1857) linking Vienna to the Mediterranean, the first and highest crossing of such a mountainous region: the line was subsequently extended to the former Adriatic fishing village of Abbazia, opening the way for its transformation into an elite health resort.[6] Using a studio of artists and writers based in Trieste, the headquarters of the parent firm Austrian Lloyd, the company heavily promoted the route as a new kind of aesthetic and theatrical experience that could be enhanced by a stay in one of the new company *Kur*-hotels along the route.[80] In the 1860s, the leading Viennese medical publisher Wilhelm Braumüller launched a comprehensive series of spa guides (*Bade-Bibliotek*), expanded and updated in the 1880s, to include all the principal spas of Austria and Hungary.

In France, the advent of the Second Empire and the return of the Napoleon family, initiated the rapid expansion of the French spas as they evolved into highly popular and fashionable leisure resorts attracting a more socially diverse clientele, and assisting upwardly mobile members of the provincial bourgeoisie with the acquisition of the social skills necessary for entry into metropolitan society.[81] A number of French spas, such as Vittel, Contréxeville, Vichy and Aix-les-Bains, followed a similar pattern of development as Wiesbaden, while Baden-Baden, thanks to Napoleon III's patronage became recognised as *Le Café de l'Europe*: the emperor was also responsible for the development of *la Route thermale* joining the Pyrenean spas of the southwest, opening them up to recreational tourism. As health tourism grew in popularity, the leading European spas expanded to cater for the influx of new visitors. New coffeehouses, restaurants, shopping arcades, libraries, theatres and opera houses gave the resorts an increasingly urban feel softened by carefully designed green spaces. Smart new hotels, pensions and villas accommodated a more socially and culturally diverse clientele whose arrival substantially changed the nature of sociability: greater numbers of visitors meant that people ceased to mingle so much, preferring to remain within their own social groups when dining and participating in social events. The fragmentation of spa society was accentuated by an increase in the numbers of private clinics catering for wealthy invalids, reinforcing the distinction between visitors who were seriously ill and those who were there primarily for recreational purposes. At the same time, the spas still functioned as centres of transnational diplomacy and other forms of social networking.[82]

From the 1860s onwards, political developments began to impact on the spa trade. In Italy the arrival of the Risorgimento (1861) heralded the renewal of the spas, as they became popular summer resorts. In Germany, Prussian supremacy signalled the closure of the Rhineland casinos, to the advantage of the French spas where the cost of redevelopment was encouraging a more proactive attitude to spa promotion by the spa authorities. Faced with the loss of income from the casinos, the German spas were forced to reinvent themselves as luxurious health resorts by investment in new facilities and amenities in order to stay competitive in an increasingly international marketplace. This was accentuated by the growing Franco–German rivalry, which meant that French spa doctors – unlike the aggressive marketing tactics of their German neighbours who had long cultivated wealthy British customers, even to the extent of learning English – also began to take an interest, particularly as Franco–German relations deteriorated. The defeat of France by Germany in 1870 with subsequent loss of Alsace-Lorraine and Aix-le-Chapelle/Aachen heralded the onset of an era of 'thermal nationalism' as the French bourgeoisie retreated to their own spa resorts. In the following decades, thermal nationalism also left its mark in Central Europe as, for example, after the Ausgleich of 1866, the Hungarians favoured their own resorts around Lake Balaton and in the Carpathians.

Conclusion

In conclusion, as this brief overview demonstrates, in their organisation, design and culture, as leisure settings, spa resorts functioned as important vectors of transnational cultural transfer across a wide range of fields, from architecture and manners to music and garden design, all of which played a part in the formation of the leisure practices influencing the way that different social groups defined and fashioned themselves. Whether initiated by princely rivalry, civic pride or entrepreneurial ambition, the driving force behind the receptivity of the spas to foreign models and influences was competition as they were forced to change and innovate in order to stay abreast of their rivals by adapting to the changing tastes, sensitivities and requirements of their customers. Among the principal agents of transmission were the architects, designers and gardeners who created the built and 'natural' environments framing spa life. Equally influential were the ambitions and enterprise of the spa owners, municipal authorities, spa doctors and local entrepreneurs who instigated, commissioned, approved and financed innovation and development, while foreigners, such as migrant shopkeepers, musicians and other cultural workers also played their part. Just as important were the international visitors, the presence of which was so important to the reputation of the spas as places of cosmopolitan sociability, who brought with them the habits and manners, tastes and fashions informing leisure practices elsewhere. As commercial growth, improved transport and communications created an increasingly wealthy, mobile and well-informed clientele, the leading spas were forced to change and adapt in order to retain their custom and to maintain their reputations as fashionable resorts. The following decades would see a massive investment in the infrastructure of recreational tourism across Europe as the urban bourgeoisie flocked to new leisure settings along the coast, in mountains and inland lakes, despite which the international spas continued to hold their own, catering for both the *mondaine* elites who combined pleasure and therapy with useful networking, and the wealthy bourgeoisie attracted to the spas by the heady combination of elite presence, splendid amenities and therapeutic environments.

Notes

1 E. Dvorjetski, *Leisure, Pleasure and Healing: Spa Culture and Medicine in Ancient Eastern Mediterranean* (Brill: Leiden/Boston, 2007), pp. 83–123.

2 M. de Montaigne, *The Complete Works, Essays, Travel Journal, Letters*, trans. D. Frame (London: Everyman, 2003), pp. 1074–1079, 1246–1247.

3 For example, E. Mansèn, 'An image of paradise: Swedish spas in the eighteenth-century', *Eighteenth Century Studies*, 31:4 (1988), 511–516.

4 W. Kaschuba, 'German *Bürgerlichkeit* after 1800: culture as symbolic praxis', in J. Kocka and A. Mitchell (eds.), *Bourgeois Society in Nineteenth Century Europe* (Oxford: Berghahn, 1993), pp. 393–422.

5 P. Borsay, *The English Urban Renaissance: Culture and Society in the Provincial Town, 1660–1770* (Oxford: Oxford University Press, 1991), pp. 150–172.

6 P. Borsay, 'Town or country? British spas and the urban-rural interface', *Journal of Tourism History*, 4:2 (2012), 56–57.

7 Cited in A. Rauch, 'Les Vacances et la nature revisitée (1830–1939)', in A. Corbin, *L'avènement des loisirs, 1850–1960* (Aubier, Paris: Flammarion, 1995), p. 83.

8 L.W.B. Brockliss and C. Jones, *The Medical World of Early Modern France* (Oxford: Oxford University Press, 2004), pp. 313–316.

9 V. Krins, 'Spa, de la cure à la villégiature: Transformations d'une ville aux 18ᵉ and 19ᵉ', in V. Eidloth (ed.), *Europäische Kurstädte und Modebäder des 19. Jahrhunderts* (Stuttgart: Konrad Theiss, 2012), p. 118.

10 H. Lietzmann, 'Des Reichsgrafen Franz Anton von Sporck Kukus-Bad: ein Beitrag zur Kulturgeschichte Böhmens um 1700', *Archiv für Kulturgeschichte*, 55:1 (1973), 138–165.

11 R. Krueger, *Czech, German and Noble: Status and National Identity in Habsburg Bohemia* (Oxford: Oxford University Press, 2009), p. 58.

12 T. DaCosta Kaufmann, *Court, Cloister and City: The Art and Culture of Central Europe, 1450–1800* (London: Weidenfeld and Nicolson, 1995), pp. 362–364.

13 J. Steward, 'The spa towns of the Austrian-Hungarian Empire and the growth of tourist culture: 1860–1914', in P. Borsay, G. Hirshfelder and R-E. Mohrmann (eds.), *New Directions in Urban History: Aspects of European Art, Health, Tourism and Leisure since the Enlightenment* (New York, Munich and Berlin: Waxmann, 2000), p. 91.

14 G. Bonsanti, 'Heilbade zu heilen: Der Fall der Montecatini der Toskana', in Eidloth (ed.), *Europäische Kurstädte*, pp. 131–142.

15 D. Mackaman, *Leisure Settings: Bourgeois Culture and the Spa in Modern France* (Chicago: University of Chicago Press, 1998), pp. 75–79.

16 R. Michaelis-Jena and W. Merson, *A Lady Travels: The Diaries of Joanna Schopenhauer* (London: Routledge, 1989), pp. 114–116, 120.

17 L. Zeman, 'The towns of the West Bohemian spa triangle in the context of the European spa heritage', in Eidloth (ed.), *Europäische Kurstädte*, pp. 96–97.

18 C. Tilitzki and B. Glodzey, 'Die Deutsche Ostseebäder in 19. Jahrhundert', in R. Bothe (ed.), *Kurstädte in Deutschland zur Geschichte einer Baugattung* (Berlin: Frölich und Kaufmann, 1984), p. 525.

19 Zeman, 'The towns of the West Bohemian spa triangle', p. 98.

20 L. Parshall, 'C.C.L. Hirschfeld's concept of the garden in the German Enlightenment', *Journal of Garden History*, 13:3 (1993), 125–172.

21 Zeman, 'The towns of the West Bohemian spa triangle', p. 96; S. Grotz, 'Aspekte zur Architurgeschichte des Bades', in S. Grotz and U. Quecke (eds.), *Balnea: Architekturgeschichte des Bades* (Marburg: Jonas, 2006), p. 22.

22 Zeman, 'The towns of the West Bohemian spa triangle', p. 95.

23 Krims, 'Spa, de la cure à la villégiature', p. 110.

24 P. Borsay, 'Pleasure gardens and urban culture in the long eighteenth-century', in J. Conlin (ed.), *The Pleasure Garden from Vauxhall to Coney Island* (Philadelphia: Pennsylvania University Press, 2013), pp. 29–48.

25 L. Grenier, *Les Villes d'eaux en France* (Paris: Institut Français d'Architecture, 1985), p. 277.

26 H. Lempa, *Beyond the Gymnasium: Educating the Middle Class Bodies in Classical Germany* (Lanham: Lexington, 2007), pp. 163–193.

27 P. Borsay, 'Walks and promenades in London and provincial England in the long eighteenth century', in L. Turcot and C. Loir (eds.), *La Promenade au tournant des XVIIIe et XIXe siècles (Belgique-France-Angleterre)* (Brussels: University of Brussels, 2011), pp. 79–95.

28 Cited in E. Schmidt, 'Kuranlagen des 19. Jahrhunderts in Deutschland: Landsc haftsarchitektur, Nutzungsangebot, Beitrag zur Stadtstruktur', in Eidloth (ed.), *Europäische Kurstädte*, p.174.

29 E. Wegner, 'Staatsbad Brückenau', in Bothe (ed.), *Kurstädte in Deutschland*, p. 266.

30 Zeman, 'The towns of the West Bohemian spa triangle', p. 95.

31 K.E. Wood, *Health and Hazard: Spa Culture and the Social History of Medicine in the Nineteenth Century* (Newcastle: Cambridge Scholars, 2012), pp. 38–59.

32 M. Conan, 'Royal gardens and city life in Paris (1643–1789)', in M. Conan and C. Whangheng (eds.), *Gardens, City Life and Culture: a World Tour* (Washington, DC: Dumbarton Oaks Trustees for Harvard University, 2008), pp. 73–89.

33 R. Rotenberg, 'Biedermeier gardens in Vienna and the self-fashioning of middle-class identities', in Conan and Whangheng (eds.), *Gardens, City Life and Culture*, pp. 111–122.

34 K. Wurst, *Fabricating Pleasure: Fashion, Entertainment, and Cultural Consumption in Germany, 1788–1830* (Detroit: Wayne State University, 2005); J. van Horn Melton, *The Rise of the Public in Enlightenment Europe* (Cambridge: Cambridge University Press, 2002), pp. 79–122.

35 R. Kassel-Mikula, 'Feudale Gartenkunst: Öffentliches Grün in "Mein Garten"', in R. Kassel-Mikula (ed.), *Wiener Landschaften* (Vienna: Museen der Stadt Wien, 1994), p. 85; G. Hajós, *Romantische Gärten der Aufklärung, Englishe Landschaftskultur des 18. Jahrhunderts in und um Wien* (Vienna: Böhlau Verlag, 1989).

36 N. Green, *The Spectacle of Nature: Landscape and Bourgeois Culture in Nineteenth Century France* (Manchester: Manchester University Press, 1990), p. 72; J. Aubert, *Dans le nord et l'est: les villes d'eaux d'autrefois* (Lyons: Horvath, 1994), pp. 37–38.

37 A. Auer, *Kurstadt Wien* (Vienna and Munich: Jugend und Volk, 1985), pp. 36–38.

38 Kassel-Mikula, 'Feudale Gartenkunst', p. 90.

39 B. Fuhs, *Mondäne Orte einer vornehmen Gesellschaft: Kultur und Geschichte der Kurstädte 1700–1900* (Hildesheim: Olms, 1992), pp. 58–67.

40 B. Hahn, 'A dream of living together: Jewish women in Berlin around 1800', in E. Bilski and E. Braun (eds.), *Jewish Women and Their Salons, the Power of Conversation* (London and New York: The Jewish Museum NY and Yale University Press, 2005), pp. 149–150.

41 J. Steward, 'The affective life of the spa', in D. Picard and M. Robinson (eds.), *Emotion in Motion: Tourism, Affect and Transformation* (Farnham: Ashgate, 2012), pp. 217–232.

42 R. Rotenberg, *Landscape and Power in Vienna* (Baltimore, MD: John Hopkins University Press, 1995), pp. 75–79; Wurst, *Fabricating Pleasure*, pp. 184–186, 280–293.

43 H. Lempa, 'The spa: emotional economy and social classes in nineteenth-century Pyrmont', *Central European History*, 35:1 (2002), p. 42, footnote 10.

44 U. Quecke, 'Von Badenkarren und Schaluppen: Zur Geschichte des Seebadens an Nord- und Ostsee', in Grötz and Quecke (eds.), *Balnea*, p. 123. See also A. Corbin, *The Lure of the Sea, the Discovery of the Seaside 1750–1840*, trans. J. Phelps (London: Penguin 1994), pp. 257–258.

45 O. Kurilo (ed.), *Seebader an der Ostsee im 19. und 20. Jahrhundert* (Munich: Martin Meidenbauer, 2009).

46 M. Hascher, 'Modebäder und Eisenbahn: Zur Frage des Beitrages der Technikgeschichte zum möglichen Welterbestatus Europäischer Kurstädte', in Eidloth (ed.), *Europäische Kurstädte*, pp. 160–161.

47 Mackaman, *Leisure Settings*, pp. 29–30.

48 G. Valette, 'Luchon', in L. Grenier (ed.), *Le Voyages aux Pyrenees òu la route thermale* (Tarbes: L'Institut Français d'Architecture, 1987), pp. 126–132.

49 Mackaman, *Leisure Settings*, pp. 44–46.

50 S. Layton 'Russian military tourism: the crisis of the Crimean War period', in A.E. Gorsuch and D.P. Koenker (eds.), *Turizm: The Russian and East European Tourist under Capitalism and Socialism* (Ithaca: Cornell University Press, 2006), pp. 49–50.

51 C.E. Stisted, *Letters from the Bye Ways of Italy* (London: John Murray, 1845), pp. 9, 33, 44.

52 V. Santioanni, *Montecatini Therme* (Florence: Octavo, 2000), pp. 49–50.

53 Wood, *Health and Hazard*, p. 28.

54 Wood, *Health and Hazard*, pp. 29–31.

55 E. Denby, *Grand Hotels, Reality and Illusion: An Architectural and Social History* (London: Reaktion, 1998), p. 96.

56 C. Keim, ' "Eine Welt für sich": Kurarchitektur und Kurgesellschaft in Baden-Baden im 19. Jahrhundert', in Grötz and Quecke (eds.), *Balnea*, pp. 89–91.

57 M.Bollé and T. Föhl, 'Baden-Baden', in Bothe (ed.), *Kurstädte in Deutschland*, pp.198–203.

58 Zeman, 'The towns of the West Bohemian spa triangle', pp. 96–97.

59 J. Steward, 'Moral economies and commercial imperatives: food, diets and spas in central Europe: 1800–1914', *Journal of Tourism History*, 4:2 (2012), 191–192.

The role of inland spas as sites of transnational cultural exchange **259**

60 Green, *Spectacle of Nature*, pp. 124–126.

61 Green, *Spectacle of Nature*, pp. 100–106.

62 J. Dixon Hunt, *The Picturesque Garden in Europe* (London: Thames & Hudson, 2002).

63 J. Murray, *A Handbook for Travellers on the Continent: Being a Guide to Holland, Belgium, Prussia, Northern Germany, and the Rhine from Holland to Switzerland*, 11th edn (London: John Murray, 1858), p. 238.

64 J.G. Kohl, *Austria, Vienna, Prague, Hungary, Bohemia, and the Danube, Galicia, Styria, Moravia, Bukovia and the Military Frontier*, Vol. 1 (London: Chapman and Hall, 1843), pp. 156–157.

65 Kohl, *Austria*, p. 158.

66 O. Kurilo (ed.), *Seebäder an der Ostsee im 19. Und 20. Jahrhundert* (Munich: Martin Meidenbauer, 2009).

67 J. Murray, *A Handbook for Travellers on the Continent*, 8th edn (1840), p. 218.

68 J. Steward, 'Travel to the spas: the growth of health tourism in Central Europe, 1850-1914', in G. Blackshaw and S. Wieber (eds.), *Journeys into Madness: Mapping Mental Illness in the Austro-Hungarian Empire* (New York and Oxford: Berghahn, 2012), pp. 73-77.

69 Steward, 'Travel to the spas', p. 219.

70 F. Trollope, *Belgium and Western Germany in 1833: Including Visits to Baden-Baden, Wiesbaden, Cassel, Hanover, the Hartz Mountains* (London: John Murray, 1834), p. 234.

71 Murray, *Handbook for Travellers* (1840), pp. 190–191.

72 Murray, *Handbook for Travellers* (1840), p. 119.

73 E. Whymper, *Scrambles in the Alps in the Years From 1860–9* (London: John Murray, 1871), pp. 5–6.

74 Mackaman, *Leisure Settings*, p. 58.

75 A.B. Granville, *The Spas of Germany*, Vol. 2 (London: H. Colburn, 1837), pp. 80–81.

76 E.J. Carter, 'Breaking the bank: gambling casinos, finance capitalism, and German Unification', *Central European History*, 39 (2006), p. 190.

77 Murray, *Handbook for Travellers* (1840), p. 220.

78 I. Bradley, *Water Music* (Oxford: Oxford University Press, 2010).

79 J. Steward, 'The culture of the cure in nineteenth-century Austria', in S.C. Anderson and B.H. Tabb (eds.), *Water, Leisure and Culture: European Historical Perspectives* (Oxford and New York: Berg, 2004), pp. 30–31.

80 F.C. Wiedmann, *Von Wien nach Triest, Reisehandbuch für alle Stationenen der k.k. priv. Südbahn Wiedmann*, 2 vols (Trieste: Öesterreichischen Lloyd in Triest, 1856); W. Kos (ed.), *Die Eroberung der Landschaft: Semmering, Rax, Schneeberg*, Niederösterreichische Landesaustellung Schloss Gloggnitz, Wien: Falter, 1992), p. 260.

81 Mackaman, *Leisure Settings*, pp. 123–124.

82 D. Blackbourn, 'Fashionable spa towns in the nineteenth century', in Anderson and Tabb (eds.), *Water, Leisure and Culture*, pp. 9–22.

12

Coastal resorts and cultural exchange in Europe, 1780–1870[1]

JOHN K. WALTON

Towns have always been engines of cultural exchange, but certain urban types have been more active in promoting this than others. Particularly important have been capital cities, inland spas and other regional and local centres of polite society and recreational gatherings. From the early eighteenth century in England, and rather later in Europe, the seaside resort was to add to the list of urban centres of cultural exchange. Seaside settings brought together temporarily displaced members of metropolitan society, or societies, in pursuit of health, pleasure and fashionable display; and they also brought regional and local elites into contact with national or international social pacesetters, affording opportunities for social emulation and basking in reflected glory. In this sense, the most prominent seaside resorts acted as capital cities in miniature, disseminating metropolitan manners and fashions to the provinces. Although the same happened in many inland spas, coastal leisure was increasingly more expansive, inclusive and 'open' than that that to be found at the spa, less trammelled by the restricted formalities of the assembly room, pump room and hotel.

Apart from functioning as important sites for cultural exchange, the phenomenon of the seaside resort with all its key features – from bathing machines, medical discourses, social etiquette and commercial strategies to architectural forms – was also itself subject to an intense traffic of cultural exchange. Originating in England in the early eighteenth century, the model of the seaside resort as a commercial entity and destination for medical recovery spread to the Continent by the late eighteenth century, becoming subject to a process of constant innovation, mutation, specialisation, imitation and emulation throughout Europe and the world in the course of the nineteenth century. This chapter analyses the transfer of the key concepts, practices and techniques of the seaside resort throughout the British Isles and the Continent in the period 1780–1870, and discusses the ways in which – and the extent to which – we can interpret seaside resorts as important platforms of cultural exchange: as places that brought cultures into juxtaposition and promoted innovation, emulation and the dissemination of novelty: as solvents of custom and tradition, encouraging social mobility and at the same time challenging and reinforcing conventions and class, gender and (trans)national identities.

The rise and spread of the British seaside resort

The seaside holiday and resort as commercial entities – over and above traditional sea-bathing activity – spread across Europe from eighteenth-century England, and developed different traditions in different countries and settings. It should be stressed that popular sea-bathing traditions with deep roots, pulling together issues of health, ritual observance, enjoyment and sociability, were by no means the preserve either of England or of Western Europe, as Waleed Hazbun has rightly emphasised with reference to Tunisia and the Islamic Mediterranean, where he is able to document indigenous customs operating alongside the imported practices.[2] They might themselves prove exportable, as in the case of Irish migrants to the north-eastern United States, who took their pre-industrial popular mid-August sea-bathing customs to Coney Island and Boston's Revere Beach.[3] But, *pace* the widely-cited Alain Corbin, sea-bathing as an organised activity under medical supervision, forming the basis for investment in accommodation and infrastructure and for the development of a fashionable holiday 'season' based on recreation, sociability and display, was an English development of the early eighteenth century, whether we locate its origins on the Mersey estuary at Liverpool or on the coast of north Yorkshire.[4]

From such beginnings it spread rapidly during the second quarter of the eighteenth century, in remote rural settings such as Allonby on the Solway Firth as well as at Margate and Brighton, within relatively easy reach of London. By the late eighteenth century, every English coastline had its sea-bathing settlements, and at this point the fashion spread to northern Europe, meeting up with the related artistic celebration of the North Sea coastal environment, which was in evidence somewhat earlier at Scheveningen, another potential point of origin for the commercial European seaside (but one that failed to spread to other places on its own account).[5] It was during the nineteenth century that the new sea-bathing fashion swept across the continent, from France and the coasts of the North Sea and Baltic to the Spanish Atlantic coast and parts of the Mediterranean (and also into Australasia and the Americas), mutating as it went in response to changing cultures and environments, and in the process generating the development of international elite resorts at favoured locations along the Atlantic and Mediterranean coasts. It should be emphasised, however, that these remained few and far between until at least the late nineteenth century, and up to the Franco–Prussian War, most international resorts were either spas or centres of 'high culture' associated with the legacy of the Grand Tour.[6]

Although eighteenth-century England was the birthplace of the European seaside holiday 'industry' (an industry with tangible 'plant' but an essentially intangible 'product', apart from income generated directly from accommodation and services, which is very hard to disentangle and quantify convincingly), its own seaside resorts remained overwhelmingly domestic in demand and character, thereby limiting the scope for international cultural exchange in the country that developed the most extensive and flourishing coastal resort network of the nineteenth century. This was an export industry only in that Britain increasingly exported holidaymakers to European resorts (and occasionally further away, even in the nineteenth century): what it produced on the balance of trade, therefore, was invisible imports, especially from France.

There was very little return traffic; but there was also internal trade within the United Kingdom, which at times had its own implications for cultural exchange within the 'four nations'. On the North Wales coast, for example, seaside resort development along the route of the Chester and Holyhead Railway from the 1840s onwards brought English residents as well as holidaymakers into what had been a non-conformist Welsh-speaking area dominated by agriculture and (more recently) slate quarrying, with English landowners directing and profiting from the economic activities.[7] Culture clashes focused especially on Sunday observance and bathing customs as well as language issues, and the picture was complicated by the high levels of out-migration from the area to (especially) Liverpool, the honorary 'capital of North Wales', which brought families into contact with English urban life and opportunities while the migrants sustained their culture through Welsh-language chapels and associated institutions.[8] English visitors to the Scottish coast were much fewer in number, while the Scottish working-class invasions of seaside resorts in northern England (especially Blackpool, Morecambe, Whitley Bay and Scarborough) were a matter for the twentieth century, especially after the First World War cut off access to the Isle of Man and curtailed the services of the Clyde paddle steamers.[9]

The case of 'colonial' (or at least constitutionally anomalous) Ireland in the nineteenth century is particularly interesting. Here, visitors from England and Scotland contributed to seaside economies, especially at Bray, a few miles south of Dublin; and Cusack has argued that seaside resort development in nineteenth-century Ireland was dominated by large landowners from English aristocratic families, who sought to impose their Protestant Ascendancy versions of townscape, values and conduct on the 'uncivilised' Catholic locals. This would certainly fit in with Matthew Arnold's idea, which he thought to have general validity, that the Thames estuary resort of Margate was 'a brick-and-mortar image of English Protestantism, representing it in all its prose, all its uncomeliness – let me add, all its salubrity'.[10] But we should remember that not all English resorts looked like Margate.

This 'Englishness' of the English seaside was reinforced by the enduring lack of overseas visitors to the coastal resorts, despite the intermittent presence of diplomats and continental exiles (whether deposed monarchs or itinerant revolutionaries), especially on the south coast. Those who sojourned at the English seaside derived little cultural novelty or stimulation, although there is a fanciful theory that Louis Napoleon (the later Napoleon III) took the idea of broad boulevards and urban planning back to Paris from his experience of Lord Street during his brief stay in Southport in 1846. He also stayed in Bath on several occasions: for example for six weeks in 1846 he resided in the Pulteney Hotel (now the Holburne Museum) at the top of Pulteney Street – a very impressive example of a broad eighteenth-century boulevard. If either of these cases could be substantiated, it would be an important example of cultural exchange originating in a watering place; but the other side of the coin is that Charles Scarisbrick, one of the key landowning influences on the early development of Southport, was clearly influenced by the time he spent in Paris as a young man, and this is a much more likely direction of flow.[11]

United States diplomatic representatives reported from contrasting coastal resorts. Nathaniel Hawthorne also lived in Southport, during 1856–1857, but – in spite of the alleged interplay of French influences – he found it provincial and dull, its holidaymakers displaying a 'well-to-do tradesmanlike air'. Hawthorne, with his antiquarian and literary interests, might have preferred Whitby, where his compatriot James Russell Lowell enthusiastically shared his delight at the ramshackle and picturesque attributes of the quaint 'old town' in the early 1880s.[12] Meanwhile the presence of an elderly and decidedly bourgeois Karl Marx as a regular summer visitor to Ventnor, on the Isle of Wight, probably contributed little, in itself, to processes of cultural exchange. More influential, if only by reinforcing stereotypes through amusement and irritation, were the 'German bands' who were a regular feature of the summer season at coastal resorts across England and Wales throughout the second half of the nineteenth century, in conjunction with the waiters and other international migrant workers who took their skills to these seasonal labour markets.[13]

Fittingly, it was J.A.R. Pimlott, the author of an excellent pioneering book on the history of holidays in England, who first pulled together the importance of changing perceptions and evaluations of landscape and environment in the origins and early development of 'formal', commercialised sea-bathing and coastal tourism, long before the work of Alain Corbin. Pimlott, in 1947, was quite clear, and firmly grounded:

> There was another reason for the popularity of the seaside which fundamentally may have been the most important of all. In the discovery of nature, the sea and the mountains, amongst the grandest and at the same time the most mysterious phenomena of nature, had a special fascination ... as far as England was concerned, the sea (was) the more important of the two ... The enthusiasm which was shown was in many respects childlike.[14]

This is not to suggest that this was a uniquely English phenomenon: it was part of a European sea-change in aesthetic perceptions (as Corbin documents), and indeed in ideas about the morality of landscape; but it was certainly, as Pimlott noticed, an essential element in the English invention of seaside tourism as a commercial proposition and an engine of urban growth and revival.

The internationalisation of the resort

The rise of formal commercialised sea-bathing and coastal tourism became a pan-European transformation, which did not occur everywhere at once and had its origins in the transmission of changing ways of seeing, responding and articulating from intellectual and artistic elites to the broader fashionable world and then down the social scale. This 'trickle-down' or, perhaps, emulative model requires further, detailed, country-specific investigation; and if it holds good, it forms an interesting contrast with the way in which 'official' medicine adopted, regulated and made fashionable popular sea-bathing practices in the previous generation, imposing notions of order, decency and classification upon them in the process of, in this case, 'trickling up' followed by the selective attempted imposition of new norms. Within this framework, however, there was a great international variety of settings, scales, markets, social mixes, trajectories, architectures, entertainments, bathing cultures and practices. There was conflict and hybridisation between classes and cultures, and sometimes nationalities; and there were degrees of openness to, and within, the negotiation of processes and outcomes.[15] The relationships between the local, the external, the national and the international varied widely between resorts, and in many cases the highest social strata were missing. Of particular interest are those resorts that became haunts of international high society, while also catering for other social groups, so that cultural exchange was inter-class between visitors as well as international between elites and inter-cultural between elites and local residents.

The coastal resort is clearly an international phenomenon in the sense that it has spread across most of the temperate and tropical globe during the nineteenth and twentieth centuries; but since its original migration across the English Channel, bringing together French and British users of summer bathing beaches in and around Boulogne and Dieppe in the intervals between wars from the late eighteenth century onwards, it has also had international dimensions in the sense of bringing people from different countries into propinquity and contact, whether in cordiality or conflict, in pursuit of health, pleasure, fashion and display.[16] This applies both to international visiting publics and to relations between external visitors, local service providers and agencies of the host government. The coastal resort was not the first modern international commercial leisure phenomenon to have such an impact: the European Grand Tour and the inland spa resort offered related opportunities for international cultural mixing, both in established centres and in newer settlements built around mineral springs, at a time when many European national polities were themselves in an emergent state.[17] The international spa resort, with its grand hotel, pump room, dancing, sociability, woodland walks and (sometimes) roulette, might provide its own cosmopolitan microcosm of high society, and this remained the case across the European mainland into the twentieth century, especially in those parts of Central Europe where the sea was a long way away.[18] But although the coastal resort emerged later, it proved to be a particularly durable, expansive and adaptable incarnation of the rapidly developing tourism industries of Europe and the modern world; and in the twentieth century some coastal resorts, beginning on Western Europe's Channel, Atlantic, Baltic and Mediterranean coasts, began to extend the role of the seaside as international melting-pot beyond the aristocratic and moneyed elites to embrace the lower middle and working classes, in a process of democratisation that the spas could not emulate.

The rise of the international coastal resort began with the spread of commercial, organised sea-bathing practices and their associated social arrangements across the English Channel from the late eighteenth century. In its earliest incarnations it entailed the sharing of beaches and amenities between French and English sea-bathers at Channel Coast ports that were developing resort functions, such as Boulogne and Dieppe, and between the English visitors and (for example) French fisherfolk, bathing attendants, hotel workers and traders. Simona Pakenham has described the growth of an expatriate British community at Dieppe, alongside the holidaymakers who arrived from Brighton and Newhaven, during the middle decades of the nineteenth century. Close relationships developed between English ladies and local servant women, while English girls from 'good families' were sent to Dieppe for convent education, and English and French families mingled in and around the Casino, exploring and testing stereotypes. Such patterns of cross-Channel interaction became common further south along the French Atlantic coast, from Normandy to the French Basque Country (and also inland, around Pau). Wherever groups of British holidaymakers and expatriates settled and clustered, they imported their own institutions (churches, chapels, golf and tennis clubs, libraries), but they also mixed with their French neighbours.[19] The British influence was to spread to the French Mediterranean with their role in the 'invention' of the Côte d'Azur.[20]

Many coastal resorts across Europe during the nineteenth century, from the Netherlands and Belgium to Finland, the Baltic and the Austro-Hungarian Empire, similarly brought neighbouring nations together in (often) uneasy propinquity, especially where power relations were unequal or one of the 'nations' was not recognised as a state; and definitions might shift as 'national' boundaries and identities ebbed and flowed.[21] But the greatest scope for cultural exchange, at all levels, was provided by those coastal resorts that became the haunts of a genuinely international 'high society', bringing together members of European (and other) royal families, aristocrats, plutocrats, financiers, arms dealers and professional gamblers.

Such places developed their distinctive identities during the second half of the nineteenth century, alongside existing inland watering places such as Bad Ems, Marienbad, Vichy or the eponymous Spa. France led the way, despite the chequered history of its own domestic relationships with royalty, empire and aristocracy. Deauville, Trouville and Biarritz were outstanding here. On the Mediterranean coast Nice and Monte Carlo or Monaco, which during the nineteenth century were respectively a climatic station and a gambling centre rather than beach resorts, were important gathering points for international

Coastal resorts and cultural exchange in Europe **267**

high society but were not actually in France, at least until Nice became part of the French state in 1860.[22] The glamour of resident royal families for the summer season was helpful but not necessary for this kind of genuinely international, melting-pot profile, with its added spice of diplomatic intrigue.[23]

The reciprocal examples of Biarritz and San Sebastián, on either side of the Franco–Spanish border in the western Pyrenees, provide early illustrations of the development of international cultural exchange through coastal tourism during the third quarter of the nineteenth century. As the Basque literary scholar Jon Juaristi has acutely observed, the regular visits paid by the French Empress Eugénie, who alternated her summers between Biarritz and Nice, to Queen Isabella II of Spain, who summered in San Sebastián, during the French Second Empire made the Basque town a centre of international high society and encouraged the development of French cultural influences there, from architecture to fashion to cakes and pastries.[24] Meanwhile Spanish aristocrats were taking advantage of favourable foreign exchange rates and turning Biarritz, especially, into a cultural extension of Castilian Spain, as the Madrid press made clear during the summers of the 1860s and 1870s. But Spain was only part of the Biarritz story. Already in 1859, when construction of the Empress Eugénie's summer palace was well advanced, the Biarritz visiting public between 1 June and 15 October officially amounted to 8,041 people, of whom 6,707 were French. We should emphasise that more than 3,000 of these were from the immediate locality, the Basses-Pyrénées and the Landes; but 670 came from Paris and its region. Into the mix, however, came not only 352 Spaniards, but also 354 English visitors, 267 Russians, 84 Latin Americans (who would heighten the Spanish flavour), 53 Romanians, 38 Prussians, and smaller numbers from several other countries. We lack similar statistics for the next 20 years, but this was a good example of the early construction of a genuinely international locus of cultural exchange, where Russian Grand Dukes, English aristocrats and (in the case of Bismarck, Prussian aristocrats) rubbed shoulders with the provincial middle classes of south-western France. Meanwhile, another observer in 1857 remarked that the Spanish contingent was drawn not only from Madrid, but also (especially) from the neighbouring Spanish provinces of Guipúzcoa, Navarra and Aragón, and that regional Spanish culinary specialities were available, including Extremadura sausage, peppers from La Rioja and even Castilian chickpeas, which were not the most obviously prestigious of offerings and underlined the importance of regional cuisine and, by extension, the transference of reassuring customs to holiday haunts, alongside the more elevated exigencies of international high society.[25]

Figure 12.1 San Sebastian, Gran Casino, 1860–1880. Collection Rijksmuseum Amsterdam.

San Sebastián's development as an international resort gathered momentum a little later, building on the cordial relationships between the French Imperial and Spanish Bourbon courts, but flowering at the point where this nexus was obliterated by the exile of Isabella II in 1868 and the downfall of Napoleon III in 1870. A related paradox was that San Sebastián's growing international visibility was greatly assisted by the building development opportunities afforded by the demolition of its fortifications on the expectation of lasting peace, while at the same time its visitor economy was stimulated by military and political events in Central Europe that disrupted the business of several gambling casinos in German spa resorts, even before the newly unified Germany introduced and enforced a ban on casino gambling. A further irony was to be experienced with the outbreak of the Carlist civil war in Spain in 1873, which led to the siege and bombardment of the now 'open' city and cut short, or at least postponed, its bid for international glory. In the interim, however, San Sebastián reaped a rich harvest from seekers after the excitements of roulette, and the associated luxuries and high-class entertainments that the profits of the tables sustained. A locally backed casino proposal in 1865, just as the new building sites in desirable locations were becoming available, did not take off, and the role of gambling in its plans was not made clear: a 'casino' could be simply a gathering place for sociable conversation and concerts. But during 1868–1869, recognised in the Madrid press as the years of San Sebastián's great leap forward into national and international prominence (even as its royal patron slipped away into exile), external speculators made their presence felt. Baron Fossard de Lillebonne, the proprietor of the existing German casino at Wildungen-les-Bains, made an initial bid, followed by Édouard Gibert and

Sophrone Sicure du Breilh. These were exotic names in the San Sebastián context, and the precedents they cited as models were Monaco, Homburg, Baden-Baden and Spa, all identified with the glamour and excitement of roulette. Two casinos, the Cursaal and the Indo, were established; and the small matter of the illegality of roulette was finessed by guaranteed revenue streams for the municipal coffers and attractive entertainment programmes. A pattern developed whereby national and local government intervened to suppress the tables at the end of every season, while turning a blind eye at the start of the new one, to the rage of conservative campaigners for local morality and against international vice. This continued until the disruptions of the Carlist wars; and even then, with the conflict raging around it, a French-run gambling casino was operating in Fuenterrabía/Hondarribia, on the Spanish side of the international Bidasoa estuary. Customers were ferried across from Hendaye on fishing boats, and again official tolerance was only suspended outside the tourist season. Meanwhile the French and other international influences on San Sebastián itself continued to take root, to flourish spectacularly at and beyond the turn of the century.[26]

Brighton, the beach and the limits of cultural exchange

Located on the boundary between land and sea, resorts and their beaches are often seen as occupying a marginal and liminal space that facilitated and encouraged cultural exchange at all levels. However, the case of Brighton, the most important resort in Britain, and its beach reveals the complexities that emerge when we look in depth at the processes of cultural exchange in a particular place. Beyond mere celebrating these complexities, a critical historical analysis also warns against any overstatement of the actual processes at work.

In his still very influential study of *Places on the Margin: Alternative Geographies of Modernity* (1991), Rob Shields presents Brighton as an exemplary, if not a typical, case of a coastal resort that brings together related characteristics of the peripheral, the liminal and indeed the carnivalesque.[27] He sees its coastal location, at the threshold between land and sea, in a debatable zone where the conventions of daily living (gender, morality, class and presentation of self) can be set aside or subverted, challenged or perhaps (by extension, and at least temporarily) hybridised, as a particularly exciting site of interaction between classes and cultures. Here, it seems, is an early but potentially classic location for cultural exchange between the metropolitan and the local, the formal and the subversive, the elite and the subordinate, the conservative

Figure 12.2 Frederick William Woledge, *Brighton: The Front and the Chain Pier Seen in the Distance*. Yale Center for British Art, Paul Mellon Collection.

and the radical. This last dichotomy can be conceived in both cultural and political terms: Brighton became an alternative pole of disreputable aristocratic culture under George IV, especially as Prince of Wales before he became king in 1820, and later a stronghold of Chartism, with its own assertive proletarian presence, while in the railway age its working-class London trippers posed problems of cultural democracy in action. This might also be expressed in terms of exchanges between the global, as embodied in London as the beating heart of the British Empire (but with few European contributions), and the local, whether based on Brighton's immediate hinterland in the predominantly rural county of Sussex, or on excursionists by rail from parochial London working-class neighbourhoods.[28]

Despite its persuasive presentation and its wide acclaim, Shield's account of Brighton and its beach as marginal space and a site of cultural exchange raises some serious problems.[29] In the first place, an important point about Brighton is that as 'London by the sea', a maritime extension of the metropolis and part of its mythology, and for two generations from the late eighteenth century the effective summer capital, it was only 'peripheral' in terms of being physically located on the English coast – and even then at the nearest point to the metropolis. London itself is situated on a tidal river, was penetrated by 'exotic' and even 'Oriental' cultures as it developed as a port with international and then global reach, and had its own Victorian (and earlier) areas of multicultural edge and risk, from Soho to Shadwell.[30] Even after Queen Victoria deserted Brighton, its exotic Orientalist Pavilion (not exactly her architecture of choice), and its intrusive and importunate crowds at the beginning of her reign, leaving a deep and carefully propagated cultural memory of the raffish antics of the prince regent and his circle and of their role in the creation of the resort, Brighton retained a high profile as a weekend destination and place of seasonal residence for fashionable and well-off Londoners, alongside the day-trippers who arrived by the London, Brighton and South Coast Railway.[31] But the phenomenon of the coastal resort as summer capital, bringing the court and ministers to the summer palace for a season and turning the national 'periphery' into the executive and administrative 'core', occurs across the globe, although mainly a phenomenon of the late nineteenth and early twentieth century in its full-blown form.[32] Even after Victoria's departure, which coincided with the arrival of the railway in the early 1840s, Brighton was only peripheral or marginal in the literal sense of its coastal geographical location: it was in many senses an extension of a world city and imperial metropolis. This must affect perceptions of its liminality.

We should also note – and this is my second point – the cultural hybridity of some of these seaside summer capitals: San Sebastián, for example, a bilingual city, Basque as well as Spanish, with a fishing port adjoining the aristocratic beach and strong French cultural influences already apparent in new urban development in the mid to late 1860s.[33] Does this challenge the idea of liminality in this context, or reinforce it? Moreover, can a summer centre of government, or of aristocratic pleasure, governed by strict behavioural conventions, dress codes and rules of formal etiquette in the 'public' places frequented by (and in many cases accessible only to) the wealthy, also be a liminal space? The role of games of chance in the casinos that were sometimes central to such resorts' identity, although of course not confined to coastal settings (where they were relatively late in appearing), brings back a suitably edgy air to the proceedings, with the ever-present and much-canvassed possibility of financial ruin or sudden spectacular gain, and the presence of adventurers and fortune-hunters among the privileged public. This was if anything enhanced by the formality that surrounded the operation of the roulette wheels, an activity that was never shared by Brighton in this form after the abolition of public gaming there in the mid-eighteenth century. But the complexity surrounding the validity and value of the concept in such settings deserves extensive comparative engagement.[34]

In the context of Brighton – my third point – the notion of the liminality of the beach as, in effect, a site of cultural exchange across imagined social

272 Towards an 'entangled history' of urban leisure culture

frontiers, is perhaps increasingly distorting with the passage of time. After the early years of the resort, with a significant focus on the beach as therapeutic site and on the presiding genius of the 'dipper', a muscular local personality who negotiated the passage between land and sea through controlled, medically supervised immersion, the beach itself became less important to the attractiveness of 'worldly' and popular resorts: as Shields himself points out, those in search of tranquil nature would go to smaller, quieter places, as a host of niche markets proliferated along the increasingly accessible coastlines of Victorian Britain and, indeed, Victorian Sussex. These were physically 'liminal' but with social characteristics that were constructed as secure and unthreatening.[35] When female, the 'dipper' herself carried something of the subsequent aura of the seaside landlady, as a powerful woman taking (in this case) physical charge of a complex and intimate set of manoeuvres and stepping outside the normal ascribed confines of her gender.[36] Liminality is certainly at issue here, in terms of the suspension of gender norms as part of a managed transition between elements and between (it is hoped) sickness and health, while negotiating an activity constructed as medical through a person without formal education, whose qualifications were based on local knowledge and physical strength. But this was a transient phenomenon in the life of the resort, as was the scopophilia of the men who haunted the vicinity of the ladies' bathing-machines (or indeed the equivalent practices of the ladies who frequented those areas of the beach where gentlemen engaged unofficially in nude bathing).[37] By the mid-Victorian period, the beach had become much less interesting to frequenters of Brighton, where the main focus of attention became the comings and goings on the promenade, where classes and cultures mixed in an increasingly controlled and consensual manner, while pubs and music halls continued to attract the working-class day-trippers from the metropolis.[38]

In any case, beaches generally in the larger resorts came to be zoned by class and cultural preference, and a measure of informal spatial segregation (usually based on people knowing their place and sticking to it) came to be normal at the developed seaside.[39] Far from being liberated from taboos or from the normative demands of a cultural script, a visitor to a resort like Brighton might well find them reinforced. This reduced the scope for direct, destabilising cultural exchange, tending rather to reinforce existing assumptions and prejudices.

Shields suggests that the arrival of the railway in 1841 'set the destiny of Brighton as a day-tripper's resort' for working-class families who patronised cafés and tearooms rather than pubs or ballrooms. This would have been

Coastal resorts and cultural exchange in Europe **273**

economically unsustainable, especially in the light of the town's continued rapid growth, while the workings of the poverty cycle always loaded the dice in favour of young people without families or older people who were free of them. Working-class couples with young families were most unusual as visitors to the nineteenth-century seaside, even in England, and vanishingly so elsewhere in Europe.[40] Pub-goers predominated among the popular classes. Shields' further identification of Brighton day-trippers with the expression of a 'collective release from the rationalised regimes of industrial labour' assumes a spread of factories and Fordism that does not match the more complex and less industrial economies of the parts of London from which the visitors were drawn, in contrast with the northern working-class visitors to Blackpool, the Isle of Man or Scarborough, although even here the work-rhythms of the mining, steel and cutlery industries, with their widespread extension of the weekend through 'St Monday', were very different from those of textile manufacture.[41] Again, any such interpretation would be even less tenable in the rest of Europe, even in the 1930s. Shields also identifies the constraints on liminal and carnivalesque tendencies in the Brighton holiday crowd with the conventions of rail travel, which is difficult to substantiate apart from the time discipline needed to catch the return train (not least because the excursion train was often a lively social melting-pot), and with the commodification of the feast through food stalls, ignoring the tendency (lamented by Brighton traders) for people to bring their own food, and the important role of the pubs in supplying the crowds with beer, that essential lubricant of most Victorian popular leisure in all urban settings, especially for men.[42]

In the circumstances described here it is difficult to see the beach at Brighton in particular, and perhaps the town or the (presumably English) seaside in general, as an 'open field for social innovation', or a socially unifying experience in which the stripping away of status indicators made for socially unmediated encounters, or 'a genuine reaching out to embrace the social totality of the national holiday', which is a very strange concept. In principle, such themes would be well worth discussing in relation to cultural exchange, but it is hard to sustain a grip on them here. Shields never makes clear when the 'new beach' was new, what forms it took, how it varied geographically and changed over time (it was certainly not 'national' in any unified sense), and how it reconciled the tensions between contrasting holiday styles, differing regional practices or externally imposed control, self-regulation and self-expression. In practice, those who 'dressed up' beyond their station at the seaside were usually soon found out (often as soon as they uttered a word, although potential status confusion was a fertile field for cartoonists and sketch writers); most public places were socially stratified, not least by price (and mid-Victorian exceptions such as Hall by the Sea at Margate were celebrated for this reason); and the rowdy excursionists of the early railway age and the mid-Victorian years soon learned to modify their behaviour and appease their 'betters', which might indeed be regarded as an outcome of cultural exchange promoting a 'civilising process', although it was more apparent from the 1880s onwards.[43] The most readily available opportunities for sexual alliance, meanwhile, were in the grand hotels, where decorous and exclusive conventions of public behaviour coexisted with opportunities for anonymous, surreptitious private enjoyment. By contrast, the seaside boarding-house was generally tightly regulated by landladies and censoriously gossipy visitors alike, as the jokes about the regime made plain.[44]

Conclusion

The rise of the seaside resort, first in England, the British Isles and then as international phenomenon, provided an important new engine of urban cultural exchange, both within, and between, nations and social classes. However, the processes of exchange were complex, and as the case of Brighton – the first of the great resorts – demonstrates, there should be no simple assumption that the seaside was necessarily a site of cultural transfer. In particular, the depth of field of exchange in resorts was limited by the nature of the gatherings. International high life clustered and excluded, directly or indirectly: participation entailed access to, and acceptance in, select areas of hotels, casinos (usually involving roulette, which was an almost essential accompaniment to sociability at this level, whether or not individuals gambled), theatres, ballrooms, assemblies, beaches and promenades. Subscriptions might be required and demanding dress codes enforced. But the demonstration effect of displays of fashionable clothing, accoutrements and behaviour would rub off on the expectations, behaviour and conversation of those middle-class visitors who also sustained the economies of all but the smallest such resorts, and took their experiences back to the capital and the provinces of France, Spain or Northern Europe.[45] How this worked in practice, what the more local, cross-class and cross-cultural influences might be (on, for example, chambermaids and needlewomen), and how this might relate to concepts such as 'liminality', offers the potential for an extended research project.

Notes

1 The editors have redrafted parts of this chapter with the permission of the author, who was not in a position to complete the final revisions.

2 Waleed Hazbun, *Beaches, Ruins, Resorts: The Politics of Tourism in the Arab World* (Minneapolis: University of Minnesota Press, 2008).

3 G. Cross and J.K. Walton, *The Playful Crowd: Pleasure Places in the Twentieth Century* (New York: Columbia University Press, 2005).

4 A. Corbin, *The Lure of the Sea*, trans. Jocelyn Phelps (Cambridge: Polity Press, 1993); A. Brodie and G. Winter, *England's Seaside Resorts* (Swindon: English Heritage, 2007); A. Brodie, 'Scarborough in the 1730s: spa, sea and sex', *Journal of Tourism History*, 4 (2012), 125–153.

5 J.K. Walton, *The English Seaside Resort: A Social History 1750–1914* (Leicester: Leicester University Press, 1983), chapter 2; J.-H. Furnée, 'A Dutch idyll? Scheveningen as a seaside resort, fishing village and port, c. 1700–1900', in P. Borsay and J.K. Walton (eds.), *Resorts and Ports* (Bristol: Channel View, 2011), pp. 126–146.

6 J.K. Walton, 'The seaside resorts of Western Europe, 1750–1939,' in Stephen Fisher (ed.), *Recreation and the Sea* (Exeter: University of Exeter Press, 1997), pp. 36–56; J.K. Walton, 'Seaside resort regions and their hinterlands in Western Europe and the Americas, from the late eighteenth century to the Second World War', *Storia del Turismo*, 4 (2003), 69–87.

7 G. Parry, '"Queen of the Welsh resorts": tourism and the Welsh language in Llandudno in the nineteenth century', *Welsh History Review*, 21 (2002).

8 R.M. Jones, 'The Liverpool Welsh', in D. Rees (ed.), *The Liverpool Welsh and their Religion* (Liverpool: Modern Welsh Publications, 1984).

9 A.J. Durie, *Scotland for the Holidays: A History of Tourism in Scotland, 1780–1939* (East Linton: Tuckwell, 2003).

10 Mary Davies, *That Favourite Resort: the Story of Bray, Co. Wicklow* (Bray: Wordwell, 2007); Tricia Cusack, '"Enlightened Protestants": the improved shorescape, order and liminality at early seaside resorts in Victorian Ireland', *Journal of Tourism History*, 2 (2010), 165–185; J.A.R. Pimlott, *The Englishman's Holiday: A Social History* (London: Faber and Faber, 1947), p. 122.

11 C. Nevin, *Lancashire: Where Women Die of Love* (Edinburgh: Mainstream, 2004); W. Lowndes, *They Came to Bath* (Bristol: Redcliffe Press, 1987), pp. 69–70; J. Liddle, 'Estate management and land reform politics: the Hesketh and Scarisbrick families and the making of Southport, 1842–1914', in D. Cannadine (ed.), *Patricians, Power and Politics* (Leicester: Leicester University Press, 1982).

12 R.E. Hull, *Nathaniel Hawthorne: The English Experience, 1853–1864* (Pittsburgh: University of Pittsburgh Press, 1980), pp. 100, 104, 116; J.K. Walton, 'Port and resort: symbiosis and conflict in "Old Whitby", Enlgand, since 1880', in P. Borsay and J.K. Walton (eds.), *Resorts and Ports: European Seaside Towns since 1700* (Bristol: Channel View, 2011), p. 134.

13 J.K. Walton, *The British Seaside: Holidays and Resorts in the Twentieth Century* (Manchester University Press, 2000), pp. 20–21; British Cartoon Archive, WH 977, *Daily Mirror*, 5 November 1912; P. Henley, *Aber Prom: A Pictorial History of*

Events and Entertainment on Aberystwyth Promenade (Talybont: y Llolfa Cyf, 2007), pp. 24–26.

14 Pimlott, *Englishman's Holiday*, pp. 106–109.

15 See, for example, A. Garner, *A Shifting Shore: Locals, Outsiders and the Transformation of a French Fishing Town* (Ithaca: Cornell University Press, 2005).

16 Walton, 'The seaside resorts of Western Europe', pp. 36–56.

17 Jeremy Black, *The British Abroad: the Grand Tour in the Eighteenth Century* (Stroud: Sutton, 2003).

18 Roy Porter (ed.), *The Medical History of Waters and Spas, Medical History*, supplement no. 10 (London: Wellcome Institute, 1990); Jill Steward, 'The spa towns of the Austrian-Hungarian Empire and the growth of tourist culture: 1860–1914', in Peter Borsay et al., (eds.), *New Directions in Urban History* (Münster: Waxmann, 2000), pp. 87–126; Douglas P. Mackaman, *Leisure Settings: Bourgeois Culture, Medicine and the Spa in Modern France* (Chicago: University of Chicago Press, 1998); Annick Cossic and Patrick Galliou (eds.), *Spas in Britain and France in the Eighteenth and Nineteenth Centuries* (Newcastle: Cambridge Scholars Press, 2006); *Journal of Tourism History*, 4:1 and 2 (2012), special issue on the international history of mineral springs resorts.

19 S. Pakenham, *60 Miles from England: The English at Dieppe, 1814–1914* (London: Macmillan, 1967).

20 M. Blume, *Côte d'Azur: Inventing the French Riviera* (London: Thames & Hudson, 1992), pp. 29–31, 34–36, 57, 61, 63.

21 J.K. Walton, 'Seaside resorts and international tourism', in Eric G.E. Zuelow (ed.), *Touring Beyond the Nation: A Transnational Approach to European Tourism History* (Farnham: Ashgate, 2011), pp. 19–36.

22 Michel Chadefaud, *Aux origines du tourisme dans le Pays de l'Adour* (Pau: Université du Pau, 1987); Gabriel désert, *La vie quotidienne sur les plages Normandes de Second Empire aux années folles* (paris: Hachette, 1983); references for Nice and Monte Carlo.

23 J.K. Walton, 'Tourism and politics in elite beach resorts: San Sebastián and Ostend, 1830–1939', in L. Tissot (ed.), *Construction of a Tourism Industry in the 19th and 20th Century: International Perspectives* (Neuchatel, Switzerland: Alphil, 2003), pp. 287–301.

24 Jon Juaristi, *Miguel de Unamuno* (Madrid: Taurus, 2012), p. 29.

25 Chadefaud, *Aux Origines du Tourisme*, pp. 370, 393–396, 470, 571–574.

26 *Revista San Sebastián*, 2 (2012), special issue on 'Casinos Donostiarras', pp. 26–29, 35–58.

27 R. Shields, *Places on the Margin: Alternative Geographies of Modernity* (London: Routledge, 1991).

28 For Brighton's history E.W. Gilbert, *Brighton: Old Ocean's Bauble*, 2nd edn (Hassocks: Flare Books, 1975), remains unsurpassed.

29 J.K. Walton, 'Histories of liminality on the coast', in T. Carter, P. Gilchrist and D. Burdsey (eds.), *Coastal Cultures: Interdisciplinary Concepts of the Coast* (Eastbourne: Leisure Studies Association, 2013). The shorter critique of Shields that follows shares some text with this publication.

30 L. Nead, *Victorian Babylon* (New Haven: Yale University Press, 2000); F. Driver, *Geography Militant* (London: Wiley-Blackwell, 2001), chapter 8.

31 Gilbert, *Brighton*.

32 Walton, 'Tourism and politics in elite beach resorts, pp. 287–301.

33 J.K. Walton, 'The waters of San Sebastián: therapy, health, pleasure and identity, 1840–1936', in Susan C. Anderson and Bruce H. Tabb (eds.), *Water, Leisure and Culture: European Historical Perspectives* (Oxford: Berg, 2002), pp. 37–52; J.K. Walton, 'Planning and seaside tourism: San Sebastián, 1863–1936', *Planning Perspectives*, 17 (2002), 1–20.

34 Gilbert, *Brighton*.

35 Shields, *Places on the Margin*, p. 89; Walton, *The English Seaside Resort*, chapter 3.

36 J.K. Walton, *The Blackpool Landlady: A Social History* (Manchester: Manchester University Press, 1978).

37 J. Travis, 'Continuity and change in English sea-bathing', in Fisher (ed.), *Recreation and the Sea*, pp. 8–35.

38 J.K. Walton, 'Respectability takes a holiday: disreputable behaviour at the Victorian seaside', in Martin Hewitt (ed.), *Unrespectable Recreations* (Leeds: Leeds Centre for Victorian Studies, 2001), pp. 176–193.

39 J.K. Walton, 'Consuming the beach: seaside resorts and cultures of tourism in England and Spain from the 1840s to the 1930s', in E. Furlough and S. Baranowski (eds.), *Being Elsewhere: Tourism, Consumer Culture and Identity in Modern Europe and North America* (Ann Arbor: University of Michigan Press, 2001), pp. 272–298; Elisa Pastoriza (ed.), *Las puertas al mar: Consumo, ocio y política en Mar del Plata, Montevideo y Viña del Mar* (Buenos Aires: Universidad Nacional de Mar del Plata, 2002); C. Aron, *Working at Play* (New York: Oxford University Press, 1999).

40 J.K. Walton, 'The seaside and the holiday crowd', in Vanessa Toulmin, Patrick Russell and Simon Popple (eds.), *The Lost World of Mitchell and Kenyon: Edwardian Britain on Film* (London: BFI Publishing, 2004), pp. 158–168.

41 Shields, *Places on the Margin*, p. 89; G. Stedman Jones, *Outcast London* (Oxford: Oxford University Press, 1970); J.K. Walton, 'Holidays and the discipline of industrial labour: a historian's view', in E. Kennedy and H. Pussard (eds.), *Defining the Field: 30 Years of the Leisure Studies Association* (Eastbourne: Leisure Studies Association, 2006), pp. 121–134.

42 Shields, *Places on the Margin*, p. 96; S. Major, *'The Million go forth': early railway excursion crowds, 1840–1860* (DPhil thesis, University of York, 2012); Gilbert, *Brighton*.

43 Walton, *English Seaside Resort*, chapter 8; Shields, *Places on the Margin*, pp. 98–99; Walton, 'Respectability takes a holiday', pp. 176–193.

44 G. Cross (ed.), *Worktowners at Blackpool* (London: Routledge, 1990); Walton, *Blackpool Landlady*; M.L. Di Domenico and P. Fleming, '"It's a guesthouse not a brothel": policing sex in the home-workplace', *Human Relations*, 62 (2009), 245–269.

45 J.K. Walton, 'Policing the Alameda: shared and contested recreational space in San Sebastián, 1863–1920', in S. Gunn and R. J. Morris (eds.), *Identities in Space: Contested Terrains in the Western City Since 1850* (Aldershot: Ashgate, 2001), pp. 228–241.

Select bibliography

Agulhon, M., *Le cercle dans la France bourgeoise* (Paris: A. Colin, 1977).

Allen, B. (ed.), *Towards a Modern Art World* (New Haven-London: Yale University Press, 1995).

Altick, R., *The Shows of London* (Cambridge, MA and London: Belknap Press, 1978).

Applegate, C., *Bach in Berlin: Nation and Culture in Mendelssohn's Revival of the St. Matthew Passion* (Ithaca and London: Cornell University Press, 2005).

Ascoli Georges, G., *La Grande-Bretagne devant l'opinion française au XVIIe siècle* (Paris: Gamber, 1930).

Audidière, S., S. Burrows, E. Dziembowski and A. Thomson (eds.), *Transferts Culturels: Studies on Franco–British Intellectual and Cultural Exchange in the Long Eighteenth Century* (Oxford: Voltaire Foundation, 2010).

Auslander, L, *Des révolutions culturelles: la politique du quotidien en Grande-Bretagne, en Amérique et en France, XVIIe-XIXe siècle* (Toulouse: Presses Universitaires du Mirail, 2010).

Bailey, P., 'The politics and poetics of modern British leisure: a late twentieth-century review', *Rethinking History*, 3 (1999), 131–175.

Bätschmann, O., *The Artists in the Modern World: The Conflict between Market and Self-Expression* (Cologne: Dumont, 1997).

Behringer, W., 'Arena and Pall Mall: sport in the early modern period', *German History*, 27 (2009), 331–357.

Bell, D.A., *The Cult of the Nation in France: Inventing Nationalism, 1680–1800* (Cambridge, MA: Harvard University Press, 2001).

Bennett, T., *The Birth of the Museum: History, Theory, Politics* (London and New York: Routledge, 1995).

Berg, M., *Luxury and Pleasure in Eighteenth-Century Britain* (Oxford: Oxford University Press, 2005).

Bevilacqua, A. and H. Pfeifer, 'Turquerie: culture in motion, 1650–1750', *Past and Present*, 221 (2013), 75–118.

Bjurström, P. (ed.), *The Genesis of the Art Museum in the 18th Century* (Stockholm: Nationalmuseum, 1993).

Black, J., *The British Abroad: The Grand Tour in the Eighteenth Century* (Stroud: Sutton, 2003).

Black, J., *The British and the Grand Tour* (London: Croom Helm, 1985).

Black, J., *France and the Grand Tour* (Bastingstoke: Palgrave, 2003).

Blackbourn, D., 'Fashionable spa towns in the nineteenth century', in S.C. Anderson and B.H. Tabb (eds.), *Water, Leisure and Culture, European Historical Perspectives* (NewYork and Oxford: Berg, 2004), pp. 9–22.

Blanning, T.C.W., *The Culture of Power and the Power of Culture: Old Regime Europe 1660–1789* (Oxford: Oxford University Press, 2002).

Blanning, T.C.W., *The Triumph of Music: The Rise of Composers, Musicians and Their Art* (Cambridge, MA: Belknap Press, 2008).

Blume, M., *Côte d'Azur: Inventing the French Riviera* (London: Thames & Hudson, 1992).

Bödeker, H.E., P. Veit and M. Werner (eds.), *Espaces et lieux de concert en Europe 1700–1920: Architecture, musique, société* (Berlin: BWV, 2008).

Bonno, G., *La culture et la civilisation britanniques devant l'opinion française de la paix d'Utrecht aux Lettres philosophiques* (Philadelphia: Transactions of the American Philosophical Society, 1948).

Borsay, P., *The English Urban Renaissance: Culture and Society in the Provincial Town, 1660–1770* (Oxford: Clarendon Press, 1989).

Borsay, P., *The Image of Georgian Bath, 1700–2000: Towns, Heritage and History* (Oxford: Oxford University Press, 2000).

Borsay, P., *A History of Leisure: The British Experience since 1500* (London: Basingstoke, 2006).

Borsay, P. and J.K. Walton (eds.), *Resorts and Ports: European Seaside Towns since 1700* (Bristol: Channel View, 2011).

Boyer, M., *L'hiver dans le Midi: L'Invention de la Côte d'Azur* (Paris: éd. de l'Aube, 2002).

Brewer, J., *The Pleasure of the Imagination: English Culture in the Eighteenth Century* (New York: Farrar, Straus & Giroud, 1997)

Brewer, J., and A. Bermingham (eds.), *The Consumption of Culture, 1600–1800: Image, Object, Text* (London: Routledge, 1995).

Brewer, J. and R. Porter (eds.), *Consumption and the World of Goods* (London: Routledge and Kegan Paul, 1993).

Brewer, J., N. McKendrick and J.H. Plumb, *The Birth of Consumer Society: The Commercialization of Eighteenth-Century England* (London: Hutchinson, 1983).

Brown, B.A., 'La diffusion et l'influence de l'opéra-comique en Europe au XVIIIe siècle', in P. Vendrix (ed.), *L'Opéra-comique en France au XVIIIe siècle* (Liège: Mardaga, 1992), pp. 283–342.

Bryson, A., *From Courtesy to Civility: Changing Codes of Conduct in Early Modern England* (Oxford: Clarendon Press, 1998).

Burke, P., 'The invention of leisure in early modern Europe', *Past and Present*, 146 (1995), 136–150.

Burke, P., *Popular Culture in Early Modern Europe* (Burlington: Ashgate Publishing, 2009).

Bury, E., *Littérature et politesse: L'Invention de l'honnête homme (1580–1750)* (Paris: PUF, 1996).

Cabantous, A., *Le dimanche, une histoire: Europe occidentale, 1600–1830* (Paris: Seuil, 2013).

Calhoun, C. (ed.), *Habermas and the Public Sphere* (Cambridge MA: MIT Press, 1992).

Carré, J. (ed.), *Londres, 1700–1900: Naissance d'une capitale culturelle* (Paris: Presses universitaires Paris-Sorbonne, 2010).

Carter, P., *Men and the Emergence of Polite Society: Britain, 1660–1800* (Harlow: Longman, 2001).

Casanova, P., *La république mondiale des lettres* (Paris: Seuil, 1999).

Chard, C., *Pleasure and Guilt on the Grand Tour: Travel and Imaginative Geography, 1600–1830* (Manchester: Manchester University Press, 1999).

Charle, C. (ed.), *Capitales européennes et rayonnement culturel, XVIIIe-XXe siècle* (Paris: Ed. rue d'Ulm, 2004).

Charle, C. *Théâtres en capitales: Naissance de la société du spectacle à Paris, Berlin, Londres et Vienne* (Paris: Albin Michel, 2008).

Charle, C., J. Vincent and J. Winter (eds.), *Anglo-French Attitudes: Comparisons and Transfers between English and French Intellectuals since the Eighteenth Century* (Manchester: Manchester University Press, 2007).

Chaubaud, G., 'Pour une histoire comparée des guides imprimés à l'époque moderne', in *Les guides imprimés du XVIe au XXe siècle. Villes, paysages, voyages. Actes du colloque de Paris de décembre 1998* (Paris: Belin, 2000), pp. 641–649.

Clark, P., *British Clubs and Societies: The Origins of an Associational World 1580–1800* (Oxford: Clarendon Press, 2000).

Clark, P., *The English Alehouse: A Social History 1200–1830* (London: Longman, 1983).

Clark, P., *European Cities and Towns 400–2000* (Oxford: Oxford University Press, 2009).

Cohen, M., *Fashioning Masculinity: National Identity and Language in the Eighteenth Century* (New York: Routledge, 2002).

Coke, D. and A. Borg, *Vauxhall Gardens: A History* (New Haven and London: Yale University Press, 2011).

Colley, L., *Britons: Forging the Nation 1707–1837* (New Haven: Yale University Press, 1992).

Conlin, J. (ed.), *The Pleasure Garden from Vauxhall to Coney Island* (Philadelphia: University of Pennsylvania Press, 2013).

Conlin, J., *Tales of Two Cities: Paris, London and the Making of the Modern City, 1700–1900* (London: Atlantic Books, 2013).

Conlin, J., 'Vauxhall on the boulevard: pleasure gardens in London and Paris, 1764–1784', *Urban History*, 35:1 (2008), 24–47.

Conway, S., *Britain, Ireland, and Continental Europe in the Eighteenth Century: Similarities, Connections, Identities* (Oxford: Oxford University Press, 2011).

Corbin. A. (ed.), *L'Avènement des loisirs, 1850–1960* (Paris: Aubier, 1995).

Corbin, A., *The Lure of the Sea* (Cambridge: Polity Press, 1993).

Cossic, A. and P. Galliou (eds.), *Spas in Britain and France in the Eighteenth and Nineteenth Centuries* (Newcastle: Cambridge Scholars Press, 2006).

Cowan, B., *The Social Life of Coffee: The Emergence of the British Coffeehouse* (New Haven: Yale University Press, 2005).

Crego, R., *Sports and Games of the 18th and 19th Centuries* (London: Greenwood Publishing Group, 2003).

Cross, G. and J.K. Walton, *The Playful Crowd: Pleasure Places in the Twentieth Century* (New York: Columbia University Press, 2005).

DaCosta Kaufmann, T., *Court, Cloister and City: The Art and Culture of Central Europe, 1450–1800* (London: Weidenfeld and Nicolson, 1995).

Davidson, D., *France after Revolution: Urban Life, Gender and the New Social Order* (New Haven: Harvard University Press, 2007).

Dixon Hunt, J., *The Picturesque Garden in Europe* (London: Thames & Hudson, 2002).

Dolan, B., *Ladies of the Grand Tour: British Women in Pursuit of Enlightenment and Adventure in Eighteenth-Century Europe* (New York: HarperCollins, 2001).

Dunning, E., Malcolm, D. and Waddington, I. (eds।)., *Sports Histories: Figurational Studies of the Development of Modern Sports* (Abingdon: Routledge, 2004).

Eagles, R., *Francophilia in English Society, 1748–1815* (Basingstoke: Macmillan, 2000).

Elias, N. and E. Dunning, *Quest for Excitement: Sport and Leisure in the Civilizing Process* (Oxford: Wiley Blackwell, 1986).

Fauser, A. and M. Everist (ed.), *Music Theater and Cultural Transfer: Paris, 1830–1914* (Chicago and London: Chicago University Press, 2009).

Furnée, J.H., '"Le bon public de La Haye": local governance and the audience in the French opera in The Hague, 1820–1890', *Urban History*, 40 (2013), 625–645.

Garrioch, D., *The Formation of the Parisian Bourgeoisie (1690–1830)* (Cambridge, MA: Harvard University Press, 1996).

Géal, P., *La naissance des musées d'art en Espagne (XVIIIe-XIXe siècles)* (Madrid: Casa de Velázquez, 2005).

Geist, J. F., *Passagen: Ein Bautyp des 19. Jahrhunderts* (Munich: Prestel Verlag, 1982).

Gerbod, P., *Les voyageurs français à la découverte des îles britanniques du XVIIIe siècle à nos jours* (Paris: L'Harmattan, 1995).

Girouard, M., *Cities and People: A Social and Architectural History* (New Haven and London: Yale University Press, 1985).

Goodman, J., P.E. Lovejoy and A. Sherratt (eds.), *Consuming Habits: Drugs in History and Anthropology* (London and New York: Routledge, 1995).

Select bibliography

Green, N., *The Spectacle of Nature: Landscape and Bourgeois Culture in Nineteenth-Century France* (Manchester: Manchester University Press, 1990).

Grieder, J., *Anglomania in France 1740–1789: Fact, Fiction and Political Discourse* (Geneva: Droz, 1985).

Habermas, J., *The Structural Transformation of the Public Sphere*, trans. T. Burger (Cambridge: Polity, 1989).

Hancock, C., *Paris et Londres au XIXe siècle: Représentations dans les guides et récits de voyage* (Paris: Éditions du CNRS, 2003).

Hardesty Doig, K. and D. Medlin (eds.), *British-French Exchanges in the Eighteenth Century* (Newcastle: Cambridge Scholars Publishing, 2007).

Harouel, J.-L., *L'Embellissement des villes: L'Urbanisme français au XVIIIe siècle* (Paris: Picard Éditeur, 1993).

Hattox, R.S., *Coffee and Coffeehouses: The Origins of a Social Beverage in the Medieval Near East* (Seattle: University of Washington Press, 1985).

Haupt, H.-G. and J. Kocka (eds.), *Comparative and Transnational History: Central European Approaches and New Perspectives* (New York: Berghahn, 2009).

Haupt, H.-G. and J. Kocka (eds.), *Geschichte und Vergleich: Ansätze und Ergebnisse international vergleichender Geschichtsschreibung* (Frankfurt: Campus, 1996).

Heller, B., *Leisure and Pleasure in London Society, 1760–1820: An Agent-centred Account* (DPhil dissertation, University of Oxford, 2009).

Hembry, P., *The English Spa 1560–1815: A Social History* (London: Athlone, 1990).

Hobsbawm, E. J., *Nations and Nationalism since 1780: Programme, Myth, Reality* (Cambridge: Cambridge University Press, 1992).

Holt, R., *Sport and the British* (Oxford: Clarendon Press, 1989).

Holt, R., *Sport and Society in Modern France* (London: Macmillan, 1981).

Hopes, J. and H. Lecossois (eds.), *Théâtre et Nation* (Rennes: Presses universitaires de Rennes, 2011).

Huck, G. (ed.), *Sozialgeschichte der Freizeit: Untersuchungen zum Wandel der Alltagskultur in Deutschland* (Wuppertal: Hammer, 1980).

Huizinga, J., *Homo Ludens* (Amsterdam: Pantheon, 1939).

Irvine, A., *Global and Transnational History: The Past, Present and Future* (London: Palgrave Macmillan, 2013).

Irvine, A. and P.-Y. Saunier (eds.), *The Palgrave Dictionary of Transnational History: From the Mid-Nineteenth Century to the Present Day* (London: Palgrave Macmillan, 2009).

Isherwood, R.M., *Farce and Fantasy: Popular Entertainment in Eighteenth-Century Paris* (Oxford: Oxford University Press, 1986).

Johnson, J.H., *Listening in Paris: A Cultural History* (Berkeley: University of California Press, 1995).

Jones, C. and D. Wahrman (eds.), *The Age of Cultural Revolutions: Britain and France, 1750–1820* (Berkley: University of California Press, 2002).

Kalifa, D., 'L'Ère de la culture marchandise', *Revue d'Histoire du XIXème Siècle*, 19 (1999), 7–14.

Kelly, J., and M.J. Powell (eds.), *Clubs and Societies in Eighteenth-Century Ireland* (Dublin: Four Courts Press, 2010).

Kümin, B., *Drinking Matters: Public House and Exchange in Early Modern Central Europe* (Basingstoke: Palgrave Macmillan, 2007).

Kurilo, O. (ed.), *Seebäder an der Ostsee im 19. Und 20. Jahrhundert* (Munich: Martin Meidenbauer, 2009).

Levenstein, H., *Seductive Journey: American Tourists in France from Jefferson to the Jazz Age* (Chicago: University of Chicago Press, 1998).

Lockitt, C.H., *The Relations of French & English Society, 1763–1793* (New York: Longmans, 1920).

Loir, C. and L. Turcot (eds.), *La promenade au tournant des 18e et 19e siècles (Belgique/ Europe)* (Brussels: Editions de l'Université, 2011).

Lorente, J.-P., *Cathedrals of Urban Modernity: The First Museums of Contemporary Art, 1800–1930* (London: Ashgate, 1998).

Lough, J., *France on the Eve of Revolution: British Travellers' Observations 1763–1788* (London and Sydney: Croom Helm, 1987).

Lowerson, J., *Sport and the English Middle Classes 1870–1914* (Manchester: Manchester University Press, 1993).

Mackaman, D.P., *Leisure Settings. Bourgeois Culture, Medicine and the Spa in Modern France* (Chicago and London: University of Chicago Press, 1998).

Malcolmson, R.W., *Popular Recreations in English Society, 1700–1850* (Cambridge: Cambridge University Press, 1979).

Marais, J.-L., *Les Societés des Hommes: Histoire d'une Sociabilité du 18e siècle à nos jours* (Vauchrétien: Éditions Iwan Davy, 1986).

Martin-Fugier, A., *La vie élégante ou la formation du tout Paris, 1815–1848* (Paris: Seuil, 1993).

Maxwell, C., *The English Traveller in France, 1698–1815* (London: Routledge, 1932).

Mcclellan, A., *The Art Museum from Boullée to Bilbao* (Berkeley: University of California Press 2008).

Mcclellan, A., *Inventing the Louvre: Art, Politics, and the Origins of the Modern Museum in Eighteenth-Century Paris* (Cambridge and New York: Cambridge University Press, 1994).

McWilliam, R., 'Melodrama and historians', *Radical History Review*, 78 (2000), 57–84.

Meinander, H., *Towards a Bourgeois Manhood* (Helsinki: Finninsh Society of Sciences and Letters, 1994).

Meinander, H. and J.A. Mangan (eds.), *The Nordic World: Sport in Society* (London: Frank Cass, 1998).

Mollier, J.-Y., J.-F. Sirinelli and F. Vallotton (eds.), *Culture de masse et culture médiatique en Europe et dans les Amériques 1860–1940* (Paris: PUF, 2006).

Montanari, M., *The Culture of Food* (Cambridge: Blackwell, 1994).

Montandon, A. (ed.), *Bibliographie des traités de savoir-vivre en Europe du Moyen Age à nos jours* (Clermond-Ferrand: Université Blaise-Pascal, 1995).

Morton, G., B. de Vries and R.J. Morris (eds.), *Civil Society: Associations and Urban Places: Class, Nation and Culture in Nineteenth-Century Europe* (Aldershot: Ashgate, 2006).

Muir, E., *Ritual in Early Modern Europe* (Cambridge: Cambridge University Press, 1997).

Newman, K., *Cultural Capitals: Early Modern London and Paris* (Princeton: Princeton University Press, 2007).

Norton, M., *Sacred Gifts, Profane Pleasures: A History of Tobacco and Chocolate in the Atlantic World* (Ithaca: Cornell University Press, 2008).

O'Byrne, A., *Walking, Rambling and Promenading in Eighteenth-century London: A Literary and Cultural History* (PhD dissertation, University of York, 2003).

Ogborn, M., *Spaces of Modernity: London's Geographies, 1680–1780* (New York and London: Guildford Press, 1998).

Ogee, F. (ed.), *Better in France? The Circulation of Ideas between Britain and the Continent in the Eighteenth Century* (Lewisburg: Bucknell University Press, 2005).

Pevsner, N., *Academies of Art, Past and Present* (New York: Da Capo Press, 1973).

Plumb, J.H., *The Commercialization of Leisure in Eighteenth-Century England* (Reading: University of Reading Press, 1973).

Pommier, E. (ed.), *Les musées en Europe à la veille de l'ouverture du Louvre* (Paris: Klincksieck-Musée du Louvre, 1995).

Porter, R., *Enlightenment: Britain and the Creation of the Modern World* (London: Allen Lane, 2000).

Porter, R. (ed.), *The Medical History of Waters and Spas, Medical History*, Supplement No. 10 (London: Wellcome Institute, 1990).

Porter, R. and M. Teich (eds.), *The Enlightenment in a National Context* (Cambridge: Cambridge University Press, 1981).

Quataert, D. (ed.), *Consumption Studies and the History of the Ottoman Empire: An Introduction* (Albany: State University of New York Press, 2000).

Ruggiu, F.-J., *Les elites et les villes moyennes en France et en Angleterre* (Paris: L'Harmattan, 1997).

Ruggiu, F.-J., *L'individu et la famille dans les sociétés urbaines anglaise et française, 1720–1780* (Paris: PUPS, 2007).

Russell, G., *The Theatres of War: Performance, Politics and Society, 1793–1815* (Oxford and New York: Clarendon Press, 1995).

Sajdi, D. (ed.), *Ottoman Tulips, Ottoman Coffee: Leisure and Lifestyle in the Eighteenth Century* (London and New York: Tauris Academic Studies, 2007).

Saunier, P.-Y., *Transnational History* (London: Palgrave Macmillan, 2013).

Schivelbusch, W., *Tastes of Paradise: A Social History of Spices, Stimulants, and Intoxicants* (New York: Pantheon Books, 1992).

Schubert, K., *The Curator's Egg: The Evolution of the Museum Concept from the French Revolution to the Present Day* (London: One-Off Press, 2000).

Sheehan, J.J., *Museums in the German Art World from the End of the Old Regime to the Rise of Modernism* (Oxford and New York: Oxford University Press, 2000).

Shields, R., *Places on the Margin: Alternative Geographies of Modernity* (London: Routledge, 1991).

Sorba, C., 'Le mélodrame du Risorgimento: théatralité et émotions dans la communication politique des patriotes italiens', *Actes de la recherche in sciences sociales*, 4 (2010), 12–29.

Stallybrass, P. and A. White, *The Politics and Poetics of Transgression* (London: Methuen, 1986).

Stedman, G., *Cultural Exchange in Seventeenth-century France and England* (Aldershot: Ashgate, 2013).

Steward, J., 'The spa towns of the Austrian-Hungarian Empire and the growth of tourist culture: 1860–1914', in P. Borsay, G. Hirshfelder and R.-E. Mohrmann (eds.), *New Directions in Urban History: Aspects of European Urban Cultural Life in the Mirror of Art, Health and Tourism* (Münster: Waxmann, 2000), pp. 87–126.

Steward, J., 'The culture of the cure in nineteenth-century Austria', in S.C. Anderson and B.H. Tabb (eds.), *Water, Leisure and Culture, European Historical Perspectives* (NewYork and Oxford: Berg, 2004), pp. 23–35.

Stobart, J., A. Hann and V. Morgan (eds.), *Space of Consumption: Leisure and Shopping in the English Town, c. 1680–1830* (Abingdon: Routledge, 2007).

Sweet, R., *Cities and the Grand Tour: The British in Italy, c. 1690–1820* (Cambridge: Cambridge University Press, 2012).

Taylor, B., *Art for the Nation: Exhibitions and the London Public, 1747–2001* (Manchester, Manchester University Press, 1999).

Thomasseau, J.-M., *Le mélodrame* (Paris: Presses Universitaires de France, 1984).

Towner, J., *A Historical Geography of Recreation and Tourism in the Western World, 1540–1940* (Chichester: John Wiley, 1996).

Turcot, L., 'Entre promenades et jardins publics: les loisirs parisiens et londoniens au XVIIIe siècle', *Revue Belge de Philologie et d'Histoire*, 87 (2009), 645–663.

Turcot, L. (ed.), *L'ordinaire parisien des Lumières* (Paris: Hermann, 2013).

Veblen, T., *The Theory of the Leisure Class: An Economic Study in the Evolution of Institutions* (New York: Macmillan, 1899).

Walton, J.K., *The British Seaside: Holidays and Resorts in the Twentieth Century* (Manchester: Manchester University Press, 2000.

Walton, J.K., 'Consuming the beach: seaside resorts and cultures of tourism in England and Spain from the 1840s to the 1930s', in E. Furlough and S. Baranowski (eds.),

Select bibliography

Being Elsewhere: Tourism, Consumer Culture and Identity in Modern Europe and North America (Ann Arbor: University of Michigan Press, 2001), pp. 272–298.

Walton, J.K., *The English Seaside Resort: A Social History 1750–1914* (Leicester: Leicester University Press, 1983).

Walton, J.K., 'The seaside resorts of Western Europe, 1750–1939,' in S. Fisher (ed.), *Recreation and the Sea* (Exeter: University of Exeter Press, 1997), pp. 36–56.

Walton, J.K., 'Tourism and politics in elite beach resorts: San Sebastián and Ostend, 1830–1939', in L. Tissot (ed.), *Construction of a Tourism Industry in the 19th and 20th Century: International Perspectives* (Neuchatel: Alphil, 2003), pp. 287–301.

Walton, J.K. and J. Walvin, *Leisure in Britain, 1780–1939* (Manchester: Manchester University Press, 1983).

Werner, M., 'Les usages de l'échelle dans la recherche sur les transferts culturels', *Cahiers d'Études Germaniques*, 28 (1995), 39–53.

Werner, M. and B. Zimmermann, 'Beyond comparison: Histoire croisée and the challenge of reflexivity', *History and Theory*, 45 (2006), 30–50.

Werner, M. and B. Zimmermann (eds.), *De la comparaison à l'histoire croisée* (Paris: Seuil, 2004).

Wurst, K., *Fabricating Pleasure: Fashion, Entertainment, and Cultural Consumption in Germany, 1788–1830* (Detroit: Wayne State University, 2005).

Zuelow, E.G.E. (ed.), *Touring Beyond the Nation: A Transnational Approach to European Tourism History* (Farnham: Ashgate, 2011).

Index

Aachen 237

access 12, 14, 21, 30, 33, 35, 37–38, 40, 55, 64, 66, 99, 106, 108–110, 157, 189, 204, 239–240, 243–245, 247–248, 250, 253, 262, 271–272, 274

adaptation 7–8, 21, 53, 59–60, 63–64, 67, 76, 84, 91, 94, 108–109, 119, 124, 141–142, 146, 152, 157, 193, 211, 246, 255, 265

Aix-les-bains 241, 245, 251, 252, 254

alehouses 11, 78–79, 163

Aleppo 161–162

amateurs 97, 140, 143

ambition 26, 118–119, 135, 143, 235–238, 255

Amsterdam 128, 162

amusement parks 153–154, 156

Anglomania 210, 218

animal sport 74, 79

Antwerp 31, 78, 133

appropriation 2, 7, 29, 49–50, 118, 141–142, 145, 163–165, 215, 221, 227, 240

arcades 24–27, 42–43, 46, 216, 239, 241, 254

archery 73–75, 78, 81, 83

architecture 31, 34, 102, 103, 108, 164, 238–240, 243, 246–247

aristocracy 5, 21, 28, 31, 53, 56, 99, 105, 127, 153, 179, 202, 212, 214–218, 222, 225, 227, 235, 237–238, 242–243, 263, 265–267, 270–271

art critics 36–37

art exhibitions 2, 28–29, 35

art union 28, 31, 33

assembly room 96–97, 105, 108–110, 140–142, 147–148, 151, 155–156, 212, 220, 237, 240, 260

assimilation 7, 126, 163, 187

auctions 25, 27, 100–101

audiences 11, 38, 47, 51–52, 55–58, 60–66, 120–121, 124, 128, 130, 133, 144–147, 172, 174, 202, 212, 214, 216–217, 227

Austria 7, 46, 118–120, 124–126, 233, 237–238, 246–247, 252–253

authority (-ies) 2, 5, 10, 55, 58, 69, 74, 148–150, 153, 157, 166–167, 169, 171, 175–177, 189, 196, 199, 205, 224, 236–237, 239, 248, 254–255

Avignon 31

Bad Doberan 240

Bad Ems 242, 248, 252, 266

Bad Homburg 252, 269

Bad Kissingen 238, 240, 249

Bad Pyrmont 240, 243, 246

Baden (Switzerland) 234

Baden (Austria) 237, 247, 253

Baden-baden 104, 246–248, 250–252, 254, 269

ball (-room) 2, 97, 105–107, 110, 147–148, 192, 213, 215, 220, 223, 229, 237, 243, 272, 274

Barcelona 30, 32, 56

288 Index

Basel 32
Bath 7, 12–13, 82, 93–116, 211–214,
216, 220, 237, 239–240, 245,
251–252, 263
behaviour 2, 5, 13, 36–39, 47, 94–95,
105, 109, 141, 157, 186,
188–190, 194–198, 200,
203–204, 221–222, 234–236,
239, 271, 274
Belgium 7, 10, 15, 117–118, 126–127,
129–130, 133–134, 266
Berlin 10, 26, 39, 43, 133, 150,
155, 176, 242, 244, 247,
249, 252
Bern 29
Biarritz 266–267
Blackpool 262, 273
Bordeaux 31, 39
Boston 261
boulevard (theatre) 24, 34–33, 49,
53–56, 58–59, 61, 63, 65–67,
198, 217, 222–225, 237, 263
Boulogne 198, 216, 265–266
boundaries (national, social, physical)
3, 6–7, 10, 15, 93–94, 99,
102, 111, 117, 188, 214,
266, 269
bourgeoisie 5, 32, 61, 82, 122,
129–130, 153, 214, 217–218,
224, 235, 241–244, 247, 249,
253–255, 263
boxing 213, 217
Bremen 32
Brighton 261, 266, 269–274
Bristol 44, 98–99, 216
Britain (Great) 3–4, 7–10, 23, 37,
42, 50, 63–65, 82, 93–96, 99,
102–104, 108–112, 176, 185,
190–191, 193–194, 196, 203,
211, 220, 226, 236–237, 240,
247, 262, 269, 272
Brussels 7, 10, 26, 31, 34, 46,
117–139
bull baiting 14, 74
business 23, 25–27, 53, 58, 100–101,
106, 111, 123, 149, 150, 162,
165–166, 168–169, 175, 190,
211, 213, 224, 250, 268

cabaret 78, 198, 214, 222
cafés 5, 21, 25, 39, 41–42, 54, 141–142,
148, 150–151, 153, 156–157,
163, 165, 177, 187, 197, 217,
220–222, 254, 272
Cairo 162
capital cities 7, 13, 21–26, 29–32, 37,
41, 53–54, 61, 94, 107, 118,
126–130, 132–135, 141–145,
149–152, 156–158, 161–163,
168, 185, 190, 196, 215,
223–225, 242, 244, 260, 262,
270–271, 274
Carlsbad 237–241, 244, 247, 249, 252
carnival (-esque) 76, 174, 219, 269, 273
casino 30, 238, 240, 243, 246, 251–252,
254, 266, 268–269, 271, 274
censor (-ship) 66, 80–81, 244, 248, 274
chamber of rhetoric 124, 126
choral society 134
church 11, 23, 43, 78, 83, 105–107, 126,
146–147, 157, 192, 251, 266
circulating library 99, 106, 109
circulation 9, 63–67, 93, 247
circus 10, 100, 102–103, 109, 153, 155,
157
clientele 109, 112, 149, 165, 167–171,
176, 235, 239, 244, 254–255
club 14, 21, 25, 28–30, 41, 72–77,
82–84, 177, 201, 219–222, 240,
266
cockfighting 14, 74–75, 79, 213, 219
coffeehouses 10, 14, 150, 161–177
commerce 5, 10, 12, 22–24, 26–28,
42–43, 51, 54–56, 58, 62, 66, 69,
72, 75, 77–78, 80, 83–84, 99,
107, 122, 135, 170, 174, 180,
212–215, 218, 220, 235–236,
245, 253, 255, 260–261,
264–266
commercialisation 3, 4, 8, 11, 13–14,
16, 56, 73, 78–79, 103, 122, 135,
163, 187, 190, 215, 217, 226,
245, 264
competition 12–13, 29, 35, 42, 55, 72,
74, 78–79, 83–84, 89, 118, 132,
135, 150, 204, 235, 237, 239,
245–247, 249, 252–255

Index **289**

concert (-hall) 2, 4–5, 11, 14, 30, 39–40, 72, 82, 96–97, 117, 122, 126–128, 130, 140, 142, 147–148, 154, 156, 159, 192, 200, 212, 215, 223, 237, 243–244, 252, 268

conduct (literature) 187–195, 199–200, 203–224, 215, 239, 263

confectioners 10, 150, 156

consumers 10, 12, 37, 95, 103, 117, 122, 164, 226

consumer culture 4, 212

consumer revolution 4, 99, 167

Copenhagen 151, 158

cosmopolitanism 104, 119, 121, 124, 130, 215, 235, 237, 240, 255, 265

court 38, 75, 78, 82, 98, 118–126, 133, 135, 143–144, 146, 167, 190–193, 223, 225–226, 235, 237, 241–242, 244, 246, 268, 271

cultural exchange 7–9, 12, 15, 37, 63, 93, 176, 186–187, 204, 210, 234, 260–263, 265–266, 268, 270–274

cultural transfer 2, 6–7, 12–16, 93, 100, 103, 109, 111, 163–164, 185, 187, 193, 211, 227, 255

curling 75

Damascus 161–162

dancing 4, 9–10, 14, 97–98, 127, 141, 187, 191, 194, 217, 225, 237–238, 244, 251–252, 265

Deauville 266

debating society 14

demand 3, 5, 9–10, 54, 60, 63, 80, 98, 100, 103, 109, 128, 146, 215, 226, 262, 272, 274

democratisation 14, 60, 66, 70, 188, 215, 265

Denmark 158

Dieppe 265–266

dissemination 8, 12–13, 67, 77, 80, 84, 109, 175, 179, 243, 260–261

distinction (social, cultural, spatial) 66, 172, 185, 189, 191, 193, 203–204, 212, 214, 225, 234–235, 254

Dresden 37, 52

drinking (house) 78–79, 82–83, 99–100, 109, 121, 124, 140, 148–150, 161–177, 200–202, 219, 239–241, 246, 250

Dublin 28, 33, 77, 110, 263

education 27, 29, 35, 98, 103, 118, 126, 128–129, 143, 145–146, 157, 211, 236, 266, 272

elite 5, 10, 15, 28, 35, 39, 41, 45, 74, 78, 81–84, 93–94, 97, 103, 105, 109, 117, 122, 127, 129, 133, 135, 140, 153, 157–158, 164, 167–168, 170, 174, 177, 189–190, 193, 195, 204, 211, 214, 217–219, 223, 230, 239, 240, 249, 252–253, 255, 260, 262, 264–265, 269

emulation 12, 26, 29–31, 33, 35, 41, 43, 46, 164, 185–186, 188, 204–205, 242, 244, 260–261, 264–265

Enlightenment 8, 13–16, 21, 29, 33, 37–38, 40, 51, 54, 72, 84, 93, 112, 149, 187, 218

entangled history (histoire croisée) 6–8, 22, 24, 94, 108, 111, 183, 211

entertainment industry 50, 224

entrance (fee) 23, 26–27, 33, 35–36, 38–40, 43, 61, 130, 152–153, 165, 254

ethnicity 1, 179

etiquette 8, 37, 164, 194, 240, 260, 270–271

fairs 22–23, 27, 53, 111, 195, 199, 201, 213, 217, 222, 230

fashion (-able) 8–9, 11, 13–14, 25, 37, 49, 53–54, 63, 73–75, 78, 83, 93–94, 96–102, 105–108, 111–112, 120–121, 124, 132, 135, 150, 152, 157, 164, 171, 174, 187–188, 192, 195, 214, 218, 221, 223, 225–226, 235, 237–240, 242–246, 254–255, 260–261, 264–265, 267, 271, 274

female 5, 34, 62, 84, 194, 220, 250, 272

femininity 5

290 Index

Finland 78, 266
fireworks 76
Florence 22, 32, 37, 75–76
football 72, 74, 77, 79, 83–84
France 4, 7, 8, 10, 13–14, 22, 29,
  31, 35, 49, 51, 53–54, 56, 60,
  76–77, 79–80, 84, 97–98,
  101, 104–105, 107, 110–111,
  119, 124, 126, 128–129, 135,
  143–144, 167, 170, 175–176,
  179, 185–186, 190, 193–194,
  196, 203, 210–213, 218–221,
  223, 226–227, 234, 237, 245,
  247, 250, 252–254, 261–262,
  266–267, 274
Francophobia 111
Frankfurt 151, 242, 245, 248–249, 252
fraternity (confraternity) 11, 83, 161
freemasonry 29, 84
Frenchification 123, 126–127, 133, 226

galleries 21–22, 24–29, 33–40, 42–47,
  203, 250
gallomania 125, 133
Gallophobia 127
gambling 9, 74–75, 82, 176, 201–202,
  213, 221, 240, 246, 251–252,
  266, 268–269
games 2, 72–84, 153, 171, 192, 213,
  252, 271
gender 4–5, 24, 28, 77, 83, 134, 212,
  218–220, 261, 269, 272
Genoa 32, 65, 170
gentry 82, 99, 109, 237
Germany 4, 7, 10, 46, 64, 78, 80,
  82, 107, 125, 143, 145, 150,
  155, 186, 234, 237–238, 240,
  244–247, 252–254, 268
Ghent 10, 31, 128, 134
global 67, 185, 270
globalisation 163
golf 75, 266
government 29, 46, 81, 119, 123–124,
  129–130, 132, 141, 143,
  145, 156, 167, 170, 175, 196,
  224–225, 246, 265, 269, 271
grand tour 8–10, 94, 101, 103, 193,
  211, 238–239, 250, 262, 265

Greece 102
guild 11, 22, 31, 75, 78, 83, 124, 170

The Hague 10, 26, 127–128
Hamburg 32
Hannover 242
health 93–94, 96, 109, 152, 154, 196,
  215, 219, 234–255, 260–261,
  265, 272
Herkulesbad 238, 246, 248
horseracing 3, 74–76, 80–82, 84, 213,
  215
hotels 149, 151, 155–156, 217, 246,
  251, 253–254, 260, 263, 265, 274
Hungary 7, 238, 253
hunting (fox and deer) 14, 74–76, 81,
  121, 243

industrialisation 10, 13, 29, 40, 51, 59,
  80, 129, 146, 156, 248, 273
influence (cultural) 7–8, 11–13, 16, 21,
  24, 26, 31, 41, 58, 65, 81, 94–95,
  99, 101, 107–108, 110–111, 121,
  125, 143, 157, 164, 185, 187,
  190, 194, 200, 211, 221, 226,
  235–240, 242, 247, 253, 255,
  263–264, 266–267, 269, 271, 274
inns 11, 74, 78–79, 82–83, 145,
  148–151, 153, 170, 223, 247
innovation 8, 12–13, 54, 76, 84,
  149, 215, 236, 245–246, 255,
  260–261, 273
intermediary 7, 95, 107
internationalisation 51, 68, 94, 96, 264
investment 44, 74, 141, 245, 253–255,
  261
Ireland 75, 77, 80, 110, 263
Istanbul (also Constantinople) 7, 9, 146,
  161–181
Italy 4, 7–8, 10, 13, 22, 50, 53–54, 63–
  65, 75, 77–78, 83, 97, 101–104,
  143, 234, 237–238, 240, 246, 254

Karlsruhe 32, 242
Kassel 238
Kiel 32
Kuks 238
kunstverein 31–32

Index

language 3, 24, 32, 51–52, 63–64, 95–96, 98–99, 106, 117, 119, 123–128, 130, 133–135, 173, 175, 177, 193, 196, 202, 218, 222, 262
lectures (public) 14, 22, 25, 29–30, 39, 58
leisure industry 94–95, 103
Liège 31, 128
Linköping 12, 140–158
Lisbon 22, 104
Liverpool 27, 44, 261–262
London 7, 9–15, 22–28, 30, 33–35, 37, 40, 54, 63–65, 73–74, 78, 80–82, 97, 99, 101, 104, 106–109, 112, 146, 148, 155, 162–163, 176, 185–205, 211, 213–218, 221–227, 236, 241, 261, 270–271, 273
lower class(es) 163, 168, 171, 188, 200, 214, 226, 239
Lucca 246
Lyon 31, 52

Madrid 23, 30, 32, 35, 45–46, 267–268
male 3, 5, 9, 81, 84, 134, 157, 165, 219, 221–222, 227
Malta 76
Mannheim 242
Margate 245, 249, 261
Marienbad 240, 246, 266
Marseilles 31, 36
masculinity 5, 72, 83, 220
mass culture (proto-) 5, 50, 63, 67, 214
media 72, 80, 82, 84, 105
men (gentlemen) 1, 5, 24, 30, 78, 97, 103, 105, 141, 165, 193–194, 202, 211, 216, 218–219, 221–223, 272
metropolis 27, 40, 51, 106–107, 109, 185, 196, 270–272
Metz 31
middle class(es) 4, 10, 15, 30, 33, 45, 121–123, 129, 133, 147, 150, 153, 157, 176–177, 190, 211–212, 214, 227, 267, 274
migrant 10–11, 26, 78, 105, 108, 149, 170–171, 174, 255, 261–262, 264
Milan 32, 64–65, 111
Monaco 266, 269

monarchy 35, 43, 127, 224, 236
Monte carlo 266
Montecatini 238, 240, 246
Montmorency 243
morality 53, 149, 196–197, 239, 264, 269
Munich 48, 243
Münster 75
museums 11, 21–29, 32, 37–41, 44, 47–48, 234

Nantes 31
Naples 32, 75, 97, 103, 242
national identity 15, 75, 110, 112, 117, 129, 133, 135, 223, 261
nationalism (-istic) 2, 6, 8, 13, 15–16, 72, 108, 111–112, 134, 255
Neo-classicism 29–30, 102–103, 108, 119, 239–240, 247, 250
The Netherlands (also Holland) 10, 64, 82, 101, 110, 118, 127, 143, 266
networks (social, cultural, spatial) 8, 12, 63, 67, 109, 174–176, 196, 202, 235–237, 244, 249, 253–255, 262
New York 75
Newhaven 266
Nice 216, 266–267
nobility 37, 98, 140, 143, 143, 157, 215, 223, 226, 235, 238, 241, 244, 244
Norrköping 9, 140–158
novelty 24, 38, 57–58, 64, 141, 146, 261, 263
Nuremberg 32

opera (house) 2, 5, 24, 30, 46, 50, 52, 54, 60, 64–66, 68, 117–135, 144–145, 153, 197, 199, 214, 216, 217, 223, 252, 254

pantomime 55–56, 60, 144
Paris 7–10, 12–15, 22–26, 29–32, 34–38, 40, 49–51, 53, 55, 58–59, 60–61, 63–65, 67, 76, 95, 97–101, 103–104, 107, 111, 118, 120, 122, 124, 126, 128, 130–132, 134–135, 146, 151, 162–163, 167, 185–205, 210–225, 237, 241–243, 247, 252, 263, 267

parks 5, 121–122, 141–142, 144, 151–157, 193, 200–202, 235, 238, 240–244, 248, 250–251
patriotism 111
patronage 28, 30–31, 73–74, 127, 144, 237, 245, 254
Pau 49
pleasure garden 12, 14, 109, 122, 152, 187, 201, 212–223, 215–216, 220, 237–238, 241
police 58, 167, 188–189, 196–200, 203–205, 224, 226, 236
politeness 14, 37, 42, 105, 121, 124, 148, 157, 187, 190, 195, 202–203, 218–220, 237, 239, 242, 260
popular class(es) 273
popular culture 2, 10, 177
popularisation 60, 65, 70
Portugal 64, 175
Prato 75
printing presses 13, 238
privilege 39, 54–55, 58, 117, 144, 167, 199, 271
professionalisation 9, 23, 28, 40, 54, 75, 96, 133, 143, 170–171, 214, 266
promenade 14, 39–40, 72, 151–152, 155, 187, 192, 194–198, 212–214, 217, 223, 234, 238, 240–242, 245, 247–248, 272, 274
prostitutes 5, 165, 201, 217, 239
provincial towns 7, 24, 73, 93, 141–145, 150, 156, 158, 211–212
Prussia 133–134, 244, 246, 254, 262, 267
pubs 23, 171, 201, 272–273
public opinion 25, 37, 41, 175
public sphere 14, 21, 24, 26, 33, 41, 43, 48, 51, 117, 121, 172, 189, 224

reference (cultural) 2, 100, 118, 185–187, 189, 195, 204, 239, 250
Renaissance 22, 78, 102, 238, 240
resistance (cultural, social, political) 7, 9, 11, 94, 108, 172, 177, 185–186
restaurants 141–142, 148–151, 153, 153, 155–157, 254
Richmond 75

romanticism 9, 15, 26, 30–31, 37, 39–40, 60, 66, 109, 134, 250
Rome 8, 32, 37–38, 42, 76, 95, 98, 101–104, 132
Rotterdam 128
Rouen 31
rugby 72
rural 12–13, 67, 77, 245, 253, 261, 270
Russia 170, 175, 237, 246

Sadlers Wells 217
Saint Petersburg 38
salons 21, 25, 29, 34–36, 39, 41, 46–47, 70, 104, 132, 171, 177, 218, 220–221
San Sebastián 267–271
Scarborough 211, 262, 273
Scheveningen 261
schweizeri 150–151, 153, 155
seaside resorts 2, 8–9, 12–13, 72, 93, 109, 216, 240, 245, 253, 260–277
sentimentalism 16, 51, 53, 57–58, 65–66, 94, 111, 203
sex 9, 45, 202, 219, 274
shopping (shopping street) 4, 23–26, 39, 42, 46, 99–100, 106, 110, 121, 162, 200–201, 212, 215, 220, 234, 237, 243–244, 251, 254
skating 75, 79, 154
sociability 14, 74, 81, 99, 109, 117, 161–177, 205, 218, 220, 225, 237, 240–241, 251, 254–255, 261, 265, 268, 274
Southport 263
Spa (Ardennes) 237, 240, 245, 252–253, 266, 269
spa 2, 4–5, 8, 11, 13–14, 93–112, 152, 156, 212, 214–215, 234–255, 260, 262, 265, 268
Spain 7, 29, 32, 38, 45, 64, 118, 175, 267–268, 274
sport 1–4, 7, 11, 14, 72–84, 201, 213, 217, 219, 225
state (support, supervision, ownership) 21, 35–36, 58, 81–82, 119, 126, 133–135, 157, 167, 172, 174–175, 177, 216, 224, 245–246, 252, 267

Index

status (social) 5, 37, 97–98, 109, 112, 118, 124, 167–168, 170, 214, 246, 273

Stockholm 10, 37, 46, 79, 140–158

Strasbourg 31

Stuttgart 32

subscription 31, 45, 75, 97, 99, 124, 130, 135, 140, 146, 212, 274

suburb (-an) 54, 61, 94, 214

suppression 83, 119, 166–167, 175, 246, 269

Sweden 7, 9–10, 79, 87, 140–158

taste 2, 8–9, 11, 35–36, 61, 66, 93–100, 105, 111, 118, 132, 134–135, 162–163, 165, 214, 220, 226, 235–237, 241–243, 245–250, 255

taverns 78–79, 82, 141, 156, 163, 169, 214, 219, 221

tax 82, 166–167, 170, 175, 252

teaching 97–99, 128

Teplitz 237, 246, 248–249

theatre 2, 4–6, 9, 12–14, 27, 29, 39–40, 49–67, 72, 95–96, 107, 109, 111, 117–135, 140–148, 152–157, 172–174, 187, 192–196, 197–199, 201–204, 214–217, 220, 224, 226, 229, 233, 238, 243, 251, 254, 274

tivoli (park) 154, 247

Toulon 31

Toulouse 75, 215–217

tourism (tourist) 2, 6, 8–9, 13–15, 37, 40, 94, 97, 103–104, 210–211, 215, 217–220, 222, 227, 235–237, 240, 243, 245, 247–248, 250, 253–255, 264–265, 267, 269

translation 13, 53, 57, 64, 71, 96, 102, 106–107, 124, 146, 170, 175, 191, 193, 196, 210–211

transnational exchange (flows, culture) 2, 6–8, 11, 13, 15–16, 21, 63, 67, 93–97, 106, 109–112, 130, 134, 142, 234–236, 239, 254–255

transport 12, 54, 236, 245, 248, 255

travel (-ler) 8–10, 14–15, 37–38, 50, 83–84, 96, 102–104, 117, 120, 124, 143–144, 147, 149, 151, 162, 169, 171, 173, 176, 186, 193, 210–227, 235, 237–238, 243, 245, 247–248, 250, 273

Trieste 32, 253

Trouville 266

Turin 32, 64

universalism 15, 61, 111–112, 119, 130, 135

upper class(es) 29, 41, 152–153, 155, 157, 165, 171, 212, 216, 223

Uppsala 146

urbanisation 3–4, 15, 72, 78, 80, 84

Utrecht 128

vauxhall (waux-hall) 12, 54, 122–123, 148, 152–153, 187–188, 194–195, 197, 214–217, 220, 240–241

vectors 8, 94, 99, 103, 105, 236, 255

Venice 10, 22, 64, 104, 150, 170

Versailles 97–98, 111, 119, 121, 190, 238

Vicenza 102

Vichy 237, 245, 266

Vienna 10, 26, 37, 46, 75, 118–119, 124, 126, 162, 237, 242–244, 247–248, 252–253

voluntary association 72

Weimar 239, 242

Whitby 263

Wiesbaden 245–249, 252, 254

women (ladies) 1, 5, 25, 62, 70, 83, 97–98, 101, 104–105, 107, 111, 140–141, 148, 165, 193–194, 198–199, 211, 214, 216–222, 234, 250, 266, 272

working class(es) 3–5, 10, 15, 30, 214, 262, 265, 270, 272–273

zoo 153